HARDBOILED ACTIVIST

HARDBOILED ACTIVIST

THE WORK AND POLITICS OF DASHIELL HAMMETT

Ken Fuller

Praxis Press
Glasgow

Published by Praxis Press
Email: praxispress@me.com

Distributor: Unity Books.

Praxis Press
c/o Unity Books
72 Waterloo Street
Glasgow
G2 7DA
Scotland
Great Britain
T: +44 141 204 1611
E:enquiries@unitybooks.co.uk
www.unitybooks.co.uk
www.facebook.com/unitybooksonline/

Photos: © Julie M Rivett

Printed by Lightning Source

© Ken Fuller 2017

All rights reserved. No part of this publication may be reproduced, distributed, or transmitted in any form or by any means, including photocopying, recording, or other electronic or mechanical methods, without the prior written permission of the publisher, except in the case of brief quotations embodied in critical reviews and certain other noncommercial uses permitted by copyright law. For permission requests, write to the publisher at the address above.

ISBN 978-1-899155-06-4

TABLE OF CONTENTS

PREFACE (i)

CHAPTER 1: IRONIES, PARADOXES AND CONTRADICTIONS 1

CHAPTER 2: SEARCHING FOR THE SOCIALIST 23

CHAPTER 3: THE DARKENING VISION 63

CHAPTER 4: HOLLYWOOD 123

CHAPTER 5: BROADWAY 155

CHAPTER 6: FOGGY GLIMPSES 193

CHAPTER 7: THE HARDBOILED ACTIVIST 225

CHAPTER 8: HARDBOILED TO THE END 253

CHAPTER 9: DRY 283

BIBLIOGRAPHY 317

INDEX 323

ABOUT THE AUTHOR 335

Preface

Dashiell Hammett is sometimes portrayed as a "Marxist writer," usually by observers who are themselves not Marxists. The truth is that he was a Marxist and a writer—although not at the same time. Thus, as indicated by this book's subtitle, Hammett's work and politics are almost, but not quite, separate subjects. What is often misidentified as an already developed Marxist outlook in some of the stories and the novels—particularly *Red Harvest*—is in fact nothing more than a deepening alienation from the corrupt society in which he lived.

This alienation led Hammett, an avowed atheist, into nihilism and despair, such that by the early 1930s he was flirting with suicide. His darkening outlook had, along with his precarious medical condition, long led him into a life of reckless excess, drinking, gambling and womanizing as if there were no tomorrow.

By the mid-1930s, he had completed all the stories and novels he would ever write. It was not merely that he had exhausted his material, but because the corrupt society that had so revolted him was now in addition suffering the effects of the Great Depression, and what could his usual protagonist, a lone private eye, possibly achieve in the face of such overwhelming odds? His fiction had nowhere to go, the world was meaningless, man powerless.

Ironically, it was the Depression that produced the factors giving rise to a new optimism in Hammett: not the mass unemployment and wage-cutting of employers, but the resurgent US labor movement which combated them; not the development of fascism in Europe, mimicked by the most reactionary circles in the USA and elsewhere, but the upsurge of broad anti-fascist movements at home and abroad. And then, in Hollywood of all places, he was introduced to Marxism, which drew these factors together and gave him a completely new way of looking at the world. Suddenly, life was no longer meaningless and Hammett threw himself into political activity. He would remain a Marxist for the rest of his life.

≋

The aims of this book are straightforward: to demonstrate, in considering Hammett's published work, that it contains few if any traces of Marxism; to track his political development in the 1930s, providing an explanation of why he would have been attracted to what many (including some of his biographers and critics) would characterize as "Stalinism," and then show his continuing commitment throughout the 1940s and 1950s; and finally to investigate why, despite the foregoing, he still failed to write. Along the way, there are occasional remarks regarding Hammett's literary merits but, as I am not a literary critic, these are of secondary importance; there is, however, a separate chapter on Hammett's contribution to the plays (or some of them) of Lillian Hellman, with whom he had a relationship spanning 30 years.

Chapter 1, a brief biographical sketch, is followed by a consideration of Hammett's published work, with a chapter each on the magazine stories, the five novels, his published screen stories, and the Hellman plays.

In Chapter 6, I attempt to unravel Hammett's political trajectory, and this necessitates a discussion of Hellman's unreliable recollections on this subject. At one stage, I was ready to conclude, such was Hammett's dissolute lifestyle, that, while he was obviously committed to the international communist movement, he probably never became a formal member of the Communist Party of the USA (CPUSA). This view was strengthened by the suspicion that any communist party would have had second thoughts before admitting such a person into its ranks, and by the fact that there seemed to be absolutely no concrete evidence that he had joined. And then, in one of the most recent of his biographies, a small detail, probably of importance to no one but me: he once showed his party membership card to his daughter Jo. This has been convincingly confirmed by Josephine Hammett Marshall, now 90, via her own daughter, Julie Rivett. So, yes, Hammett did join the party.

If any chapter is going to set the fur flying, it is probably Chapter 7. Too often, those who write about Hammett either gloss over his political beliefs or attack them. Of course, such writers have every right to challenge political positions with which they disagree, but if this is all they do, they end up telling us more about themselves than they do about their subject, and in a biography this rather defeats the object. Another tactic, as if to "excuse" Hammett for his adoption of positions which the biographer or commentator finds unacceptable, is to imply that he must have been drunk at the time or that he was an innocent abroad, "duped" into following each and every CPUSA/Soviet policy turn. Quite simply, this was not Hammett.

In Chapter 7, therefore, I examine a number of positions for which he is attacked, placing them in context, correcting factual errors, and explaining them as they appeared to others at the time, and as they would have appeared to Hammett. As it becomes perfectly obvious that Hammett's politics were as hardboiled as his fiction, this chapter gives the book its title. I realize that in adopting this approach I run the risk of being dismissed as a "Stalinist," but I tend to agree with E. H. Carr in this regard. "Of course," the esteemed historian of the Soviet Revolution wrote in *New Left Review* in 1978, "I know that anyone who speaks of the achievements of the Revolution will at once be branded as a Stalinist. But I am not prepared to submit to this kind of moral blackmail."[1]

Chapter 8 traces Hammett's political activity in the postwar years, through his court appearance and prison term to his death in January 1961. The final chapter investigates the various reasons why Hammett was unable or unwilling to complete any fiction project after the mid-1930s, and puts forward possibilities not previously considered.

≈

Thanks are due to Raymond Chandler biographer Judith Freeman, who kindly put me in touch with Hammett's granddaughter Julie

Rivett, to Julie herself for her readiness to answer my questions and providing both portraits of Hammet used on the cover and the inside pages of this book, and likewise to Richard Layman. I must also recognize the generosity of Jacob Zumoff who, despite planning to embark upon a similar project, having reached the same conclusion as I regarding the timing of Hammett's adoption of Marxism, sent me his articles. And, finally, a big thank you to Kenny Coyle of Praxis Press, without whom this volume would not have appeared.

Readers in Britain and Ireland may question my use of US English. This is explained by the fact that, before an approach by Praxis Press, it had been my intention to seek publication in the USA, where interest in Hammett is greatest; given that this edition, despite being issued by a British publisher, will, thanks to the distribution arrangements, be widely available in the USA, it seems prudent to leave things as they are.

Some of my interpretations may be questioned, but hopefully I have succeeded in avoiding factual errors; should this prove not to be the case, the fault is mine alone.

Ken Fuller,
Tagbilaran City,
June, 2017.

NOTES
1   E. H. Carr, "The Russian Revolution and the West," *New Left Review*, 1/111/September- October, 1978.

1 Ironies, paradoxes and contradictions

A century ago, a tall, thin young man turned up at the Baltimore office of the Pinkertons' National Detective Agency to begin work, first as a clerk, later as an operative. Large parts of the world were in flames. The previous year, Europe had embarked upon wholesale slaughter as constituent nations sent young men, just like this thin youth, to kill each other in order to resolve which nation would retain its colonies, which would lose them to a foe. Now, in 1915, the Industrial Workers of the World (IWW or Wobblies), the militant trade union organization formed a decade earlier, would adopt a resolution at its convention opposing that bosses' war.

While rival capitalisms fought for dominance in Europe, there was a war of sorts within the USA, as labor confronted capital. The Socialist Party had its strongest base in Oklahoma — 12,000 paid-up members, a hundred of whom had been elected to local office; in Arkansas, Louisiana, Oklahoma and Texas alone, there were no less than 55 socialist weeklies.[1] Often the bosses played rough and, in January 1915, IWW organizer Joseph Hillstrom, widely known as Joe Hill, was arrested on a trumped-up murder charge, tried and, despite a vigorous defense campaign, executed in November.

It is likely that this world was as incomprehensible to our thin youngster as it was to most of his peers. Despite having already demonstrated inclinations to drunkenness and womanizing (the first of these would last, despite interludes of sobriety, until he was convinced that further indulgence would carry a death sentence, the second until his equipment failed), he was a serious reader who sought to discover how the world worked, although while he may have gained what he would later call "foggy glimpses" of the truth, it would be many years before these sharpened and developed into real understanding.

Looking at the span of his whole life — he would die at the age of 66 — we can now see that it bristled with ironies, paradoxes and contradictions. He would enlist in the Army after the USA joined the bosses' war. As he graduated to the post of Pinkerton operative, he would find himself fighting the bosses' domestic war against organized labor, helping to break a strike. He was just doing a job the best way he could, but although he apparently did not at this stage conclude that he was on the wrong side, he would soon come to suspect that it was not the right one. Small wonder, then, that when he turned to detective fiction his stories had a distinctly nihilist flavor, for the man who was still unable to decide what to believe obviously believed in nothing. For a while, believing in nothing suited his lifestyle, as he frittered away the considerable money he received from his novels and his work in Hollywood, drinking, whoring and gambling. But a man — especially a serious-minded one who has come from a humble background and now finds himself in the company of empty-headed hedonists — can only do so much of that before he begins to question the purpose and value of his life.

Then, as fascism gained power in Europe and Japanese militarism was on the rise, our tall, thin, now middle-aged man with the striking shock of white hair finally saw beyond the fog and threw in his lot with the working class. Like his fiction, his political viewpoint was hardboiled and he supported Joseph Stalin, thereby unsettling biographers and critics yet unborn.

≈

Samuel Dashiell Hammett was born in 1894 in Maryland. His parents were of French and Scottish stock; although his mother's maiden name was Bond, she was connected via her own mother to the De Chiell family, from which Sam acquired his middle name.[2] One branch of the Hammett family claimed that "the first American Hammett was an indentured servant," while another insisted he was "a scoundrel and a thief who was transported from England for stealing."³

The family could not be described as poor, for by 1827 it owned a 200-acre farm, and it was in the three-story farmhouse that young Sam was born. There was also a store called "Hammettville," and it is possible that the area around it was also known by this name. If the family had influence, however, it was not without limits, as Sam's father Richard, who had served as a justice of the peace, found when he jumped the party-political fence, reckoning — wrongly as it turned out — that he would stand a better chance of gaining state office as a Republican. His Democratic party-mates proved particularly unforgiving, and it seems that staying in Hammettville was not a healthy option, so Richard took his family to first Philadelphia and then Baltimore, where they stayed with Sam's maternal grandmother.⁴

Richard found employment as a manufacturer's agent, a street-car conductor, clerk and seafood salesman, and finances were precarious.⁵ At one stage, his wife Annie worked as a private nurse to supplement the family income. Young Sam was an omnivorous reader, tackling Immanuel Kant's *Critique of Pure Reason* at the impossibly young age of 13 and managing to complete it, even if he did not understand it.⁶ Often, he would read through the night and turn up to school late as a result. Hammett would later tell the editor of *Black Mask* that his secondary education lasted "a fraction of a year."⁷ He didn't start first year until he was 14, and was just months into it when his father Richard's financial problems compelled his son to take a job as a messenger for the Baltimore and Ohio Railroad. Here too, Hammett had difficulty turning up on time, although by now the stimulant/soporific responsible was more likely to be alcohol. (Working children of this era, particularly those who would evolve into writers, tended to be introduced to alcohol early in their careers: Jack London was a drunkard at the age of 15.⁸) One week, Hammett was late every day and the boss called him in. He later told the story to Lillian Hellman, who recounted it in her introduction to a posthumous collection of his stories:

> His employer told him he was fired. Hammett said he nodded, walked to the door, and was called back by a puzzled man who said "If you give me your word it won't happen again, you can keep your job." Hammett said,

"Thank you, but I can't do that." After a silence the man said, "Okay, keep the job anyway." Dash said that he didn't know what was right about what he had done, but he did know that it would always be useful.[9]

He had a number of other jobs, and Symons says that his brother Richard recalls him chalking up share-prices for a brokerage firm.[10] Later, of course, he became a Pinkerton operative. The Pinkertons' Baltimore office was in the Continental Building, thus supplying Hammett with the name of the fictional agency that would feature in his Continental Op stories and novels. Hammett was trained by the assistant manager of the branch, James Wright, upon whom Hammett would base the middle-aged, overweight Op. Among the basic rules Wright taught Hammett was "be objective, never become emotionally involved with a client or anyone else connected with a case"[11] — this would later inform Sam Spade's cold-blooded approach to Brigid in *The Maltese Falcon*. According to Hammett's partner, Phil Haultain, Hammett was "at the very top," a "wonderful investigator. Sharp. Really knew his business." Another colleague, Jack Knight, describes him as one of the agency's "star performers." Hammett himself was rather more modest, saying that he was "a bit overrated" due to his ability to "explain away my failures, proving them inevitable and no fault of mine."[12]

In 1918, following the USA's entry into World War I, Hammett enlisted in the Army, but he never left the country, being posted just a few miles away from home in the Motor Ambulance Company. In October, he contracted the 'flu' that was killing millions and was found, in addition, to be suffering from tuberculosis, which was probably inherited from his mother. Even so, he was promoted to sergeant and honorably discharged in May 1919, following which he began a phase characterized by periodic hospitalization and, when his health would allow, renewed employment with the Pinkertons (possibly on a part-time basis some of the time).

Hammett was tall, very thin, and yet handsome, a man who attracted the attentions of women; he was a dandy, a drinker and a womanizer, having contracted his first dose of gonorrhea at the age of 20. At the veterans' hospital in Tacoma, he was tended by Josephine Annis Dolan and, although she outranked him (she was a lieutenant), they began a relationship and Josephine (known as Jose) became pregnant.[13] By the time he received this news, Hammett was in another military hospital in California, where he had been sent for the desert air, but he immediately decided to do the decent thing, and they were married in 1921.

There would appear to be little certainty regarding the order in which events occurred during this period, as Symons seems to think that Hammett returned home from the Army, regained his health and then took a posting at the Pinkertons' Spokane office, but was then admitted to the Cushman hospital in Tacoma six months later,[14] while Layman has Hammett later recalling that "his most exciting work as a detective came during the Anaconda strike of 1920-1921 when the huge mining corporation finally broke the IWW attempt to unionize the miners,"[15] and he would have worked out of the Spokane office for this assignment.

Hammett and Jose moved to San Francisco, where Hammett continued his employment with the Pinkertons. During this brief period, he claimed to have worked on several big cases, including that involving Fatty Arbuckle, the comedy star accused of rape, in which he gathered evidence for the defense. Layman, however, says that Hammett's stories of this period became "implausible as time passed," and that when he talked of working on four big cases, "his involvement in each case is suspect."[16] As his health deteriorated again, he was forced to work part-time during the fall and winter of 1921, and Layman says that he could only have worked from the San Francisco office for eight months at the most, with four months being more likely.[17] According to Vince Emery, he helped break a San Francisco dock strike during this brief period, so his strike-breaking was not confined to the mines.[18] In mid-February 1922, Hammett gave up the gumshoe trade for good, too ill to continue.

≈

Hammett's first daughter Mary had been born in October 1921 and so now, out of work, he needed to supplement his disability pension and thus turned his hand to writing. But this required some preparation, and Nolan says that he took morning classes in journalism for some 15 months, before deciding that the world of advertising was more attractive;[19] Emery, however, says that the Munson School offered courses for secretaries, but not reporters, and so Hammett dropped out once he had learned to touch-type.[20] During this period, he maintained his voracious reading habit, in the afternoons attending San Francisco's Civic Center Library where, he later said, he acquired his college education.

He dabbled in advertising, creating both text and illustrations; his first customer, a shoe store, rewarded his efforts with a sample of its wares. But he also began to submit prose to various magazines, and in October 1922 he was rewarded with the publication of a very brief comic piece entitled "The Parthian Shot" in *The Smart Set* which, edited by the estimable H. L. Mencken and George Jean Nathan, would publish more of his humorous pieces over the next few months. But Hammett also wrote stories, and in December 1922 the previously rejected "The Barber and His Wife" found a home at *Brief Stories*.

A more significant development came that same month with the publication of "The Road Home" in *The Black Mask*. Here, apart from a hiccup in 1926, Hammett found a ready market for his stories, and soon he was concentrating on crime tales and, with the publication of "Arson Plus" in October 1923, detective mysteries featuring his unnamed, middle-aged, portly sleuth, the Continental Op, who would feature in 26 stories and novelettes and two novels.[21]

In a move down-market aimed solely at making money, *The Black Mask* had been launched in 1920 by Mencken and Nathan with capital of a mere $500. Publishing adventure stories, mysteries, westerns and romances, within a year its circulation had reached 125,000 and Mencken and Nathan had sold their interest for $12,250.[22] It was a "pulp" magazine, a reference to the cheap wood-pulp paper on which such publications were printed, and its stories were required to be fast-paced with abundant action. It was in *The Black Mask* that the "hardboiled" crime story is said to have originated, and although Hammett was not the first practitioner (this is usually credited to Carroll John Daly, who first appeared in *The Black Mask* in May 1923), it is widely accepted that he was the one to have rescued the detective story from the libraries and country cottages of a picture-postcard rural England, imbuing it with a dose of realism and artistry.

Although Hammett continued to submit stories and articles elsewhere, most went to *The Black Mask*, but in 1926 he had a falling out with editor Phil Cody and parted company with the magazine for a while. He advertised his services in the *San Francisco Chronicle* and was snapped up by jewelry-store owner Albert Samuels, who employed him as his advertising manager. Samuels paid more than *The Black Mask*, and Hammett suddenly found that life was a little easier, earning around $350 per month[23] — which was just as well, because in May that year Josephine Rebecca, his second daughter, was born.

Hammett's success at Samuels' was short-lived, for in July 1926 he collapsed in a pool of blood and was therefore unable to remain in post, although for a while he continued on a freelance basis. Help was at hand, however, as in November 1926 Captain Joseph T. Shaw took over as editor of *The Black Mask*. Shaw's first action was to drop the definite article from the name of the magazine; the second was to coax Hammett back, promising to pay him the $300 he insisted he was owed and purchase his stories at the rate of four cents a word.[24]

Thus, Hammett returned to *Black Mask* in February 1927, but after three stories he began serializing *Red Harvest*, which would be his first novel, and this would be the pattern until November 1930, when he made his last appearance in the magazine: a serialized novel followed by a single stand-alone story.

After *Red Harvest* came *The Dain Curse*, *The Maltese Falcon* and *The Glass Key*. By this stage, Dashiell Hammett saw himself as a novelist rather than a mere writer of stories for the pulps. Ironically, there was only one more novel in him — *The Thin Man* — and this would be offered elsewhere, because he was now able to command higher fees and by this time he was doing lucrative work in Hollywood anyway.

His family life, meanwhile, was over. Having lived apart from Jose and his daughters for some time, partly on health grounds, in late 1929 the separation became permanent when Hammett, accompanied by novelist and screenwriter Nell Martin, left for New York.

His third novel, *The Maltese Falcon*, published in February 1930, was dedicated to Jose. In 1937, they would get a divorce in Nogales, Mexico, although it was doubtful whether this would have been recognized in the USA; it was never put to the test, as neither attempted to marry again. According to Layman in his commentary in Hammett's *Selected Letters*, the divorce was occasioned by the fact that Lillian Hellman, with whom Hammett had commenced a 30-year relationship in 1930, had become pregnant and was urging him to marry her; but then she had an abortion, following which the matter was never raised again.[25] There is, though, a possible flaw in Layman's account: while he says that Hellman became pregnant in the fall of 1937, the divorce was granted on 26 August,[26] a fact noted by Layman in his earlier *Shadow Man*.[27]

His daughter Jo Hammett gives an account in her memoir of Hammett visiting their house in Santa Monica, speaking to Jose alone for some time and then, following a rustle of papers, leaving by the front door without saying goodbye to his daughters; when Jose appeared, she was teary-eyed, suggesting that, although she had signed up for the divorce, she would have preferred not to have.[28] Hammett continued to support his family while he had the means to do so — in the 1950s, when the US authorities ensured that was no longer possible, Jose would be forced to return to nursing — but even before the divorce he was not always prompt in sending funds, and in 1932 a desperate Jose wrote to publisher Alfred Knopf explaining that he had only sent $100 in seven months and that the children needed clothes and "proper food."[29] By this time, Hammett was receiving Hollywood money, but was squandering it.

Hammett should have been solvent by this time. *The Dain Curse*, although vastly inferior to its predecessor, had sold better than *Red Harvest*, going through three printings in two months; *The Maltese Falcon*, published to critical acclaim in February 1930, sold even better, requiring seven printings in the first year.[30] Paramount had bought the rights to *Red Harvest* (this appeared as *Roadhouse Nights* in February 1930) and now Warner Bros. bought the rights to *The Maltese Falcon* (the first movie based on the novel was released in May 1931). In April 1930, he began reviewing mysteries in the *New York Evening Post*, a further source of income that would last six months.

Hammett's fourth novel, *The Glass Key*, departed from the detective genre and entered the world of political bosses. Serialized in *Black Mask* between March and June 1930, it was eventually published in the USA (dedicated to Nell Martin, who had by this time split with the author) in April 1931, having appeared in Britain three months earlier. With five printings in the first two months alone, by the end of 1933 the critically-acclaimed novel had sold 20,000 copies.[31] Hammett sold the film rights to Paramount, which released the movie version in June 1935. His own work in Hollywood began as early as 1930 and would continue until 1939. By the mid-1930s, Hammett was earning $100,000 a year.³²

He returned to New York during this period, writing the first 18,000 words of a novel entitled *The Thin Man*, but then he laid it aside. It was the second half of 1932 before Hammett, back in New York, began work on the second version of the novel in earnest, completing it in May 1933.

Perhaps surprisingly, given what for the time was a stunning income, Hammett still had occasion to write short stories. Between March 1932 and March 1934, he wrote and published no less than 13, all of which were published in "slicks," i.e. magazines printed on high-quality paper. It is perhaps ironic that one of the qualities often ascribed to Hammett's hero the Continental Op was loyalty, but that Hammett himself placed not a single story with *Black Mask*, the magazine which had lured him back from the world of advertising, and that whereas previously his novels had been serialized in *Black Mask*, his final book went to *Redbook* (in fact, his agent had persuaded *Cosmopolitan* to pay $26,000 for the completed manuscript, but Knopf had stepped in to claim first rights.)³³ These stories were written simply because Hammett needed the money; and that he needed it, given the substantial income outlined above, is a measure of his profligacy.

The days of short stories would soon be over, however, because *The Thin Man* turned out to be a gold mine for Hammett. The novel sold 34,000 copies in the first 18 months, but this was just the beginning, and Layman estimates that between 1933 and 1950 Hammett must have earned almost a million dollars from the book itself, the movies, the characters of Nick and Nora Charles, and the various spin-offs.³⁴

By 1934, Hammett's financial situation (or, at least, his income) had improved considerably. In January, he began writing the text for a comic strip called *Secret Agent X-9* at the suggestion of William Randolph Hearst, whose King Features syndicated it; he continued this until late April the following year, when he turned over the writing to the graphic artist, Alex Raymond. (Comically, the comic strip gave rise to the Federal Bureau of Investigation's first investigation of Hammett, as director J. Edgar Hoover thought that the character was based on an FBI agent.³⁵) Hammett, it seemed, was on particularly good terms with the Hearst empire,³⁶ for it syndicated his old stories³⁷ and the *Cosmopolitan* to which the rights to *The Thin Man* were nearly sold was Hearst's

9

International/Cosmopolitan.[38] In 1935, he signed a lucrative contract with MGM, for which he wrote the second and third *Thin Man* stories, but as fast as the money rolled in, Hammett would spend it or give it away.

Hammett's problems with TB seemed to be at an end, but his health during the 1930s often suffered as a result of the kind of life he led. In 1931, drinking heavily, he became ill and depressed and contemplated suicide. Hellman says she asked him why he was thinking of suicide, but there "wasn't any answer, except for the feeling that everything was over."[39] In January 1936, after a West Coast gathering of *Black Mask* writers (where he met Raymond Chandler for the first and only time), he flew to New York and checked into a hospital until early February for "a little rest."[40] Many of his medical problems could be traced to his heavy consumption of alcohol, although he was not an alcoholic, being able to remain sober for months at a time. In 1938, having been dry for 14 months, he fell off the wagon and suffered a nervous breakdown, whereupon he was again flown to New York and hospitalized.[41] By this time, Hammett's writing career was over, for he never completed another story, novel or (with the exception of the screenplay of *Watch on the Rhine* in 1943) movie.

≈

Returning to New York meant returning to Lillian Hellman.

Hellman was born in 1905 in New Orleans, although during her childhood half of each year was often spent in New York. In late 1925, she married Arthur Kober, a playwright and press agent, and by 1930, at which time she met Hammett, she was in Hollywood, working as a reader for MGM. She and Hammett began a relationship that would last until his death 30 years later, although even during periods when they were sleeping together one or the other would often take other partners. The different approach Hammett took with *The Thin Man* is explained by his relationship with Hellman: he was Nick Charles and she was Nora. Hellman would later say that "she recognized their word-for-word dialogue in several of the novel's sequences."[42]

Hammett seems to have been the dominant partner in the relationship, and long after his death Hellman would say that he "used his age to make the rules." According to her recollection, however, it was Hammett who asked her to "stop juggling" (taking other partners), and "I did stop for long periods, although several times through the years he said, 'Don't start that juggling again.'"⁴³ This does not ring particularly true, because Hammett often took other partners (sometimes prostitutes), and Hellman herself in the second volume of her memoirs describes how she phoned him from New York and was surprised to find the call answered by a woman claiming to be his secretary; thinking that he had no secretary and calculating that it would have been 3 am in California when she placed the call, she took a flight to Los Angeles, smashed the soda fountain in his rented mansion to pieces and then flew back to New York.⁴⁴

There is, however, a widely-acknowledged problem with Hellman's reliability. Hammett's daughter Jo says that Hellman's "official profile" of Hammett "aimed to provide a dreamlike fictional image without particular reference to fact." She describes Hellman as "manipulative, mendacious, bad-tempered" but also "funny, generous, high-spirited." Jo Hammett's solution was "to think of Lillian in the same way I think of cholesterol. There is good cholesterol and bad cholesterol. They often work at odds, but they're in the same system, use the same name, and can't be separated out."⁴⁵ In her "Foreword" to the *Selected Letters*, she says that her father's letters to Hellman "give some balance to her share in his life. They put in proportion the myth of the Great Romance, which she dramatized and exploited after his death."⁴⁶ Peter Wolfe says that Hellman maintained that "the dearth of information surviving Hammett comes less from neglect than from design. She argues well. The little that Hammett left to posterity makes him look like a man who covered his tracks."⁴⁷ She may have argued well, but maybe she did not argue honestly, for after his death she discouraged research into his life, wishing to control his image.⁴⁸

Often with Hellman, then, it is impossible to know precisely where the truth lies. In the two examples given, for example, it is difficult to believe that the philandering Hammett would ask her to "stop juggling," and the story of the soda fountain destroyed by a Hellman who had managed to sustain her jealous rage through a 2,500-mile flight also strikes one as far-fetched. It is less difficult to accept Hellman's assertion that the sexual side of their relationship lasted only a decade. Interviewed by Diane Johnson, the biographer she approved for Hammett, she recalled an occasion at the start of the 1940s when Hammett began drunkenly pawing her, suggesting that they make love; when she refused to entertain him in his drunken state, he is said to have decided there and then that he would never again have sex with her, a vow he kept,[49] although Dorothy Gallagher says that Hellman "told the story both ways."[50]

As we will see in Chapter 5, Hammett made a considerable contribution to Hellman's career as a playwright, and it might be said that this collaboration was a continuation of his own creative activity.

In May 1939, Hammett and Hellman moved onto the 130-acre farm she would call Hardscrabble in New York state, and although Hellman obviously considered it hers (and, indeed, it may well have been purchased with solely her money), Jo Hammett recalls that Hammett had once told her mother that "he and Lillian both put so much money into it that he didn't know what was whose."[51] Long after his death, Hellman was ready to concede this, writing that "Hammett and I owned a large farm..."[52] Hammett would spend considerable time here, and while it might be thought that such an idyllic site might be conducive to creative endeavor, it unfortunately provided too many excuses not to write — shooting, fishing, catching turtles, bird-watching, etc.

Along with Hellman, Hammett became heavily involved in progressive causes in the second half of the 1930s. For now, suffice it to say that his activity may be broadly divided into several areas. He undertook trade union work, specifically with the Screen Writers' Guild; his anti-fascist activity consisted of support for the Republican forces in Spain and opposition to anti-Semitism and Nazi activity in Germany; this led in turn to support for the Soviet Union. When the House Un-American Activities Committee was formed and began its anti-communist crusade (this would become muted after the USA entered World War II), he campaigned against it and was unafraid to undertake activity which, as when he campaigned for election rights, clearly allied him with the Communist Party of the USA. And, needless to say, he attracted the attention of the FBI.

≈

The USA entered World War II in December 1941. Hammett sprang a surprise on his friends when in 1942 he tried to re-enlist in the Army. He was, however, turned down and therefore spent that summer teaching at the Writers School in New York. In September that year he tried again and, at the age of 48, was accepted (according to Nolan, the problem had been not his history of tuberculosis, but his teeth, which he had pulled to gain acceptance).[53]

Hammett was first assigned to Fort Monmouth, New Jersey for training in a signals outfit. He then spent the first ten days of July, 1943 at Camp Shenango, Pennsylvania, which was reserved for those considered subversive; when Eleanor Roosevelt learned of the nature of the camp, she complained to her husband, who had the men dispersed. Attached to 14th Signal Service Company, Hammett was eventually posted to the bleak Aleutian Islands, off Alaska, and if being stationed at Shenango was considered the equivalent of being under house arrest, says Layman, maybe the windswept island of Adak, where Hammett was assigned, performed the same function.[54] Even so, Hammett took to the barren island, and indeed to Army life, and it is generally reckoned that these were his happiest years.

The FBI, apparently oblivious to the fact that in the USA, as in much of the world, broad anti-fascist alliances were the order of the day, attempted for two years to track Hammett down in the Army. J. Edgar Hoover first wrote to the Military Intelligence Service in October 1942, merely advising the MIS for its "appropriate consideration" of the fact that the Dashiell Hammett who had enlisted "on or around September 18" was "President of the League of American Writers, a Communist front organization."

The MIS replied that the War Department files indicated that Hammett was neither "a member of the military establishment [nor] a civilian employee of the War department. Therefore, no investigation of this person is contemplated by this Service."[55] Johnson interprets this to mean that the Army was simply unable to locate Hammett, and Layman thinks that this was because his name had been misspelled "Dashiel" on induction records.[56] There is, however, an obvious problem with this version: the fact that the Army was able to tag Hammett as a subversive, and therefore a candidate for Camp Shenango and the isolated Adak, is inconsistent with its claim that it was impossible to locate him. Is it not possible that the MIS's reply to Hoover (and particularly its final sentence) was the Army's way of telling the FBI director to mind his own business? It was July 1944 before the FBI was able to confirm that Hammett was in the Army.

Nolan says that Adak was a "real haven" for Hammett,[57] and this did indeed seem to be the case. All inquiries concerning his writing plans (and plans is virtually all he had had for some time) would be fruitless while he was serving his country. His hectic schedule of political activity was at an end for the duration of the war, as were whatever problems he might have been experiencing with Hellman. And he had no choice but to be sober; doubtless he was grateful for the respite from the meaningless round of social activity that had only been manageable with alcohol. In addition, there is every indication that he was indulged by his superiors on Adak, while his peers, half his age, idolized him.

Given the latitude allowed Hammett, it would appear that Layman is probably correct in his assumption that Adak served the same purpose as Camp Shenango: in such an isolated outpost (the Japanese had earlier withdrawn from the Aleutians) what harm could a few left-wingers do?

By February 1944, he was tempted by the possibility of a job that would take him through the Aleutians and to various other parts of Alaska, "though I'm not nuts about being on the loose in the Army. Being part and parcel of a definite outfit at a definite station is pleasanter for me, gives me more of a feeling of belonging, and that's one of the nicer Army feelings." A few days later, he confessed that the *Adakian*, the camp newspaper he edited, was beginning to bore him, and "I'm trying to keep myself from taking something I don't really want just because it is something else."[58] Nevertheless, in the latter part of 1944 he did take the job, travelling from island to island, delivering an orientation course. Then, after a spell back on Adak, in April 1945 he was transferred to Fort Richardson, Anchorage, where he ran a program on the post radio and edited a monthly magazine for "Information-Education" personnel.

Throughout this period, he apologized to various correspondents that he was unable to get a furlough, but one wonders whether he tried very hard. He was probably subject to conflicting impulses at this stage. On the one hand, there was the obvious question of how he would handle a return to civilian life, what with his inability to write. On the other hand, he found the return to military discipline at Fort Richardson irksome. Then again, premature rumors of a German surrender were circulating, and he began thinking about quitting, as he was "bored pissless."[59] It was perhaps no accident that just as the

Army expected more discipline of him, Hammett gave it considerably less, taking to the bottle and missing deadlines. When his nervous young lieutenant called him in, Hammett readily agreed that he was doing neither himself nor his country any good by remaining in the Army, and immediately arranged his return to civilian life.[60]

He had at least regained the rank he had earned in World War I: sergeant.

In leaving his haven, of course, Hammett was returning to all the things that might have led him to seek it in the first place. Back home, he resumed his political activity, undeterred by the anti-communist phobia being fomented in the country. He also tried to write fiction again, and it is perhaps significant that his first attempt was about a drunken man who had just been discharged from the Army, perhaps thinking that the last few years might provide him with some autobiographical material; but this attempt, like those that would follow, failed.

And he drank. Layman claims that Hammett "craved the sense of camaraderie that alcohol gives," which strikes one as curious, given the fact that camaraderie cannot have been completely absent from the left-wing circles into which Hammett had once again inserted himself, but maybe Layman has in mind the point made by Jo Hammett, who thinks her father was basically "a shy person and needed the confidence of the bottle for business and social occasions."[61] This period came to an abrupt halt when Hammett suffered a collapse and entered hospital in December 1948 and was told by the doctor to give up drink if he didn't want to die in the next few months, whereupon he stopped drinking for good.

Even before he went dry, however, Hammett would turn up for the course on mystery writing he taught at the CPUSA-supported Jefferson School of Social Science, where guests like Howard Fast or John Howard Lawson would put in an appearance. Living most of the time at Hardscrabble Farm, in December 1945 he had taken a small apartment in the city, and although he thought this would be a good place to write, its main value was its proximity to the Jefferson school, because although he might teach it, he was still unable to write. Hammett still contributed to Hellman's plays, but he failed to write one himself, even though in 1946 he had promised *The Good Meal* to producer Kermit Bloomgarden, who had made arrangements for its production.[62]

But he still had a comfortable income. Apart from book royalties, in 1946 a Sam Spade radio series commenced, lasting until 1950; another was called *The Fat Man*, based on the character of Gutman in *The Maltese Falcon*; and, of course, there was the long-running *Thin Man* series. He made no contribution to the programs, cheerfully admitting that his only duty was to receive the weekly check — although he had his daughter Mary (who, suffering from mental illness, for a time stayed with him in the New York apartment) credited as writer of *The Fat Man*, arranging for her to receive the check. The three radio shows generated a weekly income of $1,200.[63]

After play-doctoring for Kermit Bloomgarden in the summer of 1949, in the following year he was lured back to Hollywood to write the script for *Detective Story* for William Wyler, but this simply did not work out, and he returned to New York.

≋

Hammett's political activity in the postwar years will be discussed in greater detail in Chapter 8. The organization which would have the biggest impact on his life, however, was the Civil Rights Congress of New York (Hammett was its president), as he chaired its bail fund committee, and when four communists skipped bail he and the other trustees were hauled before the judge. Hammett pleaded the Fifth Amendment, refusing to answer questions regarding the four men or the identity of bail fund donors. He and the other trustees were sentenced to six months' imprisonment for contempt of court.

Hammett served his time (less two weeks for good behavior) without complaint (despite, according to his daughter, fainting in the food line on one occasion,[64]) and it is possible that he looked upon his jail term in the same way as he had approached his time in the Army — as a respite from the pressures of life outside (there were similarities: the guards called him "Mr. Hammett," for example).

But prison was the easy part. When he came out on December 9, 1951 he would find that the tax authorities had slapped an attachment to earnings on him for unpaid back taxes to the tune of $100,629.03,[65] Hellman was also hit with a tax demand for $175,000,[66] and this meant that Hardscrabble Farm had to be sold. Given the atmosphere of anti-communist hysteria and the blacklisting, royalties would be scarce anyway (the books of Hammett and other "subversives" were removed from US libraries overseas), but any that did trickle in would go straight to the Internal Revenue Service. The three radio shows based on his characters were cancelled. Thus in 1952 Hammett moved into the gatehouse on property owned by Dr. Samuel Rosen in Katonah, New York for a minimal rent.

≋

In 1955, Hammett had a heart attack while staying with Hellman in Martha's Vineyard, although he didn't realize what had happened as he didn't visit the doctor until a month later, therefore casting doubt on Nolan's claim that it was a "major" attack."[67] His financial situation would remain grim for the rest of his life; in January 1957 a court assessed his federal income tax liability at just under $141,000. Apart from the occasional outing and spells in Martha's Vineyard or in hospital, he lived the life of a hermit in Katonah, writing no fiction that was really going anywhere, and even his correspondence was practically confined to his daughter Jo and Hellman. After a spell in hospital in March 1958, he told Hellman that his health would not permit him to live alone anymore and that he would be entering a Veterans' Hospital; instead, Hellman persuaded him to move in with her in New York City.

November 1960 marked the 30th anniversary of his meeting Hellman. The date was marked by a note signed by Hammett, reading in part: "The love that started on that day was greater than all love anywhere, anytime, and all poetry cannot include it." It continued: "I did not then know what treasure I had, could not, and thus occasionally violated the grandeur of this bond." But in 1978 Hellman confessed to Johnson that she "wrote this and presented it to Dash for his signature."[68]

Late in 1960, Hammett was diagnosed with lung cancer, and he died on January 10 the following year, aged 66. Despite an attempt by J. Edgar Hoover to prevent it, he was buried in Arlington National Cemetery, as he had wished and as was his right as a veteran of two world wars.

NOTES

1. Howard Zinn, *A People's History of the United States, 1492-Present*, revised and updated (New York: HarperPerennial, 1995), 332.
2. Julian Symons, *Dashiell Hammett* (San Diego/New York/London: Harcourt Brace Jovanovich, 1985), 5.
3. Richard Layman, *Shadow Man: The Life of Dashiell Hammett* (New York and London: Harcourt Brace Jovanovich/Bruccoli Clark, 1981), 3.
4. William F. Nolan, *Dashiell Hammett: A Life at the Edge* (London: Arthur Barker, 1983), 3, 4-5. Nolan thinks that Richard Hammett sold the farm but this seems not to have been the case. The Hopewell and Aim farm was bought in 1827 by Samuel Hammett, Richard's grandfather, but it was barren. He willed it to his children, but the store (Hammettville) went to his oldest son Samuel Bisco Hammett, Dashiell Hammett's grandfather. Hammettville was sold in 1889 and the family moved into the house on the farm. See Richard Layman, *Shadow Man*, 4, and Diane Johnson, *The Life of Dashiell Hammett* (US title *Dashiell Hammett: A Life*), (London: Picador, 1985), 13-14.
5. Symons, 6.
6. Johnson, 15-16.
7. Dashiell Hammett to the editor of *The Black Mask*, November 1924; Dashiell Hammett, *Selected Letters of Dashiell Hammett, 1921-1960*, ed. Richard Layman with Julie M. Rivett (Washington D. C.: Counterpoint, 2001), 27.
8. Philip S. Foner, "Jack London: American Rebel," *Jack London/American Rebel*, ed. Philip S. Foner (New York: Citadel Press, 1964), 11.
9. Lillian Hellman, "Introduction," Dashiell Hammett, *The Big Knockover* (New York, Vintage Books, 1989), xvii.
10. Symons, 6.
11. Nolan, 9. Ward points out that "James Wright" had been a favorite alias for Pinkerton undercover operatives since the 1870s, thus placing a question mark over the identity of Hammett's manager. See Nathan Ward, *The Lost Detective: Becoming Dashiell Hammett* (New York: Bloomsbury, 2015), 8.
12. Nolan, 25, 27, 29 fn.
13. According to Jo, Hammett's second daughter, after her mother

died in 1980, Hellman told her that her sister Mary had not been fathered by Hammett. Jo says that she eventually "saw this for what it was — a prime example of Lillian re-writing life so it played better." See Jo Hammett, *Dashiell Hammett: A Daughter Remembers*, ed. Richard Layman with Julie M. Rivett (New York: Carroll & Graf Publishers, 2001), 169. This particular argument continues: Carl Rollyson, *Lillian Hellman: Her Legend and her Legacy* (New York: St. Martin's Press, 1988), 542, claims that only Hellman and a psychiatrist whom Hammett had told were parties to the secret, while Joan Mellen says that Hammett admitted to Rose Evans, his housekeeper, that Mary was not his biological daughter. See Joan Mellen, *Hellman and Hammett: The Legendary Passion of Lillian Hellman and Dashiell Hammett* (New York: Harper Collins, 1996), 247. But a later Hellman biographer, Deborah Martinson, says that the Hammett family point to a letter written by Hammett nine months prior to Mary's birth, in which he expresses his love for Jose after a night together. Deborah Martinson, *Lillian Hellman: A Life with Foxes and Scoundrels* (Berkeley: Counterpoint, 2005), 78.
14 Symons, 10.
15 Layman, *Shadow Man*. 16.
16 Ibid., 23. Sally Cline points out that by the time of Arbuckle's second trial, Hammett had already left the Pinkertons. See Sally Cline, *Dashiell Hammett: Man of Mystery* (New York: Arcade Publishing, 2014), 33.
17 Layman, 22.
18 Vince Emery, commentary, in Dashiell Hammett, *Lost Stories*, ed. Vince Emery (San Francisco: Vince Emery Productions, 2005), 40. However, Ward tends to agree with Layman regarding the unlikely nature of such claims: "Some of the jobs [during his last months as a Pinkerton], such as working the docks for the strikebreaker Blackjack Jerome or climbing a smokestack to search for missing gold, seem physically ambitious feats for a tubercular man whose weight fluctuated during this time between 132 and 126 pounds, nearly 20 pounds below his healthy weight." See Ward, *The Lost Detective*, 58
19 Nolan, 35.
20 In Dashiell Hammett, *Lost Stories*, 43-44. Cline has it that Hammett entered the Munson school "as part of his vocational rehabilitation

to train as a reporter" and finished in May 1923 after 15 months. Cline, 35.
21 Johnson, 48. Nolan (47, fn.) comes up with a slightly different total: 36 stories, counting the two novels as eight.
22 Nolan, 36. Cline is therefore mistaken when she claims that Mencken and Nathan continued to be Hammett's "editors" when he began to submit to *The Black Mask*; by this stage, they were no longer even proprietors. See Cline, 42.
23 Emery, commentary, in Dashiell Hammett, *Lost Stories*, 229.
24 Ibid., 232.
25 Layman, commentary, in Dashiell Hammett, *Selected Letters*, 62. According to Rollyson, Hellman had a total of seven abortions. Carl Rollyson, 33.
26 Johnson, 141.
27 Layman, *Shadow Man*, xvi.
28 Jo Hammett, 95-98.
29 Johnson, 106.
30 Layman, *Shadow Man*, 113.
31 Ibid., 121.
32 Robert L. Gale, *A Dashiell Hammett Companion* (Westport: Greenwood Press, 2000), 170.
33 Nolan, 118.
34 Layman, *Shadow Man*, 141.
35 Symons, 107.
36 This is not to imply that Hammett had a high opinion of the Hearst press, for in *The Dain Curse*, when Gabrielle expresses doubt that her cure for morphine addiction will be easy, the Op says, "You've been reading the Hearst papers," effectively dismissing them as sensationalist. See Dashiell Hammett, *The Dain Curse* in *Five Complete Novels* (New York: Avenel Books, 1980), 261.
37 Emery, commentary, in *Hammett, Lost Stories*, 267.
38 Layman, *Shadow Man*, 132. In early 1937, Hearst offered Hammett $50,000 to write a screen story for his lover, struggling screen actress Marion Davies, but Hammett turned it down. (Johnson, 135).
39 Johnson, 102, 103.
40 Nolan, 156.
41 Johnson, 151. Although in his *Shadow Man* Layman says that

Hammett had fulfilled his obligations to the studio regarding *Another Thin Man*, in his commentary in *Selected Letters*, 133, he says that the job was still unfinished when Hammett had his breakdown.

42 Nolan, 130. Hellman made this remark in "A Still Unfinished Woman," *Rolling Stone*, February 24, 1977 (interview by Christine Doudna).
43 Lillian Hellman, *An Unfinished Woman*, in *Three* (Boston: Little, Brown, 1979), 212.
44 Lillian Hellman, *Pentimento*, in *Three*, 462.
45 Jo Hammett, 9.
46 Josephine Hammett Marshall, "Foreword," Dashiell Hammett, *Selected Letters*, x.
47 Peter Wolfe, *Beams Falling: The Art of Dashiell Hammett* (Bowling Green: Bowling Green University Popular Press, 1980), 1.
48 See, for example, Layman *Shadow Man*, ix-x.
49 Johnson, 170-171.
50 Dorothy Gallagher, *Lillian Hellman: An Imperious Life* (New Haven and London: Yale University Press, 2014.), 67.
51 Jo Hammett, 110.
52 Lillian Hellman, *An Unfinished Woman* in *Three*, 202.
53 Nolan, 184. Layman (*Shadow Man*, 186) gives the impression that both conditions had initially counted against him, and that he had been turned down more than once.
54 Layman, *Shadow Man*, 188.
55 Quoted in Johnson, 173-174.
56 Layman, *Shadow Man*, 187.
57 Nolan, 194.
58 Dashiell Hammett to Lillian Hellman, February 29, 1944, March 5, 1944; *Selected Letters*, 290, 296.
59 Dashiell Hammett to Lillian Hellman, April 28, 1945; *Selected Letters*, 431-432.
60 Johnson, 207. In a letter to his daughter Mary dated August 15, 1945 (VJ Day), Hammett said that he had made a "lucky guess" the previous week in applying for his discharge. *Selected Letters*, 444-445.
61 Layman, *Shadow Man*, 204; Jo Hammett, 49.
62 Emery, commentary, in *Lost Stories*, 332-333.

63 Layman, commentary, in *Selected Letters*, 451.
64 Jo Hammett, 148.
65 Johnson, 248. Layman (*Shadow Man*, xvii) puts the figure at $111,008.60.
66 Nolan, 224.
67 Johnson, 279, Nolan, 230.
68 See *Selected Letters*, 622-623.

2 Searching for the socialist

The fact that in the mid-1930s Dashiell Hammett would publicly align himself with radical causes has persuaded several observers that his political development must have occurred earlier, and that his "socialism" — his "Marxism," even — is apparent as early as the 1920s in some of the stories he wrote for the pulps. This is mistaken, as we will see in this chapter. The evidence indicates that his political development was a slow, lengthy process, and that the leap into its socialist stage occurred after he had effectively ceased to write. What some writers *mistake* for socialism, or Marxism, is mere anti-capitalism, which is not necessarily the same thing at all. Anarchists and nihilists (the position that best describes Hammett's bleak outlook until the mid-thirties) can be described as anti-capitalists, but this does not make them socialists or Marxists.

≈

Hammett's short stories and novelettes may be divided into five periods: those written before his first appearance in *The Black Mask*; those written between the latter date and Phil Cody taking over as editor; those written while Cody was editor; those written during Joseph Shaw's editorship of the magazine; and those written after Hammett left the magazine.

The first six pieces fall into the categories of humor and satire, although half of them never achieved magazine publication.[1]

- "The Parthian Shot" (October 1922, *The Smart Set*)
- "Immortality" (November 1922, *10 Story Book*; as Daghull Hammett)
- "Fragments of Justice" (unpublished, possibly 1922)
- "The Breech-Born" (unpublished, written between 1922 and 1924)
- "A Throne for the Worm" (unpublished, written early 1920s)
- "The Barber and His Wife" (December 1922, *Brief Stories*; as Peter Collinson[2])

Hammett first struck it lucky in *The Smart Set*, the prestigious magazine run by H. L. Mencken and George Jean Nathan, although "The Parthian Shot" is very brief. Similarly, "Immortality" is a single-paragraph joke. At this stage it would seem that Hammett had no interest in writing about crime, for in these early pieces he commented on the world he saw about him, satirizing jurors ("Fragments of Justice"), the little man who is henpecked at home and bullied in the office but who becomes a giant in the barber shop ("A Throne for the Worm"), and jealousy and its consequences ("The Barber and his Wife"). He continued to submit material to *The Smart Set* for a year (it is possible that "The Breech-Born" was intended for this market, being the short, clever kind of squib he had previously sent it), and it is likely that for a time he harbored illusions of joining the ranks of the magazine's more illustrious contributors (F. Scott Fitzgerald, Sinclair Lewis, Aldous Huxley, Somerset Maugham, etc.).

≈

The humorous pieces did not, particularly when they were not published, pay the bills, and so Hammett then went down-market, publishing his first story in *The Black Mask* in December 1922. This was the first of 24 stories before Cody's arrival, but these were not all, as we now see, published in *The Black Mask*.

- "The Road Home" (December 1922, *The Black Mask*; as Peter Collinson)
- "The Master Mind" (January 1923, *The Smart Set*)

- "The Sardonic Star of Tom Doody" (February 1923, *Brief Stories*; as Collinson; aka "The Wages of Crime")
- "The Joke on Eloise Morey" (June 1923, *Brief Stories*, No. 4)
- "The Vicious Circle" (June 15, 1923, *The Black Mask*; as Collinson)
- "Holiday" (July 1923, *The New Pearsons*)
- "The Crusader" (August 1923, *The Smart Set*; as Mary Jane Hammett)
- "The Green Elephant" (October 1923, *The Smart Set*)
- "Arson Plus" (October 1, 1923, *The Black Mask*; as Collinson)
- "Slippery Fingers" (October 15, 1923, *The Black Mask*; as Collinson)
- "Crooked Souls" (October 15, 1923, *The Black Mask*; aka "The Gatewood Caper").
- "The Dimple" (October 15, 1923, *Saucy Stories*)
- "Laughing Masks" (November 1923, *Action Stories*)
- "It" (November 1, 1923, *The Black Mask*; aka "The Black Hat That Wasn't There")
- "The Second-Story Angel" (November 15, 1923, *The Black Mask*)
- "The House Dick" (December 1, 1923, *The Black Mask*; aka "Bodies Piled Up")
- "Itchy" (January 1924, *Brief Stories*)
- "The Tenth Clew" (January 1, 1924, *The Black Mask*)
- "The Man Who Killed Dan Odoms" (January 15, *The Black Mask*)
- "Esther Entertains" (February 1924, *Brief Stories*)
- "Night Shots" (February 1, 1924, *The Black Mask*; aka "The Judge Laughed Last")
- "The New Racket" (February 15, 1924, *The Black Mask*)
- "Afraid of a Gun" (March 1, 1924, *The Black Mask*)
- "Zigzags of Treachery" (March 1, 1924, *The Black Mask*)

After "The Road Home," an adventure story set in Burma rather than a crime tale, it was six months before Hammett's second appearance in *The Black Mask*, but by this time he had already started writing about crime for other publications. During this period, two of his stories might be classified as adventure, six as humor or satire, and 16 crime (although the edges were sometimes blurred: "The Green Elephant," for example, is a satirical crime story, while "The Second-Story Angel" might be called a humorous crime story).

It is evident, however, that by the end of the period he saw crime as his subject and *The Black Mask* as his market, for while only 14 of the 24 stories were published there, the frequency increased as time passed.

Hammett's experiences with the Pinkertons were useful in more ways than one. Not only was he provided with material, but Emery says that as a detective himself, Hammett had learned to remember details of clothing and to describe them well in his reports, although he had greater success with men's than women's attire.[3] Nolan says that Phil Geauque, manager of the Pinkertons' San Francisco office, had, having admired his reports, encouraged Hammett to be a writer.[4]

Although Hammett is credited with developing (if not inventing) the hardboiled detective story, it is a fact that even some of his crime tales are not particularly hardboiled. Indeed, some do not have an urban setting.[5] Cawelti has pointed out that some of Hammett's early material, inheriting the pulp tradition, resemble westerns. This is true enough, for "Afraid of a Gun" (March 1924) has a Jack London flavor to it, even though the background is a bootlegging operation, and the mark of some of Hammett's predecessors like the western writer Owen Wister is often evident. "Arson Plus" and "The Man Who Killed Don Odoms" (January 1924) both have rural settings. *The Black Mask* itself, both before and after it lost the definite article from its title, often featured a western scene on its cover. Nolan goes further, agreeing with those critics who say that "the private detective is a direct carryover from the lone western gunfighter..." They are, he says, "basically, the same man."[6]

And while Hammett, like Chandler, had little time for the "classic" detective story purveyed by the likes of Arthur Conan Doyle and Agatha Christie, where the crime is solved due to the brilliant mind of the investigator, he sometimes adopted the formula himself, and possibly this was inevitable once Hammett had created, in the Continental Op, his counterpart of Doyle's Holmes and Christie's Poirot. The Op is unnamed, middle-aged and overweight, and one suspects Hammett wanted to make him as little like himself as possible. He made his first appearance in "Arson Plus" in October 1923, and appeared in eight of the stories in this second period. In his first outing, he is Holmes in American garb; "Slippery Fingers," which appeared a fortnight later, has traces of the English murder mystery to the extent that there is even a body in the library! "Night Shots" (February 1, 1924) also seems to be a case for Holmes rather than the hardboiled Op.

Gradually, however, the hardboiled formula firmed up, and

Hammett obviously felt that it was a winner. Just as interesting, and in a sense even more so, are the stories in which Hammett departed from this formula, for these provide evidence that he was seeking to be more than a pulp writer. "Holiday" (July 1923), an autobiographical piece in which the protagonist spends a few days in Tijuana, is full of atmosphere, a clear indication that he was capable of more than detective stories. "The Crusader," published in *The Smart Set* the following month, is a satire on the Ku Klux Klan.

In October 1923, Hammett made his last appearance in *The Smart Set* with "The Green Elephant," in which Joe Shupe, newly embarked (not very successfully) on a life of crime, accidentally comes into possession of the proceeds of a robbery. The hoard (or, rather, the fear that it will be stolen from him) makes his life a misery, and he is almost relieved when he is arrested by Prohibition agents, whose attention he has attracted by his suspicious behavior. This story says a lot about Hammett's attitude to money, and in just a few years time he would demonstrate that he could spend it and give it away faster than it came in — no matter how fast that was. It is possible that he also saw Shupe's hoard as a metaphor for the burdens of fame that he suspected might shortly be coming his way.

October 1923 also saw the birth of the Op, who appeared in three *Black Mask* stories that month. Two of these were by "Peter Collinson," the nom de plume Hammett had first adopted the previous December — an indication that he was anxious to maximize the financial return on his creation.

Indeed, Emery says that Hammett developed the Op because he needed to increase his income, and felt that a series of stories about a single detective might achieve this, as the writing would call for less invention each time and he would therefore be able to write more; he might also acquire a following and, thus, a higher rate.[7] Even so, at this stage Hammett still wrote the occasional story outside of this formula. "Laughing Masks" (November 1923), concerns Russian émigrés, one of them a beautiful woman whose father has been murdered by his brother in order to gain control of his wealth. But rather than indicating a cautious incursion into political territory (although Hammett sent the piece to *Action Stories* rather than *The Black Mask*), this marked his first attempt at a non-American theme, and this would be followed by others.

Hammett was most entertaining when he combined crime with satire. The main character in "The Second-Story Angel" (November 1923) is a writer of crime fiction who is persuaded by a female burglar that, if he allows her to go free and then supports her, she will provide him with sufficient material to allow him to profit from the investment. He eventually finds that several other writers have fallen for the same line — a comment, surely, on the commercial reality of the crowded field in which Hammett operated. "Itchy" (January 1924) is a delightful tale in which Floyd "Itchy" Maker attempts to emulate the gentleman crook of fiction and swiftly comes to grief; this is Hammett giving his opinion of one branch of the "traditional" crime story. The following month's "Esther Entertains" demonstrates that Hammett was probably making no idle boast when, a little later, he told Blanche Knopf that he was thinking of writing a "stream-of-consciousness" novel; he also shows that, unlike Chandler, he has experience of women and knows how to write about them.

But sometimes the stories were just not up to scratch. In his Hammett biography, Layman describes stories such as "Slippery Fingers," "Bodies Piled Up," "Night Shots" and "One Hour" as lethargic, and Hammett as "a lazy writer, producing facile intrigues on schedule."[8] Hammett would probably be the first to agree.

≈

Phil Cody became the editor of *The Black Mask* in April 1924, and it is perhaps significant that Hammett's next five stories all appeared in that magazine and all featured the Continental Op.

- "One Hour" (April 1, 1924, *The Black Mask*)
- "The House on Turk Street" (April 15, 1924, *The Black Mask*)
- "The Girl with the Silver Eyes" (June 1924, *The Black Mask*)
- "Death on Pine Street" (September 1924, *The Black Mask*; aka "Women, Politics and Murder")
- "The Golden Horseshoe" (November 1924, *The Black Mask*)
- "Who Killed Bob Teal?" (November 1924, *True Detective Stories*)
- "Nightmare Town" (December 27, 1924, *Argosy All-Star Weekly*)
- "Magic" (probably mid-1920s, unpublished)
- "The Lovely Strangers" (probably mid-1920s, unpublished)

- "Tom, Dick or Harry" (January 1925, *The Black Mask*; aka "Mike or Alec or Rufus")
- "Another Perfect Crime" (February 1925, *Experience*)
- "Ber-Bulu" (March 1925, *Sunset Magazine*; aka "The Hairy One")
- "The Whosis Kid" (March 1925, *The Black Mask*)
- "The Scorched Face" (May 1925, *The Black Mask*)
- "The Hunter" (1924 or 1925, unpublished)
- "Corkscrew" (September 1925, *The Black Mask*)
- "Ruffian's Wife" (October 1925, *Sunset Magazine*)
- "Dead Yellow Women" (November 1925, *The Black Mask*)
- "The Gutting of Couffignal" (December 1925, *The Black Mask*)
- "The Nails in Mr. Cayterer" (January 1926, *The Black Mask*)
- "A Man Named Thin" (March 1961, *EQMM*)
- "The Assistant Murderer" (February 1926, *The Black Mask*)
- "Creeping Siamese" (March 1926, *The Black Mask*)
- "Seven Pages" (probably 1926, unpublished)
- "Faith" (1926, unpublished)

Although it is often said that it was Joseph Shaw who encouraged Hammett, it is possible that Phil Cody has been given less credit than he deserves in this regard, for Layman notes that the new editor "insisted that the quality of the writing in his pages be elevated, championing Hammett as a model for his other writers and imposing what might be called the *Black Mask* editorial formula on his authors." When Cody asked Hammett for his opinion of a recent issue of the magazine, Hammett "offered perceptive criticism of each story in the issue, concluding with the comment that three of the stories 'simply... didn't mean anything. People moved around doing things, but neither the people nor the things they did were interesting enough to work up a sweat over.'"[9] Nevertheless, there would eventually be a falling-out between Hammett and Cody.

Some of the 25 stories written during this two-year period are frankly undistinguished. The first, "One Hour," initially offers the promise of social comment, as we learn that the employer who has been killed in a road accident has recently fired two employees for being Wobblies (members of the Industrial Workers of the World, with which Hammett had come into contact during his Pinkerton days), but then retreats, as the two men never appear in the story. "The House on Turk Street" is a straightforward robbery-murder thriller, with no social comment. There are few indications in these stories that Hammett might be acquiring a socialist outlook. In "The Girl with the Silver Eyes," for example, he describes Roy Axford as "a mining man who had a finger in at least half of the big business enterprises of the Pacific Coast; and his word on anything was commonly considered good enough for anybody."[10] There are, of course, capitalists who are considered trustworthy — at least by other capitalists — but a socialist would not normally depict such a character positively. "Death on Pine Street," originally rejected by Cody, can only be called a damp squib, as it ends with the revelation that the victim's death was caused by the accidental discharge of a policeman's gun.

Occasionally, we come across a detail that might — just might — be intended to stand for some more significant sickness in the system. In "The Golden Horseshoe," for example, we learn that although postal inspectors (bear in mind that the U.S. Mail was once regarded with the kind of reverence usually reserved for the Constitution and the Declaration of Independence) are forbidden to assist private investigators except in limited circumstances, this hurdle can be overcome by simply lying to the man, as this will provide him with an alibi, "and whether he thinks you're lying or not doesn't matter."[11]

And then we come to "Nightmare Town." This long story concerns a town entirely populated by crooks (or their converts), where every business is a scam intended to deny "the syndicate" its share of what began as a bootlegging operation. The law, the postal service, the bank, the medical profession and the insurance business are all in it together, along with church ministers and civic officials. "There's a hundred corporations in Izzard that are nothing but addresses on letterheads — but stock certificates and bonds have been sold in them from one end of these United States to the other."[12]

It's tempting to believe that the town of Izzard, which in the finale goes up in smoke, preceded by deaths too numerous to count as the central character fights to escape its environs, stands for the entire capitalist system in the USA. Quite possibly this was Hammett's intention, but the town is brought to grief not by organized workers but by Hammett's protagonist, a drunken adventurer. If the story *was* intended as an anti-capitalist metaphor, Hammett at this stage was akin to the anarchist who believes it is sufficient to crush the oppressors with a single, devastating blow in order to usher in the brotherhood of man.

Around this time, Hammett wrote a truly curious story that at first glance could not conceivably have come from the pen of a Marxist. In his commentary preceding the previously unpublished "Magic" in the 2013 collection *The Hunter and Other Stories*, Layman speaks of Hammett's "enthusiastic interest in the supernatural" and his appreciation of Arthur Edward Waite, author of *The Brotherhood of the Rosy Cross* (1924),[13] but infuriatingly he does not cite his sources, although it is possible that Layman merely assumes this from the reference to the Waite book in *The Dain Curse*.[14] Similarly, an "enthusiastic interest in the supernatural" may have been assumed from the "temple" aspects of the plot of *Dain* and similar quackery portrayed in some short stories.

"Magic" is overwritten — so much for Hammett's praise of the short sentence (see below) — and awkwardly phrased: apprentices "shifted their knees on the floor behind him and breathed with unguarded noisiness through open mouths."[15] Nevertheless, there are some promising aspects to the story.

Strait the magician (who name is presumably patterned on that of the aforementioned Waite) is asked by a supplicant to cause a certain woman to love him. Although the woman concerned turns out to be in a relationship with Strait, he conjures up a demon to do the deed. Strait admits that his act is little more than "mountbankery" and "charlatanism," but when his apprentice nevertheless refers to his accomplishments, he counters, "Must I be less adept than politicians and recruiting sergeants and the greenest of girls?"[16] Well, here indeed is political comment, albeit buried in a story that was never published at the time.

But Hammett also uses the story to comment upon his own situation, having Strait tell his apprentice, Simon, "In this nonsense you've learned you'll find the satisfaction a man has in doing what — no matter how silly — he can do skillfully." Although admitting that the woman was his own lover, "Strait did not seem to mind. He confessed he had not played the man's part. He said Simon would understand, when his day came, that to the extent one becomes a magician one ceases to be a man. And he added that this same thing might hold true of sailors and jewelers and bankers..."[17] And writers?

Here, one feels, is the real point of the story for, like Chandler after him, Hammett was burned by the dismal realization that he was merely a "pulp writer." He aspired to greater things, but he was also a realist, acknowledging that as a professional writer he might earn a living writing what he on one occasion dismissed as "junk"[18] and sometimes even do it well enough to earn public praise as well as dollars, but he would have to forsake his real love in order to do this.

"Magic," in fact, testified to the truth of this, for while he was managing to earn a living and attract public attention by writing his crime stories, this story was destined to gather dust for almost a century.

Several pieces that Hammett wrote during this period indicated a desire to broaden his horizons and get off the pulp treadmill. "The Lovely Strangers," part romance, part detective story, about a serial bigamist flushed out by a practical joke played by a green young man in love with the intended victim, was, although unpublished at the time, possibly intended for one of the "slicks," the up-market magazines which, like the *Saturday Evening Post*, were printed on more expensive, shiny paper than the "pulps."

Whenever he could, he published in magazines other than *Black Mask*; "Another Perfect Crime," for example, appeared in *Experience*. It must be conceded, however, that by itself this did not necessarily denote a desire to improve the quality of his fiction, as it may have been born of the need to maximize his income.

The story entitled "Ber-Bulu," (aka "The Hairy One") which appeared in *Sunset Magazine* in March 1925, was, however, startlingly different. Set in Tawi-Tawi in the Sulu archipelago, this reveals a fair knowledge of this Muslim area of the Philippines: Hammett knew about the *anting-anting* (an amulet thought to protect the wearer) and that a local Muslim leader was a "datto" (although the spelling is more often "datu").

"Forty dollars Mex" doesn't sound right at first, as the currency was Philippine pesos, but Hammett had obviously learned somewhere that although the Philippines had used its own mint since 1861, Mexican currency was widely available. As Hammett's only venture outside the USA was a short trip across the Mexican border to Tijuana, his knowledge of the Sulu archipelago possibly arose from his omnivorous reading habits — and he cannot have missed events in the Muslim areas of the Philippines that from time to time hit the headlines, as when, in 1906, the US colonizers slaughtered over 600 men, women and children at Bud Dajo, Sulu.[19]

It must be said, however, that Hammett makes no display of solidarity with the colonized Muslims (called "Moros," from the Spanish for "Moors"), and displays the racism typical of both the time and most American settlers. "Knock him [a Moro] around," says the narrator, "or get a laugh on him, and you can do what you will with him — and he'll like it."

Warned of Jeffol, the Moro whose woman he has appropriated, the glowering giant Levison says, "He is a nigger and I can handle a dozen of him."[20] But Hammett ensures that Jeffol, a recent convert to Christianity, gets the better of Levison by using the example of the Samson story and, shearing him, renders him ridiculous — and weak-chinned.

In "The Hunter," written in 1924 or 1925, Hammett paints the private detective as he really is. For Fred Vitt, detection is not a vocation but just a job he happened to land ten years earlier, since when he has become skilled in an occupation he often finds distasteful. Employed to discover the man who has been forging the checks of the owner of a box company, he homes in on Close, the man's book-keeper. Close is not a criminal but a poorly-paid employee; he is thin, his clothes frayed, while his employer is a large man with a ballooning red face — and probably an adulterer, as three of his legitimate checks have been made out to a woman.

Close, it turns out, has bills to pay, having taken in an abandoned wife with two small children. Vitt browbeats him into submission in front of the woman and her two howling children, forcing him to confess. Having dropped off the couple at the local jail, Vitt instantly dismisses them from his mind, his thoughts turning to a mundane errand his wife has asked him to run on his way home.

This story was unpublished, and we must therefore assume that editors who would not bat an eyelid at multiple murders, no matter how gruesome, recoiled from this stark illustration of what one working man will do to another due to their respective roles within the capitalist system.

In a sense, it was the most brutal, hardboiled piece Hammett ever wrote, and the one which (whether or not he realized it) most clearly sounded a note of class politics. While the cold-blooded professionalism of Vitt, which had its roots in what Hammett had been taught at the Pinkerton agency, laid the basis for the development of Sam

Spade in *The Maltese Falcon*, this story (written, significantly, in the more objective third person, unlike the first-person Op stories) sadly did not herald further attempts to use the private detective genre to lay bare the inhumanity of the system.

Despite the occasional excursion into new fields, Hammett returned to the *Black Mask* treadmill. "Tom, Dick or Harry" (January 1925) sees the Op acting as little more than a modern-day Sherlock Holmes. In "The Whosis Kid" (March 1925) Hammett lays down a couple of markers for the future — all the villains try to double-cross each other, while the Op, making no attempt to prevent the title character from frisking a woman, remarks "I'm no Galahad."[21]

In "The Scorched Face" (May 1925), the Op is called upon to save several female members of the upper middle class (and at least one millionairess) from the blackmailing leader of a religious cult who has photographic evidence of their sexual abandon while under his hypnotic influence; this tale is saved by an effective sting in the tail as the Op, about to burn the photographs, finds one of his cop friend's rich wife. "Corkscrew" (September 1925) is practically a western in which the Op has the rough element kill each other so that the development company that has hired him via the Agency can sell its land. He seems to have no moral scruple about this. Because he has it in mind to employ his own, rather more lethal, way of cleaning up the town, the Op rejects advice from the few morally upright citizens of Corkscrew, as when he is harangued by the minister:

> "To refrain even for an hour from punishing wickedness is to be a partner to that wickedness, brother. You have been inside that house of sin operated by Bardell. You have heard the Sabbath desecrated with the sound of pool balls. You have smelled the foul odor of illegal rum on men's breaths! Strike now, brother! Let it not be said that you condoned evil from your first day in Corkscrew! Go into those hells and do your duty as an officer of the law and a Christian!"
>
> This was a minister: I didn't like to laugh.[22]

One can imagine Hammett, a decade or so later, reacting in the same way to a harangue by a left-wing critic of Soviet policy.

There is in Hammett's second outing in *Sunset Magazine*, "Ruffian's Wife" (October 1925), at least a spark of political understanding. Very unusually, this is told solely from the point of view of a woman who has previously worshipped the god-like husband (an early Indiana Jones type) but now is horrified as she sees him at first cowed by the sight of a gun in the hand of an opponent (a fat man by the name of Leonidas Doucas, a possible prototype for *The Maltese Falcon's* Gutman), and then killing the man in a fight. She now suspects that her adventurer husband might, stripped of his courage, be "no more than a shoplifter on a geographically larger scale, a sneak thief who crept into strangers' lands instead of homes..."[23]

Further signs that Hammett was, if not trying very successfully to break out of the detective thriller genre, to at least do something different within it, came in the next two Op stories. "Dead Yellow Women" features Chang Li Ching, who heads an anti-Japanese movement in China after the death of the nationalist leader Sun Yat Sen (the story is bang up to date, as Sun had only died a few months before its appearance) and is running guns to the nationalists.

Hammett here ventures into the world of imperialism and its opponents, and while most of the time he gets it right, he never explains why Lillian Shan, whose father had supported the Manchu dynasty to the extent that the Chinese population of San Francisco ("mostly from Fokien and Kwangtung, where democratic ideas and hatred of Manchus go together"[24]) had tried to keep him out of the USA, should now be working with Chang.

Nevertheless, Hammett has Lillian give a clear explanation of the anti-imperialist case. "Chang Li Chang," she tells the Op, "is one of the leaders of the anti-Japanese movement in China. Since the death of Sun Wen — or Sun Yat-Sen, as he is called in the south of China and here — the Japanese have increased their hold on the Chinese government until it is greater than it ever was. It is Sun Yat-Sen's work that Chang Li Ching and his friends are carrying on."[25]

A page later, he makes sure Lillian places the current situation in its historical context:

> "Since the day of Taou-kwang [the Daoguang Emperor who ruled from 1820 to 1850; the First Opium War occurred during his reign.] my country has been the plaything of

more aggressive nations. Is any price too great for patriotic Chinese to pay to end that period of dishonor?"[26]

Although the story is not without interest, and provides evidence of an anti-imperialist stirring in Hammett, it is marred by the presence of too much "Fu-Manchu" stuff, particularly in its depiction of Chang, and careless racism. The Op enlists the aid of Cipriano, a Filipino, of whom Hammett has the former remark: "At night, like all the Filipinos in San Francisco, he could be found down in Kearney Street, just below Chinatown, except when he was in a Chinese gambling-house passing his money over to the yellow brothers."[27] At one point, the Op says, "An odor came to me — an unmistakable odor — the smell of unwashed Chinese."[28]

Furthermore, Hammett's anti-imperialism is hardly consistent. It is noteworthy that while Lillian Shan talks of "more aggressive nations," the only culprit she mentions is Japan; Hammett provides her with no dialogue outlining the role of British — or, for that matter, US or French — imperialism. This is not a small matter, because Japan had taken the decision to industrialize and militarize because it could see that China's failure to do so had allowed the leading European powers to humiliate that huge country.

Despite the Op's, and therefore Hammett's, obvious sympathy with the nationalist cause in China, he muses:

> I had no proof that I could tie on Chang, couldn't get any. Regardless of his patriotism, I'd have given my right eye to put the old boy away. That would have been something to write home about. But there hadn't been a chance of nailing him, so I had to be content with making a bargain whereby he turned everything over to me except himself and his friends.[29]

Why would he be so keen on "nailing him?" We must assume that Hammett's anti-imperialism was insufficiently developed to overcome the cold-blooded, "professional" approach to the job of detection; but we must also allow for the fact that he was writing for *The Black Mask*, as it must be doubted that Phil Cody would have countenanced one of his authors given vent to a full-throated anti-imperialist cry.

Chang writes the Op a flattering note, on which the Op reflects, thereby closing the story: "You can take that any way you like. But I know the man who wrote it, and I don't mind admitting that I've stopped eating in Chinese restaurants, and that if I never have to visit Chinatown again it'll be soon enough."[30] Why so unpleasantly racist? And why that awful title?

Just as interesting is "The Gutting of Couffignal" (December, 1925), in which the villains, as in 1923's "Laughing Masks," are Russian nobility. The Op's assignment is at first entirely lacking in excitement, as his job is to guard the presents at a wedding on the island of Couffignal, an isolated place inhabited by the very rich and the minimum possible number of tradesmen required to sustain them. The Op's attitude to this clientele is decidedly lacking in respect.

> The higher these roads get, the farther apart and larger are the houses they lead to. The occupants of these higher houses are the owners and rulers of the island. Most of them are well-fed old gentlemen who, the profits they took from the world with both hands in their younger days now stowed away as safe percentages, have bought into the island colony so they may spend what is left of their lives nursing their livers and improving their golf among their kind. They admit to the island only as many storekeepers, working people, and similar riffraff as are needed to keep them comfortably served.[31]

The guests should impress the Op but, of course, they do not.

> The world had been well represented. There had been an admiral and an earl or two from England; an ex-president of a South American country; a Danish baron; a tall young Russian princess surrounded by lesser titles, including a fat, bald, jovial and black-bearded Russian general...[32]

When the well-armed Russian contingent sets about stripping the island to its last dollar, the demographic drawbacks of Couffignal become obvious, as the Op observes that "You can't fight machine guns and hand grenades with peaceful villagers and retired capitalists."[33]

After the Op has nabbed the Russian princess, she explains her plight:

> "There are so many Russians who were once somebodies and who now are nobodies that I won't bore you with the repetition of a tale the world has grown tired of hearing. But you must remember that this weary tale is real to us who are its subjects. However, we fled from Russia with what we could carry of our property, which fortunately was enough to keep us in bearable comfort for a few years."[34]

She confirms the essentially useless nature of the former nobility — of which, we suspect, the Op is already aware. In London, they had opened a loss-making Russian restaurant, then tried teaching music and languages. "In short, we hit on all the means of making our living that other Russian exiles hit upon, and so always found ourselves in overcrowded, and thus unprofitable, fields. But what else did we know — could we do?"[35]

When the princess tries first to buy him off, then offers him her body, the Op counters with a simple exposition of his approach to his job, which may have mirrored Hammett's view of his own.

> "Now I pass up about twenty-five or thirty thousand of honest gain because I like being a detective, like the work. And liking work makes you want to do it as well as you can. Otherwise there'd be no sense to it. That's the fix I'm in. I don't know anything else, don't enjoy anything else, don't want to know or enjoy anything else."[36]

Having failed to buy him, the princess runs for the door. Ever the professional, the Op puts a bullet in her leg. So much for the former Russian nobility. It's tempting to conclude that here is evidence of Hammett's developing communist sympathies, but it must be realized that the Op has done this job on behalf not of the revolution but the member of the US nobility who has employed him.

In 1924, Hammett had submitted the vast majority of his stories to *The Black Mask*, but two of these were rejected. In a letter to the editor in August 1924 (Phil Cody edited the magazine from April 1924 to October 1926), Hammett accepted the medicine, confessing that the Continental Op had "degenerated into a meal-ticket" as his creator had "fallen into the habit of bringing him out and running him around whenever the landlord, or the butcher, or the grocer show signs of nervousness." He really should, he said, stick to what he *wanted* to write.[37]

Layman rather hard-heartedly says that Hammett's letter "does not ring true,"[38] as Hammett, having said that the stories were not worth rescuing, went ahead and used them anyway. Layman fails to consider that it simply was not possible for Hammett to place the demands of art above those of the landlord, the butcher and the grocer, as apart from his disability pension all he had to support his family was the proceeds of his writing, and pulp writers were notoriously low-paid. In addition, Hammett was sick with TB again in 1924, and he was forced to rent separate accommodation for his wife and child in order to guard against infection.[39] It was, therefore, a desperately poor Dashiell Hammett who, rather than discarding the two stories, succeeded in getting Cody to accept a presumably amended version of "Death on Pine Street" (aka "Women, Politics, and Murder") in September that year, and placed "Who Killed Bob Teal?" with *True Detective Stories* in November.

Less than two years later, a further difference arose with Cody when, in response to the latter's demand for more action, Hammett submitted "The Nails in Mr. Cayterer," featuring the effeminate poet-detective Robin Thin, which appeared in the January 1926 issue of the magazine.[40] This was followed in February by "The Assistant Murderer," in which Hammett emphasized the spectacular ugliness of the detective Alex Rush. Hammett, it seemed, was in revolt; he also claimed that Cody owed him $300,[41] and he was threatening to leave unless he received increased payments for his stories. Erle Stanley Gardner, another *Black Mask* stalwart, told Cody that he was willing to take one cent per word less if this was transferred to Hammett, but the magazine's owner, Eltinge Warner, vetoed the arrangement.[42] Thus, Hammett's first stint at the magazine was approaching its end.

Hammett wrote a second Robin Thin story entitled "A Man Named Thin," but this was not published until March 1961, shortly after his death. Presumably, however, it was written soon after "The Nails in Mr. Cayterer." The second story is a spoof, but clever and amusing, and evidence of the range of Hammett's skills; but he's back in the Sherlock Holmes mode, the solution of the crime relying solely on the genius of the detective.

In February 1926 came "The Assistant Murderer," and apart from the novelty of its exceptionally ugly detective, this is notable only for Hammett's invention of awkward-sounding words like "frightenedly."[43] Given that Hammett would demonstrate in his correspondence that he was concerned by the sounds of words and phrases, one is led to suspect that this story was dashed off in a hurry, and that he simply could not be bothered, possibly because it was destined for Cody, to smarten it up. It was also one of those Hammett stories, a mystery in the traditional mode, where one only understands what has been happening when the detective gives his explanation at the end — more a "whatshappening" than a "whodunit." This is another indication of haste and carelessness.

In March 1926 came "Creeping Siamese," another "whatshappening," a completely unbelievable tale in which once again the Op solves the mystery Holmes-style. This was Hammett's last story for *The Black Mask* for almost a year, as he now left to try his hand at advertising.

≈

However, if Hammett was showing clear signs of wearying of the detective genre, this did not mean that he had given up on writing as a whole, for there is evidence that in 1926 he was trying his hand at other genres. It was during this time that Hammett wrote the unpublished "Seven Pages," which consists of a string of apparently autobiographical fragments. With more of them, one feels, he could have produced an impressionistic book of memoirs.

And then there was "Faith," an unpublished story about cannery workers, one of whom is a Wobbly. Here, says Layman in his commentary on the story in *The Hunter and Other Stories*, is evidence of an early awareness by Hammett of "progressive labor causes."[44] Well, hardly early, as Hammett was now 32 and had come into contact with

Wobblies during his Pinkerton years; it would be truer to say that this was one of the earliest indications of Hammett's interest in the labor movement, but that interest had come rather late.

One of the cannery workers, Feach, refuses to join in a condemnation of the job by Morphy, a man who sings satirical Wobbly anthems ("There'll be pie in the sky when you die," etc.). Feach claims there must be a god because for five years at every place he's worked (first at his own farm, which, along with his family, was taken from him) he's been hit by disaster. He curses God, challenges him, but nothing happens, so he sets fire to the bunkhouses where the Polish workers are housed, and then uses the familiar logic of the believer in the irrational to explain his behavior. "Maybe I done it," he said complacently, "and maybe Something used me to do it."[45]

"Faith" remained unpublished until it was included in the collection *The Hunter and Other Stories* in 2013. Whether Hammett tried to place it is uncertain, but its obvious atheism would probably have earned it a rejection slip, so Hammett need not have let this deter him from writing about the working class, particularly as the 1930s got underway. But he never did.

During this period, Hammett contributed articles to *Western Advertising*, and according to Johnson wrote its book reviews (on advertising).[46] One of his pieces for this journal, appearing in October 1926, was significantly called "The Advertisement is Literature." In this, he quotes Anatole France's view that the most beautiful sentence is the shortest. And although he would be credited as pioneering realistic dialogue in his stories and novels, here Hammett takes the view that simplicity and clarity cannot merely be lifted from life but must be created by the artist:

> Simplicity and clarity are not to be got from the man in the street. They are the most elusive and difficult of literary accomplishments, and a high degree of skill is necessary to any writer who would win them. They are the most important qualities in securing the maximum effect on the reader. To secure that maximum desired effect is literature's chief goal…[47]

In this Hammett was obviously discussing, more than merely advertising prose, his approach to his own writing, although it is true that not all of his sentences are short and beautiful. But the fact that he laid out this philosophy in *Western Advertising* is significant, as it indicated that writing was to him, as detection had been, just a job that he happened to be doing and it would have meaning for him only if he did it well. Moreover, it seemed to matter little to him whether the subject matter was crime or advertising. With such a "formalist" approach, it is perhaps not surprising that his writing contains less social comment than might be expected.

He did, in fact, plan a novel called "The Secret Emperor" during this period, and while this might be described as political, the surviving fragment indicates that Hammett was still a long way from adopting a Marxist viewpoint. The hero, Captain Elfinstone, is described in Hammett's notes as the "foremost intelligence man of his time...35, gaunt, powerful flat muscles, copper hair and eyes, bony mouth and chin, nose like a knife."[48] Elfinstone is, we gather, a war hero and often in the public eye, and he appears cast in the Bulldog Drummond mold of the period, a stolid, unflappable WASP standing between a villainous (and somewhat darker-skinned) conspirator and the democracy as practiced by the victorious allies in the recent war. (Physically, Hammett made Elfinstone an exaggerated version of himself, a practice which he adopted only very gradually in his published novels.)

Elfinstone, currently reorganizing the police detective bureau in an unnamed northwestern city, is summoned to Washington by retired General Dolliard, who says that papers have been removed from his safety deposit box which, if made public, will result in his "utter, absolute ruin."[49] After Elfinstone has spent a day inquiring into the company responsible for the safety deposit box, the papers miraculously reappear, and Dolliard tells him to cease the investigation. Later, however, as a disgusted Elfinstone refuses to see him, Dolliard insists on a meeting, and uses his wife to trick him into it. As the investigator catches sight of Dolliard in his hotel lobby, he turns away, whereupon the general pulls out a pistol and, after a struggle, ends up dead. Elfinstone is now besieged by problems: he is arrested and, although a top-notch lawyer has been assigned to represent him, Mrs. Dolliard's testimony at the inquest leads the jury to disregard his claim of self-defense; as he is released on bail, he learns that he has been sacked by the northwestern city for breach of contract; a woman he knows only as the partner of a jailed swindler is suing him for breach of promise, and a scandal sheet is implying that he has been having an affair with Mrs. Dolliard. He calls the latter and asks to meet, telling her that he has information of vital importance to her. She at first refuses, but relents when he mentions the name "Brefina." At her house, he indicates that he has a pretty good idea of the contents of her late husband's papers. But there the fragment ends.

The lawyer representing Elfinstone has been appointed by Seth Gutman, whose acquaintance he had made the previous day — and in very curious circumstances. Elfinstone had seen Gutman's daughter, Tamar, at Dolliard's house on the day of his arrival in Washington. He had no opportunity to speak to her, but spent considerable time ogling her. As Hammett gives his characters no interior life (a failing which will persist throughout the five published novels), we have little idea what might be on Elfinstone's mind and it therefore comes as something of a shock when, just a day later, he goes to her home, confesses his love for her and asks her to accompany him on his return to the northwest; they can be married on Saturday. She, after a moment of resistance, agrees — as does her father, Seth Gutman, to whom she now introduces him.

Even if we were granted access to Elfinstone's, thoughts, it is doubtful whether these scenes would ring true. The Gutmans, however, may have had their reasons for so readily agreeing to Elfinstone's rash proposal, for Hammett's notes for the novel indicate that Seth Gutman (a surname Hammett would later use for one of the villains in *The Maltese Falcon*), who has no chance of becoming President of the USA because he is Jewish, plans to rule the country by proxy, amassing compromising information on candidates.[50] For whatever reason, Hammett abandoned "The Secret Emperor" and never revived it.

≈

Joseph Shaw was brought in as editor of *Black Mask* (as, with the dropping of the definite article, the magazine was now called) when Phil Cody was promoted to the positions of circulation manager and vice-president of the magazine's parent company. Shaw not only wooed Hammett back, but encouraged him to write longer stories.[51] Layman

43

says that the period which now began, lasting until 1930, when he completed his fourth novel, was the most productive of Hammett's life, as he wrote almost 60 book reviews (of detective mysteries for the *Saturday Review of Literature*) between 1927 and 1929,[52] two novelettes,[53] four stories and four novels (each of which was serialized in *Black Mask*).[54]

Hammett's stories in this period were as follows. The serialized novels are clearly indicated.

- "An Inch and a Half of Glory" (June 10-17, 2013, *The New Yorker*)
- "The Big Knockover" (February 1927, *Black Mask*)
- "The Advertising Man Writes a Love Letter" (February 26, 1927, *Judge*)
- "$106,000 Blood Money" (May 1927, *Black Mask*)
- "The Main Death" (June 1927, *Black Mask*)

RED HARVEST
- "The Cleansing of Poisonville" (November 1927, *Black Mask*)
- "Crime Wanted — Male or Female" (December 1927, *Black Mask*)
- "Dynamite" (January 1928, Black Mask)
- "The 19th Murder" (February 1928, *Black Mask*)

- "This King Business" (January 1928, *Mystery Stories*, but written in 1927)

THE DAIN CURSE
- "Black Lives" (November 1928, *Black Mask*)
- "The Hollow Temple" (December 1928, *Black Mask*)
- "Black Honeymoon" (January 1929, *Black Mask*)
- "Black Riddle" (February 1929, *Black Mask*)

- "The Sign of the Potent Pills" (unpublished, written some time between 1927 and 1929)
- "The Diamond Wager" (possibly rejected by *Blue Book* in 1927, but published by *Detective Fiction*, as Samuel Dashiell, in 1929)
- "Fly Paper" (August 1929, *Black Mask*)

THE MALTESE FALCON
- "The Maltese Falcon, Part 1" (September 1929, *Black Mask*)

- "The Maltese Falcon, Part 2" (October 1929, *Black Mask*)
- "The Maltese Falcon, Part 3" (November 1929, *Black Mask*)
- "The Maltese Falcon, Part 4" (December 1929, *Black Mask*)
- "The Maltese Falcon, Part 5" (January 1930, *Black Mask*)

- "The Farewell Murder" (February 1930, *Black Mask*)

THE GLASS KEY
- "The Glass Key" (March 1930, *Black Mask*)
- "The Cyclone Shot" (April 1930, *Black Mask*)
- "Dagger Point" (May 1930, *Black Mask*)
- "The Shattered Key" (June 1930, *Black Mask*)

- "Death and Company" (November 1930, *Black Mask*)

≈

In "An Inch and a Half of Glory," probably written in 1926 but unpublished at the time, a man, at no great danger to himself, rescues a child from a burning building. At first he is embarrassed by his newly-won heroic status, but then misses it when it becomes old news. He becomes arrogant and is fired from his job at the railway inquiries desk, and loses a succession of others for much the same reason. He enters a second fire and this time barely escapes with his life, rescuing a kitten. Having realized that his problems stem from the first fire, he leaves town before celebrity can ambush him again. It is possible that Hammett was commenting here on his own ambivalent attitude to celebrity. We also find in this story that, five years into his writing career, he is still inventing awkward words like "venturesomeness," although the paragraph in which he employs it strikes a class attitude.

> It seemed there was no place for venturesomeness in the modern world. Courage was the one thing for which business had no use — not only could not use it, but did not want to have it around. If your employer learned you were not a sheep or a worm — a timid, docile sheep or worm — he immediately got rid of you.[55]

It is possible, of course, that this challenge to the preferred mode of the employer-employee relationship was sufficient to earn the story its rejection slip.

Certainly, such "venturesomeness" was absent from the story marking Hammett's return to the pages of *Black Mask*, apart from a single simile: "The room was as black as an honest politician's prospects."[56] "The Big Knockover" (February 1927) is certainly hardboiled, with scores of dead, but it is a barely credible tale in which criminals from all over the country descend on San Francisco to "knock over" two banks at the same time.

Three months later, Hammett returned with the sequel, "$106,000 Blood Money," and it is possible that, in writing longer stories like these, he considered himself in training for the novels that would soon follow; these two linked stories were, in fact, published as a short novel entitled *Blood Money* in 1943, although Hammett apparently thought the stories unworthy of this treatment.

The sequel sees the Op on the trail of the brains behind the "big knockover," the elderly Papadopolous. One of the few things of note in this story is Hammett's depiction of the amorality of the society, as when one character, having cheated his brother out of $15,000, doesn't turn a hair when he is killed but shows up when he hears that a reward has been placed on the head of the killer.

The story features Jack Counihan, an erring rich boy who, while employed by the Continental Detective Agency, turns to crime. Near the end of the tale, the Op tells him: "So you were meat to Papadopoulos's grinder. He gave you a part you could play to yourself — a super-gentleman-crook, a mastermind, a desperate suave villain, and all that kind of romantic garbage."[57] This is Hammett thumbing his nose at the traditional (and usually English) private detective. It is also significant, though, that one of the Op's concerns is that exposure of Counihan as a bad guy will tarnish the reputation of the Agency.

The same month as "The Big Knockover" appeared in *Black Mask*, Hammett's short satire, "The Advertising Man Writes a Love Letter" was published in the humor magazine *Judge*. His next *Black Mask* story after "Blood Money" was "The Main Death" (June 1927), which is notable for its illustration of another of the main tenets of Hammett's detection creed, as the Op refuses to become involved in his client's marital affairs, effectively covering for the man's wife.

In November 1927, the first episode of what would become *Red Harvest* appeared in *Black Mask*, and Hammett was on the road to becoming a novelist. By February 1928, the fourth and final episode appeared, and a year later it was published in book form by Knopf, with a dedication to Joseph Shaw.

Unwittingly, Shaw had, by encouraging Hammett to write longer stories, effectively lost him as a contributor of *Black Mask* stories, for it was not until November 1928 that he next appeared in the magazine – and this was merely the first installment of his next book, *The Dain Curse*, which was followed by the remaining three episodes until February 1929. There was then a break of several months until "Fly Paper" appeared in August of that year, followed by the five installments of *The Maltese Falcon* (September 1929-January 1930).

Again, just a single story separated this from the serialization of the next novel, *The Glass Key*. This, in turn, was followed by a stand-along story in November 1930, and this was the last time Hammett appeared in *Black Mask*.

As far as publication went, the serialized "Red Harvest" and "Dain Curse" were punctuated only by "This King Business," which appeared in *Mystery Magazine* in January 1928. As it is thought that this was written earlier, Hammett was probably occupied exclusively at this time with what would be his first two novels.

"This King Business" is a curious little tale in which the Op installs a US citizen as king of a fictitious Balkan country in a "revolution" in which there appears to be no conflict of class interests. We might suspect that he's merely illustrating how regimes are first installed and then discarded by the USA, but this hardly seems to be the case, as he offers the examples of Albania, (which after World War I "offered its crown to one of the wealthy American Bonapartes. He didn't want it. He was an older man and had already made his career."[58]) and Persia (whose Shah is "a Russian soldier who went in there after the war, worked himself up until he had the army in his hands, became dictator, then Shah."[59])

In the latter case, certainly, Hammett's grasp of recent history appears to have been rather weak. because nothing like that happened.[60] Grantham, the young American who has invested $3 million in this dubious "revolution," takes it all seriously, and when the Op suggests they make their escape, responds:

> "No. You go. I shall see it through. These people have trusted me, and I shall — "
>
> "My God, that's old Doc Semich's [the toppled president's] line. These people haven't trusted you — not a bit of it. I'm the people who trusted you. I made you king, understand? I made you king so you could go home with your chin up — not so you could stay here and make an ass of yourself! I bought help with promises. One of them was that you'd get out within twenty-four hours."[61]

The man who will be taking over from Grantham after the abdication that the Op has arranged hurls the previous strong man from a balcony, to be torn to pieces by the mob. The Op objects that "I hate mobs, lynchings — they sicken me. No matter how wrong the man is, if a mob's against him, I'm for him. The only thing I ever pray to God for is a chance some day to squat down behind a machine gun with a lynching party in front of me."[62] Is Hammett here revealing something of his own philosophy? Was this identification with the underdog, regardless of the circumstances, to develop during the next decade into a firm class outlook?

Having secured the escape of Grantham and his girlfriend and the return of the $3 million, the Op returns to San Francisco "to quarrel with my boss over what he thought were unnecessary five- and ten-dollar items in my expense account."[63] The Op may be a hireling, but he's a proletarian hireling.

After the conclusion of the serialization of "The Dain Curse," Hammett wrote or published a couple of stories that did not appear in *Black Mask*. "The Sign of the Potent Pills" did not appear anywhere, in fact, until it was published in *The Hunter and Other Stories* in 2013. For the period (it is thought, based on the address on the manuscript, to have been written between 1927 and 1929[64]), this is a very poor effort, starchily-written with awkward turns of phrase and falling between too many stools. Was it a comedy, a thriller, a satire? Hammett didn't seem to know.

"The Diamond Wager," possibly rejected by *Blue Book* in 1927, but published by *Detective Fiction* two years later (with Hammett billed as "Samuel Dashiell"), has a stab at the gentleman jewel-thief sub-genre, which Hammett had satirized in January 1924's "Itchy." That he would resort to a sub-genre he held in contempt can only mean that he was desperate for both money and ideas.

"Fly Paper," the only story to appear in *Black Mask* (August 1929) between the latest two serials, has the Op working for the rich ("The Hambletons had been for several generations a wealthy and decently prominent New York family."[65]), but at long distance, as he attempts to trace a missing daughter who, preferring the underworld to a comfortable bourgeois existence (a frequent theme in Hammett), dies there.

After the completion of "The Maltese Falcon" series, "The Farewell Murder" (February 1930) sees Kovalev threatened with death by Don Sherry, a man he supposedly ruined as a result of a deal involving overpriced military equipment ten years earlier. The story is distinguished only by the eccentric spelling of "barytone,"[66] which, as it is used more than once, cannot be a misprint, and the fact that Hammett, in another example of careless racism, has the Op refer to Sherry's black companion as "the dinge."[67]

In November that year, after the completion of "The Glass Key" series, "Death and Company" would mark the last appearance of both Hammett in *Black Mask* and the Continental Op in his fiction.

≈

Novelist he might be, but Hammett was not yet a prosperous one. The first printing of *Red Harvest* was only around 3,000 copies, although this was followed by a second printing in March 1930 and a third a year later.[68] The evidence suggests that Hammett was motivated by the prospect of a healthy financial return in these years. For example, by submitting to *Black Mask* almost nothing outside of his serialized novels, he would have been looking for two paydays for the same material — one when the installments were accepted by the magazine and another when they appeared in book form.

Almost a year before *Red Harvest* was published, he was writing to Blanche Knopf to tell her that he hoped to finish a second novel, *The Dain Curse*, the following month, and that he'd already sold the serial rights to *Black Mask*. He was also thinking of writing a stream-of-consciousness novel, although this might be delayed if his discussions with the Fox studio regarding *Red Harvest* bore fruit[69] (neither project saw the light of day).

With *The Dain Curse* due to be published in July 1929 (the dedication this time was to Albert Samuels, the jeweler for whom he had briefly worked), the previous month Hammett wrote to Harry Block, a Knopf editor. Having already sent Block the manuscript of *The Maltese Falcon*, he asked him how soon he could use another. "I've quite a flock of them outlined or begun, and I've a couple of groups of connected stories that can be joined in a whole just as I did with *Red Harvest* and *The Dain Curse*. The best of them were written just before *Red Harvest*, a group that would make a book as exciting as *Red Harvest*, though less complicated, with *The Big Knock-Over* as title." He added that he also had 250,000 words of stories featuring the Continental Op and therefore suggested a collection, although he would jettison 50-60,000 words. He also had a horror story; a "pure plot" detective story; a "political murder mystery"; a novel akin to *The Maltese Falcon*, and an underworld mystery. Phew![70] A month later, however, he told Block that he had reread some of the "novelettes" and no longer considered them worth the effort.[71]

This was a man in a hurry. But why? Was he anxious to publish as much as possible, providing for his family, before his health let him down for good? Or was he merely interested in receiving as much money as soon as possible? Even when the movie money began to roll in, however, Hammett was so extravagant that, hard up, he resorted to the better-paying "slicks" to publish 13 short stories in 1932-34. In addition, he wrote six other stories in the 1930s (the latest, possibly, in 1936) that were unpublished at the time.

- "On the Way" (March 1932, *Harper's Bazaar*)
- "A Man Called Spade" (July 1932, *The American Magazine*)
- "Too Many Have Lived" (October 1932, *The American Magazine*)
- "They Can Only Hang You Once" (November 1932, *Collier's*)
- "A Knife Will Cut for Anybody" (c. 1932, unpublished)
- "Nelson Redline" (c. early 1930s, unpublished)
- "Monk and Johnny Fox" (c. early 1930s, unpublished)
- "The Cure" ("So I Shot Him," Winter/Spring 2011, *The Strand Magazine*, but written early 1930s)
- "Woman in the Dark, Part One" (April 8, 1933, *Liberty*; later published as a stand-alone novel)
- "Woman in the Dark, Part Two" (April 15, 1933, *Liberty*)

- "Woman in the Dark, Part Three" (April 22, 1933, *Liberty*)
- "Night Shade" (October 1, 1933, *Mystery League Magazine*)
- "Albert Pastor at Home" (Autumn 1933, *Esquire*)
- "The Thin Man" (December 1933, *Redbook*)
- "Two Sharp Knives" (January 13, 1934, *Collier's*)
- "His Brother's Keeper" (February 17, 1934, *Collier's*)
- "This Little Pig" (March 24, 1934, *Collier's*)
- "Week-end" (unpublished, mid-1930s)
- "Action and the Quiz Kid," (unpublished, c. 1936)

"On the Way" (March 1932, *Harper's Bazaar*) is set in Hollywood. Hammett amuses himself by using one of his old stories, "Laughing Masks," as a movie title. Kipper, the main character, wants to get out of Hollywood. He's willing to marry Gladys, but he still wants to leave, and maybe this reflected Hammett's own ambivalence about Tinsel Town and its attractions. Probably correctly, Rollyson thinks that these two characters are based on Hammett and Lillian Hellman,[72] as Kipper has obviously been an inspiration to Gladys, but is as ambivalent about their relationship as he is about Hollywood.

This was followed by three Sam Spade stories which appeared in a four-month period. Here, Hammett was cashing in on the popularity of the lead character of his best book and, as the quality declines with each story, it is clear that he is writing solely for money. "A Man Called Spade" is a competent whodunit that mostly takes place in the apartment of a murder victim, but Hammett has retreated to the traditional, Holmes-style formula. "Too Many Have Lived" is another traditional whodunit, with no social implications; by the end, it is a tired creation, gasping for breath as Spade is forced to explain how he has reached his solution, there being little chance that the reader will work it out unaided. The third whodunit, "They Can Only Hang You Once," has all the action taking place in one house, where there have been two murders; it is barely credible, and one winces as Hammett throws away his greatest creation — Sam Spade.

And yet in the existing fragment of "A Knife Will Cut for Anybody" there is an indication that Hammett was willing — but, at the end of the day, maybe not able — to do rather better by Spade. Layman says that this was written in the same period, "when Hammett was torn between cranking out quick crowd pleasers and struggling to meet his own literary ambitions,"[73] and that it and "The Darkened Face," an unfinished novella, "are two versions of the same tale."[74] There is at least one indication in the fragment that Hammett is ready to take more care and employ more subtlety than he has with the other three Spade tales, and even to make the occasional social comment.

When the police lieutenant asks an acquaintance of a dead woman whether she "came to America" after she had come into control of her estate, the man is confused as, being Argentine, she was already in America in her homeland. "To North America?" he asks.[75] Hammett here is pointing to that arrogance — or ignorance — displayed by many citizens of the USA when they assume that the word "America" applies to their country alone; Hammett handles this subtly, but it's there for anyone who notices it, and it holds out the possibility that this story would have been of a much higher order than the other three. But, of course, he never completed it. Maybe there were days when he could not be bothered with quality.

The unpublished "Nelson Redline"[76] is of interest because allusions to social conditions are plentiful. There is a reference to the unemployed, thus situating the story in the 1930s, and the narrator has previously been "associated with a workers' paper that had killed itself by a shortsighted policy of specialization upon the case of the unemployed, who couldn't give it the material support it needed."[77] The other point of interest concerns the character Martin Karbo who, told there is a fire in the office building where he works, dives through the door and goes down in the elevator, leaving his colleagues behind him. Later, Karbo explains to the narrator that, being convinced that he will be an important artist, he takes no chances with his life. Hammett's narrator, who has not held Karbo's escape from the fire against him, now finds this embarrassing and unpleasant, and thus avoids Karbo in future. Unfortunately, if Hammett is attempting to make a point about what makes an artist, he misses the target, for the narrator does not explain why he suddenly finds Karbo repugnant; and one is tempted to suggest that had Hammett taken more care of his own health he may have enjoyed a greater capacity to develop his own art.[78]

"Monk and Johnny Fox," also unpublished, is a curiosity of just over three pages, mostly dialogue, that seems incomplete. Why Johnny Fox, who makes only a brief appearance, should share the title is a mystery — unless this was intended to be part of a larger work.

This also seems to be the case with "The Cure," finally published in *The Strand Magazine* in 2011 as "I Shot Him," because although on the very first page the narrator tells us that he is there to put the bully Rainey in jail, this is never explained, and at the end of the tale it is Rainey who, having challenged a man who is afraid of water to jump in the river, is drowned.

The three-part "Woman in the Dark" (April 1933) takes us back to the more familiar ground of the mystery tale, in this case well-told with a strong opening, and it is clear that Hammett was taking more care with this, at a time when his writing career was almost at an end. The revelation at the end of "Night Shade," published in October that year, that the central character is black is held by some to signify that Hammett's social conscience was awakening, but in truth it is a slim tale. The title character in "Albert Pastor at Home" is a boxer who, thrown out of the ring for an infringement, returns home to find his small business-owner father subject to extortion. Having dealt physically with those responsible, he then returns to his own business — extortion!

"The Thin Man," (December 1933) was, of course, *Redbook*'s edited version of the novel that Knopf would publish in 1934, which will be discussed in the next chapter.

"Two Sharp Knives" (January 1934) is not really a mystery, as the murderer, a policeman, having been discovered, explains that, by forging a wanted poster, he has seen a rich man jailed and, by murdering him in his cell, sought to marry his widow and live on the inheritance. However, the widow is not party to the plot and it is never explained how the deputy came by the photograph he used for the wanted poster.

Hammett's final two published short stories appeared in *Collier's*. "His Brother's Keeper" (February 1934) is a boxing tale of a fight that is supposed to be thrown, and fraternal loyalty, and this certainly demonstrated that Hammett could write non-crime stories.

The same might be said of "This Little Pig," which appeared the following month. Hammett strikes an autobiographical note — and an immodest one at that — in this Hollywood story of studio intrigue and ambitions, when he has a producer inquire of Bugs Parrish, whom he has asked to "sex up" a script, "Is the stuff you write going to be like anybody else's? That's what I'm counting on — the

Parrish touch — the angle you got that nobody else can come anywhere near."[79]

Sadly, although this compliment was accurate enough when applied to its author, Hammett's writing days — at least under his own name — were almost over. So far, only two other stories of his from this period, both unpublished at the time, have been discovered. In "Week-End," a young woman spends a disappointing weekend with her boyfriend in San Francisco before he goes to New York. As she travels home afterwards, a "muscular pain in her side brought familiar fears,"[80] and although we are presumably expected to find this significant, Hammett never explains it. "Action and the Quiz Kid" has the narrator describing how his older brother exploits a 14-year-old boy, taking him for all he's got. Although Layman cites this as evidence of Hammett's "late interest in character as opposed to plot,"[81] there is barely room in this three-and-a-half pager for character development.

≋

Because it is known that Hammett became active in left-wing causes in the second half of the 1930s, and that he was suspected of being a member of the Communist Party of the USA by this time, some writers, Peter Wolfe above all, make the mistake of assuming that he held such views at an earlier date, seeing a Marxist subtext in his work. Hammett, says Wolfe, "was wooed by Marxism in the 1920s or 1930s," despite the fact that there is not even circumstantial evidence to underpin such a claim for the 1920s. He says that the late date (1931) of "Death, and Company" and the fact that the guilty party owns a manufacturer's agency, "stir Marxist undertones." Wolfe notes that in "$106,000 Blood Money," "San Francisco now crawls with angry, sold-out criminals looking to raise traveling money for a ticket home. Their scramble for money depicts life under capitalism to the Marxist Hammett..." In this same story, a "rich man's son acts as a deep-cover agent for the robbers and thus discredits the Agency in the same way that Soviet infiltrators like Guy Burgess, Donald MacLean, and Kim Philby smirched British security in the 1950s."[82] Quite how — or why — Wolfe makes this connection is beyond comprehension.

If Hammett had not been, at a much later stage, a self-proclaimed Marxist, would Wolfe — or anyone else — make such an assertion? Of course not, and if there is anything surprising in the ground we have covered so far it is that there are virtually no indications that Hammett was a socialist or a Marxist in the 1920s, despite the fact that the event which Hellman claims changed his life forever is said to have occurred in 1917 (see Chapter 3).

We have seen that in his first period Hammett wrote humor and satire, and while there are just six pieces, three of them unpublished, it would probably not be too wide of the mark to suggest that he was at this stage aiming for the prestige on *The Smart Set*, perhaps thinking that the money would follow.

Realizing that this was unrealistic, he then settled on crime as his main subject, although it is worth noting that his first crime stories were sent to *Brief Stories* rather than *The Black Mask*, and that his first appearance in the latter magazine was with an adventure story. It is also true that his early crime stories were not particularly hardboiled, with some straying into the western genre. Unlike Chandler, Hammett did not subvert the "traditional" mystery formula, and sometimes made use of it. Even as the "hardboiled" formula took shape, however, Hammett often departed from it during this period, for example with "Holiday," "The Crusader," "The Green Elephant," "The Second-Story Angel," "Itchy," and "Esther Entertains." Thus, a quarter of the stories written during this 24-story period show Hammett trying to broaden his range, but the demands of "the landlord, the butcher and the grocer" always brought him back to crime.

While Cody was editor of *The Black Mask*, there was, apart from the occasional suggestion, no indication that Hammett was coming to a socialist, let along a Marxist, outlook. And when he did write something that might be taken as a parable of a corrupt capitalist system, like "Nightmare Town," it was both overblown and overflowing with violence. In this same period, he wrote the strange story "Magic," and the story itself, along with Layman's mention of Hammett's "enthusiastic interest in the supernatural," suggests that he was still looking around for something in which to believe. But even this curious tale voices Hammett's contempt for professional politicians and alludes even more strongly to his frustrated hopes as a writer. And so the Hammett of the mid-1920s might be seen as conflicted, a man who had turned his back on formal religion but was uneasy with life without a center, a writer who composed violent crime stories but had his eyes on higher things — but even here he was unsure of his ability to attain them, and so was constantly driven back to the *Black Mask* treadmill.

Hammett did broaden his horizons during the Cody period, although not all of his attempts to do this found their way into *The Black Mask*. "Ber-Bulu" was set in a foreign location and the plots of "Dead Yellow Women" and "The Gutting of Couffignal" were based on the political situations of China and Russia, but his budding anti-imperialism (which also raised its voice in "Ruffian's Wife") was unable to trump his racism.

If there is one story that more clearly than any other points to Hammett's dilemma during this period, it is surely the unpublished "The Hunter." Here, he is saying, "You want a private eye story? OK, I'll give you one, but I'll tell it as it is, with no frills or exaggerated violence." And that's what he did, depicting the private investigator as a soulless man who works for money and in so doing will often bring real misery to ordinary men, women and children who are possibly better human beings than him and who, had somebody not been paying him, he would have left alone.

While on the one hand the story gives an objective view of what a heartless economic system will cause people to do to each other, on the other it lays bare the bleakness at the center of Hammett's fiction — and his life. This, one suspects, is the kind of detective that Hammett had been, and the only way he could deal with that was to adopt a "professional" approach, having the Op, and later Sam Spade, take a certain pride in their abilities, and steering clear of emotional involvement in their cases. Vitt, the detective in "The Hunter," is a nihilist and so, we must suspect, was Hammett, as he had rejected religion and as yet believed in nothing which might give his life meaning.[83] Thus, the town of Izzard in "Nightmare Town" must be completely destroyed rather than cleansed.

By early 1926, tiring of his genre and at odds with Cody, Hammett was staging something of a revolt. But instead of beginning to express socialist ideas or turning to more proletarian subjects, he simply wrote about the gay detective Robin Thin and invented a detective, Alex Rush, who was distinguished by his ugliness. True, he wrote the unpublished "Faith," but this was more concerned with panning religion than promoting an alternative to either the supernatural or the kind of employment offered by the cannery.

In early 1926, it was not just *The Black Mask* that he left, but fiction itself, and his new occupation was in advertising — writing, a cynic might say, a different kind of fiction. Not only did he do it, but he made claims for its literary status. Even after his collapse at Samuels, he continued to write advertising copy on a freelance basis because, said his wife Jose, he "didn't want to go back to writing his stories" as he "thought he could make more money as an advertising man."[84]

And, of course, it was money that lured him back to *Black Mask* — the return of the $300 he felt he was owed, a higher rate per word, and the freedom to write longer stories. Joseph Shaw, who had taken over as editor, later said that "Hammett told his stories with a new kind of compulsion and authenticity. And he was one of the most careful and painstaking workmen I have ever known."[85] It was during the Shaw period that Hammett developed as a novelist, discussion of which is more appropriate for the next chapter.

If one were expecting a breakthrough in Hammett's short stories, it surely would have come in the final period, after he had left *Black Mask* for the second and last time, and after the onset of the great capitalist crisis of overproduction signaled by the stock-market crash of late October 1929. But, as indicated earlier, these later stories were written for money, so we have three Sam Spade tales along with the more promising unfinished one. Yes, there were attempts to break away from the crime genre, but only the unpublished "Nelson Redline" refers to social conditions (and that fleetingly, as the story is more concerned with the role of the artist). Discussing the stories of the Shaw period, Symons says they contained plenty of violence, but they said "no more than this is the way such people behave, take it or leave it."[86]

Would Hammett be able — or willing — to work political content into his novels?

NOTES

1 The unpublished stories are to be found in Dashiell Hammett, *The Hunter and Other Stories*, ed. Richard Layman and Julie M. Rivett (New York: The Mysterious Press, 2013); Layman has estimated the dates these were written.
2 Layman says that "Peter Collins" was "turn-of-the-century carnival and theater slang" for a nonexistent person. In *Red Harvest*, Hammett has the badly shot Reno say that he has "no more belly left than Peter Collins." See Richard Layman, *Shadow Man: The Life of Dashiell Hammett* (New York and London: Harcourt Brace Jovanovich/Bruccoli Clark, 1981), 38, and Dashiell Hammett, *Red Harvest* in *Five Complete Novels* (New York: Avenel Books, 1980), 140.
3 Vince Emery, commentary, in Dashiell Hammett, *Lost Stories*, ed. Vince Emery (San Francisco: Vince Emery Productions, 2005), 50.
4 William F. Nolan, *Dashiell Hammett: A Life at the Edge* (London: Arthur Barker, 1983), 35.
5 John G. Cawelti, *Adventure, Mystery, and Romance* (Chicago: University of Chicago Press, 1976), 165, quoted in Peter Wolfe, *Beams Falling: The Art of Dashiell Hammett* (Bowling Green, Ohio: Bowling Green University Popular Press, 1980), 12.
6 Nolan, 60.
7 Emery, commentary, in Dashiell Hammett, *Lost Stories*, 107.
8 Layman, *Shadow Man*, 49.
9 Richard Layman, "Introduction," Dashiell Hammett, *The Hunter and Other Stories*, 2, 3.
10 Dashiell Hammett, "The Girl with the Silver Eyes," *Crime Stories and other Writings* (New York: The Library of America, 2001), 150.
11 Dashiell Hammett, "The Golden Horseshoe," *Crime Stories and other Writings*, 222.
12 Dashiell Hammett, "Nightmare Town," *The Dashiell Hammett Megapack* (Wildside Press LLC, 2013), location 3213.
13 Layman, "Commentary," Dashiell Hammett, *The Hunter and Other Stories*, 66.
14 The Op suggests that Owen Fitzstephan go to the Leggett house to pump the latter's wife for information. He agrees, saying "Suppose I go out there tomorrow afternoon — to borrow a book.

Waite's *Rosy Cross* will do it." Dashiell Hammett, *The Dain Curse* in *Five Complete Novels*, 165.
15 Dashiell Hammett, "Magic," *The Hunter and Other Stories*, 84.
16 Ibid., 78, 79.
17 Ibid., 80, 88.
18 Julian Symons, *Dashiell Hammett* (San Diego/New York/London: Harcourt Brace Jovanovich, 1985), 18.
19 See, for example, Thomas M. McKenna, *Muslim Rulers and Rebels* (Manila: Anvil Publishers, 2000), 88-89.
20 Dashiell Hammett, "Ber-Bulu," *Lost Stories*, 214, 219.
21 Dashiell Hammett, "The Whosis Kid," *Crime Stories and other Writings*, 344.
22 Dashiell Hammett, "Corkscrew," *The Big Knockover: Selected Stories and Short Novels*, ed. Lillian Hellman (New York: Vintage Books, 1989), 255.
23 Dashiell Hammett, Ruffian's Wife," *The Dashiell Hammett Megapack*, location 3863.
24 Dashiell Hammett, "Dead Yellow Women," *The Big Knockover*, 189.
25 Ibid., 240.
26 Ibid., 241.
27 Ibid., 194.
28 Ibid., 217.
29 Ibid., 246.
30 Ibid.
31 Dashiell Hammett, "The Gutting of Couffignal," *The Big Knockover*, 3-4.
32 Ibid., 4.
33 Ibid., 16.
34 Ibid., 31.
35 Ibid., 31-32.
36 Ibid., 33.
37 Dashiell Hammett to the editor of *The Black Mask*, August 1924; Dashiell Hammett, *Selected Letters of Dashiell Hammett, 1921-1960*, ed. Richard Layman with Julie M. Rivett (Washington D.C.: Counterpoint, 2001,) 26.
38 Layman, *Shadow Man*, 59.
39 Diane Johnson, *The Life of Dashiell Hammett* (US title *Dashiell Hammett: A Life*), (London: Picador, 1985), 36.

40 Layman, commentary, Dashiell Hammett, *Selected Letters*, 28.
41 Emery, commentary, Dashiell Hammett, *Lost Stories*, 228.
42 Nolan, 62.
43 Dashiell Hammett, "The Assistant Murderer," *Crime Stories and other Writings*, 501.
44 Richard Layman, "Commentary," Dashiell Hammett, *The Hunter and Other Stories*, 66.
45 Dashiell Hammett, "Faith," *The Hunter and Other Stories*, 99.
46 Johnson, 310, note 8.
47 Dashiell Hammett, "The Advertisement is Literature," *Western Advertising*, October 1926, quoted in Johnson, 54-55.
48 Quoted in Johnson, 56.
49 Dashiell Hammett, *The Hunter and Other Stories*, ed. Richard Layman and Julie M Rivett (New York: The Mysterious Press), 2013, e-book edition, location 5016. Currently, the surviving fragment of "The Secret Emperor" is only published in this e-book, where it appears as bonus material.
50 Johnson, 57.
51 Layman (*Shadow Man*, 81) says this encouragement began in 1925, which can hardly have been possible as Shaw did not take over the editorship until November 1926, a fact Layman acknowledges in the later *Selected Letters*, which he edited.
52 Symons, 47, says that these reviews "are often scathing in their condemnation of highly esteemed works in the genre. He was particularly hard on S.S. Van Dine..." Van Dine (William Huntington Wright), author of the Philo Vance novels, had at one time edited *The Smart Set*.
53 The term "novelette" was also used by Raymond Chandler to describe his own long stories, but it would be a mistake to think that the term was originated by either man; Nolan (40, fn.) explains that it was a pulp-magazine term for a story of between 8,000 and 20,000 words
54 Layman, *Shadow Man*, 81-82.
55 Dashiell Hammett, "An Inch and a Half of Glory," *The Hunter and Other Stories*, 106.
56 Dashiell Hammett, "The Big Knockover," *The Big Knockover*, 384.
57 Dashiell Hammett, "$106,000 Blood Money," *The Big Knockover*, 448.

58 Dashiell Hammett, "This King Business," *The Big Knockover*, 137.
59 Ibid., 144.
60 Possibly, Hammett was thinking of the Persian Cossack Division, formed in 1879 and modeled on the Russian Cossack divisions in the Caucasus. While Russian officers had indeed been seconded to the Persian Cossack Division, after the Russian Revolution of 1917 their duties were transferred to Iranian officers. A military coup in 1921 saw the emergence of Reza Khan, a general in the Cossack Division, who became prime minister in 1925 and later Shah, establishing the Pahlavi dynasty.
61 Dashiell Hammett, "This King Business," *The Big Knockover*, 164.
62 Ibid., 169.
63 Ibid., 170.
64 Richard Layman, "Commentary," *The Hunter and Other Stories*, 12.
65 Dashiell Hammett, "Fly Paper," *The Big Knockover*, 38.
66 Dashiell Hammett, "The Farewell Murder," *Crime Stories and other Writings*, 754.
67 Ibid., 775.
68 Layman, *Shadow Man*, 96.
69 Johnson, 71-72.
70 Dashiell Hammett to Harry Block, June 16, 1929; *Selected Letters*, 49-50.
71 Dashiell Hammett to Harry Block, July 14, 1929; ibid., 50.
72 Carl Rollyson, *Lillian Hellman: Her Legend and her Legacy* (New York: St. Martin's Press, 1988), 44. Mellen is almost certainly wrong when she assumes that Gladys is a screenwriter, for she is asked whether the man who has just given her a contract is "putting you in Laughing Masks" (Dashiell Hammett, "On the Way, *The Hunter and Other Stories*, 175), which suggests she is an actress. Joan Mellen, *Hellman and Hammett: The Legendary Passion of Lillian Hellman and Dashiell Hammett* (New York: Harper Collins, 1996), 59.
73 Richard Layman, "Commentary," *The Hunter and Other Stories*, 279.
74 Ibid., 280.
75 Ibid., 284.
76 Despite Layman's advice that, with the first page missing, Hammett had written "Nelson Redline" on the second, it is open to doubt whether this was, indeed, the intended title, as Redline is

not the central character. See Richard Layman, "Commentary," Dashiell Hammett, *The Hunter and Other Stories*, 67.
77 Dashiell Hammett, "Nelson Redline," *The Hunter and Other Stories*, 113.
78 There was the occasional element of self-preservation in Hammett for, having overturned an ambulance during his brief spell in the Army during World War I, he vowed never to drive again; but this instance was completely eclipsed by his almost suicidal drinking.
79 Dashiell Hammett, "This Little Pig," *Lost Stories*, 270.
80 Dashiell Hammett, "Week-End," *The Hunter and Other Stories*, 171.
81 Layman, "Commentary," *The Hunter and Other Stories*, 12.
82 Peter Wolfe, 5, 49, 69-70, 70-71.
83 Zumoff notes: "What distinguishes Hammett's vision from both Communism and fascism is that he seems not to have any vision of a purified society." See J.A. Zumoff, "Politics and the 1920s Writings of Dashiell Hammett," *American Studies Journal*, 52.1 (2012), 92.
84 Nolan, 64.
85 Ibid., 67.
86 Symons, 38.

3 The darkening vision

In his letter to Blanche Knopf of March 20, 1928, Hammett claimed that he was "one of the few — if there are any more — people moderately literate who take the detective story seriously...Some day somebody's going to make 'literature' of it...and I'm selfish enough to have my hopes, however slight the evident justification may be."[1]

There is rather more modesty to this claim than at first meets the eye, for to be able to make it Hammett must, at least for the time being, have abandoned hopes of reaching higher. This is confirmed by the quotation-marks he puts around the word "literature," the equivalent of a sneer, while the phrase "however slight the evident justification might be" is clearly a reference to the previous six years' output of pulp stories.

He may not be considered mainstream, but he will strive to be the best at what he does — precisely the philosophy of detection he has given the Continental Op and will soon inject into Sam Spade.

It would be a mistake, however, to look upon the novels as a complete departure from the magazine stories, because when he wrote this letter the final episode of what would become *Red Harvest* had appeared in *Black Mask* the previous month, and his next three novels — *The Dain Curse*, *The Maltese Falcon* and *The Glass Key* — would be serialized in its pages between November 1928 and June 1930, although he would amend these for publication in book form. Nevertheless, it is valid to ask whether the novels did, as Hammett hoped, achieve the status of literature.

But the major question for this chapter is whether there is, as some claim, evidence of Hammett's Marxism in the novels. How correct is Symons when, having observed that Hammett had little to say about the morality of his characters in the short stories, he says that he "now moved to work that offered social criticism of the world he was depicting, the more devastating because it was mostly implicit"?[2]

Red Harvest (1928)

The Continental Op, still unnamed, is assigned to a case in Personville (popularly known as Poisonville), a mining town. The town is ugly and, due to its belching smelters, grimy. The uniformed cops the Op passes upon his arrival are unshaven, ill-clad, or smoking on duty, and we know immediately that this is a town where something is dreadfully wrong.

The Op meets a character with a red tie and asks him if it has any significance. The man introduces himself as Bill Quint, an Industrial Workers of the World (IWW) organizer, and explains that for four decades Personville has been owned — "heart, soul, skin and guts"[3] — by Elihu Willsson, owner of the mining corporation, the bank, the two newspapers and, at least in part, "nearly every other enterprise of any importance. Along with these pieces of property he owned a United States senator, a couple of representatives, the governor, the mayor, and most of the state legislature."[4] Willsson has allowed his son Donald, on whose behalf the Op is in town, to take over the running of the newspapers, which he has done with a reform agenda, but before the Op can meet him, Donald is murdered.

During the war years, the IWW had won improvements in wages and conditions, but in the post-war slump of 1921, Willsson Sr. struck back, tearing up the wartime agreements. Against the advice of Quint, who had been sent to assist, the miners had struck, playing into Willsson's hands as he hired "gunmen, strike-breakers, national guardsmen and even parts of the regular army" to break the union, succeeding after eight months of bloodshed. But Willsson was left with a problem, as during the conflict he had ceded control of the city to his thugs, and now he was unable to shake them off, as they "had too much on him."[5] The police department is rotten: when gangsters need to make a backdoor escape as detectives attack the front of their casino, the uniformed branch provides them with a vehicle.

All of the major characters in the book are blemished, with the exception of Bill Quint, who is nevertheless powerless and quickly disappears from the drama. Dinah Brand is a high-class prostitute and blatantly mercenary in her relationships. She brags that she even made money out of Quint, from whom she learned when the strike was to start and when it was to be called off, thus allowing her to make profitable investments. She admits that she sold Donald Willsson information which he was then unable to use because it would have resulted in his father going to jail along with his hired gangsters.

The murder of Donald Willsson is soon solved — he was killed by a bank clerk who, in love with Dinah Brand, became incensed when he thought that Donald had won her with his money. With this out of the way, the Op is now employed by Elihu Willsson who, in desperation, gives him a check for $10,000 and asks him to investigate all corruption and organized crime in the town. When Willsson later tries to cancel their written agreement, the Op refuses, telling him that he intends to clean up the town.

Unlike Chandler's Marlowe, the Op is no white knight, and he will turn this job into a war, getting away with as much as he can while the "Old Man" at the Continental Detective Agency office is unaware of all the facts. He tells his colleague Mickey Linehan that "there's no use taking anybody into court, no matter what you've got on them. They own the courts…" When Mickey asks what he intends for Elihu Willsson, the Op replies "Maybe ruin him, maybe club him into backing us up. I don't care which."[6]

The Op plays the gangsters off against each other, so that they finally wipe each other out. Talking to Dinah Brand (who is later murdered), he says that he could have persuaded Willsson to support him so that he could have taken the legal route. "But it's easier to have them killed off, easier and surer, and, now I'm feeling this way, more satisfying…It's this damned town. Poisonville is right. It's poisoned me." And a few seconds later: " I've got hard skin all over what's left of my soul, and after twenty years of messing around with crime I can look at any sort of murder without seeing anything in it but my bread and butter, the day's work. But this getting a rear out of planning deaths is not natural to me. It's what this place has done to me."[7]

As the novel builds to its conclusion, there is extensive carnage as Reno's men, using pipe-bombs in addition to the usual artillery, battle it out with Pete the Finn's gang. With all the leading gangsters dead, the Op tells Willsson to advise the governor that the city police had got out of control and that he should bring in the National Guard. "I'm told that the mayor and the governor are both pieces of your property. They'll do what you tell them. And that's what you're going to tell them."[8] He tells Willsson that he'd like to believe that Dinah Brand had been killed by someone that the old man had sent to retrieve his love letters. "By God, I'd like to top off the job by sending you to the gallows." When Willsson offers him the job of police chief, the Op tells him to go to hell.

At the novel's close, then, the gangsters have been vanquished and Willsson will, in the Op's words, have his city back, "all nice and clean and ready to go to the dogs again."[9] Everything has been solved, but nothing has been solved.

There are signs that Hammett has taken care with *Red Harvest*, as one finds few of the awkward phrases that dot the magazine stories; instead, on one occasion, he even employs the archaic "just as leave,"[10] meaning "prefer." But the violence is just as crude as in the pages of *Black Mask*, and if this was used in the short stories to assuage the appetite of a down-market readership, here it does little to persuade the reader that the author has any higher aims (even though some of the violence in the serialized version was, at the urging of Blanche Knopf, left out of the novel).

Although most of the characters are stereotypes, there is some character development, as when the corrupt police chief Noonan is sickened by all the killing and weakens, while the Op himself, "poisoned" by "Poisonville," finds himself enjoying himself as he manipulates the mayhem. But Hammett takes the shortcut, having his characters simply announce that this is so rather than giving them interior lives. Most of the dialogue is hardboiled and humorless, with one exception. Hiding from thugs, the Op and Dinah Brand find themselves sharing an outdoor blanket throughout the night, during which there occurs this sparkling little exchange.

> "Are you married?"
> "Don't start that."
> "Then are you?"
> "No."
> "I'll bet your wife's glad of it."[11]

Charming, but it seems to belong to another novel.

The Op is possibly more irreverent than in the short stories. Fired upon from across the street while in his hotel room one night, he looks for something to throw at the light and uses a Gideon Bible. His attitude to Elihu Willsson is in stark contrast to that of Chandler's Marlowe toward Gen. Sternwood in *The Big Sleep*, deciding that, rather than deserving respect, he is "too old and sick to be smacked."[12] As we shall see presently, however, this Op behaves rather differently than the one encountered in the earlier magazine stories.

It is impossible to say how much effort Hammett put into revising the serialized story prior to its publication as a novel, but there are indications that he made up the story as he went along, failing to remove the evidence when he had finished. For example, very early on he introduces Donald Willsson's French wife. Not only is she an important character, having witnessed the murder of her husband, but Hammett takes a bit of care with her, giving her the trace of an accent, and letting us know that her father-in-law considers her a "French hussy" and, as such, capable of murdering his son. We fully expect her to be harboring a secret, or to be revealed as being a member of a conspiracy — at least developed into a major character of some sort. Instead, after the Op and the police chief Noonan have questioned her, she makes no further appearance. It is as if another idea had come into Hammett's head as he was drafting the story, causing him to drop whatever plans he had for Mrs. Willsson.

The same can be said for Bill Quint, the IWW man who thinks Donald Willsson was a "lousy liberal."[13] Had Hammett intended to turn this into the political novel that so many people think it to be, Quint would surely have been an important character. But no, Quint, having been used by Hammett to explain the history of Personville, wanders offstage quite early on; and we never catch sight of any of Quint's members in this mining city.

≈

Yes, there *is* social comment in *Red Harvest*: Personville is a town that has been poisoned by an unrestrained capitalism, so much so that even the Op is transformed into a bloodthirsty manipulator of life and death. Nolan thinks that Hammett is "redressing old wrongs" in *Red Harvest*, the writer having "developed a deep political conscience" between 1917 and 1927.[14] "Some critics," Nolan says, "have described the novel as a Marxist assault on capitalism…"[15]

Wolfe, citing Thompson, talks of a "Marxist attack on free enterprise" that continues "through the whole work."[16] The novel, says Wolfe, was written "to show how capitalism maims and mangles the individual and how unbridled freedom degenerates into chaos and the rule of force."[17] The same critic rightly complains that the novel "moves forward by agglomeration, not internal development. The pattern doesn't suit the book, trivializing the violence growing out of New World energy by failing to link it to characters we care about." He surely goes too far, however, when he claims:

> This substitution of excess for creative energy stems from the Marxist impulse behind *Red Harvest*. The belief that capitalism destroys character and that the creed of rugged individualism destroys individuality might explain the flatness of the people in the book; Hammett's people don't relate to each other, but to the dynamics of local mob rule. Sincere political sermonizing, though, doesn't always produce good art, especially in the novel, with its traditional commitment to individuality.[18]

But where is the "political sermonizing" in *Red Harvest*? There is none. And there is no "Marxist impulse" behind the novel, any more than the book is a "Marxist attack on free enterprise."

Of Hammett's biographers, it is only Layman who does not accept the "Marxist" interpretation of *Red Harvest*, although not necessarily for the right reasons. Layman says that Quint's arguments are "unpersuasive." Well, Quint doesn't really put forward any arguments and, anyway, just because he is an IWW organizer doesn't mean, necessarily, that he's a Marxist. Layman further says that Quint gave Dinah Brand information about the strikers' plans that she used to make money, the implication being that Hammett could hardly have been guided by a "Marxist impulse" in writing *Red Harvest* if he had the supposedly Marxist Quint do such a thing. But there is no reason to suppose that Quint gave her the information for that reason. He and Brand had a sexual relationship, and this could have been part of the pillow-talk. Layman is much nearer the mark when he says: "There are no masses of politically dispossessed people in *Red Harvest* — only a detective and a group of crooks."[19]

Thompson makes a similar point when he remarks that, apart from the Op, "alternatives to corrupt behavior are nowhere to be seen..." and that even he fears that he will suffer the same degeneration as the other characters.[20] But then Thompson takes a step too far, dipping his toe into a Marxist interpretation by referring to Marx's theory of alienation: "the Op feels that the natural connection between him and his work has been poisoned by the materialistic society of Personville. As a result, he now feels a stranger to himself, one whose conscious self has somehow been forced to disassociate from his real self."[21]

But what is this "work" from which he feels alienated? The Op is, after all, a private eye, hiring out to employers of labor and owners of capital — not quite what Marx had in mind when he wrote of the alienation of labor.

≈

The assumption that *Red Harvest* is Hammett's Marxist denunciation of capitalism (it is certainly a denunciation of capitalism but not a Marxist one) arises from knowledge acquired long after the novel was published: that, according to Lillian Hellman in her 1976 memoir *Scoundrel Time*, Hammett told her that in 1917 the Anaconda Copper Company had offered him (he was then a Pinkerton operative), $5,000 to murder the IWW organizer Frank Little, and that this changed the way he looked at the world;[22] that in the late 1930s Hammett became active in organizations inspired by the Communist Party of the USA, of which he was thought to be a member; that he did jail-time in 1951 for refusing the name names during the McCarthy period, and that around this time he acknowledged (to his brother) that he was a Marxist. Only the first of these milestones concerns us here.

While there is no doubt whatsoever that Frank Little was murdered (not by Hammett: Hellman says he rejected the proposition) in 1917, it is by no means indisputable that Hammett was ever made such an offer. In 1917, he was working out of the Pinkerton's Baltimore office. Anaconda, Montana is, as the crow flies, 3,042 kilometers from Baltimore, and thus it is highly unlikely that Hammett, regardless of his prowess as an operative, would have been assigned there.

Of the Little murder, Layman says: "That story of Hammett's peripheral involvement is implausible, though his telling such a tale is likely. Hammett's accounts of his days as a detective are always suspect..."[23] As we saw in Chapter 1, however, after Hammett's Army service he took a posting at the Pinkerton's Spokane office, and in 1920-21 is said to have been strikebreaking during the Anaconda strike, when the IWW was broken.[24] Spokane is just 379 kilometers from Anaconda and 507 kilometers from Butte.

George Everett reduces Hammett's role in strikebreaking even further. Hammett, he says, was "more than likely" in Baltimore in 1917 as a "rookie operative." In May 1920, he transferred to the Pinkertons' Spokane office, where the agency had been retained by the Anaconda company to break a strike in Butte. But Hammett only worked there until November 6, when he was hospitalized at the Cushman Institute in Tacoma, Washington.

"If Hammett did spend time in Butte," says Everett, "it seems unlikely that he could have arrived before June 1920 as strikers grudgingly returned to the underground mines without achieving any of their goals. The following April, the company shut down the mines citing falling copper prices and they stayed closed until June 1922." On this account, then, Hammett was certainly not strikebreaking into 1921, and it is far from certain that he had first-hand experience of the 1920 activity; Everett speculates that if he was not an active participant, Hammett may have learned of the details of the Butte strike from colleagues or, of course, from his future wife Jose, who had been in Butte during 1917, at the time of Little's murder.[25]

J. A. Zumoff not only takes the view that the Little story is "almost certainly false," as Hammett was not in Montana at the time, but points out that studies of the Butte strike and contemporary reports make no mention of Pinkerton involvement.[26]

If the offer to murder Frank Little was never made, it obviously could not have been a life-changing event for Hammett. However, it is entirely possible that his experiences of strikebreaking, either first- or second-hand, in 1920 gave him a jaundiced view of capitalism, and it certainly influenced *Red Harvest*. Elihu Willsson justifies his behavior by telling the Op that "if I hadn't been a pirate I'd still be working for the Anaconda for wages, and there'd be no Personville Mining Corporation."[27] Willsson's company is obviously based on Anaconda, but Nolan is not really correct when he says that Hammett is redressing old wrongs in *Red Harvest*. If he were, the Continental Detective Agency, rather than a horde of gangsters, would be the strikebreaking force. In 1920 (if not in 1917) the Pinkertons were the strikebreakers, so rather than redressing old wrongs he is, perhaps, trying to atone for past sins, but even this interpretation errs on the side of the charitable because Hammett, whether in *Red Harvest* or elsewhere, never has a bad word to say about the Agency. Zumoff points out that the Op stories *"whitewash* the Pinkertons' anti-labor activity" and "disappear the class struggle entirely and present a prettified image of the Pinkertons."[28]

Nevertheless, the Op buckles down to work and ensures that Personville is rid of the corrupt police chief and the gang-leaders who have taken over the city. Is this not proof that the Op is, on Hammett's behalf, waging a "Marxist attack on free enterprise?" Not at all. As noted earlier, the Op does behave differently in *Red Harvest*, and this lies in his departure from his usual "professional" approach, by means of which he normally just gets the job done, avoiding all emotional involvement and never adopting a moral position. This time, he goes so far as to ignore the wishes of his client, Elihu Willsson when, the murder of his son solved, he tells the detective to call off the wider task of cleansing the city. But the Op's motives are purely personal rather than political, as he explains to gangster Max Thaler after Noonan, the police chief, has tried to have the detective killed: "You want to be let alone. There was a time when I wanted to be let alone. If I had been, maybe now I'd be riding back to San Francisco. But I wasn't. Especially I wasn't let alone by that fat Noonan."[29] (And here, contrary to Thompson's assertion, the Op, far from being alienated from his "work," is taking control of it.) Yes, the Op refers to Elihu Willsson as the "czar of Poisonville,"[30] but rather than leading a revolution, the detective is in fact *employed* by that very czar, and at the end of the novel he hands him back his city, "ready to go to the dogs again."

Red Harvest is not a Marxist novel — not because Hammett "never used his fiction as a forum for his political beliefs,"[31] as Layman would have it, but because Hammett at this stage was not a Marxist. Whatever might be his political associations and activities in the future, there is no evidence whatsoever to suggest that by the late 1920s Hammett had progressed beyond the bleak nihilism of the unpublished short story "The Hunter," written a few years earlier, in which the detective has no belief outside of doing the job to the best of his ability, regardless of whose lives are damaged in the process, and "Nightmare Town" (December 27, 1924, *Argosy All-Star Weekly*), in which the only remedy for a town whose every business is crooked is complete destruction.[32] True, *Red Harvest* marks progress of a kind, because Personville is cleansed rather than destroyed, but Hammett recognizes that this can only be a temporary victory; and he has assembled no forces in the novel which might bring about a more permanent solution.

The Dain Curse (1929)

Given that Hammett published so swiftly, it is perhaps not surprising that his second novel has all the hallmarks of a potboiler. It is a stinker.

Eight diamonds (Hammett was probably assisted by knowledge gained in the employment of Albert Samuels, to whom this novel is dedicated) have been stolen from Edgar Leggett, who has been experimenting on them in his home laboratory. Two strangers have been seen, quite separately, lurking in the vicinity of the house.

The Op interviews Mrs. Begg, a former servant of Leggett's, who tells him how surprised her employer had been when Gabrielle (now his stepdaughter) and her mother Alice Dain turned up out of the blue in 1923. Leggett married Alice shortly after Mrs. Begg left his employment.

One of the men seen near the Leggett house is found murdered. This is Upton, who in New York had had his own detective agency; he and one of his operatives, Harry Ruppert, had done time for attempting to bribe a jury. A man answering Ruppert's description was observed leaving the scene of Upton's murder. He was also the second man watching the house.

When Gabrielle disappears, Leggett and his wife claim that she's gone to the mountains with friends, but they appear very vague about this. She is traced to the Temple of the Holy Grail, which Eric Collinson, her boyfriend, describes as a cult. "It's the fashionable one just now. You know how they come and go in California."[33] The Op forces his way into the temple and is directed to the fifth floor, where he and Collinson find Gabrielle in a drugged state. They take her home.

Upon their arrival, they are told that Leggett has committed suicide. The police and a doctor are present (although there is no mention of police vehicles outside the house), along with Owen Fitzstephan, a novelist acquaintance whom the Op had asked to see if information could be gained from Alice Leggett.

In Leggett's alleged suicide note, he says that his real name was Maurice Pierre de Mayenne, and that he was born in France but educated in England. Returning to France to study painting, he had married Lily Dain, Alice's sister, but later realized that it was Alice that he loved. Having murdered Lily, he fled to London with Alice and his five-year-old daughter. There he was arrested and returned to Paris, where he was convicted and sentenced to life imprisonment on Devil's Island. After some time, he escaped from the island with another prisoner who later died.

Leggett then found work at a British mining company in Venezuela, where he was befriended by a man called Edge who later killed his employer and absconded with the contents of the company safe. Although he had refused to be a part of this plan, Leggett, afraid that a police investigation would uncover his record, accompanied the thief to Mexico, where it became apparent that Edge was fully aware of his past. When he tried to get away from Edge, there was a fight in which Leggett killed the thief in self-defense.

Eventually, Leggett ended up in San Francisco, where he took his current identity and later sent for Alice and Gabrielle. In the meantime, however, Alice had employed Louis Upton to search for Leggett, and thus his employee Ruppert had been sent to South America and succeeded in tracing his movements as far as Mexico, learning along the way of the three deaths with which, regardless of his innocence,

Leggett might be convicted, given his record. Upton, possibly having followed the trail of Alice, eventually found Leggett in San Francisco, and demanded money. Leggett gave him the diamonds in part-payment while he raised the cash. He had planned to kill Upton, having first faked the burglary, but Ruppert, who presumably had a grudge of his own, beat him to it. Ruppert had then visited Leggett, returning the diamonds and demanding money in their stead; Leggett had killed him and stowed his body in the cellar.

In the Avenel edition of Hammett's collected novels, we are, thus far, but 33 pages into *The Dain Curse*, four pages of which are taken up by this explanatory suicide note. A further seven pages is devoted to the Op's unveiling of the truth (despite, in some cases, the slimmest of clues — the very thing for which Raymond Chandler would later criticize the "traditional" school of mystery writing).

The Op immediately pronounces: "He didn't commit suicide...He was murdered."[34] Gabrielle points at her stepmother, accusing her of being the murderess, but it turns out that the murder she had witnessed had been of Ruppert, not of her father. The Op says that Leggett had a substantial bundle of money on him and clearly intended to disappear.

The note he left makes no mention of suicide and is addressed to the police, not his wife or daughter. Leggett had not sent for Alice and Gabrielle: they had traced him to San Francisco, hence his surprise upon their arrival. Upton had demanded money from Alice, not Leggett. Possibly, she had Ruppert kill Upton.

Having then silenced Ruppert, she had told Leggett the whole story and persuaded him to take the blame before shooting him. It is the Op's belief that, 15 years earlier, Alice and not Leggett had killed Lily, but Alice now says that she had trained five-year-old Gabrielle to do it, as a game with an unloaded gun, but on the day in question had suggested she play the game with her mother, who was sleeping. Alice tells Gabrielle that she is "cursed with the same black soul and rotten blood that she [Lily] and I and all the Dains have had..."[35] Alice grabs a gun and attempts to make her escape, but is caught by Fitzstephan; the gun discharges, leaving her dead.

This Chapter VII resembles nothing more than a Victorian denouement in which Holmes reveals all. But why did Alice confess, if she was intent on escaping? The Op says that this is because she had already been acquitted of her sister's murder in Paris, but this is a little thin. After a further two-and-a-half-page chapter of explanation, the case appears to be closed and the Op is assigned to another case.

≋

By this stage, however, Hammett has less than a third of a novel. Therefore, he has the Op receive a call from the Old Man, the detective agency's branch manager, telling him that the "Leggett matter is active again."[36] And thus we enter Part Two, which gives us 21 pages of story followed by a seven-and-a-half-page explanation of what we have just seen.

A disturbed Gabrielle is now the ward of Madison Andrews, the family lawyer who has, upon the recommendation of Dr. Riese, the family physician, allowed her to return to the temple, with former Leggett employee Minnie Hershey acting as her maid, in the hope that it will calm her and restore her sanity. After an initial improvement, however, Riese notes a dramatic worsening of Gabrielle's condition, and so he and Andrews agree that someone — the Op — should be assigned to keep an eye on her.

Here, the Op makes the acquaintance of Joseph and Aaronia Haldorn, who run the temple. At night, having vainly awaited the promised arrival of Dr. Riese, the Op wakes after a snooze to find himself drugged. He goes to Gabrielle's room, but her bed is empty. Eric Collinson arrives on the doorstep, and they stumble upon Gabrielle on the ground floor. She claims to have killed Dr. Riese in a religious ritual; her nightgown is bloodstained, and she carries a long dagger. They find Riese's body by the altar. Gabrielle says they should not be surprised, given that she is afflicted with the Dain curse.

The Op goes upstairs to Minnie's room, where he is attacked by an apparent apparition. "I didn't believe in the supernatural — but what of that?" he says. "The thing was there."[37] Having escaped, downstairs he and the young couple are accosted by the Haldorns' young son, who urges the Op to save his mother, who is about to be killed by her husband. They find Aaronia tied to the altar, and Joseph wielding a knife over her. The Op kills him.

End of second story. The Op then gives his long explanation to his novelist friend Fitzstephan, and at this stage the only function the latter performs is to listen while the detective divulges his ingenious solution of the mystery. At the end of the novel, however, Hammett will find a more substantial, if completely unexpected, role for him.

The Haldorns, explains the Op, had been actors until deciding to follow the example of a fellow thespian who, having forsaken the stage for the pulpit, was now "riding in Packards instead of daycoaches."[38] Hammett mentions some of the religious fakers like Aimee Semple McPherson who were so common in California. The Haldorns ran the racket — separating rich believers in the supernatural from their money — while Tom Fink, who had formerly "been in charge of the mechanical end of most of the well-known stage magicians' and illusionists' acts" piped the drug to the rooms and created the "phantoms." Aaronia had discovered that Joseph had been physically attracted to Gabrielle, hence the former's appearance on the altar. Minnie had fallen for the mumbo-jumbo and so when told by a "spirit" to save her mistress, she had killed Riese.

≈

So here we are, the second denouement behind us and still only halfway into the novel. This time the Op receives a telegram from Eric Collinson and is once more recalled to the case.

Gabrielle is by now more convinced than ever that she has inherited the "Dain curse," her bad blood leading her to commit evil deeds. Having married Collinson, she is staying in an isolated cottage on the coast, a sanctuary suggested by Fitzstephan, who had completed a novel there the previous year. Her new husband is murdered and the third part, during which the Op, more gentle and mild on this outing, cures her of both her belief in the "curse" and her morphine addiction, consists of a search for the murderer. The revelation of his identity also serves to tie the three components of the novel together, although not without stretching credulity to breaking point.

Called to the small settlement of Quesada by Collinson's telegram, upon his arrival the Op finds that his client has already met his death by being pushed over a cliff, and that Gabrielle is missing. The Op is now retained by Collinson's father. Fitzstephan receives a ransom note, demanding $10,000 for Gabrielle.

The local marshal, Dick Cotton, tries to frame Harvey Whidden by planting some of Gabrielle's belongings under his mattress. It turns out that the two men have never really clicked, and matters are not helped by the fact that Whidden is having an affair with Cotton's wife. When questioned by the sheriff and District Attorney, she readily supplies an alibi for Whidden on the night of Collinson's murder. She is then found strangled, having written an account in which Whidden's alibi is retracted and he is now named as Collinson's killer. The local law enforcement officers, with the Op, are led to a cave, where they find that Whidden has indeed been holding Gabrielle. Whidden is killed in the encounter.

Are we there yet? No, not quite. Even Collinson's father is asking the Old Man why the investigation is still ongoing if the murderer has been found, but the Op holds out for another week, as he hopes to pull all the loose ends together. It's not entirely clear what these loose ends might be, and the novel is such an unholy mess that we are forced to doubt whether Hammett knows precisely where he is going with it. In fact, in the remainder of the novel there is precious little investigation.

In the meantime, the Op has urged the Old Man to use his influence to have Tom Fink and Aaronia Haldorn released on bail (although it is far from clear who would come up with the bail money) as they might, if tailed, lead to a broader explanation. The cynical reader suspects, however, that Hammett's hope is that, if allowed to wander through the remaining pages, these two characters will spark an idea or two in the author's mind. If this is, indeed, Hammett's aim, it fails.

Tom Fink turns up at the Op's hotel in Quesada with the intention of disclosing that he is the step-father of Harvey Whidden. As he and the Op start to converse in the hotel corridor, an explosion rocks the Op's room and Fitzstephan is almost killed. Well, that's an idea, but all it achieves is the enhancement of the fantastic nature of the approaching denouement. The Op is also visited by Aaronia Haldorn. He tells her that she's been wasting her time attempting to throw suspicion on the lawyer Madison Andrews (a red herring which deserves no elaboration here). In response to her question, he tells her that he knows "the answer," whereupon she tries to kill him. This encounter is unexplained at the time.

In effect, at this stage of the novel Hammett has abandoned any attempt to fashion a believable conclusion, and more time is devoted to the Op's ministrations to Gabrielle, whom he takes through a cold-turkey cure for her morphine addiction and convinces her that the Dain curse is non-existent — that, in fact she has inherited the nobler qualities of her father. But even this is rendered unbelievable by having Gabrielle claim as she suffers withdrawal symptoms that she killed Dr. Riese and had persuaded Joseph to kill his wife; she says that she had been working with Whidden, had got him to kill Collinson for her and that, as they needed money, they had faked her kidnapping; even the bomb which disfigured Fitzstephan, she says, had been her doing, having manufactured it in her father's laboratory. Why should she make such claims? Or are we expected to believe that withdrawal symptoms have produced these delusions? It makes no sense at all.

Just as unconvincing in its way is the Op's borderline confession of love for Gabrielle as, when she asks why he has taken such trouble with her, he says, "I'm twice your age, sister, an old man. I'm damned if I'll make a chump of myself by telling you why I did it, why it was neither revolting nor disgusting, why I'd do it again and be glad of the chance."[39] This declaration may have been believable had Hammett drawn Gabrielle differently, but she has almost no forehead, her lobeless ears are pointed at the top like an animal's, her chin is also pointed, and for as long as any of the male characters have known her she has been emotionally disturbed. Despite these drawbacks, Joseph Haldorn, Eric Collinson, Owen Fitzstephan (as we shall see) and now the Op have all been attracted to her, two of them to such an extent that they were prepared to kill for her. Hammett makes no attempt to explain this fascination.

The case is "cracked" when Fitzstephan, visited by the Op in hospital, tells him that Fink had handed him the bomb and that he, Fitzstephan, not knowing what it was, had needed to conceal his link to the Temple and the fact that Fink had a reason to kill him. Fink, the Op says, was worried that if Fitzstephan continued with his rampage of murder, the truth about the Temple murder would come out and he, too, would be hung. Fitzstephan now reveals that he is Alice's cousin.

The five-and-a-half-page "explanation" is given by Fitzstephan, in court. Alice was not just his cousin but had also been, in New York, his lover. The Temple had been his idea, "though he kept his connection with it a secret, since everyone who knew him knew his skepticism; and his interest in it would have advertised it as the fake it was."[40]

Fitzstephan had had to kill Alice to keep her quiet. He had also killed Leggett. He became attracted to Gabrielle, growing more determined when she rebuffed him. Riese had stumbled upon a meeting between the Haldorns and Fitzstephan at the Temple, and so he had to die. Aaronia then became aware of Fitzstephan's true interest in Gabrielle, and so it was planned that she should die also. After Collinson married Gabrielle, Fitzstephan, who knew Whiddon from the previous year, paid him to kill Eric. Whiddon, thinking that Fitzstephan had double-crossed him, took Gabrielle hostage. Fitzstephan's final victim had been Mrs. Cotton. For good measure, Fitzstephan concludes with the opinion that Alice, not Gabrielle, had killed Lily.

At the end, Gabrielle tells the Op that she "can't really make myself believe that all that actually happened to me."[41] The reader has the same problem.

≈

Layman records that Harry Block, Hammett's editor at Knopf, thought that *The Dain Curse* was "too complex, that the three sections were too independent, and that reader interest lagged between the sections." Hammett himself thought the reason for this was that it had been originally written as a serial for *Black Mask*.[42] According to Symons, Joseph Shaw had insisted that each of the four installments be separate stories,[43] but this makes little sense because there were four installments but only three stories. Then again, why would Shaw insist upon separate stories for *The Dain Curse* when this had not been the case with *Red Harvest* and would not be expected of *The Maltese Falcon* and *The Glass Key*?

While Hammett is said to have made many changes in the "novelization" process, this major flaw in the book — three stories, each with its own denouement — was not overcome. Hammett seems not to have had the patience of a Chandler who, while he certainly cannibalized short stories in order to make a novel, completely rewrote them in the process, with the result that the join is only really noticeable in *The Big Sleep*, his first novel. As we saw in Chapter 2, Hammett in this period was a man in a hurry, anxious to publish as much as possible as soon as possible, and this haste — and, it must be said on this occasion, his contempt for his readers — certainly took its toll, and Hammett was as far away as ever from raising the status of the hardboiled mystery to "literature."

There are indications that Hammett was quite aware of just how bad this novel was. He mocks himself when, in explaining the set-up at the Temple of the Holy Grail and the murders committed on its premises, he has the Op ask Fitzstephan: "You actually believe what I've told you so far?" and, when Fitztephan replies in the affirmative, tells him that he has a childish mind.[44] There is more self-mockery later, as Hammett has Fitzstephan tell the Op, "Nobody's mysteries ought to be as tiresome as you're making this one."[45]

There are also passages where Hammett seems to pose the "literature" of the mainstream novel against the more tawdry (but more remunerative) product over which he is currently laboring. It is surely worthy of note that Hammett makes Fitzstephan a novelist whose physical appearance resembles Hammett's own. The Op had known Fitzstephan five years earlier, when they had been involved in a case in New York. Fitzstephan had then been 32, making him now 37 (Hammett would have been 35 when the novel was published); he is described as "a long, lean, sorrel-haired man...with sleepy gray eyes, a wide, humorous mouth, and carelessly worn clothes; a man who pretended to be lazier that he was, would rather talk than do anything else, and had a lot of what seemed to be accurate information and original ideas on any subject that happened to come up, as long as it was a little out of the ordinary."[46] Apart from the "carelessly worn clothes" (a mark, perhaps, of the "literary" man) this is a passable description of Hammett.

Fitzstephan reminds the Op that he had once offered to present him with a set of his books. "Yeah," says the Op. "But I never blamed you. You were drunk." The novelist responds that the Op had not been "tight enough to take the books." The Op explains: "I was afraid I'd read them and understand them...and then you'd have felt insulted."[47]

They discuss their respective jobs.

> "We're different," I said. "I do mine with the object of putting people in jail, and I get paid for it, though not as much as I should."
>
> "That's not different," he said. "I do mine with the object of putting people in books, and I get paid for it, though not

as much as I should."

"Yeah, but what good does that do?"[48]

This is the hardboiled Hammett debating with the more refined Hammett, and the former appears to be winning. Towards the novel's close, Hammett comes close to comparing his own occupation to the charlatanism of quack religion, when the Op explains that to Fitzstephan "the cult was a combination of toy and meal-ticket: he liked influencing people, especially in obscure ways, and people didn't seem to be buying his books."[49]

There is, needless to say, no evidence of Marxism in this poor novel. One of the few critical references to the contemporary socio-political culture comes when Fitzstephan describes a friend as having "the most consistently logical and creditable reasons for having done the most idiotic things. He is" — as if this explains it — "an advertising man."[50] But this is also gently self deprecating, as Hammett had written advertising copy for the San Francisco jeweler Albert Samuel, and contributed several articles on the subject to *Western Advertising*.

Wolfe says that the Temple of the Holy Grail's "large following among San Francisco's elite lets Hammett criticize both social institutions and trends in organized religion at one stroke,"[51] but this is clutching at straws.

Evidence that the Op's morality can extend across racial lines is provided when, following the murder of Dr. Riese, Collinson urges him to shift the blame away from Gabrielle. Outraged, the Op asks whether he should shift it to the Haldorns' Filipino servants (these are, unfortunately, usually referred to as "boys"), so that one of them might hang instead.

But one thing that is present in *The Dain Curse* — and to a disturbing extent as it is heaped upon one poor woman — is Hammett's antiblack racism. Minnie Hershey is a black servant, and the Op views her as a servant and little else; his attention, when he deigns to pay her any, almost always focuses on her color. She lives in "a Negro neighborhood, which made the getting of reasonably accurate information twice as unlikely as it always is."[52] Because she is a "mulatto" she naturally falls for the religious swindle at the temple — the "poor boogie."[53] Another character refers to Minnie's boyfriend as "the shine,"[54] while the Op's colleague Mickey Linehan sees Minnie as "the dark meat."[55]

It may be all very well for apologists to point to such expressions as being part of the cultural norm of the late 1920s, but a socialist, let alone a Marxist, would not have employed them — unless, perhaps, to show the character uttering them in a negative light. We learn, in passing, that Minnie is in jail for the murder of Dr. Riese, but there is of course no mention of the Op providing evidence to save her from the gallows.

It is worth remembering that, as his daughter Jo points out, Hammett "had begun life with the usual racial biases...His Maryland ancestors had been slave owners, and his early stories are full of the normal stereotypes..."[56] But here he was on his second novel, and he had still not shaken off his racism.

The Maltese Falcon (1930)

Hammett, possibly realizing that he had to try harder after the mess of *The Dain Curse*, now dispensed with the Continental Op and the first-person narrative and introduced Sam Spade, who outdoes the Op in patter, ruthlessness and his easy relationships with women. No white knight, he has no reservations about sleeping with his female client — or his partner's wife.

Reduced to its essentials, the plot of *The Maltese Falcon* is very simple.

San Francisco private detective Spade is visited by Miss Wonderly, who spins a yarn about a missing sister, who has allegedly absconded with a Floyd Thursby. Spade's partner Miles Archer is assigned to be at the hotel where Wonderly is to meet Thursby that night and to tail him thereafter. Later that night, Spade receives a call that Archer has been murdered and visits the scene. Thursby is also found dead, and at first the police want to hang one or both murders on Spade — Archer's because there is talk of Spade having an affair with his wife Iva, and Thursby's on the assumption that Spade would have been interested in avenging his partner.

The next day, Miss Wonderly admits that her original story was a pack of lies and that her name is Brigid O'Shaughnessy. She wants to retain Spade's services as she is in danger, but she refuses to explain the circumstances. She does, however, tell him that she met Thursby in the Orient, and that they had arrived in San Francisco from Hong Kong the previous week. Thursby, she says, killed Archer.

Joel Cairo, effeminate and perfumed, comes to the office, telling Spade that he wishes to locate a statuette of a bird, offering $5,000 for the job. Brigid, meanwhile, is still refusing to give Spade further details, so he appears reluctant to proceed with the case. When she asks, "Can I buy you with my body?"[57] he says he'll think about it.

Spade arranges a meeting between Cairo and Brigid at his apartment. Cairo suspects that Brigid has the statuette; she tells him that she'll have it in a week, maybe less. After an episode in which the police visit the apartment (prodded to do so, it later transpires, by Iva Archer, who is jealous, having seen Spade enter the apartment house with Brigid), Brigid tells Spade that her original role had been to help get the falcon from its owner, a Russian called Kemidov, but then they discovered that Cairo intended to desert them, so she and Thursby turned the tables on him.

Spade asks his secretary Effie to put Brigid up for a few days and is then called to the hotel of Caspar Gutman, who is also in search of the falcon. Spade gives him until 5.30 to explain exactly what the falcon is and then returns to his office, where he is told by Effie that Brigid never arrived at her home. Spade locates the taxi she had used and is told by the driver that he dropped her at the Ferry Building.

Gutman meets the deadline Spade has given him, explaining that when the Order of the Hospital of St. John of Jerusalem settled in Malta, Emperor Charles V of Spain demanded payment of one falcon a year, and the first year the falcon, thanks to the wealth of the order, took the form of a gold statuette encrusted with jewels. In the succeeding centuries, the statuette made its way around North Africa and Europe until a Greek dealer found it in a Paris shop in 1911, but he was murdered and the bird stolen. It took Gutman a further 17 years to track it down to Kemidov, who was living in Constantinople. He employed Thursby, Cairo and Brigid to steal it for him, but they stole it for themselves instead. Gutman offers Spade $25,000 when he hands over the falcon, and a similar sum when he arrives in New York, or, alternatively, 25 percent of whatever he receives for the bird. But then Gutman drugs him, leaving him unconscious in his hotel room.

The following day, Spade learns that Joel Cairo has been interested in the arrival of a ship called *La Paloma* from Hong Kong. Effie arrives in the office from checking out the veracity of Gutman's story of the falcon with her cousin, a history lecturer, and tells Spade that one of the ships at the pier is on fire — *La Paloma*.

Later that day, a seven-foot man enters the office and drops dead. He is Jacobi, captain of *La Paloma*, and he's carrying the falcon. Effie takes a call from an apparently distressed Brigid, urging Spade to come to Gutman's hotel immediately. Having stashed the falcon, Spade arrives to find Rhea, Gutman's daughter, apparently drugged. He attempts to walk her into consciousness, and she manages to mumble an address to which Brigid has been taken, following which he puts her to bed and calls a hospital. He then hires a car and driver to take him to the address in an outlying town, only to find the house deserted.

When he returns to San Francisco, Spade goes to the hotel to be told that no one is in the Gutman suite and that someone has called the Emergency Hospital to a nonexistent sick girl. He arrives home at midnight to find Brigid waiting for him on the street. Gutman, Cairo and Wilmer Cook, a young thug employed by Gutman (although Wilmer is in a homosexual relationship with Cairo) are waiting for him inside.

When Gutman dramatically reduces his offer to $10,000, Spade reluctantly agrees to produce the falcon but argues that, given the fact that three murders have been committed, they will need to hand the police a fall-guy, and he suggests Wilmer, or Cairo. Cairo would be ideal, Spade says, because he actually did kill Thursby and Jacobi, and if there are worries about what he might tell the police he could be conveniently killed resisting arrest. When it is suggested that Spade consider Brigid for this role, we think he is bluffing when he says he'll consider it.

During the discussion, loose ends are tied up or explained. On the night of the first two killings, Wilmer had brought Thursby to Gutman, but he had been loyal to Brigid, and so Wilmer had followed him back to his hotel and killed him. When Brigid had the taxi drop her off at the Ferry Building, she had been on her way to *La Paloma*, where she met Jacobi (to whom she had entrusted the falcon in Hong Kong). Cairo and Gutman, now working together, had calculated that Jacobi must have the falcon and had turned up, accompanied by Wilmer, while Brigid was on board with Jacobi.

In searching the ship, Wilmer had accidentally started a fire. Jacobi and Brigid, having pretended to agree to Gutman's terms, had then managed to flee the others, and were only relocated the following day, when Jacobi again escaped, although not before being mortally wounded by Wilmer. In order to send Spade on his fool's errand while the search for Jacobi continued, Brigid had been "persuaded" to call him in apparent distress.

When Spade produces the falcon, Gutman immediately takes a penknife to it, discovering that it is a lead copy. Exit Gutman and Cairo (Wilmer, having not relished playing the role of fall-guy, has absconded earlier).

Alone with her now, Spade tells Brigid that he knows that her intention had been that Thursby and Archer should shoot it out. If Thursby was killed, she would be rid of him at last, and if Archer had died she would have made sure Thursby was arrested for it. When the confrontation failed to occur, she killed Archer herself. Therefore, regardless of what he might feel for her, he intends to hand her to the police.

This was a new kind of hero, as hardboiled as they came.

≈

Hammett gives us several creations of note in *The Maltese Falcon*, such that it stands head and shoulders above its predecessor — and, for that matter, *Red Harvest*. Caspar Gutman, the fat man obsessed by his pursuit of the statuette, with his refined British turn of phrase, was strong enough to carry his own radio series in the late 1940s (although, as Gutman is killed offstage at the end of *The Maltese Falcon*, it would be more accurate to say that the character in *The Fat Man* was based on him). The gay relationship between Joel Cairo and Wilmer Cook was fairly new to US fiction in 1930. Harry Block, Hammett's editor at Knopf, had tried to persuade him to make changes here, but Hammett told him that "I would like to leave them as they are, especially since you say they 'would be all right perhaps in an ordinary novel.' It seems to me that the only thing that can be said against their use in a detective novel is that nobody has tried it yet. I'd like to try it."[58] Hammett describes Wilmer Cook as a "gunsel," and the editor was obviously unaware that this referred to a young homosexual in a relationship with an older man, and so it passed into the language as meaning a gunman.[59]

But the most vivid creation is Sam Spade. The detective is tall like

Hammett and looks "rather pleasantly like a blond satan"[60] — and, of course, he shares a forename with Hammett. He is a hard man. Visiting the site of Miles Archer's demise, he has absolutely no interest in taking a close look at the body and, having told the police that he will break the news to Archer's wife Iva, he calls Effie Perine, his secretary, and asks her to do it. Spade and Iva have been lovers (in fact Iva visits the office and asks Spade whether he killed Miles), but when Effie asks him whether he will marry her now that her husband is dead, Spade finds the suggestion silly. Counters Effie,

> "She doesn't think it's silly. Why should she — the way you've played around with her?"
> He sighed and said: "I wish to Christ I'd never seen her."
> "Maybe you do now." A trace of spitefulness came into the girl's voice. "But there was a time."
> "I never know what to do or say to women except that way," he grumbled, "and then I didn't like Miles."[61]

The last thing Spade tells Effie when he leaves the office is to have the "Spade & Archer" sign removed from the door and replaced with "Samuel Spade."

Spade is ruthless. At their first meeting, Joel Cairo tells him that he has made inquiries about him and has been assured "that you were far too reasonable to allow other considerations to interfere with profitable business relations."[62] He displays ample evidence of this lack of sentimentality when, at the end of the novel, he tells Brigid he's going to turn her in for the murder of Miles Archer, despite the fact that he's slept with Brigid, despite the fact that he loathed his partner. Does he love her? "'I think I do,' Spade said. 'What of it?' The muscles holding his smile in place stood out like wales. 'I'm not Thursby. I'm not Jacobi. I won't play the sap for you.'"[63] He tells her that she did him no harm when she killed Miles Archer, but when "one of your organization gets killed it's bad business to let the killer get away with it."[64] Here, the "professional" code of the detective, previously adopted by the Continental Op, is back in play.

After he's told her that he's turning her in, Brigid says he must know whether or not he loves her:

"I don't. It's easy enough to be nuts about you." He looked hungrily from her hair to her feet and up to her eyes again. "But I don't know what that amounts to. Does anybody ever? But suppose I do? What of it? Maybe next month I won't. I've been through it before — when it lasted that long. Then what? Then I'll think I played the sap. And if I did it and got sent over then I'd be sure I was the sap. Well, if I send you over I'll be sorry as hell — I'll have some rotten nights — but that'll pass."[65]

Of the three women in the novel, the only one for whom Spade shows any real affection is Effie Perine, his secretary, who according to Nolan was based on a cousin of Hammett who had the same name.[66] He touches her, he kisses her, he rests his head against her hip as she stands by his chair, he jokes with her, and he does all of this in a non-sexual, non-threatening manner that seems perfectly natural and relaxed. So Spade is not correct when he tells Effie — of all people! — that "I never know what to do or say to women except that way."

The easy, affectionate relationship that Hammett depicts between Spade and Effie is something that, say, Raymond Chandler would never have been able to manage, because Hammett was a womanizer who genuinely liked women. He was used to them, used to talking to them, used to being intimate with them — experience that Chandler lacked.

It is tempting to theorize that this relaxed style arises from the fact that there is no sexual relationship between Spade and Effie, but this does not stand up: the same easy, bantering style can be seen in Hammett's correspondence with women he has slept with, whether his wife Jose, long-time companion Hellman, or Peggy O'Toole, a secretary at Albert Samuels who may well have provided part of the inspiration for Effie.

But is this right? There was apparently another side of Hammett's relations with women. For example, we know that an actress sued him for assault in 1932, and that he is said on one occasion to have punched Hellman so hard on the jaw that he knocked her down.[67] A psychiatrist would probably employ words like "transference" to explain the fact that Spade punches and slaps the two gay characters

Joel Cairo and Wilmer Cook. And one does get a bit of a jolt when, seeking an explanation for Spade's affection for Effy, we turn back to the first page and see her described as having a "shiny boyish face."[68] But so little is known of Hammett's private life, and his work, unlike Chandler's, contains so few indications of a gay inclination (although, as we shall shortly see, there is one in *The Glass Key*), that such speculation must be fruitless.

≈

Symons says that with *The Maltese Falcon* Hammett had come "to realize the limitations of a first-person narrative" as "no action can be described, no motive assessed or speculation made, outside that individual's perceptions."[69] This is of course perfectly true, but even though Hammett adopts the third-person narrative for this novel he makes no attempt to go beyond the limitations he had previously been subject to, as all the action is seen from Spade's perspective, and we are left as ignorant of the interior life of the other characters as we are of Spade's.

Although the novel marked a great advance on his previous work, and it has been widely praised as such, it is far from flawless. The simple basic plot is surrounded by a great deal of padding. For example, the plot summary above makes no mention of Sgt. Tom Polhaus and Lt. Dundy; it has no need to, because they are not essential to the plot and their several appearances do not advance the action at all — although we must allow that Lt. Dundy establishes what became the template for the fictional relationship between the American private detective and his slower-witted and often hostile counterpart in the local police force.

Polhaus and Dundy are central to Chapter VIII, as they enter Spade's apartment after Joel Cairo, having been attacked by Brigid, screams for help, but the action goes nowhere as Dundy ponders who can be charged with what, until Spade unconvincingly claims that the three of them had decided to play a joke on the police. Similarly, Chapter XV sees Spade being harassed by the district attorney, but this plays no part whatsoever in developing the plot.

It is Wolfe's view that "Rhea Gutman's presence in *Falcon* carries weight. That her father has been searching for the bird as long as she has been alive shows the extent of his obsession..."[70] But in fact she is introduced into the story for the sole purpose of sending Spade on a fool's errand in what is basically a wasted chapter. Hammett probably realized the gratuitous nature of bringing in a supposedly drugged Rhea merely to misdirect Spade, as the next time Spade meets Gutman, he has the latter say that the act "served its purpose," to which Spade remarks, "Anything would've."[71]

Towards the end of the novel, Chapters XVIII and XIX are simply long-winded, the first containing a long discussion concerning the merits of this or that fall-guy, or having a fall-guy at all, while the second features a pointless episode in which Gutman palms one of the ten $1,000-dollar notes he gives to Spade, causing Spade to have Brigid disrobe in the bathroom to convince him that she has not taken the money.

It should be remembered that this particular novel, like its two predecessors, had first appeared in serialized form in *Black Mask*, and it is probable that Hammett, who was paid by the word, was stretching the material to ensure that it filled five installments and maximized his income.

As we have seen earlier, Hammett has fun by employing the obscure word "gunsel." In the same way, although for the opposite reason, in one scene he has Spade ask Wilmer Cook how long he's been "off the gooseberry lay." While this term seems vaguely obscene, it merely refers to the theft of clothes from a washing-line.

Then again, he has Spade use the archaic "as lief" (*Red Harvest*'s "as leave") when he says "I'd as lief not have him think there's anything to be kept quiet,"[72] meaning "I'd gladly not have him..." Hammett's care for words and their usage is again apparent when he has Spade chide Effie for referring to "the *La Paloma*" which, he says, as it contains two definite articles, "is a lousy combination."[73] In view of this, it is surprising that Hammett himself still employs the odd howler, although by no means as often as in his previous work. There is at least one made-up word that makes us cringe: Cairo's eyes, we are told, "became unangry."[74] Time after time, Hammett uses the ungainly "corridor-door."[75] Equally inelegant are "his other hand gripping her other arm"[76] and "A trembling in his knees began to shake the knees of his trousers."[77]

Hammett was still, we are led to suspect, writing in haste.

Does *The Maltese Falcon* contain social comment, giving an indication that its author is, or is on the way to becoming, a Marxist? It does not.

True, Spade tells Brigid O'Shaughnessy: "Most things in San Francisco can be bought, or taken."[78] Also, as in some of Hammett's previous work, most of the characters are thoroughly corrupt and untrustworthy. Gutman employs a crew to steal the falcon from Kemidov, the Russian; Brigid, Joel Cairo and Floyd Thursby double-cross Gutman; Brigid and Thursby then betray Cairo before he can double-cross them. In San Francisco, Thursby breaks the mold by refusing to betray Brigid, and this confirms him in Spade's eyes as a "sap." Although on several occasions Gutman says that Wilmer is like a son to him, he nevertheless agrees to sacrifice him because "if you lose a son it's possible to get another — and there's only one Maltese Falcon."[79] As Zumoff points out, however, Hammett did not discover corruption, which had been widely opposed for decades — including by reactionary forces like the Ku Klux Klan.[80]

And, as previously, Hammett is merely painting a picture of how things are; he makes no investigation of how they might have got that way, even less of how a society producing such creatures might be transcended. Wolfe unwittingly undermines his own thesis, i.e. that Hammett is a Marxist, when he notes that there is "little moral struggle, the characters having already lost their battles with conscience. Before they come to us, they have decided to rob, deceive a husband, wife, or business associate, steal — even kill — for the falcon."[81] There is, in other words, still no dialectical development in Hammett's work, as there would be in that of a Marxist.

In discussing *The Maltese Falcon*, Wolfe tries for two bites of the cherry, suggesting that Hammett (presumably in addition to being a Marxist) has some form of Freudian father complex, as he says that Spade, "in his skirmishes with Lieutenant Dundy and District Attorney Bryan, kicks against the father — his punitive, obedience-exacting society."[82] This case has also been made by Johnson, and we may as well dispose of it here. Johnson, Hammett's first biographer, asserts that "paternity is central to Hammett's work," citing the relationship between the Continental Op and the Old Man, his manager, and that "the central theme in two of his novels, *The Glass Key* and *Red Harvest*, is the murder of a son by his father,"[83] Wolfe repeats this two-fathers-killing-their-sons (and in only five books!) charge.[84]

There is no reason to quarrel with Symons's assertion that Hammett "loved his mother and constantly quarreled with his father,"[85] and we know from Layman that Hammett said that "he would never treat a woman the way his father treated his mother."[86] But it is a far stretch indeed to infer from this that much of Hammett's work, and his world outlook, stems from his problematic relationship with his father. The Op's relationship with the Old Man, for example, is warm and respectful most of the time, although when the Op breaks the rules he will be chastised.

As for *Red Harvest*, one wonders how carefully Johnson and Wolfe have read the novel, because not only is the death of Donald Willsson *not* the central theme, but he is killed not by his father but by a jealous bank clerk who lusts after Donna Brand! Even in *The Glass Key*, while there is no doubt that Senator Henry kills his son, the death seems to have been unintentional. The Freudian interpretation simply does not hold water.

The closest thing to a guide to Hammett's philosophical outlook at the time he wrote *The Maltese Falcon* is surely the Flitcraft story.

Spade tells Brigid the story of a man called Flitcraft, happily married with two sons and a successful real estate business, who simply disappeared one day during his lunch-break, having made generous provision for his family.

Five years later, after a man answering Flitcraft's description had been seen in Spokane, his wife approached the detective agency where Spade was employed at the time. Spade found him easily enough, and discovered that the new life he had built was remarkably similar to the one he had left: he had a new wife and baby, his own home and a successful automobile business. Flitcraft explained how, on that day five years earlier, he had been on his way to lunch when a beam had fallen from a construction site, narrowly missing him. "He felt like somebody had taken the lid off life and let him look at the works."[87]

> "What disturbed him was the discovery that in sensibly ordering his affairs he had got out of step, and not into step, with life. He said he knew before he had gone twenty feet from the fallen beam that he would never know peace

again until he had adjusted himself to this new glimpse of life. By the time he had eaten his luncheon he had found his means of adjustment. Life could be ended for him at random by a falling beam: he would change his life at random by simply going away."[88]

Spade explains Flitcraft's eventual choice of an almost identical life as follows: "He adjusted himself to beams falling, and then no more of them fell, and he adjusted himself to them not falling."[89]

What do the critics have to say about this? Symons relates the story to Hammett himself, saying that hitherto he had "done his best to order his life sensibly, without much success. For several years afterward, however, he made no attempt to order it at all."[90] True enough, so...Nothing.

The brave Wolfe maintains that the "main thrust of the Flitcraft story...comes in Spade's reason for telling it — to advise Brigid indirectly that, bedazzled though he may be for the moment, he will revert to the mentality of the private detective and arrest her for murdering Miles Archer, unless she talks him out of it."[91] Maybe, but probably not. Wolfe concedes, by the way, that no Marxist interpretation can be placed upon the Flitcraft story. "The Marxist belief that quantitative changes lead to qualitative ones doesn't apply to all imaginative literature written by Marxists (unlike the Marxist-inspired plays of Bertolt Brecht, which argue man's changeability and perfectibility)."[92]

The key to the story surely lies in the fact that Flitcraft ends one life in Tacoma and begins another in Spokane. Tacoma was where Hammett was treated for tuberculosis and where he met his wife. Tuberculosis was his falling beam. In Spokane, he was possibly a strike-breaker.

Nunnally Johnson explains Hammett's wild behavior by "an assumption that he had no expectation of being alive much beyond Thursday..."[93] Jo Hammett, the author's daughter, recalls that he once told her the Flitcraft story. "What I remember is his delight in the story — as if it were a gift he had received that was just right. As a boy he had wanted to find the Ultimate Truth — how the world operated. And here it was. There was no system except blind chance. Beams falling."[94] In part, of course, the acceptance of such an outlook was little more that a convenient justification for Hammett's own irresponsibility.

Dashiell Hammett believed in no deity. The universe had no particular reason for existing. The society in which he lived was corrupt and riddled with criminality. Life was meaningless. Once his beam had fallen in Tacoma, it didn't really matter if he went to Spokane to break strikes. It was just a job, and he might die soon anyway. This was the view not of a Marxist but of a nihilist.

The Glass Key (1933)

Hammett's penultimate novel is set wholly in the world of corrupt politics, but *The Glass Key* is even less of a Marxist denunciation of the system than *Red Harvest*.

Ned Beaumont (in Scottish slang from at least the late 19th century, a "ned" has referred to a lout or hooligan; Hammett's father was of Scottish stock) describes himself as "a gambler and a politician's hanger-on"[95] — to Paul Madvig, political boss, gangster, and owner of the Log Cabin Club, a gambling joint. With an election in the offing, Madvig has thrown in his lot with Senator Ralph Henry. The latter, Beaumont warns Madvig, is "one of the few aristocrats left in American politics… That's why I'm warning you to sew your shirt on when you go to see them, or you'll come away without it, because to them you're a lower form of animal life and none of the rules apply."[96]

Madvig is obsessed with the Senator's daughter, Janet, but his relationship with the family is complicated by the fact that he has previously warned Janet's brother Taylor, a ne'er-do-well, to stay away from his own daughter.

As political boss, Madvig has the city officials in the palm of his hand. When a bookie leaves town with Beaumont's winnings, Madvig readily agrees that Beaumont be sworn in as a deputy sheriff. Political considerations alone act as a restraint on Madvig. When Beaumont asks him to quash the prosecution (for murder) of the brother of Walt Ivans, a member of his group, Madvig argues that the time is not right; he'll be able to do something after the election, but not now. But such accommodation of respectable opinion has repercussions on both sides of the legal and political divide, and Beaumont warns him:

"Everybody knows Walt Ivans's been working for you

down in the Third Ward and is a member of the Club and everything and that you'd do anything you could to get his brother out of a jam if he asked you. Well, everybody, or a lot of them, is going to start wondering whether you didn't have the witnesses against his brother shot and frightened into silence. That goes for the outsiders, the women's clubs you're getting so afraid of these days, and the respectable citizens. The insiders — the ones that mostly wouldn't care if you had done that — are going to get something like the real news. They're going to know that one of your boys had to go to Shad [Shad O'Rory, a political and economic rival] to get fixed up and that Shad fixed him up. Well, that's the hole Shad's put you in — or don't you think he'd go that far to put you in a hole?"[97]

Madvig's prospects are further dimmed by the death of Sen. Henry's son Taylor, as suspicion comes to rest on the political boss; not only had he warned Taylor to stay away from his daughter, but she, having continued to see Taylor Henry secretly, now embarks upon a campaign of writing anonymous letters, implicating Madvig.

For his part, Madvig denies the allegations because, we are led to believe, he is afraid that any appearance of guilt will end his hopes of marrying the dead man's sister. Even though he has received some of the anonymous letters, Farr, the loathsomely supine District Attorney, is still deferential to Beaumont who, representing Madvig, meets him regularly, but even this particular worm is beginning to turn.

The wheels begin to come off of Madvig's election campaign when he resolves to have the police close down Shad O'Rory's nightclubs, a decision that leads to counter-attacks by O'Rory, who warns the political boss, "It's going to mean killing," because "I'm too big to take the boot from you now."[98] Beaumont warns Madvig that "Our coppers aren't used to bothering with Prohibition-enforcement. They're not going to like it very much."[99]

Later, Beaumont tells Madvig that if the aim is to have the whole city administration re-elected, it's hardly sensible to present the electorate with a crime wave just before the election. He tells Madvig that he's allowed himself to be outsmarted. "First you let the Henrys wheedle you into backing the Senator. There was your chance to go in and finish an enemy who was cornered, but that enemy happened to have a daughter and social position and what not..."[100]

Beaumont appears to break with Madvig, following which O'Rory asks him to go to the press and spill the beans on Madvig's involvement in the Taylor Henry killing and "the dirt on how he's running the city."[101] The newspaper is another rotten institution in this thoroughly corrupt city, as its publisher is deeply in debt to a company owned by the candidate opposing Henry in the Senate race, so he "does what he's told and prints what he's told to print."[102] Apart from the Taylor Henry killing, O'Rory wants Madvig's sewer-contracts exposed, but this proves to be another area where Madvig has been restrained by political considerations, as Beaumont tells him, "He let his profits go to keep from raising a stink."[103]

When Beaumont tries to leave, O'Rory's gorilla Jeff Gardner gives him a savage beating, following which Beaumont is held prisoner until, having started a fire in his room, he escapes from the alternative accommodation to which he is moved.

After several days in hospital, Beaumont is told by a minor character called Harry Sloss (actually the name of a member of staff at Albert Samuels' jewelry business where Hammett had worked as an advertising agent) that on the night of the Henry killing he and a companion, Ben Ferris, saw Taylor Henry and Madvig arguing at the spot where Henry's body was later found. Ferris has already been to the DA with this information. Beaumont suggests that Sloss go to the DA and tell him that he had been unable to recognize the two men arguing. When Sloss seeks payment, Beaumont says he'll be given "a soft job after the election, one you'll have to show up on maybe an hour a day."[104] Beaumont then goes to see the DA himself. Farr at first claims no progress in the Henry killing, until Beaumont divulges that he knows that Ben Ferris has made a statement, whereupon an embarrassed Farr gives the impression that he's dismissed this evidence. When Beaumont asks whether Farr thinks Madvig should allow himself to be arrested for the killing, Farr says that it isn't for him to tell Madvig what to do. Beaumont leans across Farr's desk to whisper that it's also "not for you to do much Paul wouldn't tell you to do."[105]

Beaumont tells Madvig that support is slipping away and that he'll lose the election unless the Henry killing is resolved. After some prevarication, Madvig claims that he had killed the young man but that it had been an accident, Taylor Henry having cracked his skull on the pavement after Madvig had taken away the stick he had been waving. He says he hadn't confessed and pleaded self-defense because "I want Janet Henry more than I ever wanted anything in my life and what chance would I have then, even if it was an accident?"[106]

Shortly after this, Beaumont forces a confession out of the dead man's father, who says that although Taylor had died in the circumstances described by Madvig (although Beaumont later tells Janet that he is not convinced it was an accident), it had been he who had been responsible. Madvig, having been rebuffed by Janet, had left the Henry house with Taylor in pursuit. The senator, not wishing, as he puts it, to lose the "friendship" of Madvig, had followed, and an argument had ensued between him and his son. Madvig, it is now apparent, has been covering for Senator Henry for purely political reasons.

Madvig now accepts that defeat at the polls is inevitable, saying that he will wait out the next four years, "cleaning house and putting together an organization that will stay put." Shad O'Rory is dead, and "I'm going to let his crew run things for the next four years. There's none of them that can build anything solid enough for me to worry about. I'll get the city back next time and by then I'll have done my housecleaning." He could win now, "but I don't want to win with those bastards."[107] Madvig's reference to "housecleaning" should not, of course, be taken to mean that his future administration will be honest, merely that it will be loyal, and in this regard the situation at the end of *The Glass Key* is very similar to that in *Red Harvest*.

≈

As so often in the past, in this novel Hammett sometimes coins a phrase so awkward that one wonders what he must have been thinking. In one scene, for example, Beaumont is "watching the blond man [Madvig] from the ends of his eyes."[108] The "ends of his eyes?" It has no meaning, and suggests haste, lack of care; we certainly know there was haste in the writing of *The Glass Key*, because we have it from Hammett himself that, falling behind schedule, he put in a 30-hour stint to catch up.[109]

Then, as in "The Farewell Murder," the last story Hammett wrote for *Black Mask* before the serialization of this novel, there is the curious use of the word "barytone" again. "The white-haired man said: 'Fine, Paul. How's yourself.' His voice was a musical barytone."[110] Rather than a spelling mistake, it seems this was Hammett trying to display a little erudition, as "barytone" is a word in classical Greek in which the last syllable is unaccented. As he uses the word incorrectly, this attempt misfired. That this was a recent affectation can be gleaned from the fact that in *The Dain Curse*, which in serial form appeared a year before "The Farewell Murder," Joseph has a "baritone voice".[111]

On the other hand, in some scenes we can see the characters before us as they play their roles.

> Whisky knocked cigarette-ash on the floor and returned the cigarette to the left side of his mouth. He snuffled. "How long you going to be gone?"
> Ned Beaumont held a coffee-cup half-way between the tray and his mouth. He looked thoughtfully over it at the sallow young man. Finally he said, "It's a one-way ticket," and drank.[112]

It is easy to see why Hollywood wanted Hammett. But this ability to see the characters in action and to describe what he sees also has its downside, for as Nolan points out "We are never allowed inside any of the people…we see them all once-removed; we are forced to judge them strictly on what they say and do."[113]

For example, while Ned Beaumont is unlike any other leading character in the Hammett novels, we are left guessing as to how or why he moves from one position to another. Beaumont may be hardboiled, but he's not superhuman. Hit in the stomach, or after too much whisky, he'll vomit. When his taxi is in a collision with another, he trembles, as he does after finding Taylor Henry's body. He bites his nails and picks nervously at his mustache. And when he's badly beaten and held prisoner by O'Rory's men, he tries to commit suicide with a rusty razor blade found on the bathroom floor. But why has he volunteered to take such a beating from Jeff Gardner, O'Rory's pet gorilla? When he is seen to break with Madvig, what is his motivation? And when, at the end of the novel, he decides to leave for New York, taking Janet Henry with him (just as, at around the same time, Hammett departed for

New York with the writer Nell Martin, to whom the novel is dedicated) what has led him to this decision? What, for that matter, are Janet Henry's intentions in accompanying him? This third-person novel, by failing to give its characters an interior life, never even attempts to answer such questions.

Beaumont resembles Hammett. He is tall, and only "the flatness of his chest hinted at any constitutional weakness."[114] Like Hammett, Beaumont is something of a dandy, who knows you shouldn't wear silk socks with tweeds, or brown shoes with a blue suit, and he keeps a handkerchief in his breast pocket.[115] Rather as in Raymond Chandler's *The Little Sister*, almost every character in *The Glass Key* is corrupt and motivated by pecuniary gain. And yet Janet Henry seems to hint that Beaumont himself is not totally corrupted when she remarks of his spacious, high-ceilinged apartment, "I didn't know there could be any more of these left in a city as horribly up to date as ours has become."[116]

But this leads to more questions: if Beaumont was plucked from the gutter by Madvig just over a year previously, where did he acquire his taste in architecture and clothes? But maybe Hammett is here pointing to the essential hypocrisy of this character who knows that wearing tan shoes with a blue suit is a crime but sees nothing wrong with having the case against a murderer aborted. And as Beaumont is so obviously deliberately drawn to resemble his creator physically, is Hammett telling us something about the void at the center of his own being?

On several occasions, *The Glass Key* sounds a religious note which biographers and critics appear to have missed. Less than a third of the way into the novel, "Paul Madvig arrived at Ned Beaumont's rooms as the bells in the grey church across the street were ringing the Angelus."[117] The Angelus is the prayer in which the angel Gabriel appears to Mary and advises her that she is to give birth to Jesus. In the discussion which takes place between Madvig and Beaumont, differences between the two men emerge, with the political boss declaring for action against Shad O'Rory and Beaumont urging caution. Later in this chapter, Beaumont buys a one-way ticket to New York and publicly breaks with Madvig.

In the speakeasy where the break takes place, the barman serves them pretzels, the origin of which is thought to date back to the medieval monasteries, where they were devised as a means of circumventing the Church prohibition on certain ingredients during Lent; later, they also became associated with Easter.[118] It is in the following chapter that Beaumont's departure for New York is postponed by his imprisonment and beating by Jeff Gardner. Later in the novel, when Beaumont encounters Gardner in a nightclub, the latter declares that his former victim must be "a God-damned massacrist...You know what a massacrist is?" In tagging on that question, Hammett obviously intends that we give the word close attention — and, I would suggest, particularly the "crist." The suggestion is, therefore, that Beaumont has offered himself for crucifixion on Madvig's behalf.

Hammett is known to have been non-religious, and in particular to disdain the Catholic Church, but at the same time he certainly had a knowledge of the Bible, which he sometimes employed in his fiction. In this very novel, for example, Beaumont tells Janet Henry that she's opted to play the role of Judith.[119] His story "Ber-Bulu" had of course been based on the biblical story of Samson, and according to Emery the hirsute character's name, "Levi-son," was inspired by the tribes of Israel.[120] So was Hammett drawn by religion at this stage in his life? Probably not, but the chances are that he was feeling empty and pondering moral alternatives. Beaumont tells Janet Henry, "I don't believe in anything, but I'm too much of a gambler not to be affected by a lot of things,"[121] but a little earlier he is seen "smoking and staring at the grey church across the street...His teeth crushed the end of his cigar."[122] As he illustrated with the Flitcraft parable in *The Maltese Falcon*, Hammett found life meaningless, and the indications are that this situation was becoming ever less tolerable. He was looking for something to believe in, but he had not yet found it.

It is extremely doubtful that Hammett had embraced Marxism at this stage. Wolfe is simply wrong when he says that in this novel "the Marxist novelist, Hammett, accepts corruption and vice as facts of urban life."[123] It is Hammett the nihilist who accepts these things, for he was still closer to the more nihilist of hardboiled writers like Horace McCoy than to Marxism. Once again, it is Layman who hits the nail on the head, commenting that *The Glass Key* is "remarkably apolitical" in that no stance, liberal or conservative, is adopted.[124] Where is the working class in *The Glass Key*? It still has to put in an appearance in Hammett's work. Then again, if Hammett had been a Marxist, he would have known a thing or two about dialectics, a knowledge which would surely have enabled him to give Beaumont an inner life and show us how and why his perceptions and intentions develop and change throughout the novel.

In *The Glass Key* there is a theme of male bonding, as when Beaumont tells Janet Henry, "You're right about my being Paul's friend. I'm that no matter who he killed."[125] Wolfe, citing Kenney and Bazelon, wonders whether the relationship — or, at least, the attraction — is sexual. "In *Glass Key*, the motives are often sexual. Kenney says that the friendship between Beaumont and Madvig is 'so intense that it seems at times to approach the homoerotic.' In concert, Bazelon calls Madvig 'almost, indeed, a homosexual love-object' for Beaumont. It is difficult to find evidence supporting this argument."[126] The text is ambivalent on this score. At times, the relationship between the two men seems fraternal, as when, early on in the novel, Madvig asks Beaumont, "Why haven't you been out to the house?...Mom was saying last night she hadn't seen you for a month."[127] The last scene in the book conveys a different impression, however: Beaumont tells Madvig that he's leaving for New York; Madvig asks him to stay, but Beaumont refuses.

> Ned Beaumont said: "Janet is going away with me."
> Madvig's lips parted. He looked dumbly at Ned Beaumont and as he looked the blood went out of his face again. When his face was quite bloodless he mumbled something of which only "luck" could be understood, turned clumsily around, went to the door, opened it, and went out, leaving it open behind him.
> Janet Henry looked at Ned Beaumont. He stared fixedly at the door.[128]

Two decades later, that scene would have an echo in the closing scene of Chandler's *The Long Goodbye*, after Philip Marlowe has told Terry Lennox that their friendship is at an end.

> He turned and walked across the floor and out. I watched the door close. I listened to his steps going away down the imitation marble corridor. After a while they got

faint, then they got silent. I kept on listening anyway. What for? Did I want him to stop suddenly and turn and come back and talk me out of the way I felt? Well, he didn't. That was the last I saw of him.[129]

While, however, it is fairly certain that Chandler was a repressed gay whose works contain a number of homoerotic representations, it is only in *The Glass Key* that this note is struck in Hammett's work (his life was, of course, unlike Chandler's, somewhat over-supplied with women), and so it would be hardly possible to pursue the point.

The title of the novel comes from a dream that Janet Henry has in which she and Beaumont are lost in a forest; starving, they come upon a small house in which they can see a table piled with food. The door is locked, but they find the key under the door-mat. When they open the door, however, they discover that hundreds of snakes are writhing on the floor. In Janet's first version, they relock the door and climb onto the roof, from where Beaumont reaches down and unlocks the door again. The snakes all slither off into the forest, after which Janet and Ned enter the house and relieve their hunger. In her second version, the key, being glass, shatters just as they force the door open, and the snakes slither all over them. Much has been made of this by various of Hammett's interpreters,[130] but it is surely significant that Janet tells Beaumont how the dream really ended after her father has been unmasked as the killer. Even allowing that the reference to serpents in the garden is biblical, implying temptation, all the dream means is that the mystery of the Taylor Henry murder, once unlocked, will let out an ugly truth.

The Thin Man (1934)

In Hammett's first stab at *The Thin Man* in 1930, he retains the third-person viewpoint followed since *The Maltese Falcon*.[131]

John Guild is a private detective sent to investigate Walter Irving Wynant, who has deposited a check that has been altered from $1,000 to $10,000. Wynant lives in the mountain village of Hell Bend. Upon arrival, Guild discovers that Wynant, who is said to be crazy, has apparently murdered his secretary, Colombia Forrest, and absconded.

According to the Hopkinses, Wynant's caretakers, Forrest had told him that she was leaving his employment to get married and, as their relationship had been sexual, he had killed her in a fit of jealousy.

Wynant is "very tall — well over six feet — and thin. Won't weigh more than a hundred and thirty, they say. You know he's tubercular..."[132] This could be Hammett, except that Wynant has a long beard and neither smokes nor drinks. The missing man has written on science, philosophy and anthropology, his latest book being entitled *Knowledge and Belief*, but a reviewer friend of Guild's tells him that "the magazine stuff he's been doing lately — since *Knowledge and Belief* — I know is tripe and worse."[133]

Colombia Forrest had returned to the house from the city, driving a car that is found to belong to Charles Fremont. Wynant's own car is missing. Guild visits the Fremont house and is told by the sister Elsa that Charles was due to marry Forrest the following day. He had first met her in a speakeasy when she had been with a Helen Robier. Guild doesn't believe what he's being told. As they talk, a shot from the street narrowly misses Fremont. Guild and Fremont, who has caught sight of the shooter and identifies him as Wynant with his beard shaved off, search the area and find Wynant's car, abandoned and wiped clean of prints.

That night, Guild goes to a restaurant, the Manchu, as he has been told that Wynant was seen by a Hell Bend neighbor entering it earlier. He is surprised to discover that Elsa Fremont sings at the restaurant.

At Wynant's bank the following day, Guild discovers that he had been writing checks for a Laura Porter, who over several months has received almost all he had deposited. Guild then visits Laura Porter's bank and gets her address. He goes to the apartment house where, according to Fremont, Forrest's friend Helen Robier lives, but is told that Robier had been killed in a car accident some time earlier. When Guild, joined by Boyer, the young and inexperienced District Attorney from Hell Bend, visit Laura Porter's rooming house, the landlady identifies a picture of Forrest as Porter.

In Laura Porter's room there are signs that Wynant has been there to shave off his whiskers. Back at the bank, they find that Porter's account is almost empty, as she had withdrawn $12,000 in cash the previous day. When opening the account she had given Wynant and Francis X. Kearney, owner of the Manchu, as references.

A news report quotes former police magistrate "Erle Gardner" (a playful reference to Erle Stanley Gardner, who had been a contributor to *Black Mask* before going on to write his lucrative series of Perry Mason novels) as saying that Forrest had been convicted of shoplifting three years earlier, but the sentence had been suspended when Wynant reimbursed the store and took her on as his secretary.

At the Fremonts', Elsa says her brother has gone to Hell Bend. When she denies having heard of Porter, Guild says her brother must have. She tells Guild that Charles manages a couple of fighters for a living, one of them Sammy Deep, a Chinese boxer. Charles, having got Elsa the singing job, knows Kearney.

Guild and Boyer learn that Fremont never arrived at Hell Bend. They drive out to the town and learn that a telegram arrived for Wynant at 2.05 on the afternoon of the murder, but no one had answered the door. The Fremont car had been there, but Wynant's had not. Guild speculates that Forrest may have been packing, or she may have already been dead. Guild now thinks Wynant innocent. He and Boyer question the Hopkinses, Guild saying that they should be charged, as their story makes no sense.

At the Manchu, in the early hours of the morning, the owner Kearney says he's never heard of Porter, although that means nothing, as people often ask him to stand as references for their friends. Kearney reminds Guild that he sent a friend of his, Deep Ying, to jail recently, adding that his brother works at the restaurant. Deep Kee comes over and they have a friendly conversation.

When Guild sees Elsa home, she asks him to remain with her. He stays a while, during which she attempts to seduce him, but Guild, unlike Spade and prefiguring Chandler's Philip Marlowe, never mixes business with pleasure. Before he leaves, Elsa urges him to search the house, as she's nervous. He does so, and returns to tell her that he's found her brother's body in the cellar, and that it looks like suicide. When he suggests that Charles killed Columbia Forrest, she tells him that he was at the Boxing Commission at the time in question.

≈

And there, after 18,000 words (the count is Nolan's), the fragment ends. Symons thinks this first version was abandoned because it was

"was disappointing to the writer, as it is to the reader,"[134] but in all honesty the reader is not particularly disappointed. It is typical Hammett, and while it is true that on this outing he shows no sign of further development as a writer, the awkward phrasing is absent, and the plot is not cluttered with bodies. The story does show signs of becoming very convoluted, and this may have deterred Hammett from proceeding further; then again, after 18,000 words a fair amount of territory has been covered and he possibly doubted his ability to extend the material to novel length; or he may simply have been unable to see where the plot was going. Faced with one or more of these problems, Hammett would not have been the first writer to, having approached his desk with a leaden heart, cast his eye over the manuscript and put it aside in exasperation. In his case, this point was reached after a break of two years during which he had met Lillian Hellman and moved into a completely different social milieu — and that, of course, was another reason for starting afresh.[135]

In the eventual novel, Hammett retains few elements from his first attempt: the name of Wynant for the alleged murderer who has disappeared, although the forename is changed to Clyde; Wynant is described almost exactly as before; the name of the original private detective, John Guild, is now given to a police lieutenant; and, as before, Wynant's secretary has been murdered. But the detective is not even a detective any longer, for Nick Charles, (his father's name had been Anglicized from Charalambides by an immigration officer on Ellis Island) is married to the daughter of the late owner of "a lumber mill and a narrow-gauge railroad and some other things" and "I quit the agency to look after them."[136] Nick, 41, and Nora, 26, are socialites, living the kind of alcohol-fueled existence inhabited by Hammett and Hellman (to whom the novel is dedicated).

The first word in *The Thin Man* is "I." Hammett seems to have determined at the outset to announce this return to the first-person perspective, for in so doing it is as if he is also confessing (to those he may have led to expect better things, but mostly to himself) that he has also returned to the mystery novel.

THE DARKENING VISION

≈

Nick and Nora, from San Francisco, are spending the Christmas-New Year break of 1932 at a luxury hotel in New York. Nick comes across twenty-year-old Dorothy Wynant in a speakeasy. Some eight years ago he worked for her father, an inventor, when he had been threatened by a former colleague called Kelterman, who alleged that his ideas had been stolen. The following day, Nick gets a call from Herbert Macaulay, Wynant's lawyer, and they have lunch together, when Macaulay tells Nick that he hasn't seen Wynant since October,

The following day, the newspapers announce that Wyant's secretary, Julia Wolf, has been found shot dead in her apartment and that the police are looking for Wynant, whose former wife, visiting the apartment in search of him, discovered Wolf's body. Nick describes Wynant as "Tall — over six feet — and one of the thinnest men I've ever seen. He must be about fifty now, and his hair was almost white when I knew him. Usually needs a haircut, ragged brindle mustache..."[137] Apart from the 12-year age difference and the poor grooming, this could be Hammett.

According to the press, Julia's body was identified by an Arthur Nunheim (who, calling himself Albert Norman, has already called Nick to ask that they meet to discuss a proposition), who has linked her to a gangster. As Nick, Nora and Dorothy are having breakfast the following afternoon, Dorothy's parents arrive — her mother Mimi and her new husband Christian Jorgenson. Mimi says that according to the papers Wolf was killed by her lover, a gangster called Morelli. Mimi, keen to locate Wynant, says she's worried for the sake of the children, because although she has no further claim on Wynant (she agreed to a lump-sum divorce settlement), her children Dorothy and Gilbert have, and the family is now broke. She asks Nick to help, but he is not interested.

The next morning Nick is awoken by Nora to find he is attended by armed gangster Shep Morelli, who says he didn't kill Julia Wolf. The police announce their presence at the door of the suite, whereupon Morelli shoots and grazes Nick's chest. This incident provokes in Nick the first flicker of interest in the case. "I don't know what I'm going to do," he says, "because I don't know what's being done to me. I've got to find out."[138]

Dorothy, who has arrived back at the suite reporting that her mother has beaten her, says Mimi and Chris left their apartment together on the day of the murder — after 2.30, close to 3.00. Nick asks her why Mimi wants to find Wynant and she replies "For money. We're broke. Chris spent it all."

Nick receives a telegram from Wynant asking him to contact the lawyer Macaulay to discuss taking over the investigation of the Wolf murder. Nick tells police lieutenant John Guild what he knows: Wynant told Macaulay on October 3 that he had to leave town for a while, and Macaulay has the impression that he's working on an invention. Wynant has arranged it so that the lawyer can convert his stocks into cash whenever he needs it. Guild now says that $28,500 has been withdrawn from Wynant's account since his disappearance, and Macaulay has had to sell a few things to provide that amount. Guild reveals that, two years before she worked for Wynant, Wolf served six months on a "badger-game charge" — an extortion scheme in which a man is usually tricked into a compromising position by a woman — "under the name of Rhoda Stewart."[139] Guild says Wolf was alive at 2.30pm when Mimi called her, and at around 3pm when Macaulay phoned. He divulges that Nunheim, who identified Wolf as a friend of Morelli, occasionally acts as a police informer.

Macaulay receives a letter from Wynant asking him to persuade Nick to find the murderer, regardless of cost. He says he saw Wolf the night before her death, when she gave him the $1,000 he had requested (Macaulay has said that he had provided her with $5,000). She said she was unwell and wanted to leave her job. For a year, he says, he and Wolf and merely had an employment relationship. He asks that the location of Sidney Kelterman be investigated, as his current work involves the ideas Kelterman had accused him of stealing.

Nick and Nora visit the Pigiron Club, a speakeasy owned by Studsy Burke, whom Nick sent to prison some time ago. Burke tells him that Nunheim used to come to the club, chasing Julia. Nick and Guild pay Nunheim a visit, but he escapes. He is later shot with the same pistol used to kill Julia Wolf.

Mimi asks Nick what penalty she might face for concealing evidence. She says she has found proof of Wynant's guilt but she has hidden it. Nick tells her that her new husband Jorgenson is in reality Wynant's former rival Kelterman. Gilbert, Wynant's teenaged son, has intercepted a letter from Jorgenson's first (and still current) wife.

In a longish scene at the Pigiron Club, Shep Morelli tells Nick he had known Julia Wolf since they were children in Cleveland, and he's pretty sure she was stealing from Wynant. Julia, having learned shorthand in prison, was sent by an agency to Wynant, and she looked upon employment with him as an investment, paying big dividends in the long run. She told him of her record. Morelli and she were only friends, but Wynant was jealous and so they stopped seeing each other in October, as she was unwilling to jeopardize her investment. He thinks Nunheim knew Wynant's whereabouts. During this scene, a fat man starts to remonstrate with Nick regarding Nunheim, but is beaten into silence by guests and a waiter before he can say more. This incident will turn up again in the second *Thin Man* sequel Hammett will write for the screen.

When Nick and Nora take Dorothy to her home, they find the police there. Guild says Jorgenson has been picked up but seems innocent of the Wolf killing, as Mimi says she has the evidence implicating Wynant. She shows Nick a length of watch chain attached to a small gold knife. This, she says, was in Julia's hand when she found her, and it belongs to Wynant.

The next morning, Macaulay comes to the hotel and tells Nick that Guild has been to see him with the watch chain, and he has confirmed it as Wynant's. He says he's going to turn Wynant in. He now gives an alternative version of his movements on the day of the murder, saying that he had been followed (he describes a man like Nunheim); trying to lose his tail, he saw Wynant in a cab, driving away from the direction of Julia Wolf's apartment. He concludes by saying that Wynant has now phoned him and an arrangement has been made for him to meet Macaulay and Nick that night. Macaulay says Wynant told him to give Mimi any reasonable sum she might request.

Wynant's son Gilbert has told his sister Dorothy that he has been seeing his father, and that Wynant knows who killed Julia Wolf. Guild has stationed a man in Julia Wolf's apartment, who apprehends Gilbert when he goes there, having received a note from his father asking him to visit the apartment (he has provided a key), where he will find further instructions concealed in the pages of a book called *The Grand Manner*. Guild has his men search the apartment for the book, but it is not there. Gilbert now says he lied when he claimed he had been seeing his father; this was to impress Dorothy, who seemed no longer to admire him so much since Nick Charles has been around.

Nick is called to Mimi's place, where she tells him that Wynant has paid a visit, leaving her three bundles of bonds and a check for $10,000. Macaulay, meanwhile, has heard again from Wynant, who has cancelled their evening meeting. Earlier, Nick has urged Guild to take a look at Wynant's workshop, which has been closed since his disappearance. Guild now reveals that a dismembered body has been found there, buried under cement; most of the flesh has been burned away by lime, but the clothes buried with the body are still partially intact, including a belt-buckle with the initials D.W.Q. and a walking stick, from which Guild infers that the dead man was fat and lame.

In best Sherlock Holmes fashion, Nick immediately declares that the remains are those of Wynant, the clothes having been placed there to give a false impression. He later explains to Nora that the lawyer Macaulay killed Wynant, Julia Wolf and Nunheim. Macaulay, having lost large amounts on the stock market, had in partnership with Wolf been robbing Wynant for some time. Wynant had discovered this and, fueled partly by jealousy, had gone to Macaulay's house to confront him, but Macaulay had killed him, later transferring the remains to Wynant's own workshop. He worked with Julia Wolf to transfer the remainder of Wynant's money to themselves, but by now Julia was scared, and so Macaulay silenced her, leaving Wynant's watch chain on her body. But Nunheim had seen him leave the apartment, and then Mimi had arrived and removed the chain in the hope that she might later extort money from her former husband.

Macaulay's telephonist recalls him receiving a call from an Albert Norman (Nunheim) and that Macaulay had immediately gone out; he had, of course, killed Nunheim. The purpose of sending Gilbert to Wolf's apartment was to convey the impression that Wynant had had a key. Macaulay obviously could not appropriate Wynant's estate without suspicion falling on him, so he arranged that Mimi should receive the bonds and the check on the understanding that she would split the proceeds with him.

The Thin Man was a new departure for Hammett in that the main characters, Nick and Nora Charles, are urbane, witty and rich; the only connections with the earlier world of hardboiled detectives lie in Nick's status as a retired snooper, the amount of alcohol consumed, and the almost incidental fact that murders occur during the course of the story which are, at its conclusion, solved.

The domestic regime of Nick and Nora mirrors that of Hammett and Hellman: Nora is reading Chaliapin's memoirs (which Hammett had himself recently consumed[140]); breakfast is often taken in the afternoon; the couple find time for theater excursions and cocktail parties; and they have an obscure and expensive breed of dog called Asta (a Schnauser, in life given to Hellman by the humorist S. J. Perelman). Nora, of course, is closely based on Hellman. Hammett gives us no description of Nick Charles, although the publicity departments of Knopf and MGM would soon ensure that the character would assume the physical appearance of Hammett himself; Nick Charles/Hammett, rather than the dead Wynant, would henceforth be the Thin Man.

The setting and its characters call for sparkling dialogue and Hammett often supplies it. After he has wrestled a violent Mimi to the sofa, Nora asks Nick:

> "Tell me the truth: when you were wrestling with Mimi, didn't you have an erection?"
> "Oh, a little."[141]

When Gilbert, Dorothy's younger brother, asks about the prevalence of incest, Nick replies, "There's some...that's why they've got a name for it."[142] The novel's most wonderful line, however, is given to Guild, who tells Nick, "His story listens all right to me."[143] It is possible that Hammett has deliberately emphasized the crudity of the policeman's dialogue in order to provide a contrast to the bubbly chatter of the Charleses, although he may equally have heard it during his detective years and filed it away for future use.

As far as the writing goes, there are none of the awkward phrases that mark some of Hammett's earlier work, and he makes a point of inserting one "as lief." But there is a problem with this, as it is Guild that he has say "I'd just as lief ask you."[144] How likely is it that this would fall from the lips of the same man who says, "His story listens all right to me?" This is indicative of a wider problem, for Hammett sometimes seems to have stored a number of incidents or lines and is so anxious that they should not go to waste that he uses them rather haphazardly. For example, Gilbert asks his question about incest apropos of nothing whatever — apart from giving Hammett/Nick the opportunity to deliver the punch line. And why is it necessary to tell us that the 18-year-old Gilbert is — improbably — writing a book called *Knowledge and Belief*? In the original version of the story, of course, this was the title of one of Wynant's published works; it is as if the phrase is acting as a meme for Hammett, and he is unable to let go of it.

As in *The Maltese Falcon*, there is some padding, as when Dorothy tells Nick that she has bought a battered pistol in a speakeasy for $12. The police, who confiscate the gun from Charles's suite, later say that it is useless as a weapon, rusted inside. And there the matter dies, having served no purpose at all. There is a sign of haste when, very near the end of the novel, Nick introduces Macaulay as a former Army comrade, something Hammett has previously neglected to tell us; if he had intended to return to Chapter 2 in order to insert this information when Macaulay makes his first appearance, it obviously slipped his mind. There seems to be a similar slip, either by Hammett or his editor, when, late in the story, Jorgenson/Kelterman is referred to as "Rosewater."[145] (In some editions of the novel, this character does, in fact, go by the name of Rosewater.)

≋

Between 1930 and 1932, the US economy had contracted 27.7 percent, and in the latter year unemployment reached 23.6 percent. Since 1929, 40 percent of all banks had failed; international trade had fallen by two-thirds. In March 1932, 3,000 unemployed workers who had marched on the Ford plant in River Rouge, Michigan were attacked by company guards and police, resulting in four deaths and many injuries.The following month three-quarters of a million New Yorkers were reported to be on city relief. Since 1924, a bill had been before Congress which would have granted World War I veterans a "bonus" of one dollar a day (or $1.25 per day for service overseas).In June, 25,000 veterans and members of their families set up camp near the White House to press their case, but the bill, although passed by the House of Representatives, was heavily defeated in the Senate. The "Bonus Expeditionary Force" stayed put, however, until late July, when President Hoover ordered federal troops commanded by General Douglas MacArthur to assist police in clearing the camp. There followed the "Battle of Anacostia Flats," in which MacArthur, exceeding his instructions, sent his men into the camp, which was put to the torch. Military historian Eric Larrabee records: "One man had his ear cut off by a cavalry saber; a seven-year-old boy who ran back for his pet rabbit was bayoneted in the leg; two score more were hurt by bricks, clubs, bayonets and sabers; and an eleven-week-old baby exposed to tear gas died."[146]

Such was the time when Dashiell Hammett decided to write his most escapist novel. While the lines at the soup kitchens lengthened (not that we are given a glimpse of them — or even a mention), Nick Charles, having tired of the Wynants, suggests to his wife, "Let's go to Max's. I'd like some snails."[147] When his broker reports that he's managed to sell some bonds on which Charles had written off the loss and urges him to buy gold, Charles gives him "an order to buy some Dome Mines at 12½."[148] In the midst of the excitement of the Wynant case, Charles spends a morning on business matters, including "going over a plan we had for lowering our state taxes..."[149]

It is initially tempting to assume that social comment is completely absent from *The Thin Man* — unless Hammett wishes the whole novel to be taken as a comment on the essential meaninglessness and social irresponsibility of such an existence. That such may have been his intention is suggested when Hammett has a man at a cocktail party say, "Comes the revolution and we'll all be lined up against the wall — first thing."[150] But such hints and suggestions are far too infrequent and subtle to detract from the fact that, above all else, the intention of Hammett's novel is to entertain, and the vaguely serious points which do exist are, as we shall see, directed at himself rather than the reader.

Having said that, it is certainly the case that Hammett populates this frivolous world with characters who have few, if any, saving graces. As George Thompson puts it, "The moral vision of *The Thin Man* is dark indeed. The plot does more than unmask a villain; it shows that the villain survives only because of the corresponding greed and savagery in those around him — cannibals like Macaulay the killer can feast off others because the world is so devoid of values that he can appear as a natural part of the landscape."[151]

But it's not just those around Macaulay, it's *almost everybody in the novel*. Nick Charles has, as we have seen, no social conscience, surrounding himself with riches and numbing himself with alcohol at a time when 15 million Americans are unemployed; if his wife Nora is capable of rising above his superficiality, we are given no evidence of it. Macaulay plunders the wealth of his client and murders three people in a desperate bid to compensate for his stock market losses, attempting to fool the wartime comrade who saved his life. Julia Wolf gives her body as part of a long-term investment in Wynant, and then is an accessory to his murder. Austin Quinn, Nick Charles's broker, is infatuated with young Dorothy Wynant, the missing man's daughter; his wife Alice tells Charles, "You know I'm only staying with him for his money, don't you? It may not be a lot to you, but it is to me — the way I was raised."[152]

Dorothy herself is obsessed with Nick Charles. Her mother Mimi tells him, "If you want Dorry, take her, but don't get sentimental about it."[153] Dorothy's brother Gilbert has an interesting take on Mimi: "Mamma's not really dangerous. She's just a case of arrested development. Most of us have outgrown ethics and morals and so on. Mamma's just not grown up to them yet."[154] Ethics and morals, then, usually have no place in the grown-up world.

There is a long digression concerning a 19th-century cannibal in Colorado.[155] The story concerns Alfred G. Packer, who in 1873-74 undertook a prospecting expedition as part of a 20-strong party; months later, lost and starving, he killed his remaining five companions and ate their flesh. He was eventually convicted of their manslaughter, but pardoned in 1901. When, in the passage quoted above, Thompson refers to Macaulay as a "cannibal" he obviously sees (as must have Hammett himself) Packer's situation — adrift in the wilderness, with no law enforcement, courts; no society, indeed — as symbolizing the moral desert inhabited by Hammett's characters.

There is a sense in which the attempts of Nick Charles to resist efforts to drag him into the investigation of the Wynant case may be viewed as a parable of Hammett's desire to leave the detective genre behind. And if Hammett is the flawed and frivolous Nick Charles, he is also Wynant, the man who is supposedly working on an invention but who is, in fact, dead, just as Hammett, claiming to be at work on one novel or another in the following years, would be creatively dead. Not only does Wynant share a physical description with Hammett, but he has a sister-in-law who has fallen out with him after he has said in an interview that "he didn't think the Russian Five Year Plan was necessarily doomed to failure."[156] Later we learn that this Aunt Alice "says he's become a Communist and she's sure the Communists killed Julia Wolf and will kill him in the end."[157]

At one point in the story, Guild receives information that Wynant has committed suicide in Allentown, Pennsylvania, but this turns out to be false, appearing to serve no purpose other than to allow Guild to give forth with the only outburst of racism in the novel, as he explains to Nick that the man mistakenly thought to have been Wynant is found to have been an unemployed carpenter who "got shot by a nigger trying to stick him up."[158] At first, this strikes the reader as another of Hammett's pointless diversions, rather like the wild goose chase upon which Rhea Gutman sends Spade in *The Maltese Falcon*. On closer examination, however, it seems that Hammett was posting himself a message.

Why would Hammett have chosen Allentown as the place where Wynant might end his life? It should be recalled that in Hammett's first, uncompleted version of this story Wynant is a writer who has recently submitted "tripe and worse" for magazine publication; let us also bear in mind that in the second half of 1932 Hammett, hard up for money, had published his three inferior Sam Spade short stories in the "slicks." So why Allentown? In 1910, Allentown had been the site of the 108-day Bethlehem Steel strike; in early 1933, Lehigh Valley, in which Allentown is situated, was host to a rash of garment-worker strikes against child labor and sweatshop conditions.[159] Hammett completed *The Thin Man* in May 1933, and so he must have been aware of this strike activity as he wrote, and have chosen Allentown as a possible destination for Wynant quite deliberately. If the writer of "tripe and worse" were to perish in such a city, it would only have been so that he might be reborn in a more serious role. It might be somewhat rash, however, to assume that Hammett had in mind a literary role, as he never completed another novel. It is just as possible that with the Allentown parable Hammett was signaling his intention of leaving behind the detective novel — and maybe writing as a whole — in order to engage in political activity.

However, just as the report of Wynant's suicide turns out to be false, so was Hammett's implied intention to forsake the detective genre premature, as Hollywood — or at least the lure of its generous rewards — would drag him back to it to the extent that he would write the stories for the second and third *Thin Man* films. But it was also in Hollywood that his political activity, so absent in his life thus far, began.

NOTES

1. Dashiell Hammett, *Selected Letters of Dashiell Hammett, 1921-1960*, ed. Richard Layman with Julie M. Rivett (Washington D. C.: Counterpoint, 2001), 47.
2. Julian Symons, *Dashiell Hammett* (San Diego/New York/London: Harcourt Brace Jovanovich, 1985), 38.
3. Dashiell Hammett, *Red Harvest* in *Five Complete Novels* (New York: Avenel Books, 1980), 7.
4. Ibid.
5. Ibid.
6. Ibid. 79.
7. Ibid., 104.
8. Ibid. 134.
9. Ibid.
10. Ibid., 86. In *The Maltese Falcon* and *The Thin Man*, Hammett renders the phrase in the even more archaic form "as lief."
11. Ibid., 93.
12. Ibid., 10.
13. Ibid., 21.
14. William F. Nolan, *Dashiell Hammett: A Life at the Edge* (London: Arthur Barker, 1983), 75.
15. Ibid, 77.
16. Peter Wolfe, *Beams Falling: The Art of Dashiell Hammett* (Bowling Green: Bowling Green University Popular Press, 1980), 77; George J. Thompson, "The Problem of Moral Vision in Dashiell Hammett's Detective Novels," Diss., University of Connecticut, 1971.
17. Wolfe, 89.
18. Ibid., 91.
19. Richard Layman, *Shadow Man: The Life of Dashiell Hammett* (New York and London: Harcourt Brace Jovanovich/Bruccoli Clark, 1981), 96. Zumoff makes a similar point, remarking that this mining-town story is remarkable for the absence of miners! See J. A. Zumoff, "The Politics of Dashiell Hammett's *Red Harvest*," *Mosaic*, 40.4 (2007), 123.
20. George J. "Rhino" Thompson, *Hammett's Moral Vision* (San Francisco: Vince Emery Productions, 2007), 43, 60.
21. Ibid., 59.

22 Lillian Hellman, *Scoundrel Time* (London: Macmillan, 1976), 35-36.
23 Layman, *Shadow Man*, 13. "When he was in certain moods," says Layman, "he delighted in fooling interviewers, interested listeners, and sycophants with fabricated tales about his past and his future plans." Ibid., ix. Ward claims that the "story of Frank Little and the deadly bribe became a favorite of Hammett's," although there is scant evidence that Hammett told it to anyone apart from Lillian Hellman, Ward's source. See Nathan Ward, *The Lost Detective: Becoming Dashiell Hammett* (New York: Bloomsbury, 2015), 35.
24 The chronology in *Hammett: Crime Stories and Other Writings* (New York: Library of America, 2001), 920, records: "1920. Leaves home permanently in May; travels to Spokane, Washington, where he resumes work for Pinkerton. Serves as Pinkerton operative in Idaho and Montana, becoming involved as strikebreaker in Anaconda miners' strike."
25 George Everett, "The Seeds of *Red Harvest*: Dashiell Hammett's Poinsonville," *Only in Butte*, http://butteamerica.com/hist.htm, accessed May 2, 2015. Ward advises us that Hammett's future wife was, in fact, the adopted daughter of "Captain" William Kelly, an Anaconda executive, so she would have had considerable knowledge of both Butte and the company. See Ward, 127.
26 J. A. Zumoff, "Politics and the 1920s Writings of Dashiell Hammett," *American Studies Journal*, 52.1 (2012), 81, 82. Ward, on the other hand, claims that "scores of Pinkerton and Brown detectives roamed the town..." Ward, *The Lost Detective*, 32.
27 *Red Harvest*, in *Five Complete Novels*, 101.
28 Zumoff, "Politics and the 1920s Writings of Dashiell Hammett," 84.
29 *Red Harvest*, in *Five Complete Novels*, 45. Ward's assertion that the Op, in order to free Personville, "burns down much of the town... using hell-raising techniques cribbed from agitators like Frank Little" is extremely wide of the mark. See Ward, *The Lost Detective*, 37.
30 Ibid., 10.
31 Layman, *Shadow Man*, 96.
32 Zumoff rightly sees "Nightmare Town" as the "prototype" of *Red Harvest*. In dismissing claims that the novel is in any way "Marxist," he makes the very pertinent observation that, quite apart

from the level of the author's political consciousness, *Black Mask*, in which the novel was first serialized, "tended to be a pro-law-and-order journal, at times even running sympathetic stories about the Ku Klux Klan." The world of the novel, Zumoff says, can be read as "one of nihilist cynicism," and its "political ambiguity...reflects Hammett's half-way status." J. A. Zumoff, "The Politics of Dashiell Hammett's *Red Harvest*," 122, 126, 132.
33 Dashiell Hammett, *The Dain Curse* in *Five Complete Novels*, 167.
34 Ibid., 178.
35 Ibid., 183.
36 Ibid., 187.
37 Ibid., 203.
38 Ibid., 209.
39 Ibid., 282.
40 Ibid., 287.
41 Ibid., 291.
42 Layman, *Shadow Man*, 101, 103.
43 Symons, 52.
44 *The Dain Curse* in *Five Complete Novels*, 214.
45 Ibid., 249.
46 Ibid., 154.
47 Ibid.,155.
48 Ibid.,157.
49 Ibid., 287.
50 Ibid., 211. George Thompson thinks that he *does* see a Marxist influence in the novel, arguing that Hammett's language, as Fitzstephan comes to look upon Gabrielle as his property, "suggests the Marxian view that the capitalistic system must eventually corrode from within," and that possibly "Hammett chose to focus on the family unit — in particular the Dains — to suggest the Marxian view that corrosion of the human spirit in a materialistic society is both gradual and inevitable." See Thompson, *Hammett's Moral Vision*, 91. But even if he had been a Marxist at the time, Hammett would not have needed to focus on the family in order to do this.
51 Wolfe, 99.
52 *The Dain Curse*, in *Five Complete Novels*, 152.
53 Ibid., 212.
54 Ibid., 162.

55 Ibid., 168.
56 Jo Hammett, *Dashiell Hammett: A Daughter Remembers*, ed. Richard Layman with Julie M. Rivett (New York: Carroll & Graf Publishers, 2001), 90.
57 Dashiell Hammett, *The Maltese Falcon*, in *Five Complete Novels*, 332.
58 Hammett to Harry Block, July 14, 1929; *Selected Letters*, 51.
59 Dashiell Hammett, *The Maltese Falcon*, in *Five Complete Novels*, 367. A hilarious misuse of the term "gunsel" occurs in William Manchester's memoir of his military service in the Pacific War. During a peaceful interlude, Manchester is a sergeant relaxing with his men after an evening of alcohol-fueled discussion. "I remember sprawling on my left hip, looking almost affectionately at my gunsels, one by one." William Manchester, *Goodbye Darkness: A Memoir of the Pacific War* (New York: Dell Publishing Co., 1982), 343.
60 Hammett, *The Maltese Falcon*, 295.
61 Ibid., 311.
62 Ibid., 326.
63 Ibid., 437.
64 Ibid., 438.
65 Ibid., 439.
66 Nolan, 90.
67 Dorothy Gallagher, *Lillian Hellman: An Imperious Life* (New Haven and London: Yale University Press, 2014), 44.
68 Dashiell Hammett, *The Maltese Falcon*, in *Five Complete Novels*, 295.
69 Symons, 62.
70 Wolfe, 22. Sally Cline is the latest to subscribe to this interpretation, closely following Johnson as she argues that paternity is "pivotal to an understanding of Hammett's writings." She also thinks that Willsson "effectively contrives to get his son, Donald, killed…" See Sally Cline, *Dashiell Hammett: Man of Mystery* (New York: Arcade Publishing, 2014), 14.
71 Dashiell Hammett, *The Maltese Falcon*, in *Five Complete Novels*, 410.
72 Ibid., 313.
73 Ibid., 397.
74 Ibid., 340.
75 For example, ibid., 321.
76 Ibid., 402.
77 Ibid., 417.

78 Ibid., 330.
79 Ibid., 424.
80 Zummoff, "Politics and the 1920s Writings of Dashiell Hammett, 85.
81 Peter Wolfe, 19.
82 Ibid., 114.
83 Diane Johnson, *The Life of Dashiell Hammett* (US title *Dashiell Hammett: A Life*), (London: Picador, 1985), xv.
84 Wolfe, 22.
85 Symons, 6.
86 Layman, *Shadow Man*, 8.
87 Hammett, *The Maltese Falcon*, in *Five Complete Novels*, 335.
88 Ibid., 336.
89 Ibid. Cline for some reason thinks that the Flitcraft story is "non-fiction." Cline, 76, 77.
90 Symons, 71.
91 Wolfe, 125.
92 Ibid., 20.
93 Nunnally Johnson, *The Letters of Nunnally Johnson*, ed. Doris Johnson and Ellen Leventhall (NY: Knopf, 1981), 315, cited in Johnson, *The Life of Dashiell Hammett*, 124.
94 Jo Hammett, 101.
95 Dashiell Hammett, *The Glass Key*, in *Five Complete Novels*, 543.
96 Ibid., 447.
97 Ibid., 485.
98 Ibid., 488.
99 Ibid., 485.
100 Ibid., 491.
101 Ibid., 497.
102 Ibid., 515.
103 Ibid., 497.
104 Ibid., 548.
105 Ibid., 550.
106 Ibid., 554.
107 Ibid., 587.
108 Ibid., 445.
109 James Cooper, "Lean Years for the Thin Man," *Washington Daily News*, March 11, 1957, cited in Layman, *Shadow Man*, 115.

110 Dashiell Hammett, *The Glass Key*, in *Five Complete Novels*, 487.
111 Dashiell Hammett, *The Dain Curse*, in *Five Complete Novels*, 192.
112 Dashiell Hammett, *The Glass Key*, in *Five Complete Novels*, 493.
113 William F. Nolan, *Dashiell Hammett: A Casebook* (Santa Barbara: McNally & Loftin, 1969), 69.
114 Dashiell Hammett, *The Glass Key*, in *Five Complete Novels*, 474.
115 One definition of "Beaumont" found on www.urbandictionary.com has it that, used as slang, the word means "elegantly over the top." Accessed May 30, 2015.
116 Dashiell Hammett, *The Glass Key*, in *Five Complete Novels*, 543.
117 Ibid., 482.
118 http://en.wikipedia.org/wiki/Pretzel, accessed July 27, 2014.
119 The Book of Judith is accepted by Catholics but considered by Protestants to be part of the Apocrypha. Judith uses her beauty to gain access to Holofernes, leader of an invading army, and then lops off his head.
120 Vince Emery, commentary, Dashiell Hammett, *Lost Stories* (San Francisco: Vince Emery Productions, 2005), 225.
121 Dashiell Hammett, *The Glass Key*, in *Five Complete Novels*, 562.
122 Ibid., 546.
123 Wolfe, 130.
124 Layman, *Shadow Man*, 118.
125 Dashiell Hammett, *The Glass Key*, in *Five Complete Novels*, 546.
126 Wolfe, 140; William Patrick Kenney, "The Dashiell Hammett Tradition and the Modern Detective Novel," Diss., University of Michigan, 1964, 86; David T. Bazelon, "Dashiell Hammett's Private Eye," in *The Scene before You: A New Approach to American Culture*, ed. Chandler Brossard (New York: Rinehart, 1955), 188.
127 Dashiell Hammett, *The Glass Key*, in *Five Complete Novels*, 445.
128 Ibid., 588.
129 Raymond Chandler, *The Long Goodbye* [1953] (London: William Heinemann/Chatto & Windus/Octopus Books, 1977), 614.
130 See, for example, Wolfe, 144. The "glass key breaks if jammed into the wrong lock or turned too sharply in the right one. Restraint, patience, and lightness of touch may help you enjoy the food without bringing on the snakes..." etc., etc.
131 This first draft would eventually appear as "The Thin Man," *City Magazine*, November 4, 1975; it would later be reprinted as "The

Thin Man: An Early Typescript" in *Hammett: Crime Stories and Other Writings*.
132 Dashiell Hammett, "The Thin Man: An Early Typescript," *Crime Stories and Other Writings*, 862.
133 Ibid., 871.
134 Symons, 93.
135 Nolan, *Dashiell Hammett: A Life on the Edge*, 128.
136 Dashiell Hammett, *The Thin Man*, in *Five Complete Novels*, 593
137 Ibid., 595.
138 Ibid., 614.
139 Ibid., 627.
140 In a 1932 letter to Hellman, Hammett says he's just finished the memoirs of "the Russian primrose," whom Layman takes to be Feodor Chaliapin. Hammett to Hellman, May 5, 1932; *Selected Letters*, 80.
141 Dashiell Hammett, *The Thin Man* in *Five Complete Novels*, 691. This was excised in the first British edition. It is during this confrontation that Nick quips to Mimi, "You must come over to our place some time and bring your little white whips." Ibid., 677. Symons thinks this is suggestive of an interest in "sadistic sexual activities," (Symons, 101.) but it is clear from the context that it is nothing of the kind, being simply a sarcastic reference to Mimi's violence towards her daughter.
142 Ibid., 711. Hammett has rescued this line from the earlier typescript, where Guild tells District Attorney Boyer, "It's happened before…That's why they've got a name for it." "The Thin Man: An Early Typescript," *Crime Stories and Other Writings*, 877.
143 Dashiell Hammett, *The Thin Man*, in *Five Complete Novels*, 702.
144 Ibid., 626. Hammett also employs the phrase in the original version of the story. See *Crime Stories and Other Writings*, 858.
145 Ibid., 698.
146 Eric Larrabee, *Commander In Chief: Franklin Delano Roosevelt, His Lieutenants and Their War* (London: Andre Deutsch, 1987), 306-307.
147 Dashiell Hammett, *The Thin Man*, in *Five Complete Novels*, 621.
148 Ibid., 628.
149 Ibid., 644.
150 Ibid., 598.
151 George Thompson, "Part VI – The Thin Man," *Armchair Detective*,

November 1974, quoted in Nolan, *Dashiell Hammett: A Life at the Edge*, 133.
152 Dashiell Hammett, *The Thin Man*, in *Five Complete Novels*, 665.
153 Ibid., 677.
154 Ibid., 641.
155 Ibid., 636-640. This is taken from Thomas Samuel Duke's *Celebrated Criminal Cases of America* (1910). Duke had been a police captain in San Francisco. In *The Maltese Falcon*, Spade's alarm clock rests on a copy of the same book; later in the novel, Caspar Gutman leafs through the heavy volume to pass the time.
156 Hammett, *The Thin Man*, in *Five Complete Novels*, 633.
157 Ibid., 640.
158 Ibid., 645.
159 See *The Nation*, May 31, 1933.

4 Hollywood

Hammett went to Hollywood in 1930, where he was put on contract by Paramount at the rate of $300 a week for four weeks, with an option for a further eight weeks and the promise of an extra $5,000 for an original screen story.[1]

This gave rise to his short screen story "The Kiss-Off" which, after adaptation by Max Martin, was transformed into a screenplay by Oliver H.P. Garrett.[2] The film, directed by Rouben Mamoulian and starring Gary Cooper and Sylvia Sidney, was released as *City Streets*. That same year, Mellen has him writing a treatment called "The Ungallant," in which a detective rescues a Russian princess.[3] According to Robert L. Gale, he may have worked on *Blonde Venus* which, released in 1932, starred Marlene Dietrich, and "definitely worked on the script of *Ladies' Man*" (1931) a William Powell vehicle.[4] Layman says that Hammett also wrote original screen stories for Republic Studios and Howard Hughes's Caddo Company.[5]

He was then signed up by Warner Bros. to write a Sam Spade story for the screen, but he made the story — called "On the Make" — too dark for the studio's taste, and so in April 1931 his third draft was rejected, Hammett having received two of the three $5,000 payments specified by his contract. He reworked the story and three years later sold it to Universal, which had it revised by Dories Malloy and Harvey Clork, who to Hammett's chagrin turned it into a light comedy called *Mister Dynamite*.⁶

Hammett may have worked on several other screen stories during this period which are now lost to us. One we do know about is *Devil's Playground*, which was never produced.

The film version of *The Thin Man*, starring William Powell as Nick Charles and Myrna Loy as his wife Nora, was a great success, and MGM wanted more of the same, and so Hammett (who had not contributed to the first film apart from writing the novel on which it was based and selling the film rights for $21,000) was contracted to write the story for a second at the rate of $2,000 per week for a maximum of ten weeks. Besieged by celebrities and starlets, and very often incapable of writing because he was drunk, it took Hammett all of those ten weeks to grind out a story occupying a mere thirty-four pages, which he submitted in January 1935.⁷ After several revisions, this became *After the Thin Man*, and was released on Christmas Day, 1936.

Amazingly, given this low rate of productivity, in June 1935 MGM gave him a three-year contract to act as assistant to producer Hunt Stromberg, with an additional $750 per week whenever he wrote "complete continuity, including dialogue for any photo-play."⁸ He persuaded the studio to purchase the rights to Albert Halper's proletarian novel, *The Foundry*, which it had first rejected, for $15,000⁹ on the basis that Hammett would work on the screen treatment; in November he signed a contract to do just this for $5,000, but he never wrote it.

Hammett wrote the third Nick and Nora Charles film, *Another Thin Man*, but after his contract ended in July 1939, having been suspended on several occasions due to transgressions on his part, his Hollywood writing career had, with the exception of occasional "script doctor" duties, effectively reached its terminus, although he would return to write the screenplay for 1943's *Watch on the Rhine*, based on the play by Lillian Hellman.

In 1949 he was asked by friend William Wyler to adapt the play *Detective Story* for the screen, and so he returned to Hollywood for the last time. He told his daughter Mary in January 1950 that he would try working at the studio this time, although he would "most likely end up working at home as usual." By the end of the month, with obviously little accomplished, he told Hellman that he was staying home to see if he might start writing the script "in big chunks. So far, no, but presently, of course."¹⁰ In February, he mentioned a discussion with "agency folk" about "a future Hitchcock picture with a piece of the take," but a week later he told Mary that movies "ought to be written by people who like seeing movies. I try not to feel as if I were slumming, but that's what it amounts to."[11] It is fascinating to speculate whether the project in question was *Strangers on a Train*, on which Raymond Chandler, who was not Hitchcock's first choice, ended up working.

In any case, Hammett would obviously not have been up to the task, as after three months he gave up on *Detective Story*, telling Wyler, "I can't do it. I just can't do it anymore,"[12] and returned the $10,000 advance.

That we are able to discuss half a dozen of Hammett's screen stories in any depth is due to the fact that Richard Layman and Julie M. Rivett (Hammett's granddaughter) have presented them to us in two recent books — *The Hunter and Other Stories* (2013) and *The Return of the Thin Man* (2012). It is important to understand that, with the exception of *Watch on the Rhine*, Hammett wrote not screenplays, but stories or treatments, and thus the term "screenplay" is not employed in the following discussion. While consideration of these treatments will give us an idea of what Hammett was in these years, it will be useful to include *The Foundry* in the discussion, as this may indicate what he was not.

The Kiss-Off

A high-school girl — who remains unnamed throughout the story — has a boyfriend who works at a shooting gallery, but they are destined to be parted for five years and then brought back together in dramatic circumstances.

The girl's stepfather Tom Cooley visits fellow-criminal Blackie and stumbles upon Agnes, Blackie's girlfriend, letting Jack Willis out of the apartment. Seeing that their relationship is at the very least affectionate, Cooley conceals himself. At the door, Blackie intervenes, dragging Agnes away, but Willis warns him: "You're making too much dough out of my booze to pick a fight with me, Blackie."[13] When he passes him in the corridor, Willis proposes to Cooley that "if anything happened to Blackie" he should take over his mob.

Blackie and his bodyguard, Slim, drink with Cooley in the apartment, then go out on business, leaving Cooley behind. Cooley calls his stepdaughter and asks her to bring his pistol to a spot just behind Blackie's apartment. He lays in wait for Blackie and, assisted by Slim's drunkenness, guns him down and hands the pistol back to the girl, telling her to dump it in the river, but she is apprehended by detectives before she can complete her mission and goes to reform school for five years.

Cooley now takes over Blackie's gang, but dismisses Slim due to his unreliability and, unaware of his relationship to the girl, takes on the boy at the shooting gallery, who he sees is a crack shot.

Five years later the girl, now 21, is home and reunited with the boy, now called the Roscoe Kid. The Kid is put off by her new hardness, so she decks herself out in bright new clothes in an ill-judged attempt to interest him, but she succeeds only in attracting Willis. Willis consults Cooley concerning the availability of the girl and is given the green light. She, meanwhile, realizes she has made a mistake with the Kid and so adopts a more demure attitude which rekindles his interest. He suggests they get out of "the racket" and go straight.

At a party to celebrate her homecoming, the girl is angered by the Kid's jealousy and he, a non-drinker, withdraws from her once more. But his obvious interest in the girl gives pause to Willis who, as he leaves, reminds Cooley of their understanding, repeating the threat he had made to Blackie. But Cooley is not Blackie: he has the Kid to protect him.

To Cooley's dismay, however, the Kid has packed his bag and is leaving. Cooley attempts to persuade the girl to urge him to stay and, when this fails, proceeds to beat her. Overhearing this, the Kid tells Cooley that he's changed his mind.

Willis now recalls Slim to active duty, putting to him the same proposition he had made to Cooley five years earlier. Slim agrees on condition that Willis assists in the removal of the Kid. They plan a trap for Cooley but Agnes, to whom Willis has just given notice in order to make way for the girl, overhears them and calls Cooley, but he has already fallen for the ruse and has left home, so she tells the girl of the trap before going to the police.

The girl thwarts the planned ambush by jamming the car she is driving in between Cooley's vehicle and that containing the bushwhackers. After shots are exchanged, the police arrive. Slim is dead and Agnes tells the police that five years ago it was Cooley who murdered Blackie. As the Kid and the girl make a break for it, Agnes shoots Willis. Having hidden overnight in a sewer, the couple make their way out of town, the girl throwing the Kid's guns into the river at the spot where she had intended to dispose of her stepfather's pistol five years earlier.

They take a train for a distant destination, the Kid smiling as he hands the conductor his ticket.

≈

Hollywood was getting what it had paid for with this story, as it is original and hardboiled. As we have come to recognize, however, with Hammett (and, indeed, other practitioners of the genre, like Horace McCoy) the latter term often implies nihilism: most of the relationships are strictly cash-based and, as so often in Hammett, the loyalties of the crooks shift whenever financial opportunity beckons. While it may be objected that the relationship between the girl and the Roscoe Kid does not conform to this cynical outlook, it is surely a possibility that the sentimental ending was dictated by Hammett's knowledge that Hollywood would not buy a product that was unduly pessimistic. The ending is, in addition, unrealistic: why would the Kid, after five years in the employment of Tom Cooley, during which time he must surely have been called upon to use his weapon, suddenly decide that he must quit "the racket?" It is also unlikely that the reform school in which the girl has been incarcerated provided driving lessons!

Hammett surely wrote "Kiss-Off" solely for the money, dashing off seven handwritten pages immediately upon arrival in Hollywood,[14] so eager for the first $5,000 bonus that he could not be bothered to give the girl a name.

On the Make

Gene Richmond, a seedy private eye, is ejected from one city (presumably San Francisco) and quickly establishes himself in another (probably Los Angeles). All the rules Hammett devised for the Continental Op are discarded, as Richmond cons money from his clients, having Helen Crane, his secretary (who, having just completed a prison sentence for helping her previous employer defraud clients, has been employed due to her proven ability to keep a secret), write up expenses for operatives who don't exist. The only operative in his employment, in fact, is Babe Holliday, a young woman with whom he has a longstanding relationship that is, one gathers, often more than professional.

In the main plot, stockbroker Herbert Pomeroy has foolishly provided start-up capital for a bootlegging operation which, unknown to him, has branched out into narcotics. As the goods are brought ashore from the *Carrie Nation*[15] at night, there is gunfire and an undercover narcotics agent is left dead. Detective Gene Richmond receives a call from Ward Kavanaugh, Pomeroy's lawyer. They meet, and the lawyer, without naming his client, outlines his plight. Richmond points out that the client could be charged with first-degree murder, even though he was nowhere near the scene. Having traced Kavanaugh's earlier call to Pomeroy's home, Richmond names the client and tells Kavanaugh that he'll take the job for a $25,000 retainer, although the eventual bill may be as high as $200,000. Later that night, Richmond meets Barney, an underground snitch, from whom he learns that a crook called Cheaters Neely is on the run.

The next day, Neely and his boys (Happy Jones, Buck and the Dis-and-Dat Kid, previously seen in the *Black Mask* story "The Big Knockover") arrive at Pomeroy's mansion and invite themselves to stay while the stockbroker decides how he will help them out of the mess they're in. Kavanaugh summons Richmond to Pomeroy's mansion, where he is just in time to prevent Pomeroy from writing Neely, whose demands have boiled down to getaway money, a large check.

While Neely and his gang stay at the mansion, Richmond seeks to persuade them that he will look after them if they behave themselves. When Neely tells him that all they want is a getaway stake, he objects, "But what's in that for me?"[16] Over the next two days, while the Neely gang play poker, smash glasses and drop cigarette ash over the carpets, Richmond makes the acquaintance of Pomeroy's daughter Ann.

While he certainly milks as much money from Pomeroy as possible, it seems that Richmond is not serious about protecting Neely, for he makes several visits to the city to arrange his downfall. Here, he visits Barney, his snitch, who, begging him to keep his name out of it, tells him that ten pounds of cocaine has been delivered to Rags Davis at the Sutherland Hotel. Back in his office, Richmond calls Joe King at the FBI and, in return for confirmation that the murdered man was a narcotics agent, advises King of the whereabouts of the cocaine.

Richmond now finds that he has to calm his secretary as, increasingly concerned by his fraudulent methods, she tells him that she has no wish to return to prison. He then receives a call from Joe King, who tells him that there is no sign of the cocaine in Rags Davis's hotel room and that the suspect refuses to crack. Richmond asks him to bring Davis to him, and then tells his office boy to call Barney and have him come to the office immediately. Knowing that a face-to-face meeting between Davis and Barney can only result in the latter's death, Richmond ponders the dilemma for a few seconds before concluding: "That's his hard luck."[17]

Upon seeing Davis in Richmond's office, Barney is stricken with terror, but Richmond persuades him to "make a clean job of it," promising him "all the protection you need."[18] Seeing that he is sunk whatever he says, Barney tells Richmond and King that Davis has a second room at the hotel, following which Davis confesses.

Richmond returns to Pomeroy's mansion to find that a number of guests, family friends, have arrived. It is now clear that there is a mutual attraction between Richmond and Ann Pomeroy. He tells her that in the course of working on this case he has had to do some unpleasant things.

> She puts a hand on one of his, says softly, earnestly, "You're doing them for me — for Father and me. I ought to be forced to hear what you're having to do."
>
> He says drily: "I'm getting paid for it. I'm a hired man doing his job."
>
> She puts both hands on his and corrects him tenderly: "You are a friend — savior."
>
> He looks around in embarrassment, sees that the bridge games have broken up and some of the players are coming toward them. He rises with evident relief.[19]

Richmond plans another trip to the city, telling Pomeroy that he will need $5,000 to pay for the travel expenses of his informant, whose life is now in danger. In his office the next morning, he peels off $1,000 from the bundle of notes that Pomeroy's office has sent over, and puts the remaining $4,000 in his wallet. Having received a call from a panic-stricken Barney, he goes to his rooming house, but by the time he arrives Barney is dead. As he waits for the police, Richmond transfers the $1,000 to his wallet.

In his apartment, Babe Holliday quizzes him about Ann Pomeroy.

> "Can you keep a secret?" he asks, and then without waiting for her to answer, "I think she's the big one."
> Babe laughs. "It's probably her old man's dough that's the big one."
> He grins good-naturedly, says: "Maybe — but I find myself forgetting that sometimes."
> She pretends amazement. "Then it *is* serious!"[20]

Their conversation is interrupted by a call from the lawyer Kavanaugh, who tells him that the Neely gang has abducted Ann. Richmond dictates descriptions of Ann and her abductors to Babe Holliday, telling her to contact Joe King and the police department, before he dashes out to his car.

Outside the city, Richmond comes upon a police roadblock, which has successfully stopped the kidnappers and rescued Ann. Herbert Pomeroy has also arrived, and advises Richmond that he intends to tell the police the truth. Richmond points out that he's in the clear, as the murdered man was a narcotics agent, and Pomeroy had had nothing to do with that side of Neely's operation.

Joe King is on the scene, and explains to Richmond that his secretary has visited the Federal building and unburdened herself of her concerns: that the Neely gang were at Pomeroy's, and that Richmond had always known that Pomeroy could never be convicted of the murder and was prolonging matters in order to maximize his own financial gain. This ends Richmond's relationship with Ann.

The following day, on bail, Richmond sits in his office and considers his situation.

He pushes his hat back and mutters: "Gee, I'm smart! I got thirty thousand dollars and will probably have to go to jail or at least blow town, where I could have had ten million and the one woman that's ever really meant anything to me — maybe." He touches his forehead with the back of his hand and repeats, "Gee, I'm smart!"[21]

≈

Lest we believe that this meditation is the prelude to a conversion to the straight and narrow, Hammett closes the story by having a client call for news of progress, whereupon Richmond recommends that a further nonexistent operative be assigned to the case. Despite his recent lesson, Richmond is unreformed.

It is important to note that the version of "On the Make" that appears in *The Hunter and Other Stories* is as it was reworked by Hammett after rejection by Warner Bros. It therefore seems that the original story, turned down because of its darkness, was even more pessimistic than this one — which, as Richmond refuses to learn from his mistakes, is itself almost as noir as it is possible to get. Almost, but not quite: in reality, a man like Richmond would see only money in Ann Pomeroy, while she would almost certainly be able to tell what kind of man he was the first time he opened his mouth.

After the cavalier manner in which Hammett had dashed off "Kiss-Off," he seems to have taken care with "On the Make," which occupies almost 70 pages in the 2013 collection. Although now and again Hammett issues camera and editing instructions, the treatment often reads like a novelette. Although it would be a decade before Humphrey Bogart would be cast as Sam Spade, it is almost impossible not to imagine him reading Richmond's lines — implying, of course, that the Bogart version of Spade was more Hammett than Bogart. For all that, the story demonstrates that Hammett had still not shed his nihilism.

It would not be until 1944 that *Double Indemnity*, scripted by Raymond Chandler and Billy Wilder, would demonstrate that a portrait of unmitigated villainy could get past the censors and onto the screen. It is possible that after that experience a studio might have taken a chance with "On the Make," filming it as Hammett had intended, but by that time the rights would have been long gone.

It is a little-known fact, however, that in December 1936 echoes of "On the Make" would find their way, albeit briefly, and bearing the name of another author, onto Broadway.

Devil's Playground

Gus Wayne, a mercenary instructor in the army of a Chinese provincial military governor, is forced to flee with his comrades Bingo Kelly and Hank after he is discovered with his employer's "favorite wife."[22] Having eluded the military leader's army, their small pack train travels into Mongolia.

They eventually enter a large town, where they are thrown into jail after ignoring a curt summons from a W. Ruric. The next morning, they are visited by a beautiful woman: Wanda Ruric, who has inherited mining concessions and a great deal else from her Russian engineer father (who, it is presumed, amassed this wealth before the Russian Revolution). Nothing has been heard from the team she dispatched to work the mine, and so she asks Wayne and his comrades to investigate.

Verner, Wanda's advisor (also inherited from her father), counsels her against hiring the adventurers, but she compromises by saying that she will accompany them. Once Wayne and his comrades agree, Verner recruits his own thugs to join the expedition.

As they travel into the wilderness, pack animals die or run off, and Verner's men drive away the other workers. Bingo Kelly is killed after he overhears Verner plotting treachery with a local lama. Eventually, they arrive at the mine to find that it is being worked by white strangers. For reasons unexplained, they accuse Verner of betrayal and a battle ensues in which Hank is mortally wounded. Only Wayne and Wanda now remain. Throughout the journey, there has been sexual tension between them, but he now accuses her of being responsible for Hank's death, and she breaks down.

On the long homeward journey, they admit their love for each other. Back in the town which Wanda practically owns, however, she resumes her former arrogance, and Wayne tells her that he will leave. He resists her entreaties to stay and so she says that she will go with him, leaving her wealth behind. Riding together, their previous affection returns, leading Wayne to suggest, "Well, after all, if you'd promise honestly to behave — to stop being the Queen of Sheba — maybe we would be more comfortable back there."[23] They return to the town.

≋

Unlike Gene Richmond, then, Gus Wayne gets both the woman and her money, but the treatment, had it been produced, would have been sadly typical fare for the 1930s. It was, in any case, a step backward in political terms for Hammett. Whereas he had previously portrayed Russian émigrés in his short stories unsympathetically, and while his Chinese story "Dead Yellow Women" had bristled with stereotypes it had at least shown a basic understanding of the anti-imperialist cause. Here, however, the three US mercenaries serve a Chinese warlord with apparent authorial approval — an approval silently extended to Wanda and her late father, who have amassed a fortune by exploiting the Mongolians, who appear merely as servants or thugs. There are, of course, class differences between Wayne and Wanda, but the manner in which these are resolved suggests class collaboration rather than class struggle. And, of course, the male chauvinism is too blatant to require mention.

But then, of course, this was one of the things that Hammett wrote for money.

After the Thin Man

Nick and Nora Charles return to San Francisco after their previous adventure in New York to find that their house has been invaded by a crowd of people, many of whom are unknown to them, intent upon giving them a "surprise" homecoming party. At one point in the chaotic proceedings there are gunshots at the front door as Pedro Dominges, whom Nora recognizes as the man who, some six years earlier, had been her father's gardener, is murdered, managing to utter "Mees Selma Young"[24] before he expires. The police discover that Dominges, having made a little money as a bootlegger during the Prohibition years, owned an apartment house at 346 White Street.

As the police question guests, Nora receives a call from her distraught cousin Selma (Landis nee Forrest, definitely not Young), who begs her to keep the invitation that she and Nick have received to dine with their Aunt Katherine that evening. At the Forrest home (not, strictly speaking, the "Landis home" as Hammett calls it[25]), Nick is surprised to find that the members of the old-money family, who have previously considered him the poor (and thus barely acceptable) in-law, are making an effort to be polite to him. This, it transpires, is because Aunt Katherine has need of his services: Robert Landis, Selma's gallivanting husband, has disappeared and Katherine is anxious not that he be found necessarily, but that any scandal be kept from the public gaze. Selma, meanwhile, regrets having broken off her engagement to David Graham in order to marry the philandering Landis. She suspects that her husband has recently been entertaining a woman at the Li-Chee Club, as the management has sent her a cigarette case in the apparently mistaken belief that she left it there.

Nick and Nora visit the Li-Chee, where we find Landis ensconced with Polly Byrnes, the resident songstress with whom he has concocted a scheme whereby David Graham will pay him a substantial sum to desert Selma, following which he will go away with Polly. The club is owned by Dancer, whom we first encounter as he ejects Phil, Polly's brother, from the club, suspecting that he has come to scrounge money from her. We soon learn that Dancer is in fact in league with Polly and that they intend to separate Landis from the money he receives from Graham. Landis, meanwhile, calls Graham and says that he can wait no longer and needs the money tonight, whereupon Graham agrees to give him negotiable bonds and meet him down the street.

Landis and Polly walk to the spot agreed with Graham, but they are followed by Phil, who has been waiting outside the club.

In the restaurant, Dancer introduces Nick to his Chinese partner Lum Kee, whose brother Ying Kee Nick sent to jail several years ago. However, Lum Kee displays no animosity to Nick, later explaining that he didn't like his brother but was rather fond of his girl friend. In due course, Nick is joined by a bunch of crooks with whom he has a comfortable relationship, one of them drunkenly imparting the information that Polly lives at 346 White Street.

Dancer calls Polly's apartment, but there is no answer; when he curses that he had told her to take Landis straight to her place, Lum Kee reminds him that Landis had said he would go home first to pack a bag. Dancer leaves the club, shortly followed by Lum Kee.

Landis indeed packs a bag, but as he is about to snatch Selma's jewels from a bedside drawer she awakens and they have a brief argument. As he makes his way to the street, she takes a pistol and follows him. A policeman hears a shot and we see Landis lying on the sidewalk with Selma standing over him, pistol in hand. David Graham arrives on the scene, takes the pistol from her and tells her to return to the house and deny any knowledge of what has just occurred. Graham then disposes of the pistol in the sea.

Back at the Li-Chee, Nora asks Dancer why he sent the cigarette case to Landis's wife, but he denies responsibility, telling her that Lum Kee was unaware of the situation. Upstairs, Dancer asks Polly whether she still has "the paper" — later we will see that this refers to a check for $10,000 — as, with Landis dead, they may need this more than ever.

Nora goes to the Forrest house to comfort Selma who, she finds, has only pretended to take the sleeping pills given her by the sinister Dr. Kammer (whose role, which promises to be more significant, turns out to be simply one of tranquilizing Selma to ensure that she causes the family no scandal), and urges Nora to call David Graham or go to his apartment to confirm that he is safe and sound. Regarding her husband's death, she tells Nora that she had heard a shot and that Landis was dead by the time she came upon his body.

Nora goes to Graham's apartment and tells him that Selma did not kill Landis. He now seems to think that his disposal of the pistol may incriminate Selma, as the police might otherwise have tested it and found that it had not been fired. While she is in the apartment, Phil's face appears at the window, but by the time the policeman who has followed Nora here is forced to believe this (her declaration "I'm Mrs. Nick Charles"[26] is sufficient to bring him to his senses), Phil has escaped.

At the Li-Chee, the party has been joined by the police led by the plodding Lt. Abrams, whose first appearance followed the death of Pedro Dominges, and Caspar, Dancer's lawyer. Upon realizing that Caspar does not represent Polly, Abrams questions her alone, as a result of which she weakens and surrenders a check for $10,000 made out to her and signed by Landis. The question now is where Landis got hold of such an amount. Polly also recalls that Pedro Dominges, confirmed now as her landlord, seemed to know Landis.

As things seem not to be going at all well for him, at one point Dancer manages to flee the scene, having arranged for a waiter to plunge the club into darkness by throwing the main switch. He makes his way to Phil's apartment where, obviously thinking that Phil has killed Landis, he threatens him for having attempted to "cut yourself in on somebody else's game."[27] The next morning, Dancer turns up at the Hall of Justice and acts the innocent, claiming that with the lights out and shots being fired, he had decided it was not healthy to remain in the Li-Chee.

When Nick and Nora arrive home after a sleepless night, a stone is hurled through their front window; the note wrapped around it, written to give the deliberate impression of limited literacy, advises Nick that Phil, an ex-con, is actually Polly's husband.

At the Forrest household, Aunt Katherine is telephoning the publisher of the leading daily, enjoining him to handle Landis's death "as quietly as possible."[28] He agrees, although in fact the news is already in banner headlines. Katherine then calls a member of the family known as "the General," asking him to contact the mayor with the same request. Later that morning, the General arrives at Nick's house with the news that, the mayor having done nothing, Selma has been arrested. He asks Nick to "make the police stop being silly — to get Selma out of there right away — to put an end to all this beastly notoriety."[29]

Lt. Abrams tells Nick that the $10,000 check was perfectly legitimate, as Selma had deposited the same amount in Landis's account the day before it was written. But Nick now compares the signatures on a previous check Landis had written with the one for $10,000, pronouncing the latter a fake, the signature having been traced.

Nick and Abrams go to Phil's hotel, where they find him dead, having sustained a beating before he was strangled. Meanwhile, at the Forrest house Nora takes a call from David Graham, who tells her that he must see Nick immediately. She meets him and drives him to the apartment house previously owned by Pedro Dominges, where Abrams has asked Nick to take a look at certain anomalies. Here, Nick finds that every room has been newly carpeted apart from one which, located immediately above Polly's, had been recently rented by a man called Anderson. Graham arrives and shows Nick a note, obviously written by the same person who hurled a similar missive through Nick's window; this one says that Dancer has discovered that Phil was

Polly's husband.

In Dominges's apartment, Nora spots a photograph of him and the other servants once employed by her father; Dominges's mustache is shorter and darker than when Nick saw his body the previous day. In Anderson's room they roll back the carpet and find a hole in the floor in which is concealed a listening device. There is also a length of iron piping which, as Nick demonstrates, can be assembled into a ladder that when hung outside the window just reaches Polly's room below.

Dancer, Lum Kee and Polly are brought to the scene, soon to be joined by Selma Landis. When Abrams tells Polly that her husband has been killed, she and Dancer begin to trade accusations, which Nick interprets as Polly charging Dancer with the murder of Phil, and he accusing her of deception because she had not told him of her real relationship with Phil. It seems from this that the writer of the anonymous note has tried to plant the suspicion that Dancer has killed Phil, but Dancer swears that Phil was alive when, having beaten him up, he left his hotel room. He explains that he had been punishing Phil, as he thought he had tried to rob Landis and had been forced to kill him.

When Selma arrives, she admits that she did not write the check for $10,000 that was deposited in Landis's account, and that she had previously been constrained from telling the truth by Aunt Katherine's fear of further scandal, as she thought it had been forged by Landis.

Nick commences his Sherlock Holmes-style denouement, surmising that Dancer had sent the cigarette case to Selma and, when she returned it with a note, had forged her signature on the check, which was then deposited in Landis's account. Polly had kept Landis out of circulation, so that the bank would, had it harbored doubts about the check's authenticity, have been unable to contact him.

Red hairs, probably from a wig, were found in Phil's room, and Nick now speculates that the murderer and the mysterious Anderson are one person, and that he had rented the room above Polly's, disguised in the wig and glasses, using the place as a listening post, his object being to find the best time to kill Landis but, hearing that he and Polly were going away the next day, had been forced to bring forward his plan. But Dominges had come to his room to lay a new carpet and, despite the disguise, recognizing "Anderson" as Graham, whom he had seen when he had been engaged to Selma, told him that he was changing the lock on the apartment while he sought advice.

Graham had then followed him to Nick's house and shot him. By his dying words, "Mees Selma Young," Dominges was trying to identify his killer: "Miss Selma's young man." Nick reminds Graham that he had previously remembered the Forrests' gardener as having a long white mustache, which was the way he looked now, not his appearance six years ago.

Graham finally murdered Landis as he came out of the Forrest residence, having been deterred from committing the deed earlier by Polly's presence. Noticing Selma as she came from the house, Graham quickly drove around the block and came back to frame her by disposing of her gun. All along, he has been motivated by his hatred of Landis for taking Selma from him, while his apparently enduring devotion to her was merely an excuse to stay close until the opportunity arose to kill her husband. Phil, having witnessed the murder, had gone to Graham's apartment house to demand money, but had left when he saw that Nora was with him; his later meeting with Graham had resulted in his death.

Once Nick has completed the story, Graham obliges by falling to his death from the window, where he has been holding Nora as a bargaining chip, while she is saved by the agile Lum Kee.

≈

The point must be made that *After the Thin Man* is not all Hammett's work. As we saw earlier, Hammett's labors during the ten weeks of his contract resulted in a mere thirty-four pages. This original story was markedly different from that summarized above, as Julie M. Rivett explains:

> In the first version, Nora sneaked out to play sleuth and was knocked cold, drugged, and kidnapped by Chinese hoodlums. Pedro the ex-gardener was not present to be shot to death on the Charleses' doorstep. David was not Selma's jilted suitor but her younger brother. And Nick discovered that Polly's husband, Phil, was the murderer.[30]

The husband-and-wife team of Frances Goodrich and Albert Hackett then went to work on it, with director W. S. Van Dyke and producer

Hunt Stromberg also making contributions. This more than doubled the size of the document, a "temporary" screenplay dated April 29, 1935. There were still problems, however, not least with the motives involved in the plot, and so Hammett was rehired in June to bring some consistency to the story, which he did by salvaging "both the Hacketts' and his own best elements" and cutting Stromberg's "more fanciful digressions."[31] His final draft, which occupies over a hundred pages in *The Return of the Thin Man*, is dated September 17, 1935. Before it reached the screen, however, the Hacketts made further revisions, eliminating the shooting scene with Dominges who, a lowly janitor now, is simply found dead later in the movie; while the denouement is much the same, in this final version David Graham is led away by the police rather than falling from the window.

However, in the September 17 document, much of Hammett's own material can be readily identified as such, because to a large extent he has merely cannibalized some of his earlier work.

The scenes in the Li-Chee, for example, are taken from Hammett's original, unfinished attempt at *The Thin Man* novel, where the club is called the Manchu and the Chinese brothers, one of whom Nick has put away, are Deep Ying and Deep Kee; Lum Kee retains Deep Key's "you bet you" mannerism. The songstress in that story is Elsa Fremont, now transformed into Polly Byrnes.

A forged check also features in this earlier story, as it does in "The Hunter." In *Red Harvest*, of course, a dying character is thought to have uttered "Max," whereas he was trying to say "McSweeny," a device now adapted to add mystery to Pedro Dominges's dying words. And the nightclub plunged into darkness? Answers on a postcard.

The plot of *After the Thin Man* is decidedly clunky and unrealistic. As Dominges has no trouble recognizing Graham when he visits his room, why was he unable to do so when he rented that room? The whole business of the forged checks is excruciatingly complex, and it is not made sufficiently clear that there are, in fact, two such checks — one forged in Selma's name and deposited in Landis's account, and the second forged with Landis's name and given to Polly. No attempt is made to explain how Dancer gained possession of blank checks from Selma and Landis.

Hammett the Marxist is, of course, nowhere to be found. While Rivett assures us that in these Depression years "moviegoers welcomed an imaginative [sic] world in which class barriers were permeable and wealth was not a precondition of happiness,"[32] socialists and communists were concerned with tearing down those barriers. Hammett, on the other hand, has Nick Charles return to a San Francisco home where he and Nora are cared for by a butler, a maid and a cook. When Lt. Abrams asks Nick why he was unable to recognize the dead Dominges as the former gardener of his in-laws, he replies: "Who notices a gardener unless he squirts a hose on you?"[33] Significantly, when the old-money Forrests find that the political establishment and the media are no longer willing to do their bidding, they turn to Nick Charles to "end all this beastly notoriety," and he uncomplainingly complies. (Much of this ruling-class defensiveness would, however, be excised from the screen version.) To defend Hammett by arguing that Hollywood was unlikely to countenance the portrayal of class antagonism and or the advancing of socialist ideas is to miss the point: a Marxist would never have penned this blatant escapism.

But just a few weeks after he submitted his final manuscript, Hammett would have his opportunity to write a movie with a strong working-class theme.

The Foundry

Albert Halper's 1934 novel[34] is set in an electrotype foundry in 1928-29, with all the petty jealousies, rivalries and ripe language of both bosses and workers convincingly rendered, although at times Halper is also lyrical, as when he describes the arrival of spring in Chicago.

The Fort Dearborn Electrotype Foundry is a union shop, but only for skilled men, so no action is taken when a 14-year-old messenger is sacked for the flimsiest of reasons. Although the class contradictions are clear enough, Halper does not resort to caricature. Senior director Max'l Steuben dismisses a worker called Slavony, but then is forced to re-engage him when his skills cannot be replaced. When Slavony is absent for four days after the death of his newly-born child, Steuben pays him in full even though he is under no obligation to do so. But then, as capricious as ever, he sacks a 60-year-old janitor for the high crime of mimicking him.

The foundry sits atop a print factory, upon whose fortunes it largely depends. The president of the printery plays the role of patrician, holding annual works picnics and concerts, to which the foundry workers are also invited; but this is the same man who denies his printworkers the right to organize in a union. It is at the annual concert that young clerk and budding musician August Kafka has his modernist symphony performed, and Halper's six-page treatment of this is extremely effective and moving. The workers in the audience realize they are hearing the "music of their machines" that they have never really noticed before. This is a theme that has been building throughout the novel, as the machinery, even though it controls the men rather than them controlling it, has a strange beauty to it.

With Wall Street prices climbing skyward, the three partner-owners of the foundry have decided to chance their luck, but the Crash of 1929 ruins them, leading to a heart attack in the case of one, and the suicide of another. At the same time, the print factory is faced with an emergency and at the firm's concert the company president, previously the gentle benefactor, takes to the stage and urges the foundry workers to return to the factory in order to save the situation. Previously, the radical Karl Heitman has joined the foundry workforce and has been elected union chairman, but while he has attempted to rouse his workmates to the realities of class society they have shown no interest, thinking themselves secure in their union shop. Now, Heitman seizes the opportunity to give them a demonstration of their own power (although, as he later explains, this demonstration is principally aimed at the unorganized printworkers in the audience), publicly bargaining with the print company president and refusing to lead the men back to work until the old man has agreed to pay them triple time.

At the finale, Heitman explodes the persona of the print boss, warning his men that the "old bastard" and those like him will use the crisis to crack down on them, and that they must now look beyond their craft unionism and start thinking of organizing the workers on the floors below.

≋

Layman thinks that Hammett's signature on the contract to adapt *The Foundry* for the screen is "the earliest indication of Hammett's active pursuit of the political agenda of the Communist Party USA."[35] This is, of course, a plausible enough thesis; but it is mistaken.

Albert Halper was not a communist, and he never became one. He would later pen a sour memoir of this period, in part an outpouring of bile concerning writers more successful or more gifted than him like Irving Stone and Joseph Freeman (Halper stoops to ridiculing the latter for his physical appearance); on this account, Halper was not a very pleasant person. However, he informs us that he was constantly being urged to write something based on the four years he had spent in a foundry but, finding the label "proletarian novelist" irksome and presumably resenting the notion that he required "authenticity," he resisted. Thus, after one unpublished novel he wrote *Union Square*, which was followed by a collection of his short stories. By 1934 (by which time, it is worth bearing in mind, Halper was still only 30), unemployment had reached mass proportions and the labor movement was beginning to stir. The CPUSA looked askance at Halper, *New Masses* having panned *Union Square*, but now Halper allowed his agent to place some pieces in the journal and, possibly estimating that there would now be a market for such a book, he wrote *The Foundry*.

The novel did well, but if Halper thought that the CP would join in the praise he was destined for disappointment.

Reviewing *The Foundry* in *New Masses*, Joseph North attacked Halper's previous novel for presenting communists as "the lunatic fringe," but he acknowledged that, as unemployment and the attendant tide of protest and resistance rose, Halper himself realized the book's shortcomings. With regard to *The Foundry*, the review's title — "Still on the Fence" — summarizes North's view of Halper at this stage.[36] North berated him for having a "petty bourgeois brain" beneath his proletarian cap, and for condescension towards his characters. The characters themselves constituted "the top layer of the proletariat encrusted with petty bourgeois ideals." North said that Halper does not make clear that this is not *the* proletariat, which is why "he gets a big hand from the bourgeois critics."

But then North laughed at the fact that these same critics had missed the implication in the book's finale, i.e. that "the factory can be run *without* the bosses." North conceded Halper's ability: "He is a first rate writing man. He can spin a yarn when he has a mind to: he can, more vitally than I have seen in any of our younger American writers, give the feel, the smell, the sound of our brick and electric jungles in which the industrial proletariat lives and dies." But, a "true artist, he must experience the basic urge to go with the forces of creation. Halper...must make up his mind. Although the proletariat cannot make him a best seller it wants and needs him...But it cannot wine and dine and flatter."

Events would show that Halper was indeed more interested in literary success; ironically, it is perhaps as a result of this wrong turning that he is today largely forgotten. North was, however, too harsh on *The Foundry*, possibly as a result of the sectarianism of the period. The novel paints a realistic picture of a section of the working class, and if Heitman calls not for revolution but for the organization of the unorganized, this is a sober position, given the low level of consciousness achieved by the foundry workers at this stage. The Soviets seemed to have no problem with the novel, reprinting it and, explaining to Halper that they did not respect US copyrights, handing him two thousand rubles when he made an ill-humored visit to Moscow in 1935.

The Joseph North review was published over a year before Hammett contracted to adapt the novel, so it is clear that he was hardly following the CPUSA line. And he never followed through with the screen adaptation. There are a number of possible explanations for this. It is, for example, impossible to see how *The Foundry* could have been adapted to Hollywood's liking without it being bowdlerized, and so Hammett may have quickly realized this. Alternatively, if he was close to the CPUSA at this stage, it may have been drawn to his attention that the party was not particularly keen on the novel.

The project may simply have been blown away by the whirlwind of Hammett's personal life. After attending a get-together of former and current *Black Mask* writers on January 11, 1936 at which he met Raymond Chandler for the first and only time (Chandler later remarked upon Hammett's capacity for whisky), he flew to New York where he was treated at the Lennox Hospital for "gonorrhea, alcoholism, and exhaustion,"[37] and spent much of the remainder of the year recovering. By mid-September he was in Tavern Island, Connecticut with Hellman, collaborating on her second play, *Days to Come*, which would open (and close) in mid-December that year. Finally, of course, Hammett may simply have found the task beyond him. Sometime in 1937, MGM passed the job of adapting *The Foundry* to Noel Langley,[38] who would shortly write *The Wizard of Oz*, but the Halper novel never made it to the screen.

But the true significance of *The Foundry* with regard to Hammett is not that it was a film that he did not or could not write. His daughter Jo says that "what Gershwin had accomplished in his field — bridging the gap from Tin Pan Alley to the concert hall — was precisely parallel to what Papa wanted to do in his own."[39] *The Foundry*, with its use of the common language to depict a serious theme, indicated the kind of work of which Hammett might have been capable, had he put his mind to it.

Another Thin Man

There were clear indications that Hammett was heartily tired of the *Thin Man* formula, and in February 1937 he sold the rights to the characters of Nick and Nora Charles to MGM for $40,000. The Hacketts were also fed up with it, and sought to sink the possibility of further sequels by making Nora pregnant in their screenplay for *After the Thin Man*; the tactic failed.[40] Towards the end of 1937, Hammett wrote Hellman: "Maybe there are better writers in the world, but nobody ever invented a more insufferably smug pair of characters. They can't take that away from me, even for $40,000."[41]

Even so, he was not done yet, for MGM had persuaded him to write a third movie featuring these "insufferably smug" characters, baby and all. According to Layman, the studio negotiated a new contract under which he would be paid $5,000 for a synopsis, $10,000 on acceptance of the story and $20,000 for "a complete screen story."[42] Thus, by removing the system of weekly payments, Hammett would be rewarded only on the basis of productivity.

It turned out, however, that Hammett's story was based on "The Farewell Murder," one of his Continental Op stories published eight years earlier. This was a further indication that Hammett was running out of creative steam.

≈

Nick and Nora have arrived back in New York, from where they are to travel to the estate of Colonel MacFay, the business partner of Nora's late father, for the weekend. In their hotel suite they meet Face Peppler, a criminal associate who, now employed as a bellboy, cheerfully admits that until he was recognized by Nick it had been his intention to amass a small fortune from the hotel guests. He now discards his uniform and, hearing that Nick Jr. will be celebrating his first birthday the following week, promises to give him a party and lifts Nora's address book as he exits the suite.

Nick, Nora, Nick Jr., Nick's nurse and the dog Asta are conveyed to the MacFay estate by the colonel's chauffeur who, as they near the house, is seized by a paroxysm of terror as he sees the body of a black man in the road, a large knife protruding from his chest. The chauffeur runs off and Nick drives the vehicle back to the spot where the body was seen, but it has now disappeared. When Nick, upon arrival, explains to the housekeeper that they have lost the chauffeur, she "replies serenely: 'Oh, bless you, it's quite all right.'"[43] This is, unfortunately, a foretaste of silliness to come.

Apart from the servants and MacFay himself, the household contains Lois, the colonel's adopted daughter, Dudley Horn, who doubles up as MacFay's chief assistant and Lois's fiancé, and MacFay's secretary Freddie Coleman, who is also obsessed with Lois. The ill-tempered colonel explains that the estate is being terrorized by Sam Church who, having just finished a ten-year prison term, takes the view that MacFay is indebted to him for having taken sole responsibility for the crooked scheme that led to his imprisonment. He was at the time employed by MacFay and Nora's father, and has now threatened that MacFay will die if he is not adequately compensated. During the course of the evening, a bathhouse is set on fire and Lois's pet collie is found with its throat cut; these events, like the "dead" man in the road, are all intended to frighten MacFay into submission.

The way Dudley Horn explains it to Nick, illegal dealings with regard to a public utility "were traced as far as Church, but not as far as the Colonel,"[44] and Nick now fears that MacFay, who manages the Charles investment portfolio, may have his hand in the cash register.

The following morning, Nick goes to see Church. En route, he finds that Church's rented cottage is under surveillance by a man claiming to be a police officer. On arrival at the cottage, he finds that two others live there: the black man who the previous night was supposedly dead in the road (and who is given the racist name "Dum-Dum") and a woman called Smitty who carries a pistol concealed against her thigh. Church asks Nick about the colonel's health and is apparently surprised to discover that he is still alive, as he had dreamed for the third time that his throat had been cut (he claims that his dreams always come true after their third appearance). When Church, realizing that he stands little chance of getting money from either MacFay or Nick, appears to threaten Nick's wife and son, he receives a black eye. Church advises Nick that the three of them are leaving at noon.

Back at the MacFay house, it is confirmed that the colonel is, indeed, still alive. A little later, Horn confirms that the Church party has left on the noon train. Nick now suggests that MacFay discuss business with him and Nora, as this was the reason he had invited them for the weekend, but the colonel now confesses that this was a pretext, as he had really wanted protection against Church. Nick, concerned about the security of their wealth, is still keen to have the discussion, and, after MacFay has intimated that while he had previously been involved in illegality, he had kept Nora's father ignorant of the fact, there follows a comic sequence in which MacFay bores and confuses him (Nora has made her excuses) with an examination of their various investments.

Meanwhile, back in New York Face Peppler is using Nora's address book to phone around to her well-heeled friends, inviting them to attend Nick Jr.'s birthday party, which will also be attended by members of the underworld who hold Nick in esteem, even if they have to borrow children to gain admission. Smitty (formally Mrs. R. Culver Smith) is also in the city with Dum-Dum and Church. She calls Lt. John Guild to explain that a friend of her husband Tip, who is in prison, has asked that she be home after midnight as he has a proposition for her. She asks Guild if this is the police department trying to set her up. He advises her that this is not the case and suggests that she do as the man says so that the department can see what it's all about. A gambler called Diamond-Back Vogel (the man whom Nick had seen keeping a watch on Church's cottage) calls at the apartment, ostensibly to advise her of a scheme on which her husband Tip wants her assistance, but obviously to check on her relationship with Church. After Vogel has left, at a preordained time Church sends Dum-Dum out; he sits down in the vestibule of a building and, taking a pint of whisky from his pocket, acts the part of the drunkard.

At 1am, as Lois, unable to sleep, is in Nick and Nora's room, there is a gunshot down the hall and the lights are extinguished. MacFay is found in his room, his throat cut; a pistol, with which MacFay apparently tried to shoot his attacker, lies on the floor, and the wires have been torn from his bedside light. Both the window in his room and the front door are open. Shortly, the assistant district attorney VanSlack and a full team of policemen arrive at the house. Just like Boyer in the original typescript for the *Thin Man* novel, the inexperienced VanSlack is deferential to the ace detective. After Nick gives VanSlack the license number of the car used by the man spying on Church, the police identify the vehicle as belonging to the gambler-racketeer Vogel. VanSlack suggests they go to the city to see him and look in on Smitty.

Before they leave for the city, there is more excitement as the dog Asta is seen running around the grounds with a knife in his mouth. Nick manages to persuade the dog to surrender the weapon, and as he does so he is approached by Lois, who whispers that there is something she must tell him. When she sees a man, gun in hand, behind Nick, she pushes the latter out of the path of the bullet. Nick fires at the man and the police join in, killing Dudley Horn. Lois, who has suffered a flesh wound, is now able to complete her conversation with Nick: Dudley killed MacFay. Her suspicion, she says, was alerted when he suggested they tell the police they were together at the time of the murder, and then he began to behave strangely when he heard that the knife had been found, and placed a pistol in his pocket.

Nick and VanSlack arrive outside Smitty's apartment, where they meet Lt. Guild, who immediately provides Smitty with an alibi, as the place has been under surveillance all night; even as he says it, he realizes that she has used him for this purpose. In the apartment, Smitty tells them that her relationship with Church, who was her husband's cell-mate, has been of a professional nature, as he "needed a girl to stooge for him."[45] Vogel arrives and explains that he has been keeping an eye on Smitty for his friend Tip. As the others are diverted by a disturbance, Nick picks up a match book he has found in the apartment bearing an advertisement for the West Indies Club. As he leaves the apartment, he sees that, several floors below, VanSlack and Guild have caught Dum-Dum, finding the large knife in his waistband.

At the West Indies Club, Nick is surprised to find Nora waiting for him. (How did she know he would be there? There is an explanation, but it is so contrived that the reader may be spared it.) Dum-Dum also puts in an appearance, having demonstrated to his captors that he had been in a police drunk tank at the time of the murder. In the club, Nick meets a character called Cookie, who tells him that Church used to have a girlfriend called Linda Mills who lived at the Chestevere Apartments. He goes on to say that Church could not have been involved in the murder of MacFay because he had seen him going into Vogel's...at which point Dum-Dum and a waiter beat him into silence.

Leaving the club after daylight, Nick goes to the Chestevere Apartments and persuades the landlady to let him into Linda Mills's room, where he notes that the pillows have been placed on a chair beside the unmade bed. He also seems to find significance in a scorch-mark on the carpet, and the fact that a small hole in the wall, now covered by a picture, has been concealed by a patch of white paper. The description of Linda Mills given by the landlady could fit either Lois MacFay or Nick Jr.'s nurse.

Back at their hotel suite, Nick finds that Lois has come to stay, Nora explaining that she felt unable to leave her at the MacFay house; Nick finds her asleep in a bedroom, with no pillows on the bed. Soon, the party organized by Face Peppler gets underway, with underground figures arriving with children in tow.

Smitty receives a phone call from Dum-Dum, advising her that Church is on his way to Nick's hotel, and leaves immediately. Diamond-Back Vogel also arrives at the hotel as Nick Jr.'s nurse is pacing outside. Church enters Nick's suite via the fire escape, gun in hand, and takes Nick's wallet. Allowing Church to pin him against Lois's door, Nick announces in a loud voice that Church appears to be doing his utmost to get arrested, presumably confident that he can avoid conviction for the MacFay murder. Soon after Church takes to the fire escape, there is a gunshot, and Nick and Nora see his body on the street below; Smitty stands nearby, a gun at her feet. Lois now joins them at the window, saying that she has heard the shot.

As the police assemble all the suspects in the Charles suite, they are one by one eliminated from the inquiry. Nick Jr.'s nurse says that she has been working under an assumed name, having recently been released from prison after serving a sentence for shoplifting; after MacFay's murder, she feared that the police would identify her from her fingerprints, and so she had run away.

Vogel explains that Church had last night been at his gambling joint in the company of big business figures, and so could not have killed MacFay.

When Guild and VanSlack are still unable to work out the identity of the murderer, Nick calls them "a couple of schoolboys," and proceeds to demonstrate an "electric-cord-gun-paper-water trick" [46] which, although this is never fully explained, would have allowed MacFay's throat to be cut and then give "the murderer between five and ten minutes to get an alibi before the water soaked through and set the gun off."[47] The murderer is Lois. As Linda Mills, Lois had practiced the aforesaid trick at the Chestevere Apartments. She had also killed Church this afternoon, having heard Nick say that he seemed to be courting arrest and therefore suspecting that he was about to double-cross her. Lois, suddenly speaking like a gangster's moll, confesses all to Nick and Nora, saying that she had always hated her role as MacFay's adopted daughter and that she and Church had "found out that we talked the same language."[48]

≈

Possibly the most surprising thing about *Another Thin Man* is that Hammett was on the wagon when he wrote it (he wrote to Hellman in mid-January to say that he had been ten months without a drink.[49]) The story — at least as it appears in *The Return of the Thin Man* — bristles with inconsistencies and stretches credulity (are we to believe that the potential heiress risks all because she discovers that she and Church "talked the same language?").

Take, for example, the case of Nick Jr.'s nurse. Unnamed, she accompanies the family to the MacFay estate, but after arrival she receives not a mention. Much later, when Nick and Nora are back in New York, we are told that she is Ella Waters and that she had run away after the MacFay murder. Then there is Face Peppler, who at the end of the story becomes "Creeps." After the murder, Mrs. Bellam, the housekeeper, attends Lois in bed, telling her: "Colonel MacFay was afraid of Dudley Horn. Dudley Horn knew too much about him, even knew he was robbing that nice Mr. and Mrs. Charles." Asked why Horn felt he had to kill Nick, she explains: "If Mr. Charles had discovered his losses in going over the accounts yesterday, the estate would have had to make them good, my dear."[50] Amazingly, this sub-plot is simply dropped.

The last few pages of the screen story, in which Nick explains what has happened, is a complicated mess, and the Hacketts must have rolled their eyes when they contemplated how to make a screenplay of it.

The version that appears in *The Return of the Thin Man* is dated May 13, 1938. According to Rivett, the original document contains a lengthy passage, eliminated in later versions, in which VanSlack violently tries to implicate Nick in two murders; this was "voted off the book in favor of general readers, who might have been put off or confused by two storylines."[51] Rivett also says that it was the Hacketts who transformed Face Peppler into "Creeps" — but the change occurs toward the end of the May 1938 document,[52] and so it is possible that the change was in fact made by Hammett, who then neglected to correct the name at the start of the story.

As noted earlier, the story is certainly not original, being based on "The Farewell Murder," but the self-plagiarism does not end here, for the scene in the West Indies Club in which Dum-Dum and a waiter set about the drunken Cookie to prevent him from saying more was used in Chapter 22 of *The Thin Man*. It also lacks originality, of course, in the sense that it relies on the hackneyed Holmes-Poirot formula in which only the brilliant detective, held in awe by the authorities, can solve the crime. Moreover, the solution depends upon specialized knowledge (of the "electric-cord-gun-paper-water trick," among other things) of which reader or viewer can have not the slightest familiarity — a failing for which Raymond Chandler would later chastise the "traditional" school of crime-writers.[53]

We should remind ourselves that this was written in 1938, when Hammett was apparently a member of the CPUSA and working assiduously on its behalf; and yet here he is, peddling the same old escapism, the outlook still the same bleak nihilism as when he wrote his novels. He was writing for the money.

In late 1938, Hammett, despite his professed disdain for Nick and Nora Charles, had one last stab at a *Thin Man* treatment, a document of just a few pages intended as a sequel to the first film based on his novel, in which the Charles couple returns to San Francisco accompanied by Dorothy Wynant.

As in *After the Thin Man*, their train is greeted by reporters, and at home there is a surprise party. Herbert Macaulay, the murderer of Clyde Wynant, has escaped and, disguised as a woman, is in pursuit of Mimi, who flies to San Francisco seeking Nick's protection. Then Chris turns up and, in league with an old acquaintance called Dancer, who hangs out in Chinatown, plans to squeeze money out of Mimi. Gangster Shep Morelli from *The Thin Man* is also in town with Georgia, Chris's legal wife. During the course of the usually convoluted plot, Chris is killed and in the finale Nick pays witnesses to give false evidence in order to secure a confession from Dancer.

MGM rejected the treatment. There were several reasons why they might have done so. For one, the future of the *Thin Man* franchise was in doubt anyway, as various key players (the Hacketts and co-star Myrna Loy) were keen to bale out, and the star William Powell had colon cancer. In addition, Hammett was no longer in favor at the studio as he was playing a leading role in the Screen Writers' Guild, which MGM had opposed from the outset. Frankly, however, it is likely that the treatment would have been rejected anyway. Quite apart from a further lowering of the moral tone with Nick's purchase of witnesses, the complex plot, compressed into a few pages, is barely comprehensible, and one sometimes gets the impression of a man attempting to assemble a film from out-takes.[54]

Hammett submitted a further story called "Girl Hunt," which merely recycled his "Fly Paper" story of 1929. This too was rejected. His Hollywood career was almost over. Unknown to the world, however, even before working on the two *Thin Man* films he had been largely responsible for two Broadway plays, one a smash hit and the other a disastrous flop.

NOTES

1 William F. Nolan, *Dashiell Hammett: A Life at the Edge* (London: Arthur Barker, 1983), 110. Nolan says this occurred in 1931, but in fact it was 1930.
2 Richard Layman, "Commentary," Dashiell Hammett, *The Hunter and Other Stories*, ed. Richard Layman and Julie M. Rivett (New York: Mysterious Press, 2013), 187.
3 Joan Mellen, *Hellman and Hammett: The Legendary Passion of Lillian Hellman and Dashiell Hammett* (New York: Harper Collins, 1996), 19.
4 Robert L. Gale, *A Dashiell Hammett Companion* (Westport: Greenwood Press, 2000), 169. Gale is not completely reliable: for example, he says that the star of *Mister Dynamite* was Gene Richmond, whereas the latter is the name Hammett gave the lead character in "On the Make," the screen story on which *Mister Dynamite* was based.
5 Richard Layman, "Introduction," Dashiell Hammett, *The Return of the Thin Man*, ed. Richard Layman and Julie M. Rivett (London: Mysterious Press for Head of Zeus, 2012), 2.
6 Ibid., 170.
7 Richard Layman, *Shadow Man: The Life of Dashiell Hammett* (New York and London: Harcourt Brace Jovanovich/Bruccoli Clark, 1981). 157. A survey conducted in 1940 found that half of Hollywood's screenwriters earned less than $120 per week. The highest reported weekly salary was $3,750. This gives an indication of Hammett's high-flying status. See Gerald Horne, *The Final Victim of the Blacklist: John Howard Lawson, Dean of the Hollywood Ten* (Berkeley, Los Angeles and London: University of California Press, 2006), 140.
8 Nolan, 152; Julian Symons, *Dashiell Hammett* (San Diego/New York/London: Harcourt Brace Jovanovich, 1985), 107.
9 Albert Halper, *Good-bye, Union Square: A Writer's Memoir of the Thirties* (Chicago: Quadrangle Books, 1970), 192-193.
10 Dashiell Hammett to Mary Hammett, January 12, 1950 and Lillian Hellman, January 31, 1950; Dashiell Hammett, *Selected Letters of Dashiell Hammett, 1921-1960*, ed. Richard Layman with Julie M. Rivett (Washington D. C.: Counterpoint, 2001), 532, 534.
11 Dashiell Hammett to Lillian Hellman, February 14, 1950 and Mary

Hammett, February 22, 1950; *Selected Letters*, 537, 538-539.
12 Nolan, 212.
13 Dashiell Hammett, "The Kiss-Off," *The Hunter and Other Stories*, 191.
14 Layman, "Commentary," *The Hunter and Other Stories*, 187.
15 Hammett's sense of humor is at work here: Carrie Nation (1846-1911) was a militant temperance campaigner.
16 Dashiell Hammett, "On the Make," *The Hunter and Other Stories*, 244.
17 Ibid., 257.
18 Ibid., 259.
19 Ibid., 263.
20 Ibid., 270.
21 Ibid., 274.
22 Dashiell Hammett, "Devil's Playground", *The Hunter and Other Stories*, 201.
23 Ibid., 207.
24 Dashiell Hammett, *The Return of The Thin Man*, 25.
25 Ibid., 31.
26 Ibid., 74.
27 Ibid., 88.
28 Ibid., 93.
29 Ibid., 95.
30 Julie M. Rivett, "After the Thin Man: Headnote," Dashiell Hammett, *The Return of the Thin Man*, 13.
31 Ibid., 14.
32 Julie M. Rivett, "After the Thin Man: Afterword," Dashiell Hammett, *The Return of the Thin Man*, 124.
33 Hammett, *The Return of the Thin Man*, 30.
34 Albert Halper, *The Foundry* (New York: Viking, 1934).
35 Richard Layman, "Introduction," Dashiell Hammett, *The Return of the Thin Man*.
36 Joseph North, "Still on the Fence," *New Masses*, September 25, 1934.
37 Layman, "Introduction," Hammett, *The Return of the Thin Man*, 6.
38 Dashiell Hammett to Lillian Hellman, November 27, 1937; *Selected Letters*, 125.
39 Jo Hammett, *Dashiell Hammett: A Daughter Remembers*, ed. Richard

Layman with Julie M. Rivett (New York: Carroll & Graf Publishers, 2001), 92.

40 Julie M. Rivett, "After the Thin Man: Afterword," Dashiell *Hammett, The Return of the Thin Man*, 126. Joan Mellen, 127, is therefore mistaken when she suggests that the appearance of the baby in *Another Thin Man* was Hammett's way of keeping alive the fetus that Hellman had aborted.

41 Dashiell Hammett to Lillian Hellman, December 26, 1937; *Selected Letters*, 128.

42 Layman, *Shadow Man*, 166. On the other hand, Nolan, 161, says that Hammett was offered $40,000 for the outline of the third *Thin Man* movie. Layman's seems the likelier version.

43 Dashiell Hammett, *Another Thin Man* in *The Return of the Thin Man*, 134.

44 Ibid., 141.

45 Ibid., 194.

46 Ibid., 216.

47 Ibid., 217.

48 Ibid., 219.

49 Dashiell Hammett to Lillian Hellman, January 15, 1938; *Selected Letters*, 129.

50 Ibid., 187, 188.

51 Rivett, "Another Thin Man: Headnote," *Return of the Thin Man*, 128; Julie M. Rivett to Ken Fuller, May 31, 2015.

52 Ibid., 223.

53 See, for example, Raymond Chandler to James M. Fox, Raymond Chandler, *Selected Letters of Raymond Chandler*, ed. Frank McShane (New York: Columbia University Press, 1981), 357.

54 "Sequel to The Thin Man" can be found in *The Return of the Thin Man*, 227-233.

5 Broadway

The extent of Dashiell Hammett's contribution to the plays of Lillian Hellman is far from settled. The matter is made more complicated than it might be by the apparent tendency of biographers to be guided by their allegiance, or otherwise, to their subject.[1] There would appear to be three camps: the Hammett partisans; the Hellman denigrators; and the Hellman rehabilitators.

In his introduction to *Nightmare Town*, a collection of Hammett's stories, William Nolan (a Hammett partisan) says that Hammett worked on "nearly all of her original plays (the exception being *The Searching Wind*). He painstakingly supervised structure, scenes, dialogue, and character, guiding Hellman through several productions His contributions were enormous, and after Hammett's death, Hellman never wrote another original play."[2]

Dorothy Gallagher (a late arrival, with little of originality to say, in the camp of Hellman denigrators) endorses this latter point.[3] Hellman biographer Deborah Martinson (a rehabilitator) disagrees, arguing that those critics who imply that Hellman's plays were written by Hammett are simply wrong and that Hammett's granddaughter Julie Rivett is closer to the mark when she says that although Hammett's close involvement in Hellman's first play, *The Children's Hour* was sufficient to qualify him as co-writer, subsequent plays were Hellman's own work.[4]

Denigrator Joan Mellen (who is also something of a Hammett partisan) writes of Hellman's lack of confidence in her ability to write another play without Hammett's assistance after *The Children's Hour*.[5]

Although Hellman herself would sometimes acknowledge Hammett's assistance on a particular play or a specific speech, it was not until her later years that she became a little more open about the size of his contribution. In a 1974 interview with Bill Moyers, she *thinks* that Hammett encouraged her to resume writing (she had previously written a few short stories), although she has no idea why she decided on plays. Later in the interview, however, she acknowledges that Hammett helped her "enormously. I can't ever pay him enough gratitude for what he did beyond the obvious things that writers can help with. He was so enormously patient. And more than patient, he was honest, sometimes rather sharply and brutally honest. Without that I don't think I would have done very much."[6]

Five years later, Hellman was even more fulsome:

> His [Hammett's] effect on me was enormous. I've long had a belief, which is very possibly not the truth, that without Hammett, I wouldn't have written. I've come to think, perhaps, that I would have written, but I would have had an infinitely greater struggle, and been less good, I think, without him. He taught me, in a sense, to write. And beyond that which many people have done for many other people, he took chances that very few people will ever take, particularly people they love. He told the truth…There was a time when I thought that I would never have written anything without him. I don't think that's true any more. But I think I would have had a much harder time, so hard that I might have given up.[7]

That same year, in an interview broadcast two years later, she admitted that she was unsure whether she would have written without Hammett's influence. "It was he who teased me back into writing, annoyed me back into writing, baited me back into writing. And then watched for as long as he lived."[8]

While it is clear that on occasion Hammett did rather more than watch, we will probably never know the extent of his contribution.

We can, however, consider what is known regarding his involvement in each of the plays and in two or three of them — something not done by previous writers, as far as I am aware — consider the texts for evidence of his hand.

The Children's Hour

Karen Wright and Martha Dobie run a small private girls' school which is at last paying for itself. When one of the pupils, problem child Mary Tilford, is punished for lying, she runs away from school to the house of her grandmother and guardian, and convinces the old woman not to insist on returning her to school by claiming that Wright and Dobie have a lesbian relationship.

The grandmother, Amelia Tilford, alerts the parents of the other children, who are also withdrawn from the school. Wright and Dobie file a libel suit against the old woman but as a key witness (Dobie's aunt, Lily Mortar, who was overheard telling her niece that her jealousy over Wright's impending marriage to Dr. Joseph Cardin was "unnatural") fails to appear, they gain publicity but lose the case. Amelia Tilford later visits the two ruined teachers to tell them that, having finally got the truth out of Mary, she has asked the judge to issue a statement and will be paying in full the compensation they had sought. But it is too late: Martha Dobie, having confessed to Karen that the mere fact of the allegation had brought to her realization that she had indeed felt sexual love for her, has just committed suicide; and Karen and her fiancé Joe Cardin have split up, as she fears that the question of whether she had been in a lesbian relationship would always be between them.

≈

Hellman was not always honest in acknowledging that Hammett had suggested that she turn William Roughead's story, contained in his *Bad Companions* (1930), into a play. Hammett's daughter Jo recalls that when the source of the plot came up in conversation while the three of them were alone, Hellman failed to acknowledge Hammett's contribution, and he did not correct her.[9] In a 1952 interview Hellman went so far as to claim that she had chosen the story upon which to base the play,[10] but 13 years later she admitted that the choice had been Hammett's.[11] Three years after this, however, she claimed not to remember what convinced her that a play could be fashioned from the story,[12] and in 1970 she could not remember what led her to write that first play.[13]

Biographers — both Hellman's and Hammett's — have no doubt that Hammett had selected the story, suggesting that Hellman base a play upon it.[14] Indeed, it was only natural that Hammett would have read Roughead's recently-published book as, although a Scottish solicitor, the latter was a pioneer of the "real crime" genre. But Hammett's involvement extended far beyond this, although Hellman was not always ready to admit as much — "I don't remember very much about the writing or the casting," she wrote in her second volume of memoirs.[15] She is said to have told her lover Ralph Ingersoll, however, that Hammett had "virtually written *The Children's Hour*, steering her line by line."[16]

According to Nolan, "Hammett criticized each page, each act, each bit of dialogue. Draft after draft he would tell her, 'It's getting better, Lily. But you're not there yet.'"[17] Emery takes the view that Hammett's contribution was such that he could have claimed co-authorship.[18] Layman also credits Hammett's significant contribution to the play, saying that he and Hellman "worked on successive drafts together."[19] Mellen tells us that in a Florida Keys fishing camp in the spring and summer of 1933 Hellman and Hammett worked on the play together. "Relentlessly, he told her how bad the first draft was, and then how bad the second was, and the fifth, and the sixth. (In 1935, however, while the play was still running, Hellman told the press he had read only the fourth draft, when he made his suggestions...)" Hammett not only made suggestions but also changed speeches, consistently arguing for greater simplicity.[20] Hammett's contribution was certainly recognized by others, for publisher Alfred Knopf, having received the script, asked Hammett, "Shall I send you or rather Lillian a contract or what?"[21]

Here and there, it is possible to detect Hammett's work in *The Children's Hour*. Asked by one of the girls whether she had ever been in the movies, former actress Lily Mortar replies, "I had many offers, my dear. But the cinema is a shallow art."[22] This sounds like Hammett, for this was precisely his view of cinema, while Hellman enjoyed her work as a screenwriter. When Martha, having waxed bitter to Joe Cardin about his impending marriage to Karen, apologizes, Joe puts his arm around her, allowing her to rest her head against his chest.[23] Although he is engaged to Karen, not Martha, he comforts the latter physically, and because he does this in a perfectly relaxed, natural manner, Martha accepts the gesture. This is reminiscent of that early scene between Sam Spade and his secretary Effie in *The Maltese Falcon*, and it is probable that Hammett wrote this; it is not unreasonable to suspect that he wrote much of the wisecracking Cardin's dialogue.

The Children's Hour opened on Broadway in November 1934 and was a great success (691 performances), leading to a Hollywood offer for Hellman to adapt it for the screen; she did so, excising all references to lesbianism, and it emerged as *These Three*; this was one of several screenplays she wrote around this time. While on contract to Samuel Goldwyn, she earned $2,500 a week — more than Hammett was getting.

Days to Come

In mid-1936, Hellman rented a cottage on Tavern Island, Connecticut, where she and Hammett spent the rest of the summer working on her second play, *Days to Come*, about a strike of brush-workers. Given the strikebreaking theme, it might be reasonable to assume that Hammett's influence was on this occasion even greater than previously, and he certainly gave a positive appraisal of the final draft.[24] When the play proved to be a disastrous flop, he confessed to an error of judgment.

Set in Callom, Ohio, 200 miles from Cleveland, this second play deals with a brush factory where the owner Andrew Rodman has, due to economic circumstances, reduced wages and thereby provoked a strike by the normally placid workforce.

Rodman is portrayed as a basically decent man completely at a loss to know how to deal with economic forces beyond his control. He is therefore bullied by his lawyer-best-friend Henry Ellicott, who has in the past had an affair with Rodman's wife Julie and now takes it upon himself to call in professional strike-breakers, telling an unhappy

Rodman that the decision was necessary in order to secure a loan to tide the company over.

When union organizer Leo Whalen comes to the Rodman house with Tom Firth, the lay leader (previously a close friend of the boss), Julie tries to befriend the former but Whalen, a straight-shooter who is exasperated by the evidence of class collaboration he sees in the situation, puts her off.

Just as there is no hatred between boss and workers, so there is none between Whalen and Wilkie, the leader of the strikebreakers, and when the latter arrives at the house he and Whalen have a brief discussion of a fellow-organizer who was killed, probably by one of Wilkie's men, and of other towns they've worked. There is no animosity, just a casual discussion between two professionals who happen to be on different sides in the system.

Rodman is under the impression that the strikebreakers will be making his brushes, but Whalen assures him that this is not the way it works, and their role will be to break the strike with brute force. Whalen therefore advises the strikers against violence, counseling that once they surrender to such impulses the fight will be lost. A month into the strike, therefore, the strikebreakers complain that it's impossible to provoke the strikers into a fight, and Wilkie moans that, as Rodman doesn't really want him there, there's little for him to do.

One evening, Julie Rodman visits the strike office and tells Whalen that she wants to stay with him. Whalen laughs when she asks if he loves the poor, telling her that he hates them, but loves "what they could be."[25] She persists, telling him that she wants for herself what he has found. Whalen, half-suspecting that this is all part of a ruse thought up by Wilkie to discredit him, dismisses her as a silly rich woman in search of a world other than her own.

In the meantime, two of the lead strikebreakers have fallen out and the body of the loser is dumped in the alley behind the strike office. Whalen is taken into custody just long enough to allow Wilkie to seize his opportunity, blaming the death on the strikers. The strikebreaker tells Rodman that "somebody's been killed tonight and that somebody worked for me. If I'm going to stay in business I can't let people get the idea they can slice up my folks."[26] Some of the strikebreakers are sworn in as deputies and the long-awaited violence commences, during which Tom Firth's adopted daughter is killed. The strike is broken.

In the aftermath, Rodman tells Julie (who has never loved him) that she doesn't deserve any punishment. "Go anywhere you like. Or nowhere. Whatever is left here is as much yours as it is mine. *That's your punishment* — if you're looking for it. For the rest of your life, my wife, for all the days to come..."[27]

≈

Hellman encouraged the view that Hammett had made little contribution to *Days to Come*, telling an interviewer in 1936, just days before the play opened on Broadway, that the "urge" to write it had been on her for five or six years.[28] But how could this be if, as she was to later acknowledge, Hammett encouraged her resumption of writing, which commenced with *The Children's Hour*?

Martinson says that Hellman began to write the play in 1935 when, following her mother's death, she visited Ohio to research labor problems, but was unable to complete it until the following year, when she visited Cuba alone for that very purpose. She concedes, however, that Hammett assisted with the planning of the play.[29] There is at least one problem here: Hellman's lone visit to Cuba was in June 1936 (she had travelled there with lover Ralph Ingersoll in March), and yet Mellen tells us that in October she was still making demands on Hammett regarding the draft of the play, inspiring Arthur Kober, her former husband, to exclaim, "Here is collaboration!" After Hammett moved to Princeton, she took a revised version to him and he dutifully took out his blue pencil, deleting and simplifying. Mellen describes one of his insertions (which she infuriatingly fails to identify) as "pure Hammett." There were, apparently, several trips to Princeton,[30] and Rollyson says that the final draft was written there.[31]

Gallagher reckons that Hellman "supplied her own plot" for the play and that Hammett was not much use because he was undergoing treatment for gonorrhea and was drunk much of the time in 1936.[32] Mellen partly concurs with this, saying that when, after medical treatment in New York City, he joined Hellman on Tavern Island, he was "too sick even to read," giving the play the thumbs-up after the merest glance. In the same sentence, however, she tells us that the man who was too sick to read "turned to Ping-Pong and badminton" as an alternative![33]

After the disastrous first-night performance, during which William Randolph Hearst led his large party out of the theatre at an early stage, Hellman berated Hammett for having said that it was good. He replied, "I did indeed. But I saw it at the Vanderbilt tonight and I've changed my mind."[34] This certainly does not give the impression of co-authorship, but there are sufficient textual indications that Hammett's involvement was much greater than has been realized.

≈

First, there is the fact that *Days to Come* features strikebreakers. Hammett had, after all, worked for a company which specialized in precisely this activity. It would have been a bold Hellman indeed who wrote about such a subject with no input from Hammett. Martinson says that Hellman was knowledgeable about labor unions due to her involvement in the Screen Writers Guild.[35] While it is true that the Guild was established as a trade union in 1933, however, Hellman's activity did not commence for a few more years, and so her experience by the time *Days to Come* was written would have been minimal at best.

It is almost impossible to believe that Hellman would have been able to depict the relationship between the strikebreaker Wilkie and union organizer Whalen as purely professional, devoid of personal animosity, for where would she have gained the experience on which such an insight would have been based? These scenes surely bear the stamp of Hammett, whose Pinkerton training had taught him to avoid personal involvement in a case — a trait he had assigned to the Continental Op and Sam Spade. "There is no doubt," Rollyson concedes, "that Hellman was writing from Hammett's experience as well as from her own."[36]

Then again, as soon as Wilkie and his thugs enter the Rodman house, we experience a frisson of recognition. Surely we have been here before. But when, and where? We turn back to Hammett's more obscure (although recently-published) writings and then it comes to us: in "On the Make," the screen story that Hammett initially wrote in 1931 and, following rejection by Warner Bros., revised in 1934, gangster Cheeters Neely and his boys invite themselves to the mansion of stockbroker Herbert Pomeroy, where they stay in the hope that the latter will provide them with getaway money. Similarly, in *Days to Come* Wilkie stations his two lieutenants, Mossie and Easter, in the Rodman house (announcing this to Rodman with little concern whether he likes it or not), where they show little respect for the furnishings or accessories.

When Rodman expresses his unhappiness over the decision to call in strikebreakers, the lawyer Ellicott explains that this was a condition of the loan the company has been granted, "as you couldn't've gotten a nickel in Cleveland if you hadn't made this decision."[37] "Couldn't've." The three-word, two-apostrophe abbreviation was almost a Hammett trade mark. For example, in the story "Two Sharp Knives" (1934), he uses "he'd've," "I'd've" (three times) and "you'd've" in one paragraph.[38] There are numerous occurrences: along with the previous examples, "we'd've," "wouldn't've" and "she'd've" can be found in *The Dain Curse, The Maltese Falcon, The Glass Key*, the first and final drafts of *The Thin Man*, and the treatment for *Another Thin Man*. There are probably numerous examples to be found in the short stories and novelettes, should one care to search for them. This form of abbreviation is not found elsewhere in Hellman's work. And then there is the use by Rodman's sister of "Be still" to shut him up. This unfashionable term (even then) is found nowhere else in Hellman's work but it can be found in Hammett's — once in *Red Harvest* and twice in *The Dain Curse*.[39]

When Julie Rodman visits Whalen in the strike office, Hammett's hand is clearly evident. As Mellen says, "Lily admitted...that she had required a man to facilitate her effort to discover 'something to want, or to think,' a man 'to show me the way.'"[40] Julie Rodman wants for herself what Whalen has found, but she makes a poor job of explaining this. She tells Whalen she wants to stay. . "Sounds crazy, doesn't it? It isn't crazy for me. I know the things you're going to say about a silly, rich woman. But I've thought about it, and I know it isn't that. I have no right to come here and talk to you like this — "[41] In earlier drafts, there was apparently much more in this scene that made it clear that the Julie-Whalen duo was a thinly disguised Hellman-Hammett, but Hammett deleted much of it.[42]

We know, therefore, that Hammett edited this scene, but how much did he insert? The union organizer speaks like the lead character in a private-eye movie and, as with Gene Richmond in "On the Make," it is all too easy to imagine his lines being spoken by Bogart. The dialogue in this scene strikes one as pure Hammett. And when the two thugs, Mossie and Easter, fall out and Mossie ends up dead, the enterprise strikes one as more like a gangster movie than a Broadway play.

At this stage, there is another very concrete indication of Hammett's hand, as Wilkie explains to Rodman how the situation has changed.

> I don't think you understand. I'm not talking about Mossie. I'm not crying about that. That was his job. He got paid for it. But somebody's been killed and that somebody worked for me. If I'm going to stay in business I can't let people get the idea they can slice up my folks. And I won't. I can't make you let me keep this job. But I can't leave tonight. I'm the police here, Mr. Rodman, and if I wasn't worrying about finishing a job I was hired for, I'd have to think about that.[43]

Again, there is that jolt of recognition. This is precisely the argument Sam Spade puts to Brigid O'Shaughnessy in *The Maltese Falcon*: she has to swing because she murdered Miles Archer, as a private eye who allows his partner's killer to go free will soon find himself short of clients. Wilkie's final speech, as he departs the Rodman house, also has the ring of Hammett:

> But I want to tell you, I've worked for a lot of men, some of them deacons of the church who were breaking strikes for the good of America, but I never worked for a man before who believed I could come in, run his factory, and break his strike without walking on anybody's toes.[44]

The version of *Days to Come* which appears in *The Collected Plays* was trimmed quite extensively by Hellman, and by comparing this with the version in *Four Plays*, which she published in 1942, we can see that there were originally other lines which might have been written by Hammett. "Didn't anybody ever tell you that Christians aren't supposed to act like Christians?" Whalen asks Firth early on in the play. In the scene in the strike office, when Julie Rodman tells Whalen that her recent self-examination has not involved the services of a psychoanalyst, Whalen quips, "Oh, I thought that was the rich man's gin."[45]

In Chapter 4, I expressed the view that "On the Make" reads more like a novelette than a screen story, and Martinson correctly makes the same point about *Days to Come*, calling it "more novelistic than dramatic."[46] This is, in my view, a further sign of Hammett's involvement.

≈

Entertaining in places, *Days to Come* is a mess, and it survived a mere seven performances. Politically, it is disappointing. What would one expect of a play with such a title, written in 1935-36, about a brushworkers' strike? A large number of working-class characters? In fact, there are really only two: Tom Firth and Leo Whalen, and the play is centered around the factory-owner and his family. An optimistic ending? The strike is defeated and the title, rather than a reference to a future in which workers will enjoy the full fruits of their labor, has, as we have seen, a far less sunny meaning.

The Little Foxes

In the Alabama of 1900, the Hubbard siblings, Ben, Regina and Oscar, are fading Southern aristocracy, still growing cotton. The more visionary Ben sees the need to link up with Northern capital, and so he has negotiated a deal with William Marshall of Chicago to build a cotton mill on the plantation. The problem is that the Hubbards will be unable to meet their part of the deal without the contribution of Regina's husband, banker Horace Giddings, who is currently hospitalized in Baltimore with a serious heart condition; Regina's letters on the matter go unanswered. Eventually, their daughter Alexandra is dispatched to bring him home.

Upon arrival, although desperately weak Horace is immediately badgered to support the project. He refuses to do so, and makes it clear that, with the exception of his daughter, he wants nothing more to do with the Hubbards. Oscar's son Leo, who works in Horace's bank, tells his father that Horace has $86,000 in railroad bonds in a safe deposit box, and that he only checks on them every few months. Oscar immediately suggests that he "borrow" the bonds, which would be repaid before Horace next examines them in September.

The plan is taken to Ben who, affecting high principles, says he does not want to know any details, but if the bonds can be borrowed, he is content. But Horace checks on the bonds well ahead of schedule, and tells Regina that he will take no action against the perpetrators; instead, he will consider it a loan from himself, and thus he will get a slice of the profits from the cotton mill; he will also change his will, giving Regina only the railroad bonds and leaving everything else (including the interest in the mill), to Alexandra. However, he has an attack and, after Regina withholds his medicine, he dies of heart failure.

Regina now advises Ben and Oscar that Horace told her of their dishonesty. The price of her silence will be 75 percent of the Hubbard share of the mill's profits (previously she had jacked Horace's share up to 40 percent from a third, assuring her brothers that this would be sufficient to win Horace's support; this had been at Oscar's expense, who would be compensated by a marriage between his son Leo and Alexandra, who would inherit Horace/Regina's share). The brothers have no choice but to accept her demand.

≈

Years later, as Hammett was watching the film version of *The Little Foxes* with his daughter Jo, he greeted the opening lines ("Little foxes have lived at all times, in all places. This family happened to live in the Deep South in the year 1900") with the cry, "I wrote that! I wrote that!"[47]

As she wrote *The Little Foxes*, Hammett nagged Hellman to make improvement after improvement — to such an extent that at one point she threatened to abandon the project, while Hammett, according to Nolan, "exhausted himself" on the play and was unable to continue his novel entitled "My Brother Felix," which he abandoned in September 1938 after just seventeen pages.[48] In fact, Hammett neither completed another novel nor wrote another short story. According to Emery, the various drafts of the play make it "it plain that Hammett's participation went beyond that of a typical editor."[49]

Unusually, Hellman admitted that Hammett's contribution to *The Little Foxes* (even though the Hubbards were based on her mother's family, the Newhouses) was considerable, stating in an interview in

1965: "I had many problems writing *The Little Foxes*. When I thought I had got it right, I wanted Dash to read it. It was five o'clock in the morning. I was pleased with this sixth version, and I put the manuscript near his door with a note. 'I hope this satisfies you.' When I got up, the manuscript was outside my door with a note saying, 'Things are going pretty well if you will just cut out the liberal blackamoor chit-chat.'"[50] (This is a reference to the dialogue she had given black servants.)

In her second volume of memoirs, she says that this play "was the one that was most dependent" on Hammett, as "he was working so hard for me because *Days to Come* had scared me and scared him for my future."[51]

Hellman's biographers agree. Says Mellen: "Scrupulously and with unstinting generosity, he rewrote, edited, mulled over every word of the text," writing some of the speeches and telling her after the ninth draft that she was on her way and should now start again. " Such was his contribution, says Mellen, that he "had virtually rewritten *The Little Foxes*."[52]

≈

Unlike with the previous two plays, it is more difficult to discern where Hellman ends and Hammett begins in *The Little Foxes*, although educated guesses are possible.

At the end of the play, Regina, Ben and Oscar are at each other's throats. "Oscar, listen to him," Regina says after Ben has asked what evidence she has against Oscar and Leo. "He's getting ready to swear that it was you and Leo! What do you say to that?...Oh, don't be angry, Oscar. I'm going to see that he goes in with you." This is the standard divide-and-rule ploy, used by the Continental Op on countless occasions, clear evidence of Hammett's hand. The tactic is also evident a little earlier, when Horace Giddings predicts that Ben Hubbard will set the races against each other in the proposed cotton mill, thus enabling him to pay wages even lower than those current in the South at that time. This would appear to be Hammett's line of territory.[53]

On the other hand, the scenes in which Horace Giddings and his daughter Alexandra roundly condemn the avarice of the Hubbards[54] are most likely the work of Hellman, anxious to inflict revenge on the Newhouses for standing aloof from the less prosperous Hellmans. The Hubbards are full of cant and hypocrisy, qualities exposed in a scene between Ben and William Marshall, the Chicago capitalist. Ben, hand literally on heart, proclaims that a man doesn't involve himself in business simply for money, which, after all, is not everything, to which the more honest Marshall responds: "Really? Well, I always thought it was a great deal." The amused Marshall continues:

> You have a turn for neat phrases, Hubbard. Well, however grand your reasons are, mine are simple: I want to make money and I believe I'll make it on you...Mind you, I have no objections to more high-minded reasons. They are mighty valuable in business. It's fine to have partners who so closely follow the teachings of Christ.[55]

This is the clear-eyed Yankee capitalist gently mocking the romantic folderol with which southern proprietors (although usually of a former age, and with greater sincerity than that displayed by Ben Hubbard) cloaked their exploitation. It is probable that Hammett, a southerner himself (as, of course, was Hellman), and with the breadth of his reading more likely to have a sense of the age in which the play is set, is responsible for this.

This same sense is present in a later passage in which Ben, for all his fake "southern" sensibility convinced that the future of southern landowners like himself was determined by the outcome of the Civil War 35 years ago, speaks not just of the inevitability of a marriage with northern capital, but of the opportunity it offers. Telling Regina that the two of them are not sour complainers like Oscar and Leo, he declaims:

> The century's turning, the world is open. Open for people like you and me. Ready for us, waiting for us. After all this is just the beginning. There are hundreds of Hubbards sitting in rooms like this throughout the country. All their names aren't Hubbard, but they are all Hubbards and they will own this country some day. We'll get along.[56]

When asked, 30 years later, whether she had intended that *The Little*

Foxes should present "a picture of the evil of the coming of industrialism in the South and the implications that the modern capitalistic world is full of Hubbards," she replied: "I certainly did not. I woke up extremely surprised that anybody thought so."[57] If it had not been her intention, then it must have been Hammett's who, as we will see in the following chapter, had recently embraced Marxism.

His efforts on *The Little Foxes* paid off because the play, staged in 1939, was a success, running for 410 performances.

Watch on the Rhine

The Farrelly family house, just outside Washington, is hosting Count Teck de Brancovis, a Rumanian refugee and a frequent visitor to the German Embassy, and his wife Marthe. Theirs is a failed marriage, as at the age of 17 Marthe was pressured by her mother to marry Teck, whom she despises. Now, she and David Farrelly, son of the matriarch Fanny, are attracted to each other. Even though World War II has commenced (without, as yet, the USA), Fanny and David Farrelly are, like much of America, complacent regarding Nazism.

They are joined by Sara, the daughter of Fanny, her husband Kurt Muller and their three children. Kurt is a German anti-Nazi activist who has fought for Republican Spain and is now on the run.

Kurt hears that three of his comrades have been arrested and plans to return to Germany to rescue them by bribing the guards. He tells Fanny how he and another fighter raided the house of a local Gestapo chief. "I do not tell you the story to prove we are remarkable but to prove they are not."[58]

De Brancovis has suspected Kurt from his arrival and now tries to blackmail him, offering his silence in return for $10,000 of the resistance funds that Kurt is carrying. Having at first pretended to agree to the proposal, Kurt later tells de Brancovis, "This money is going home with me. It was not given to me to save my life, and I shall not so use it. It is to save the lives and further the work of more than I."[59] He suspects that de Brancovis intends to take the $10,000 from him and also betray him in return for a visa.

Kurt goes outside with de Brancovis and kills him. He confesses to David, Fanny and Sara, "I have done it. I will do it again. I have a great hate for the violent. They are the sick of the world...Maybe I am sick now, too."[60] Aroused from her complacency, Fanny contributes to his fund and he leaves.

≋

The play was written after the conclusion of the non-aggression pact between the Soviet Union and Germany in 1939, and several of Hellman's biographers use this fact to depict her as heroically defying the CPUSA line by continuing to promote anti-fascism. Often, apparently motivated by anti-communism (or at least anti-Sovietism), the same biographers mischaracterize the situation, as when Martinson claims: "The timing of Hellman's *Watch on the Rhine* demonstrates her personal confrontation with the fascists and their Soviet allies."[61] The Soviet Union and Nazi Germany were, of course, never allies. (This subject will be discussed more fully in Chapter 7.) Mellen, who joins in this anti-Soviet chorus, notes, however, that the first completed draft of *Watch on the Rhine* is dated August 15, 1939, shortly before the non-aggression treaty was signed.[62] Years later, Hellman would claim that she had made a start on the play even before she had commenced *The Little Foxes*, but had then thrown it away.[63]

The fact remains, however, that later drafts did maintain the anti-fascist theme. At the time, there was adverse criticism by the CPUSA, but Mellen puts her own spin on this:

> *The Daily Worker*, unwilling openly to admit Lillian Hellman had violated Party directives by encouraging the antifascist struggle at this inopportune moment, faulted her for not mentioning the working class as the leaders in the struggle for a better world. Worse, she failed to indicate "that a land of socialism has already established the permanent new life of peace and freedom." "Peace," of course, was the buzzword.[64]

Mellen notes, however, that the party-led League of American Writers awarded the play a prize at its meeting in June 1941.[65]

Johnson says that Hellman and Hammett worked on the play together in 1940-41,[66] although it is impossible to know how much of the finished product might be Hammett's. One certainly suspects that it was he who inserted the following line as an in-joke: discussing Sam Chandler, one of de Brancovis's card-playing friends at the German Embassy, Fanny tells him, "Sam Chandler has always been a scoundrel. All the Chandlers are. They're cousins of mine."⁶⁷

The play opened in April 1941 and ran for 378 performances.

≈

Hellman was unable to remember the circumstances which led to Hammett writing the screenplay for the Hollywood version of *Watch on the Rhine*,⁶⁸ and most of her biographers are similarly at a loss, but Martinson comes up with a perfectly obvious explanation: the screen rights had been bought by Paramount, and Hellman was still under contract to Goldwyn.⁶⁹ Hal Wallis paid Hammett $30,000, but on condition that, given Hammett's reputation for missing deadlines, Hellman and Herman Shumlin would guarantee delivery.⁷⁰

According to Mellen, it was at this point that Hellman turned the tables on Hammett, editing his script with a severity similar to that which he had used on her plays. In doing so, however, it seems that she excised the only truly *political* writing that Hammett had ever done.

Hammett had not viewed the play too kindly, telling Hellman that she had "ruined a great play by too much sentimentalism. Anti-fascist sentimentalism."⁷¹ Here, of course, he was hewing to the party line, which at the time concentrated on the call for peace, a policy which was similar to that of the left toward World War I, which had correctly been condemned as an inter-imperialist conflict. And this seems to have been reflected in his screenplay, the original draft of which Mellen pans as "self-indulgent, loose and baggy."⁷² She is particularly critical of an opening sequence in which the youngest Muller child is taken aback by the degree of poverty he sees out of the window during the train journey to Washington. Mellen refers to this as "uncharacteristic polemicizing about the rich and poor."⁷³ Uncharacteristic indeed! This is precisely the kind of political writing that is absent in the whole of Hammett's work but which his critics and admirers seem to imagine was there all along! He was at last a political writer, only to be censored by la Hellman, who cut the exchange.

As an example of the "sententious philosophizing" excised by Hellman, Mellen quotes the Hammett line: "We don't like to remember, do we, that they [the Nazis] came in on the shoulders of some of the most powerful men in the world."⁷⁴ It seems that Mellen is unable to distinguish class politics from "sententious philosophizing." It is her belief that Hammett's "emotional nihilism" had "led him to sentimental writing, interminable scenes, sententious speechmaking, and flabby dialogue."⁷⁵

If the examples she gives are anything to go by, however, Hammett had at last found an outlook that offered the possibility of him *overcoming* the nihilism (which was philosophical rather than emotional) which had hitherto prevented him from approaching his writing from a Marxist standpoint. But Hellman had other ideas; she received $11,500 for her editing of Hammett's script and writing additional scenes.⁷⁶ But there are some things which Hellman admired in the Hammett screenplay, in particular the poker game, merely mentioned in the stage version but now written as a scene, in which Teck de Brancovis plays with his pals at the German Embassy, neatly summing up, as Rollyson says, "the ideological, cynical, and collaborationist forces aligned against Kurt."⁷⁷

The film opened in August 1943, and Hammett's screenplay was nominated for an Oscar.

The Searching Wind

For her next play, Hellman took the theme of appeasement, a logical step from *Watch on the Rhine*. Told in flashback, the play follows the path of the Hazens, a US diplomatic family, as they make their way around a Europe in which fascism is taking hold.

In October 1922 they witness the conclusion of Mussolini's "March on Rome." Moses Taney, politician and newspaper proprietor, and father-in-law to Alex Hazen, comments that the government guns that can be heard in the background are firing at nothing, that it is all show. Emily, talking of her social engagement the previous evening, says a man called Peronne had only attended because he had thought Moses would be there, as he didn't think Moses understood the situation in Italy, which would undergo a recovery under Fascist rule. "He's an impartial judge," quips Moses. "He put up the money for Mussolini."⁷⁸

Alex, the diplomat, takes the view that, as distasteful as the situation may be, Mussolini is a necessary evil, as without him there would be a revolution. "If Mussolini can put it down that doesn't make me like him, or the money behind him, or the people. But somebody had to do it, and you don't pick gentlemen to do the job."[79] This, of course, describes a major strand of US foreign policy up to the present day.

Discussing these matters in 1944 in the family's house in Washington, Alex's son Sam, who has been wounded in Italy, seems to be saying that if people like his father had understood the forces at work in 1922, he would not have been called upon to fight there two decades later. Alex excuses himself by saying, "There are men who see their own time as clearly as if it were history [a neat way, in fact, to describe Marxists]. But they're rare, Sam."[80]

In Berlin in 1923, Alex, Emily and family friend Cassie (who throughout the two decades covered by the play is the third member of a love triangle) witness an anti-Jewish attack by Nazis. There are echoes of Italy the previous year, both in the situation and in Alex's reaction to it. He notes the misery, poverty and desperation of the people, and the fact that the police appear to avoid controlling the situation. Another character remarks that it is rumored that "somebody from Thyssen," the industrial conglomerate, was funding "those clowns outside."[81]

The play moves to Paris, 1938, where Alex is ostensibly on holiday, although he is about to send a report on the European situation to Washington. He is visited by German unofficial envoy Count Max Von Stammer, who tells him that if Germany were given "the proper freedom and cooperation we might be prepared, in time, to turn East. East. To rid Europe of the menace of Russia."[82] He urges Alex to persuade France and Britain not to go to war, but Alex appears to be affronted by the proposed deal and terminates the interview.

As Alex prepares to send his report to Washington, however, his wife Emily reminds him that if there is to be a war their son Sam will "soon be old enough to fight in it...I don't want my son to die. I don't want you to have anything to do with his dying. I don't like Nazis any better than you do. But I don't want a war. I love Sam, and I want him to be happy, in a peaceful world."[83]

Now, in 1944, Sam asks Alex if he had recommended appeasement in his report. Emily says he shouldn't blame his father too much, as nothing anybody had said would have made much difference. Then, somewhat unrealistically, Sam (a slow reader, we have been told) declares: "History is made by the masses of people. One man, or ten men, don't start earthquakes and don't stop them either. Only hero worshippers and ignorant historians think they do. You wrote me that in a letter once. You said it was what Tolstoi meant in *War and Peace*."[84]

Sam continues by telling his parents that he had never felt at home anywhere until he had entered the army, where he met down-to-earth people. At first he had bragged to these friends about the exploits of his father the Ambassador, but then one of them handed him a clipping from a society column describing a dinner party at which Emily, along with a former White Russian, a Dutch banker who had dealings with the Nazis, and a French novelist, was among the guests.

The friend had told Sam: "Glad to be sitting in mud here, Sam, if it helps to make a charming world for your folks."

> "And the rest of those people, they're all old tripe who just live in our country now and pretend they are on the right side. When the trouble came in their countries they sold out their people and beat it quick, and now they make believe they're all for everything good. My God, Sam," he said, "if you come from that you better get away from it fast, because they made the shit we're sitting in."[85]

At first, Sam says, he did not understand why he was so ashamed of that clipping but now he knew. He has already told his parents that his injured leg must be amputated. Now he tells them: "I am ashamed of both of you, and that's the truth. I don't want to be ashamed that way again. I don't like losing my leg. I don't like losing it at all. I'm scared — but everybody's welcome to it as long as it means a little something and helps to bring us out someplace."[86]

Hammett was in the army when Hellman wrote *The Searching Wind*, but Mellen says that he read it and altered some of the dialogue.[87] The latter is unlikely, for in the correspondence to which Mellen refers Hammett is not responding to the play itself but simply agreeing with comments in Hellman's previous letter. He did not receive the completed play until mid-March 1944, by which time, he acknowledged, it would be too late to get any useful advice to Hellman before the play went into "tryouts" in Delaware ahead of its Broadway opening in April. He liked the play, but thought it should have been presented in chronological order, and doubted whether the character of Cassie was really necessary — which was tantamount to saying that the love triangle itself should have been discarded. Moreover:

> The essential frivolity that fucked things up — and I take it that's the real point — isn't *shown*. No answer is provided to the question, "But what else could these people have done?" And there isn't — except, of course by inference — any statement that the kind of people who couldn't do anything else should never have been there.

Nevertheless, he thought "it is in ways the most interesting play you've done, and it's got swell stuff in it, and, as I said before, it's defter than any of the others..."[88]

Although he was probably unable to make changes to the play, this is not to say that he did not influence it. For example, Sam (Hammett's own forename) finding a home in the Army paralleled Hammett's experience, and Hellman would have picked this up from his voluminous correspondence from the Aleutians. But it is also worth noting that Hellman included in this play the points regarding the funding of Mussolini's Fascists and Hitler's Nazis made by Hammett in his draft of the *Watch on the Rhine* screenplay and then excised by Hellman (possibly because what was acceptable on Broadway would have been rejected by Hollywood). And if Hellman had objected to what Mellen calls Hammett's "sententious philosophizing" in his *Watch* screenplay, she inserted her own sermonizing into *The Searching Wind*, particularly via Sam Hazen.

The play was a hit, running for 318 performances.

Another Part of the Forest

Set 20 years before *The Little Foxes*, Hellman's sixth play relates the back-story of the Hubbard family, which is depicted as dysfunctional, held together (then thrown apart before being drawn back together again) by money. The Hubbards are a family only in the biological sense: affection is nowhere to be found, and the two sons are treated as employees by their father; the mother believes that she has lived the past 37 years, i.e. the period of her marriage, in sin.

Marcus Hubbard, the patriarch, became wealthy as a war-profiteer, but now the family store is declining. His profiteering is remembered in the area, and the family is treated by many as outcasts. Son Oscar rides with the Klan and is infatuated with a lumpen prostitute.

As an illustration of how the Hubbards are commonly regarded, when Oscar tells the prostitute Laurette to pretend "nobody knows anything about you, pretend you're just as good as them," she responds, "Pretend I'm as good as anybody called Hubbard?"[89] She later reiterates this by declaring "I'm not better than anybody, but I'm as good as piney wood crooks."[90] But the Hubbards' opinions of each other are barely more positive, Marcus telling the same prostitute, "Oscar is a liar. Always has been...And he steals a little. Nothing much, not enough to be respectable."[91]

Daughter Regina is extravagant, and wants to move to Chicago; she thinks she's in love with John Bagtry, a Confederate veteran who talks of making his fortune by fighting in Brazil, but her older brother Ben, who sees the need to link up with other sources of wealth, wants her to marry banker Horace Giddens.

Thoroughly ruthless, Marcus has no romantic illusions about the antebellum South or the economic system upon which it was based, telling John Bagtry that he never thought the Confederacy would win the Civil War. "Never, from the first foolish talk to the last foolish day."[92] Bagtry's dim-witted sister, Birdie, tells Marcus of John's intention to go to Brazil. "Of course, you know, Mr. Hubbard, the radical people down there are trying to abolish slavery, and ruin the country. John wants to fight for his ideals." Marcus suggests he consider fighting for the other side. "Every man needs to win once in his life." When Bagtree objects that he fights not for slavery but for a "way of life," as if the latter has nothing to do with the economic basis upon which it rests, Marcus does not mince his words. "Well, I disapprove of you. Your people deserved to lose their war and their world. It was a backward world, getting in the way of history. Appalling that you still don't realize it."[93] (With this pronouncement, Marcus comes close to qualifying as one of those "men who see their own time as clearly as if it were history," as Alex puts it in *The Searching Wind*, and this is really a flaw in the play, for if Marcus had really been this clear-sighted he would have known as surely as his son Ben the steps necessary to safeguard the future.)

It is Ben who sees the way forward. The Bagtry family's Lionnet cotton plantation is in decline and the family is unable to make ends meet, and when Birdie comes to Ben to ask for a loan, he quickly sees a way of gaining control of the plantation, and thus plans that his brother Oscar should marry Birdie. He tells his father that Birdie's mother would never have accepted the loan, and so Birdie has written a promissory note; the old lady probably does not have long to live and the estate is in such a parlous state that "the time would come when you'd own the plantation for almost nothing..."[94]

Ben tells his father that the requested loan is for $10,000, planning to retain half of it for his own use. When this is revealed, Marcus says he will not only refuse to make the loan but will cut Ben off. Ben then discovers Marcus's dark secret from his mentally unstable mother: during the war, Marcus had bought salt from the Union forces and sold it to the starving Confederate population for $8 for each small bag; perhaps unwittingly, he had led Union troops to a Southern training camp, resulting in the massacre of 27 Confederate volunteers, then bribing an officer to provide him with passes that would clear him of involvement. Ben uses this to bend Marcus to his will, and at the end of the play he is in the ascendant.

The loan has been agreed and the Bagtry plantation will indeed, as we have seen in *The Little Foxes*, fall into the hands of the Hubbards after the marriage of Oscar and Birdie. Regina, regardless of her feelings for John Bagtry, has agreed to marry banker Horace Giddens before he can discover that she's been sleeping with Bagtry (her incestuous relationship with her father[95] will remain under wraps).

The play ends with Ben Hubbard surveying the changes wrought in the Reconstruction period, just as in *The Little Foxes* he will proclaim that their future will be secured by an alliance with Northern capital. There are, he now says, "Big goings on. Railroads going across, oil, coal. I been telling you, Papa, for ten years. Things are opening up." But not necessarily in the South, objects Oscar, to which Ben replies:

But they are. That's what nobody down here sees or understands. Now you take you, Papa. You were smart in your day and figured out what fools you lived among. But ever since the war you been too busy getting cultured, or getting Southern. A few more years and you'd have been just like the rest of them.[96]

≈

Hellman apparently did not show Hammett this play until she had finished it, but he then told her that there were some plotting problems that needed fixing, something she had realized herself. He therefore went to work on it, but unfortunately we do not know the extent of his contribution,[97] although the strong historical sense would seem to come from him. The Hubbard-Bagtry situation symbolizes the declining Southern aristocracy's need to seek an alliance with the rising merchant class, which will itself be transformed into a capitalist class by its later marriage with northern capital. As Hellman would later deny any such intention with *The Little Foxes*, we may safely assume that it was Hammett who brought this out in the later play also. Some of the sharper dialogue (Marcus's line in which he says Oscar steals, but "not enough to be respectable" springs to mind) may also have come from Hammett.

Opening on November 20, 1946, *Another Part of the Forest* was not as popular as its immediate predecessors, running for 182 performances.

Montserrat

There is no indication that Hammett made any contribution to *Montserrat*, which Hellman adapted from the French play by Emmanuel Robles. Set in the Venezuela of 1812, much of the action concerns the attempts of the Spanish colonial authorities to pressure the young Captain Montserrat, a liberal whose sympathies lie with the Venezuelan *independistas*, into betraying the whereabouts of Simón Bolivar, the leader of the rebels. In Hellman's adaptation, many veiled references to the anti-communist hysteria then building in the USA can be found, but Hellman would have been quite capable of drawing these parallels. The play opened in October 1949 and was not a success, running for just 65 performances.

The Autumn Garden

This play, often described as "Chekhovian,"[98] concerns itself with the abandoned hopes and lowered aspirations of the middle-aged.

Constance Tuckerman, another rich woman down on her luck, owns a summer guest house (once an impressive family mansion) on the Gulf of Mexico, 100 miles out of New Orleans, where her family's main house was sold years ago. This summer, the guests include:

- Nick Denery, a painter, who spent the war in occupied France, and with whom Constance was in love 20 years ago; his wife, Nina, and their maid;
- Mrs. Mary Elllis, her daughter Carrie and her son Frederick, who is (or is he?) "engaged" to Sophie, an 18-year-old French girl whom Constance has "rescued" from poverty in France;
- General Benjamin Griggs, who led his men into Paris, and his wife Rose; their marriage is unhappy, and he wants a divorce;
- Edward Crossman, who has loved Constance for years, but who is stymied by her continuing obsession with Nick.

≈

This is the last of Hellman's plays to which Hammett made a major contribution, although, as was often the case, Hellman did not always acknowledge this. In an interview just before the play opened, she said that the play had taken her nine or ten months to write, but mentioned no involvement by Hammett.[99] By 1965, she was volunteering the information that he had written the speech by Gen. Griggs towards the end of the play.[100]

In her introduction to *The Big Knockover*, Hellman claims that Hammett, having read the play, spoke "sharp and angry, snarling. He spoke as if I had betrayed him." He told her to tear it up because "It's worse than bad — it's half good." She didn't see him for a week. Seven months later, she handed him the rewritten play. On this occasion, he was all praise, telling her that "it's the best play anybody's written in a long time. Maybe longer," although the Griggs speech needed fixing.[101]

This, of course, gives the impression that apart from two critiques, seven months apart, of the whole, Hammett's sole input was the Griggs speech. Mellen come nearer to the truth when she says that for this play Hammett reprised his role as "play doctor."[102]

Martinson has it that Hammett "marked sluggish passages...and he diagrammed the pace of the action" and completely wrote one scene (although, irritatingly, she does not tell us which one).[103] In correspondence with his daughter Jo, Hammett himself certainly gave the impression of close involvement. On September 9, 1950 he wrote that "Lillian's finished the second act of her new play and it reads awfully good."[104]

This indicates that Hellman's account is wrong, unless he is referring to the second act of a later draft; and even in the latter case, this differs from Hellman's claim that she handed him this later draft in completed form. The clincher comes in a letter to Jo four months later, when he wrote:

> We finished the last — and I think practically final — revision of Lily's play yesterday afternoon and I came up here [Hardscrabble Farm], where I hope I'll be allowed to stay till I have to go in for the new school term next week. The play reads pretty doggone swell, though you never really know till you see actors act it out. It hasn't a title yet. At the moment *Some of Us* — my suggestion — looks most likely.[105]

That "we" indicates a lengthy collaboration, and the fact that he says the revision was completed in the afternoon means that he was not speaking of his overnight revision of a single speech. Indeed, Martinson says that Hammett rewrote the Griggs speech during rehearsals.[106]

Although there is something of a consensus that Hammett did indeed write the Griggs speech, Layman points to the "evidence of her working drafts"[107] to claim that he merely reworked it. That this is so is demonstrated by Rollyson, who gives us three versions of that speech, the first two by Hellman, the last by Hammett.[108] In fact it is hard to believe that Hellman wrote any of these versions as, discussing forsaken opportunities, the "frittering away" of a life, they quite clearly all refer to Hammett, and the first version is a better candidate for Hammett's authorship because it refers to the time, ten or fifteen years earlier — precisely the time that Hammett stopped writing on his own account — when Griggs allowed the moment when he should have changed his life to pass him by.

≋

Quite apart from this single speech, there is ample evidence of Hammett's presence — as writer (or play doctor), model or inspiration — throughout the play. When Rose Griggs recalls that her mother-in-law used to say that "Southern women painted a triangle of rouge on their faces as if they were going out to square the hypotenuse,"[109] we detect the hand of Hammett, who maintained a lifelong interest in mathematics. Griggs himself says: "I started with mathematics. Seems strange now, but that's why I went to West Point — wonderful mathematics department. So I got myself two wars instead. I want to go somewhere now and study for a few years, or… Anyway, sit down by myself and think."[110] How like Hammett. That Griggs is based on Hammett is given further verification when his wife complains: "It's very hard to take seriously a man who spends the evening with a Chinese grammar. I'll never forget that winter with the Hebrew phonograph records…"[111] — surely a reference to the fact that, as Hellman often recalled, Hammett was interested in a wide range of subjects, some of which had no practical application.

Ben Griggs is desperate for a divorce, but when his wife Rose is told that she only has a year to live, she pleads with him to remain with her until the end; he tells Crossman that he may have partly welcomed the news, as it "made it easier for me to give up."[112] In like fashion, Hammett was always ready to welcome the opportunity not to write (see Chapter 9).

But if Hammett is Griggs, he is also a good part of Nick Denery, the painter who has not finished a picture in 12 years. Five years earlier, over a seven-month period Hammett had spoken in his correspondence of his intention to write a novel about a painter. Writing to his daughter Mary in October that year he said that he was actually working on the book (although such declarations by Hammett should never be taken as gospel), and that he was toying with The Changed Lock as a title. As the project was about "a middle-aged painter who comes home from the wars," such a title indicates that his subject would find difficulty re-entering his creative world — although, of course, we will probably never know.[113]

If Nick may be based on Hammett's intended creation, he also resembles the man himself, as an exchange between the painter and his wife demonstrates.

> NICK. If I haven't finished every picture I started it's because I'm good enough to know they weren't good enough. All these years you never understood that? I think I will never forgive you for talking that way.
> NINA. Your trouble is that you're an amateur, a gifted amateur. And like all amateurs you have very handsome reasons for what you do not finish — between boats and trains.
> NICK. You have thought that about me, all these years?
> NINA. Yes.
> NICK. Then it was good of you and loyal to pretend you believed in me.[114]

This sounds as if it might have been based on an argument between Hellman and Hammett. Although it is easy to believe that Hellman would be cruel enough to depict Hammett in this manner, it is less easy to believe that she would have the courage to do so while he was alive. It is possible, therefore, that these lines were written by Hammett, amounting to self-flagellation.

Drunk, Nick ends up sleeping on the bed of Sophie, the young French girl, while she takes a chair across the room. When they are discovered in the morning, a mini-scandal erupts. Nick argues with Nina, telling her that she knows this has never happened before.

> NINA. …Nicky, it always confuses you that the fifth time something happens it varies slightly from the second and fourth. No, it never happened in this house before. Cora had a husband and Sylvia wanted one. And this isn't a hotel in Antibes, and Sophie is not a rich Egyptian. And

this time you didn't break your arm on a boat deck and it isn't 1928.[115]

Here, I think, we have another Hellman-Hammett argument, as she had always found his philandering hard to accept, and had philandered herself partly in retaliation. But Hammett would have shrugged off this kind of attack (or accepted it with pride), and thus it is likely that these are Hellman's words.

A jarring note is struck, however, when Sophie suddenly turns blackmailer, threatening to publicly accuse Nick of seduction unless Nina gives her $5,000. When Nina resists, Sophie figuratively holds up a mirror to her:

> You wish to be the kind lady who most honorably stays to discharge — within reason — her obligations. And who goes off, as she has gone off many other times, to make the reconciliation with her husband. How would you and Mr. Denery go on living without such incidents as me? I have been able to give you a second, or a twentieth, honeymoon.[116]

This, it must be said, is the voice of a worldly woman, not an 18-year-old. But quite apart from its lack of realism, this scene introduces a note of melodrama that is completely out of step with the rest of the play.

The charge of melodrama (critics always employed the word pejoratively, often accompanied by the claim that she was aiming for commercial success, regardless of the artistic consequences) had been leveled at Hellman ever since *The Children's Hour*, which ends with a suicide.[117] It is interesting to speculate just how far Hammett was responsible for this. Melodrama had, after all, been his line between 1923 and the mid-1930s, and it is undeniable that those Hellman plays in which he was most closely involved are the most melodramatic of her oeuvre.

Apart from granting Hammett a 15-percent share of her royalties[118] from *The Autumn Garden*, Hellman dedicated the play "To Dash." But it was not a great success, opening in March 1951, lasting for 101 performances and losing $75,000.[119]

The Lark

Here, after a gap of almost five years during which both she and Hammett had suffered from McCarthyism and she had edited a volume of Chekhov's correspondence, Hellman adapted Jean Anouil's play *L'Alouette*, based on the story of Joan of Arc. By this time, she and Hammett were living apart, although they saw each other frequently, and there is no indication that he made any contribution to this adaptation; she recalls that he told her, "I don't think much of this St. Joan business."[120] Unsurprisingly, there are references to the McCarthy period, and it would seem from the following exchange that Hellman saw herself as a Joan, abandoned by the intellectuals who had once stood on the left (a subject to which she would return in her memoir *Scoundrel Time*).

> JOAN. The common people believe in me---
> CAUCHON. They believe in anything. They will follow another leader tomorrow. You are alone, all alone.
> JOAN. I think as I think. You have the right to punish me for it.[121]

The play did well, opening in November 1955 with Julie Harris as Joan[122] and running for 229 performances.

Candide

Again, Hammett had no input into this musical adaptation of Voltaire's satire; indeed, there was hardly room for him, as Hellman would forever after claim that the play, and her writing, had been ruined by an excess of collaborators which included Leonard Bernstein, who wrote the score. The play departs substantially from Voltaire's novella, allowing Hellman to insert contemporary references.

Candide opened on December 1, 1956 and was a flop, closing two months later after just 73 peformances.

Toys in the Attic

Julian Berniers, who left the family home some time earlier, is worshipped by his spinster sisters, Carrie and Anna. His search for a fortune has, however, come to naught, as the shoe factory he bought with his wife's money has gone under.

Now he's home again and mysteriously expects to come into a small fortune. He spends profligately on his two poor sisters and his wife Lily, only to find they no longer want what he has provided. He loses everything when Lily, fed by Carrie, informs the person from whom he's expecting to make the money that he and the man's wife (a former lover) have been in cahoots; he receives a severe beating into the bargain. Restored to poverty, he now finds that the two sisters dote upon him once more.

≈

The plot of *Toys*, Hellman conceded, came from a suggestion made by Hammett, although she did not, as was his idea, focus on Julian.[123] The play is obviously strongly biographical in that it was her father Max who had bought a shoe factory and then lost it; Max, like Julian, had enjoyed the devotion of his two sisters. The profligacy, however, is surely based on that trait in Hammett. Mellen detects no significant contribution by Hammett, although she notes that Hellman "felt insecure without his presence and approval."[124]

That approval appears to have been withheld, for when he had read it he pronounced it terrible and in need of rewriting.[125] Worse was to come. At the opening night celebration at the Plaza Hotel, Hammett let her have both barrels: "After all I've been through with you, after all I've taught you, you turn out this piece of shit!" Mellen, basing her account on the recollections of editor Richard Giroux, one of the guests, says that Hammett "named specific speeches, specific scenes. He liked none of it. Unconcerned that he was embarrassing their guests, he kept up his tirade for a long time."[126]

It would certainly appear from this that Hammett's contribution was indeed minimal. The public tended to take Hellman's part, and the play, opening in February 1960, ran for 464 performances, making it her second biggest hit after *The Children's Hour*.

After Hammett's death in January 1961, Hellman wrote only one more play. *My Mother, My Father and Me* (based on Burt Blechman's novel *How Much?*) is quite amusing on paper but on stage, despite a cast including Ruth Gordon and Walter Matthau, survived only 17 performances.

NOTES

1 This tendency is particularly noticeable in the treatment of Hellman, who elicits the bile of several writers for her silence regarding Stalin's "terror" of the 1930s, the Soviet role in the Spanish Civil War, and the Soviet-German Non-Aggression Pact of 1939 — matters which will be discussed in Chapter 7. Hellman's notoriously unreliable memoirs, and in particular her claim never to have been a member of the Communist Party, may also influence the views taken of her abilities and achievements as a dramatist.
2 William F. Nolan, "Introduction," Dashiell Hammett, *Nightmare Town*, eds. Kirby McCauley, Martin H. Greenberg, Ed Gorman (New York: Vintage Crime/Black Lizard, 1999), x.
3 Dorothy Gallagher, *Lillian Hellman: An Imperious Life* (New Haven and London: Yale University Press, 2014), 49.
4 Deborah Martinson, *Lillian Hellman: A Life with Foxes and Scoundrels* (Berkeley: Counterpoint, 2005), 96.
5 Joan Mellen, *Hellman and Hammett: The Legendary Passion of Lillian Hellman and Dashiell Hammett* (New York: Harper Collins, 1996), 83.
6 Bill Moyers, "Lillian Hellman: The Great Playwright Candidly Reflects on a Long, Rich Life," National Educational Television, April 1974, in Lillian Hellman, *Conversations with Lillian Hellman*, ed. Jackson R. Bryer, (Jackson and London: University Press of Mississippi,1986), 147, 152.
7 Peter Adam, "Unfinished Woman," *The Listener,* February 8, 1979; *Conversations with Lillian Hellman,* 225.
8 Marilyn Berger, "Profile: Lillian Hellman," KERA-TV, Dallas-Fort Worth, April 1981; *Conversations with Lillian Hellman,* 240.
9 Jo Hammett, *Dashiell Hammett: A Daughter Remembers,* ed. Richard Layman with Julie M.Rivett (New York: Carroll & Graf Publishers, 2001), 13.
10 Harry Gilroy, "The Bigger the Lie," *New York Times,* December 14, 1952; *Conversations with Lillian Hellman,* 25.
11 John Phillips and Anne Hollander, "The Art of the Theater 1: Lillian Hellman — An Interview," *Paris Review,* 33 (Winter-Spring 1965); *Conversations with Lillian Hellman,* 57.
12 Lewis Funke, "Interview with Lillian Hellman," *Playwrights Talk About Writing: 12 Interviews with Lewis Funke* (Chicago: Dramatic

Publishing Co., 1975). Interview conducted in 1968; *Conversations with Lillian Hellman*, 96.
13 "Lillian Hellman Reflects upon the Changing Theater," *Dramatists Guild Quarterly*, 7 (Winter 1970); *Conversations with Lillian Hellman*, 126.
14 See, for example, Mellen, 66.
15 Lillian Hellman, *Pentimento*, in *Three* (Boston: Little, Brown, 1979), 455.
16 Mellen, 192.
17 William F. Nolan, *Dashiell Hammett: A Life at the Edge* (London: Arthur Barker, 1983), 145.
18 Vince Emery, commentary, Dashiell Hammett, *Lost Stories*, ed. Vince Emery (San Francisco: Vince Emery Productions, 2005), 289.
19 Layman, commentary, Dashiell Hammett, *Selected Letters of Dashiell Hammett, 1921-1960*, ed. Richard Layman with Julie M. Rivett (Washington D.C: Counterpoint, 2001), 59.
20 Mellen, 67-68, 69.
21 Ibid., 71.
22 Lillian Hellman, *The Children's Hour*, in *The Collected Plays* (Boston, Toronto: Little, Brown and Company, 1972), 7.
23 Ibid., 20.
24 Nolan, *Dashiell Hammett: A Life on the Edge*, 157.
25 Lillian Hellman, *Days to Come*, in *The Collected Plays*, 107.
26 Ibid., 114.
27 Ibid.,128.
28 Lucius Beebe, "An Adult's Hour is Miss Hellman's Next Effort," *New York Herald Tribune*, December 13, 1936; *Conversations with Lillian Hellman*, 5.
29 Martinson, 114, 116, 117, 119. Hellman says that the trip to Ohio was an "atmosphere tour" in which she saw "what the people looked like and how they spoke." See the Beebe interview, 5. Be that as it may, she also noted details of a brush factory, recording details of wages and conditions, and the early drafts of the play concentrated on the strike rather than the Rodman marriage. See Carl Rollyson, *Lillian Hellman: Her Legend and her Legacy* (New York: St. Martin's Press, 1988), 91.
30 Mellen, 119, 120.
31 Rollyson, 95.

32 Gallagher, 51, 52.
33 Mellen, 117.
34 Ibid., 121.
35 Martinson, 116.
36 Rollyson, 95.
37 Lillian Hellman, *Days to Come*, in *The Collected Plays*, 80.
38 Dashiell Hammett, "Two Sharp Knives," *Crime Stories and Other Writings* (New York: The Library of America, 2001), 847.
39 Hellman, *Days to Come*, in *Collected Plays*, 127; Hammett, *Red Harvest*, in *Five Complete Novels*, (New York: Avenel Books, 1980) 65; Dashiell Hammett, *The Dain Curse*, in *Five Complete Novels*, 197.
40 Mellen, 64.
41 Hellman, *Days to Come* in *The Collected Plays*, 108.
42 Mellen, 119-120.
43 Lillian Hellman, *Days to Come*, in *The Collected Plays*, 114.
44 Ibid., 124.
45 Hellman, *Days to Come*, in *Four Plays by Lillian Hellman* (New York: The Modern Library, 1942), 126, 132.
46 Martinson, 119.
47 Mellen, 276.
48 Ibid., 167, 168.
49 Emery, commentary, Dashiell Hammett, *Lost Stories*, 298. Regardless of the extent of Hammett's contribution, it cannot be disputed that Hellman, as often was the case, was almost encyclopedic in her research, amassing 115 typewritten pages of notes regarding US life in the last two decades of the 19th century. See Rollyson, 123.
50 John Phillips and Anne Hollander, *Conversations with Lillian Hellman*, 69.
51 Lillian Hellman, *Pentimento*, in *Three*, 472.
52 Mellen, 133, 136, 149. Kessler-Harris — Alice Kessler-Harris, *A Difficult Woman: The Challenging Life and Times of Lillian Hellman* (New York: Bloomsbury Press, 2012), 98 — agrees that this was the play in which Hammett was most involved, while Gallagher, 95, has Hellman say that Hammett had "given" *The Little Foxes* to her, although she dates this in 1946, whereas *Foxes* was produced in 1939. Possibly she is thinking of *Another Part of the Forest*, the Hubbard prequel which *was* produced in 1946.

53 Lillian Hellman, *The Little Foxes* in *The Collected Plays*, 195, 171.
54 Ibid., 176, 199.
55 Ibid., 141, 142.
56 Ibid., 197.
57 Lewis Funke, *Conversations with Lillian Hellman*, 101.
58 Lillian Hellman, *Watch on the Rhine* in The *Collected Plays*, 250.
59 Ibid., 253.
60 Ibid., 260-61.
61 Martinson, 171.
62 Mellen, 172.
63 Richard G. Stern, "An Interview with Lillian Hellman," May 21, 1958; *Conversations with Lillian Hellman*, 34.
64 Mellen, 173.
65 Ibid., 174.
66 Diane Johnson, *The Life of Dashiell Hammett* (US title *Dashiell Hammett: A Life*), (London: Picador, 1985), 163. Again, Hellman's research and preparation were prodigious, amounting to 100,000 words in notes. See Rollyson, 165.
67 Lillian Hellman, *Watch on the Rhine* in *The Collected Plays*, 238. Quite why Hammett should take a dig at Raymond Chandler is, however, anyone's guess, as they had only met once and Hammett seemed to have a good opinion of him.
68 Jan Albert, "Sweetest Smelling Baby in New Orleans," 1975; *Conversations with LillianHellman*, 171.
69 Martinson, 173.
70 Layman, commentary, Dashiell Hammett, *Selected Letters*, 176.
71 Mellen, 174.
72 Ibid., 178.
73 Ibid., 179.
74 Ibid., 184.
75 Ibid., 179.
76 Ibid., 174.
77 Rollyson, 191.
78 Lillian Hellman, *The Searching Wind* in *The Collected Plays*, 286.
79 Ibid., 292.
80 Ibid., 296.
81 Ibid., 302.
82 Ibid., 311.

83 Ibid., 315.
84 Ibid., 321-22.
85 Ibid., 323-24.
86 Ibid., 324.
87 Mellen, 215.
88 Dashiell Hammett to Lillian Hellman, March 13-15, 1944; *Selected Letters*, 301-302.
89 Lillian Hellman, *Another Part of the Forest* in *The Collected Plays*, 361.
90 Ibid., 362.
91 Ibid., 371.
92 Lillian Hellman, *Another Part of the Forest* in *The Collected Plays*, 367.
93 Ibid., 367, 368.
94 Ibid., 349.
95 See ibid., 378, 379 for this revelation.
96 Ibid., 401, 402.
97 See Mellen, 252-254.
98 See, for example, Kessler-Harris, 176-177.
99 Ward Morehouse, "*Garden* Pleases Miss Hellman," *New York World-Telegram and Sun*, March 3, 1951; *Conversations with Lillian Hellman*, 23.
100 John Phillips and Anne Hollander, *Conversations with Lillian Hellman*, 64.
101 Lillian Hellman, "Introduction," *The Big Knockover: Selected Stories and Short Novels*, ed. Lillian Hellman (New York: Vintage Books, 1989), xiv, xv. She gives the same account in *An Unfinished Woman*; see *Three*, 287-288.
102 Mellen, 273.
103 Martinson, 244, 245.
104 Dashiell Hammett to Josephine Marshall Hammett, September 9, 1950; *Selected Letters*, 543.
105 Ibid., 549.
106 Martinson, 245.
107 Richard Layman, *Shadow Man: The Life of Dashiell Hammett* (New York and London: Harcourt Brace Jovanovich/Bruccoli Clark, 1981), 218.
108 Rollyson, 299-300.
109 Lillian Hellman, *The Autumn Garden* in *The Collected Plays*, 446.
110 Ibid., 477.

111 Ibid., 476
112 Ibid., 542.
113 See Dashiell Hammett to Mary Hammett, October 31, 1945; *Selected Letters*, 454.
114 Lillian Hellman, *The Autumn Garden* in *The Collected Plays*, 519.
115 Ibid., 532.
116 Ibid., 538.
117 See Kessler-Harris, 87-100 for a discussion of this aspect of Hellman's work.
118 Emery, commentary, Dashiell Hammett, *Lost Stories*, 335.
119 Mellen, 278.
120 Ibid., 316.
121 Lillian Hellman, *The Lark* in *The Collected Plays*, 582.
122 Martinson makes a major blooper by giving this credit to Julie Christie, who would have been 15 at the time. See Martinson, 275-276. This is no mere typo, as the error is repeated in a picture caption and the index.
123 Lewis Funke, *Conversations with Lillian Hellman*, 103; Mellen, 328.
124 Mellen, 329.
125 Ibid., 330.
126 Ibid., 334.

6   Foggy glimpses

For a number of reasons, Dashiell Hammett was an unlikely candidate for membership of a communist party. While, during this period, left-wing writers would have generally disdained to write for the reactionary, anti-labor Hearst press, Hammett, although he would make the occasional disparaging comment about it, seemingly had few reservations about making money from this source. The comic strip *Secret Agent X-9*, for which Hammett supplied the text, was written at the suggestion of, and published by (in his King Features Syndicate), William Randolph Hearst.[1] Commencing in mid-1936, the Hearst syndicate reprinted Hammett's earlier stories.[2]

In early 1937, around the time Hammett is thought to have joined the CPUSA, Hearst offered him $50,000 to write a screen story for Marion Davies, the press baron's lover, but this was asking too much even of Hammett, and he turned it down.[3]

Then, of course, we must consider the fact that he had formerly been a Pinkerton agent, and that his duties had possibly included strikebreaking. This was widely known, his former employment having been used by his publishers as an indication of the authenticity of his work. Of itself, this would not have necessarily debarred him from communist party membership, as long as he had drawn the appropriate lessons from the experience, and it is probably safe to assume, therefore, that the CPUSA would have required proof of his reformed character if it was to admit him into membership. The problem is, of course, that this was the only aspect of his character that *was* reformed.

It must surely be the case that few communist parties in the world would have welcomed someone with a lifestyle like Hammett's. During the Hollywood years, he earned an enormous amount of money and spent it extravagantly, gambled or gave it away, or loaned it with no realistic expectation of repayment. While he seems to have made an attempt to remember his family obligations, little of his largesse came their way, and in 1932 his wife Jose was reduced to writing what amounted to a begging letter to Alfred Knopf, Hammett's publisher.[4] He lived in classy hotels like the Roosevelt and the Knickerbocker; even while working as a script doctor, he spent large parts of his life at the Brown Derby and the Clover Club.[5] When circumstances permitted, he employed a cook and valet/chauffeur. As early as 1931, however, he contemplated suicide after drinking heavily and falling into a depression. When Hellman asked him why he was contemplating ending his life, all he could say was that he had a "feeling that everything was over."[6]

In 1934, in Hollywood to write *After the Thin Man*, Hammett rented a six-bedroom penthouse apartment at the Beverly Wilshire for $2,000 a month.[7] As the money went out faster than it came in, Hammett was often in debt; Layman cites Hellman as recalling that at one stage he owed the Wilshire $11,000, and the store where he bought his booze another $1,300.[8]

Nor did such extravagance cease after the time he is thought to have joined the CPUSA: after MGM offered him $40,000 for the third *Thin Man* film in September 1937, he moved back into the six-bedroom penthouse at the Beverly Wilshire. Nolan says that Hammett would give his barber, who attended the hotel, $30 for his morning shave — more than the man made in a week in his shop.[9] In early 1938, having fallen off the wagon after 14 months, he was found in a state of collapse at the Wilshire (where he was seriously in arrears) and, assisted by the Hacketts, the husband and wife writing team, was flown to Hellman in New York, who had him admitted to hospital, where he was found to be suffering a nervous breakdown.[10] In May that year, his doctors found that he had a "definite fear of insanity."[11]

Hammett is often referred to as an alcoholic, although, given his ability to give up drink for extended periods (and, in 1948, permanently), he was obviously not clinically dependent upon alcohol. He was, however, a notorious and chronic drunkard, and the drinking would lead to other problems — vandalism, for example. On a drunken night out with screenwriter Nunnally Johnson in Florida in 1933, Hammett smashed the windows of a department store.[12] In the autumn of 1936, he rented a house in Princeton, and by the time he returned to Hollywood the following year (at the request of his Princeton neighbors, according to Layman[13]), the place was in disrepair and the landlord was suing him for rent arrears.[14]

It was quite probably his consumption of alcohol that led him to violence against women. In 1932, actress Elise de Viane was awarded $2,500 (she had sought $35,000) in her assault case against Hammett.[15] At a party early in their relationship, Hammett knocked Hellman to the floor with a punch to the jaw; she was sometimes seen with bruises. "The violence," say Mellen, "was always there as a threat should she step out of line or say too much."[16] In 1935, he asked Hellman for $5,000, which she gave him. A week later, he was broke again, and when she asked him what he had done with the money he hit her and told her he had squandered it on a prostitute.[17]

Hammett visited prostitutes often, and paid for it with several bouts of gonorrhea. When the studio sent secretary Mildred Lewis to Hammett's rented house on Bel Air Road in the hope that he might actually produce some work, she often found herself with little to do as he slept late and often summoned prostitutes — black and Oriental by preference — from Madame Lee Francis's brothel.[18] Even after re-enlisting in the Army, before assignment to the Aleutians Hammett would have a soldier drive him into New York at weekends so he could visit "his favorite Harlem whorehouse."[19]

The sex in the Hammett-Hellman relationship lasted a decade, perhaps a little longer, but they were never monogamous, each taking other partners at will, and in this sense they were more bohemian than communist, perhaps looking upon their sexual adventures as a form of "rebellion" — but one which, of course, left the structures of bourgeois society intact. In his *An American Testament*, describing the 1920s but written in the 1930s, Joseph Freeman discusses a German woman called Greta:

> Had she been a worker, she would have had the discipline of the proletariat in the rapidly shifting conflict of our times. But she was a bohemian, and her revenge upon the bourgeois world from which she had come and which had repudiated her was to abandon its virtues along with its vices.[20]

Freeman talks of those bohemians in Greenwich Village who made a fetish of sex.

> Now it began to appear as though the bohemian, poor in material goods, insignificant in politics, made a fetish of sex partly out of a desire to absorb the culture of the "best" people. The ruling class of each society determines that society's culture, and the intellectual was voicing the decaying values of the Western bourgeoisie. In the Village I had observed that to imitate Mrs. Bloom's free and easy conduct was not merely a pleasure, but a mark of intellectual distinction; it showed a woman was "advanced," superior to the timid little girls who clung to their mothers' aprons in Flatbush or Iowa. It was disturbing to find the same type occasionally in the Party, however rarely. Of course, one could reflect that the socialist movement — as the alert Bernard Shaw had long ago observed — attracts not only those who are too good for the old order, but those who are not good enough.[21]

There was, surely, a strong bohemian strain in the behavior of Hammett and Hellman, and the breadth of the gap between this and "socialist" conduct would become apparent in 1944 when Hellman began an affair with John Melby, whom she met in the US Embassy in Moscow. Melby was a career State Department man, an anti-communist who in 1950 (he was by then officer in charge of Philippine affairs) led a mission to the Philippines, setting out the military requirements for the Philippine government's conduct of operations against the communist-led Huk Rebellion. Ironically, Melby then fell victim to McCarthyism due to his relationship with Hellman and was dismissed.[22]

In his personal behavior, there were often signs that Hammett's sympathy for lesser mortals lacked consistency. When Hammett and Hellman took Jo shopping with them, Hellman would snap at the sales assistants while a tolerant Hammett looked on.[23] At a party in the 1930s, Hammett advised a woman to leave Nathaniel West alone as "he hasn't got a pot to piss in"[24] — a curious thing for a supposed communist to have said. And his racism had not been completely eradicated: in 1931, having intended to repay a loan to Albert Samuels, his former employer, Hammett instead squandered the money on a week-long party and therefore asked Samuels for a further loan, sending his black, uniformed chauffeur with a note reading, "Give the jig the bundle. Dashiell Hammett."[25]

Doubtless there were American communists who shared some of these behavioral traits, but it must be doubted whether someone displaying *all of them* would have either qualified for, or even sought, membership in a communist party. Some such applicants were, we know, rejected: according to screenwriter Ring Lardner Jr., who would become one of the Hollywood Ten, towards the end of his life the alcoholic F. Scott Fitzgerald considered himself a communist but was thought by the CPUSA to be "too unreliable" for membership.[26] Mellen attempts to explain his extravagance by saying that his sudden wealth "burned guilt into his working-class soul." But it is difficult to see how working-class guilt could have been assuaged by lavishing jewelry and expensive clothes, including a mink coat, on Hellman — which is what Mellen then tells us he did.[27] For someone identifying with the cause of the working class, such guilt should, surely, have been generated not so much by the *receipt* of such huge sums of money but by the way it was used so self-indulgently at a time when many millions of US workers were out of work.

≋

Hammett's dissolute lifestyle was such that one is tempted to conclude that, although he eventually embraced the communist cause, formal party membership was unlikely. On this question Lillian Hellman is less than helpful.

In *An Unfinished Woman*, Hellman says of Hammett: "I do not know if he was a member of the Communist Party and I never asked him."[28]

In *Scoundrel Time*, she enlarges on this claim:

> I am fairly sure that Hammett joined the Communist Party in 1937 or 1938. I do not know because I never asked, and if I had asked would not have been answered, and my not asking, knowing there would be no answer, was typical of our relationship. I did not join the Party, although mild overtures were made by Earl Browder and the Party theorist, V. J. Jerome.[29]

These claims are not only false but ludicrous: in a draft statement to the House Un-American Activities Committee in 1952 (this part of the statement was not used), Hellman had admitted joining the CPUSA "in 1938 with little thought as to the serious step I was taking."[30] She claimed that she "stopped attending meetings or taking part in Communist Party activities in the latter part of 1940 and severed all connections with the Party."[31] Far from severing "all connections," however, in 1944 she attended Paul Robeson's 46th birthday party with Earl Browder, general secretary of the CPUSA.[32] As she was a party member, her suggestion that she did not know if Hammett was also a member, particularly as he would probably have been in the same party group, is distinctly unconvincing.

The whole problem with Hellman's testimony on this matter is that she wrote her memoirs after Hammett's death, at a time when it was no longer fashionable to have been a member of the CPUSA. She sought to distance herself from the party, portraying her role as one of a noble and disinterested defender of democracy, while romanticizing the figure of Hammett as the committed Marxist and stern teacher.

When did the transformation in Hammett's consciousness occur? Did he join the party? If so, when?

As we saw in Chapter 3, it is unlikely that the life-changing event that Hellman claims for Hammett — the offer in 1917 of $5,000 to murder labor leader Frank Little — ever happened, as he does not appear to have been anywhere near Montana at the time. Nolan's version of this claimed event looks convincing, but he relies solely on Hellman's *Scoundrel Time*.[33] It is likely, therefore, that this incident must be consigned to the realm of mythology. However, Hammett may have been involved in strike-breaking activity on behalf of Anaconda in 1920, and this activity could well have turned his stomach and set his mind on an anti-capitalist path. But it did not make him a Marxist.

We saw in Chapter 2 that while some of Hammett's short stories and novelettes could be interpreted as denunciations of a corrupt system, there was little to mark them as Marxist, and when he branched out to deal with foreign political situations his anti-imperialism was marred by racism. Then there was the nihilism of "The Hunter" which, one suspects, most accurately described Hammett's outlook at this time.

The novels followed but, as we have seen, anyone seeking signs of a steady development of a left-wing viewpoint, or the sharpening of Hammett's analysis of capitalist society, comes away disappointed. While it cannot be disputed that *Red Harvest* is an anti-capitalist novel, it is not "Marxist" — and could not be so for the simple reason that Hammett was not yet a Marxist. *The Dain Curse* was a complete failure as a novel and contained no hint of left thinking, but buried in that book is a passage that perhaps illustrates the state of Hammett's mind in this period, as the Op tells Gabrielle:

> "Nobody thinks clearly, no matter what they pretend. Thinking's a dizzy business, a matter of catching as many of those foggy glimpses as you can and fitting them together the best you can. That's why people hang so tight to their beliefs and opinions; because, compared to the haphazard way in which they're arrived at, even the goofiest opinion seems wonderfully clear, sane, and self-evident. And if you let it get away from you, then you've got to dive back into that foggy muddle to wangle yourself out another to take its place."[34]

Hammett, it is worth remembering, was a drunken philanderer during this period (and would remain so beyond it) who gave no evidence of believing in anything. Here, though, is an indication that he *wanted* to believe in something that would give his life meaning, and that he was catching a few "foggy glimpses" of it.

But progress was slow. *The Maltese Falcon*, with its Flitcraft parable, provides evidence of a persistent nihilism. Nolan says that after this book Hammett "no longer believed that the private detective made a realistic protagonist. As his view of the world continued to darken,

Hammett became convinced that the problems of society could not be dealt with one-to-one."[35] This is possible, but where is the evidence? It is doubtful that Hammett's thinking had developed to such an extent even at that late stage. Nevertheless, in *The Glass Key* Hammett seems to be seeking meaning, but this proves to be a false dawn, as the final novel, *The Thin Man,* is pure escapism.

Might the reported suicide of Wynant, the thin man who bears a physical resemblance to Hammett, in Allentown, that bed of labor unrest, signal the demise of the thriller-writer and the arrival of a new, socially active Dashiell Hammett? This is possibly what he intended, but by this time he was in Hollywood, writing for big money, his screen stories devoid of social content. Yes, he was probably struggling towards belief, looking for a reason to live, but it was not until the mid-1930s at the earliest that he found something. According to Layman, "Communism provided a more or less formal expression of values that Hammett believed in well before he joined the Party in the mid-1930s."[36] This is plausible, but apart from the anti-capitalist tone of *Red Harvest* and a few stories, and the jaundiced view of US society evident in the remaining novels, there is no hard evidence of these previously-held "values." It would probably be more accurate to say that Hammett, when he finally got to grips with it, found Marxist thought intellectually satisfying, and saw communist practice as "hardboiled" enough to do the job that a lone detective was incapable of doing. Here, finally, was something he would "hang onto." Even then, however, he would continue to live his personal life as a nihilist, an individualist.

≈

How did Hammett come to Marxism? Did Lillian Hellman introduce him to it?

Richard Layman believes that Hammett's political involvement came about "largely, though not exclusively, through Hellman's influence," and that she championed the left-wing causes to which they signed up "more vociferously than he did.[37] To what extent, then, was Hammett brought to the left by Hellman, with whom he started a relationship in November 1930? How committed was Hellman herself to left-wing causes?

There is, in fact, scant evidence that Hellman was politically involved before she met Hammett, and what little exists is unreliable. Mellen claims that Hellman had joined the John Reed Club, a cultural organization formed in 1929 under CPUSA influence, as does Emery, who also tends to the view that Hellman exerted a political influence on Hammett.[38] But although Mellen makes this claim on two occasions, she provides no source, and it is probable that Emery's own claim is derived from her book. Other biographers make no mention of the John Reed Club.

In *An Unfinished Woman*, Hellman claims to have read Lenin in her early twenties, due to her meeting with Soviet poet Vladimir Mayakovsky in New York.[39] Mayakovsky certainly visited New York in 1925,[40] when Hellman would have been 20 and completely unknown, although at that time she was working for the publisher Boni and Liveright, and so it is just possible that she had met him on the publishing circuit. Significantly, however, none of her biographers mentions a meeting with Mayakovsky; Hellman was keeping a diary as late as 1924, as Mellen cites it, and one would have thought that a meeting with Mayakovsky would have merited an entry, even if it were the only one for 1925. Clearly, the meeting may be a Hellman invention, and so, therefore, may be her claim to have read Lenin as a result of the encounter (and, it must be said, the reading of Lenin usually comes after the way has been prepared by a study of Marx and Engels, or of a popularization of their works).

Did Hellman become politically active as the Depression wrought havoc throughout the USA? Kessler-Harris finds no evidence that in 1933, a particularly dire year, "she and her friends ever talked about the political issues of the day;" she further finds that in the early 1930s "Hellman seems at first to have been uninvolved in the political scene."[41]

In her first memoir, Hellman would date what she termed her "radicalism" from 1937 when, returning from a visit to Spain (where, she claims, she met Dolores Ibarurri, "La Pasionaria," although she gives no account of either the meeting or the woman), she spent a few weeks in Paris and then traveled to London, which is where she says her radicalism began, although she does not say what, apart from mulling over her Spanish visit, led to this development. "It saddens me now," she would write, "to admit that my political convictions were never very radical, in the true, best, serious sense. Rebels seldom make good revolutionaries, perhaps because organized action, even union with other people, is not possible for them...In the next few years, I put aside most other books for Marx and Engels, Lenin, Saint-Simon, Hegel, Feuerbach."[42] One wonders why, if she was reading the first three, she bothered with the others; and, of course, she apparently forgets this claim when, seventy-odd pages later, she talks of having read Lenin in the 1920s.

In *Pentimento*, her second volume of memoirs, Hellman contradicts this chronology somewhat by, in her account of her involvement with her childhood friend "Julia," claiming that during this same European trip she had smuggled $50,000, concealed in a hat, into Germany and handed it to the anti-fascist activist in a Berlin restaurant. For a Jewish woman to have undertaken such an assignment in 1937 would certainly have betokened commitment. Even so, she writes that "I do not know when I understood what" during the early to mid-thirties, although the rise of European fascism "had shaken many of us into radicalism, or something we called radicalism..." Then, "by 1935 or 1936...new assessments had to be made fast about what one believed and what one was going to do about it...The new radicalism was what I had always been looking for."[43] The clear implication here is that her arrival at "radicalism" predated by a year or two the conversion she had earlier claimed to have occurred in London. Twenty pages later, she then throws doubt on this by having "Julia" write to her after the visit to Spain: "Good girl to go to Spain. Did it convince you?"

The problem, of course, is that there never was a "Julia," and Hellman never smuggled money into Berlin. Although Martinson accepts the essential truth of the tale,[44] other biographers have not been so charitable. Mellen, for example, consigns the whole story to the realm of fiction. Whereas Hellman claimed to have made an earlier, 1934 visit to see Julia in Vienna, where she was supposedly both a student-patient of Freud and an anti-Fascist campaigner, Mellen cites producer Herman Shumlin who found that this was simply impossible, "so consistently had he been aware in 1934 of Lillian Hellman's whereabouts."[45]

"Julia" seems, in fact, to have been based on Muriel Gardiner who, while she had been an anti-fascist in Vienna, had, unlike "Julia," not lost first her leg, then her life, to the Nazis. Gardiner wrote to Hellman after the publication of the latter's *Pentimento*, pointing to the similarities between her own life and that of "Julia," and mentioning that she and Hellman had a mutual friend in Wolf Schwabacher,[46] so it is probable that Hellman had heard Gardiner's story from the latter. Hellman claimed never to have received this letter.

There are, however, other indications that "Julia" was fiction. Hellman claims that Julia "went away to Oxford" in "our nineteenth year" (they were supposedly the same age), which would have been in 1923. She further claims to have visited her the following year, finding that although Julia was "invited everywhere in Oxford and London...the only names I remember her speaking of with respect were J. D. Bernal and J. B. S. Haldane," both scientists and both Marxists. The problem here is that Haldane had left Oxford in 1922, at least a year before Hellman has Julia arriving there. In 1924, Bernal was undertaking research at the Davy Faraday Laboratory at the Royal Institution in London, and while it is not impossible that "Julia" may have found her way there, it is unlikely.

There is a further problem with Hellman's 1937 timetable. According to her account, she left for Europe on the *Normandie* in August — probably August 25[47] — and, although the purpose of her visit was to attend a theatre festival in Moscow, she first spent "a fine time, one of the best of my life,"[48] in Paris, where she was approached by an emissary from Julia. Then she entrained for Moscow, via Berlin and her meeting with Julia, whom she says she met in October.[49]

After the Moscow festival, she spent "a few weeks" in Prague[50] before returning to Paris, where Otto Simon (one of the many pseudonyms of Otto Katz, a Comintern representative whom, as we will see, she had already met in Hollywood) persuaded her to visit Spain, where a diary entry places her on October 13.[51] Clearly, that would have been impossible if she had been in Berlin in October, en route for Moscow. The picture is further muddied by a letter from Hammett dated September 9, which he concludes with: "I hope and imagine you had a swell time in Russia,"[52] a clear implication that the Moscow festival had been and gone by the time of her claimed meeting with "Julia." The festival had, in fact, been in September, as a report in *Time* refers to it having taken place over three weeks during that month.[53] If Hellman had stayed for the whole festival, she obviously would not have had time to spend "a few weeks" in Prague before travelling to Paris and turning up in Spain on October 13.

It is, thus, difficult to separate fact from fiction in Hellman's memoirs,[54] but there is certainly no evidence that she introduced Hammett to Marxism.

≈

But might the boot have been on the other foot?

According to Mellen, it was Hammett who introduced Hellman to the writings of Engels,[55] and Gallagher says that one of Hammett's attractions for the young Hellman was "the politics she soon came to share with him."[56] Hellman herself gives the impression that Hammett was ahead of her, as when she says, "I would test my reading on Dash, who had years before, in his usual thorough fashion, read all the books I was reading, and a great many more," and that

> a woman who was never to be committed was facing a man who already was. Socialist belief had become a way of life and, although he was highly critical of many Marxist doctrines and their past and present practitioners, he shrugged them off. I was trying, without knowing it, to crack his faith, sensed I couldn't do it, and was, all at one time, respectful, envious and angry.[57]

The impression given here — of a Hammett who has long ago absorbed the classics of Marxism — is completely misleading. It was Howard Bay, Hellman's stage manager, who remembered that Hammett had given her Engels to read. "She did her best," says Rollyson, "but Bay could see that she had little interest in such material."[58] The earliest Hammett could have presented Hellman with Engels was 1939, as that was the year she first knew Bay.[59] If Hammett had been a Marxist of long standing, it is hardly likely that he would have waited a decade before providing his partner with reading material. It is therefore safe to assume that Hammett's own "conversion" had been fairly recent.

In this regard, it is interesting to note that in the spring of 1936 Hammett appeared to be researching labor matters. Living at the Madison Hotel in New York, he hired Eleanor Wolff as secretary, but she recalls that, as Hammett was not writing, she had little to do apart from bring him books from the New York Public Library.⁶⁰ Says Mellen:

> One book by Allan Pinkerton he wanted was *Strikers, Communists, Tramps and Detectives*. Another volume was called *Two Evilisms* [sic]*: Pinkertonism & Anarchism*, "by a cowboy detective who knows, as he spent twenty-two years in the inner circle of Pinkerton's Detective Agency." He wanted to know about strikes and lockouts, and union organizing and blacklisting, and about the sin of spying on workers. The Pullman strike. The Homestead strike.⁶¹

Why would he have been conducting this research if he had first-hand experience of Pinkertonism? One possibility is that his experience, particularly of strikebreaking, was rather less extensive than he had previously claimed. Another is that his reading was intended to inform his work on Hellman's *Days to Come*, which would be staged in mid-December that year. A third is that as he was now drawn to left-wing causes, he was seeking a deeper understanding of the "Pinkertonism" in which he had played a part. If so, this is an indication of just how late his commitment to the left came.

It is indisputable that both Hammett and Hellman had become radicalized by 1936-1937, and it is probable that the Spanish Civil War had a great influence on their thinking, as Republican forces, aided by the Soviet Union and progressive volunteers who formed the International Brigades, attempted to prevent a fascist takeover by General Francisco Franco, who was supported and supplied by both Italy and Germany. J. A. Zumoff reckons that "the radicalization of the 1930s — which propelled many other writers to socialism — probably affected Hammett more than the murder" of Frank Little, as claimed by Hellman.⁶²

But did Hammett join the CPUSA? Mellen mentions a 1936 dinner at Hellman's home, where a guest was V. J. Jerome, the CP leader responsible for cultural affairs. His presence, claims Mellen, "reveals that Hellman and Hammett were already Party faithful," although in fact it does nothing of the kind, as Jerome, given his role, would have welcomed the opportunity to socialize with two prominent members of the artistic community, regardless of whether they were yet party members.⁶³ We are told by Kessler-Harris that screenwriter and CP member Allen Boretz saw Hammett at a meeting in 1937, noting that he "stood in a corner and said very little...It was a Marxist study group... These were not yet Communists, if they ever did become Communists."[64] Here, we are probably witnessing the genesis of Hammett's Marxism.

Nevertheless, Kessler-Harris thinks that Hammett and Hellman were "probably members in 1936 and 1937," and she later says that, according to some, Hellman was a "'concealed' member well after 1941." FBI informer Louis Budenz would later identify Hellman as a member from 1937 to 1945, while Martin Berkeley claimed that she "attended a meeting at his California home in the late thirties." But these claims are not particularly trustworthy, as they were made during the height of the anti-communist hysteria of the early 1950s by people anxious to please the authorities.[65] Ring Lardner Jr., who *did* attend the meeting at Berkeley's house, was adamant that that Hellman was not there.[66]

Nevertheless, it is doubtless true that Hammett was introduced to Marxism in Hollywood. Before proceeding further, however, we should first dispel the confusion concerning the role of Otto Katz in the organizing of Hollywood communists and the notion that he may have recruited Hammett.

Kessler-Harris confusingly refers to Katz as a "communist double agent,"[67] while Emery uses the term "Communist recruiter" and claims that he formed the CPUSA's "Hollywood cell" in June 1937.[68] Emery's account of Hammett's political initiation in Hollywood is pure Cold War-speak — so much so that one can imagine it being used as the voice-over in an old monochrome movie cranked out by a tamed Hollywood during the McCarthy era:

> Now that historians have had access to Soviet archives, we know there was a large–scale, well-organized Communist plan to infiltrate and subvert movies, radio and publishing in many countries to convert media and news into propaganda outlets for Communist causes. The Communist Party organized a clandestine program to recruit celebrities, especially authors, and to use them as secret soldiers for Stalin, endorsing Communist agendas but never publicly admitting their Communist memberships. Hammett and Hellman were steered to promote

> Communist causes by Communist recruiter Otto Katz, "one of the most complex secret agents of his era," according to Stephen Koch in his 1994 book *Double Lives: Spies and Writers in the Soviet War of Ideas against the West*.[69]

Hammett, of course, would have been appalled or amused by this nonsense — especially from one of his professed admirers.

Jonathan Miles, biographer of Otto Katz, is little better in this regard. For example, he usually describes Katz as a "spy," whereas he was more accurately an emissary of the Communist International. That Miles does not understand the role of the Comintern is obvious when he claims that its "network would aim to overthrow capitalism by spreading the socialist vision and planting disinformation" and that "the 'fraternal parties' in the West would assist in the recruitment of secret agents and provide cover to mask their intrigues."[70] Similarly, he says that the Friends of Soviet Russia, a solidarity organization led by US communists, "gave the Comintern a foothold in North America."[71]

The Comintern (the Communist International, or Third International) was the international center of the communist movement founded in 1919, to which all national parties recognized and accepted as being communist were affiliated, sending delegates to its periodic congresses where major policies were decided and a leadership — the Executive Committee — was elected. Thus, the Comintern did not need a pro-Soviet solidarity group to establish a "foothold in North America" for it, as the communist parties of the USA and Canada were both Comintern affiliates.

The claim that the Comintern aimed to "overthrow capitalism by...planting disinformation" is, of course, incorrect, as communists recognized that the motor of history was class struggle, not "disinformation." Neither, by and large, did national parties recruit "secret agents" — if, by this, Miles means espionage agents; although there may have been exceptions, most communist parties forbade their members to engage in espionage. What local parties *would* have provided were Comintern emissaries, who were used to advise smaller parties undergoing a troubled infancy, and to assist various local parties on specific questions on which the emissary was an expert.

This, indeed, was Otto Katz's role. Born in 1895 in what would become Czechoslovakia in 1918, Katz, from a Jewish family, became a communist (in the German party, initially) and a Comintern emissary specializing in anti-fascist activity. After training in Moscow between 1931 and 1932, his assignments thereafter included work in Germany, France, the UK and, during its Civil War, Spain. He edited a book exposing Nazi brutality in Germany, and in London played a leading role in a "trial" demonstrating the worthlessness of the evidence concocted against Georgi Dimitrov and the other communists charged with the Reichstag fire.

In the mid-1930s, he was in Hollywood, having arrived in the USA in late 1935, and on his journey to the west coast speaking "forty times in three weeks,"[72] to foster the establishment of anti-Nazi groups. Once in Hollywood, working as "Rudolph Breda," Katz plugged into the German and Austrian expatriate community — Fritz Lang, Marlene Dietrich, Peter Lorre, Billy Wilder, etc. — and then moved outward. The organization he inspired was launched as the Hollywood Anti-Nazi League for American Democracy on July 23, 1936 after Breda's departure (he left Hollywood in mid-May 1936 and shortly thereafter returned to Europe.)[73]

That Katz's visit had made an impact is illustrated by the fact that in autumn that year, some 10,000 people attended a public meeting at Hollywood's Shrine Auditorium, where the subject was "The Menace of Hitlerism in America."[74] Katz served as the model for Muller in Hellman's play *Watch on the Rhine* and, reputedly, for Victor Laszlo in *Casablanca*. After World War II, he returned to Czechoslovakia, where in 1947 he organized the World Federation of Democratic Youth's inaugural World Festival of Youth and Students and was appointed political and foreign editor of *Rude Pravo*. In 1952, however, he fell victim to the Cold War paranoia sweeping much of Eastern Europe and was arrested and tried with 13 others in the "Slansky trial." After confessing to having worked with US and British intelligence, he was found guilty of treason and executed.

It is apparent from this that Katz could not, as Emery claims, have formed the CPUSA's Hollywood "cell" in 1937, because he was no longer in the USA at that stage — and, indeed, it would have been unthinkable for a foreign visitor to have interfered in such a manner: the establishment of party organizations was the business of the CPUSA. Interestingly, Hellman and Hammett receive only the briefest of mentions in Miles's biography of Katz, where they are described as "Communist sympathizers."[75] In fact, the communist party in Hollywood was organized — yes, in 1937 — by screenwriter and playwright John Howard Lawson, who had left New York in 1928, called into existence as a Hollywood writer by the arrival of sound. He played the leading role in the formation of the Screen Writers' Guild in 1933 and the following year joined the CPUSA, thereafter developing into the most influential communist in town. Says Lawson: "When the first meeting was held I gave the main report...and I was elected to be chairman of the forty people — actors, writers, directors and their wives — who were present at that first meeting. I continued as the party grew to several hundred members."[76]

Mellen claims that Hammett and Hellman became members of a "special group of the Communist Party that was so loosely organized as not to be a regular Party 'branch.' Because its members were all well-known writers, the secrecy of their membership had to be preserved."[77] This sounds plausible, echoing the experience of Howard Fast, who says that he joined the party's Cultural Section, where most of the well-known members "held their membership in secret," and where there "were no lists; we carried no cards."[78] Martin Gottfried, biographer of Arthur Miller, finds it impossible to establish whether his subject had been a CPUSA member, partly due to this same "members at large" status. He cites Elia Kazan as saying that he suspected that Lillian Hellman was one such member; Hammett is not mentioned.[79] But then Mellen confuses the picture by saying that although the "Hollywood cell" of the CPUSA was formed in July 1937, Hammett and Hellman did not attend.[80]

Layman follows Hellman's lead, saying that Hammett probably joined the CP in 1937 or 1938; by May of the latter year, says Emery, Hammett was recruiting for the party in Hollywood.[81] Johnson has it that one of Hammett's party tasks was to make sure that members paid their dues.[82] These assertions by Emery and Johnson run counter to Mellen's claim of "secret membership," as recruitment and dues-collection were by their nature semi-public activities; had Hammett been thus engaged, it is likely that we would have before us considerable testimony regarding this, thus confirming his membership. Clandestine membership by public figures was surely intended to combine a private, personal commitment to the party with a public advocacy of party-supported causes, thus giving the latter the appearance of having a broad appeal. While it is not impossible, it is therefore unlikely that Hammett was either a recruiter or a dues-collector, and that if he was a member it was in the category claimed by Mellen.

≈

Just as there is so little evidence of Hammett's party membership, so there are indications that he may not have been a member at all. This seems to have struck Nolan, who notes: "The Communist press seemed to be confused about him; they wanted to include Hammett in their ranks, but he maintained an outside, independent stance."[83] This is borne out by the fact that while he followed the party line after the Soviet Union signed its non-aggression pact with Germany in 1939 (as Hellman departed from that line by writing *Watch on the Rhine*), after the war he would have nothing to do with the CPUSA's support of the 1948 presidential campaign of Henry Wallace (while Hellman participated). Mellen's assertion that Hellman's politics "took the pattern of matching Hammett's" is not, therefore, strictly true.[84]

Kessler-Harris thinks that his letters to his daughter Mary in 1936, as Roosevelt was running for a second presidential term, and when the CPUSA had adopted the Popular Front policy, "have the ring of the insider."[85] This is not really the case, but there are two letters to Mary in that year of interest to us.

In February, Hammett tells Mary that "our" communist party in Germany has 40,000 members. This is the first of his letters with any real political content, although some of it is distinctly off-beam. For example, he predicts that Goering and Von Blomberg, whom he describes as Germany's national army commander, will break with Hitler and Goebbels.[86] In fact, General Werner von Blomberg had been minister of defense since 1933, continuing in this position when the Ministry of Defense became the Ministry of War in 1935, as well as occupying the post of commander-in chief of the armed forces. Rather than allying with von Blomberg, Goering, along with Himmler, sought to oust him, and in January 1938 he succeeded, as it was discovered that von Blomberg's new wife had posed for pornographic photographs taken by a Jew with whom she had been living, and that her mother had been a prostitute.

The fact that Hammett made no mention of the fact that the German communist party (KPD) had, following the Reichstag fire in 1933, been subject to repression by the Nazis, with all its 82 parliamentary deputies jailed and its general secretary Ernst Thaelmann placed in solitary confinement, makes him sound anything but an "insider."

In September 1936 comes the letter to which Kessler-Harris refers, and while it is true that this contains a very effective, simple guide to the situation in Spain (an indication that Hammett could have turned his hand to the popularization of political issues if he had had a mind to), his paragraph on the CPUSA's electoral policy is less convincing.

> No, there's no truth in the statement that the Communists are supporting Roosevelt; that's just the old Hearst howl. *They've* been against Roosevelt from the beginning and, though *they'd* rather have him elected than [Alf] Landon, it's only because *they* think he'll do less harm. Meanwhile, *they're* busy trying to get all the votes *they* can for *their* own presidential candidate, Earl Browder. *They* don't expect to win, of course, but the idea is that if the Communists and Socialists and Farmer-Labor interests make a pretty good showing this time, the Democrats will try to win their support by doing something for the workers between now and the next election. If the Republicans get in, all the workers can expect is a kick in the seat of the pants no matter what happens.[87] (Emphases added.)

While the second half of this paragraph is a competent summation of CPUSA electoral aims, the first half is not quite correct. William Z. Foster in his history of the CPUSA describes the party strategy as follows:

> The position of the Communist Party in the 1936 elections, in line with its general attitude toward the New Deal, was one of objective, but not official support for Roosevelt. At its ninth convention (in New York, June 24-28, 1936), the Party took the stand that the central issue of the campaign was "democracy versus fascism," and it pointed out that the major forces of reaction and fascism were ganged up

behind Landon. It called for "the concentration of all forces of the working class and its allies in the fight against the Republican-Liberty League-Hearst combination and for the defeat of its plans in the elections of 1936." The Party directed its main fire against Landon. As for Roosevelt, while the Party realized that he had made certain concessions to the toilers, it correctly asserted that he had made bigger "concessions to Hearst, to Wall Street, to the reactionaries." It declared that Roosevelt's "middle course" was "not a barrier to reaction and fascism," and that the Party could not therefore give him a full endorsement. Consequently, the Party put up its own national ticket, Earl Browder and James W. Ford. It was on the ballot in 34 states. The type of campaign which the Party carried on, however, calling for the defeat of Landon at all costs, militated against the Party polling its own full potential vote in the elections — hence its ticket received only 80,181 votes.[88]

It is surprising that Hammett, who would join or support a number of anti-fascist organizations, seems to have missed the fact that for the CPUSA the central issue in this election was "democracy versus fascism." If he was a party member, therefore, he was not a very attentive one. However, it is noteworthy that while in February Hammett speaks of "our" communist party in Germany, when discussing the US communists in September he employs the third person: "they" and "their." One possible interpretation is that in talking of "our" communist party in Germany Hammett was asserting his allegiance to an international movement, while domestically he was not (yet?) a member of "their" communist party.

To give Hammett credit, he does end the September 1936 letter by leaving us in no doubt regarding his class loyalty, telling Mary: "be in favor of what's good for the workers and against what isn't. Follow that, and you may not be the most brilliant person in the world, but at least you'll be able to hold your head up when you look in the mirror."[89] This was new, and a firm indication that he had certainly moved to the left.

Despite the many assumptions of Hammett's party membership, there is precious little hard evidence, and it is almost possible to believe that he felt himself to be part of an international movement and was more than willing to work closely with its national contingent, the CPUSA, but without becoming a formal member, therefore leaving himself free to ignore policies with which he disagreed. But there *is* evidence of his party membership. It is still sparse, but it's telling, and in one case it's a clincher.

There is, for example, the diary entry by Arthur Kober, Hellman's former husband, indicating that on February 22, 1940 he attended, in Rollyson's words, "some kind of study group headed by Hammett," at which Kober understood very little.[90] Could this be anything but a party group? And if Hammett was leading the discussion, is this not evidence (not conclusive, maybe) that he was a party member?

Hammett's daughter Jo told Rollyson of an occasion when the party ordered him to tell a friend that the program he wished to implement had not found favor, even though he, Hammett, believed it was sound.[91] It is difficult to reconcile this Hammett, meekly following a party instruction, with the one who willfully ignored a complete policy — support of Henry Wallace's presidential campaign — in 1948, and one has even greater difficulty picturing a Hammett "almost in tears" when given this assignment, but the fact remains that such a thing could not have occurred unless he was a party member.

Sally Cline's 2014 biography of Hammett is dotted with minor inaccuracies and has only one new thing, albeit a very significant new thing, to say: that Hammett had once shown his party card to his daughter Jo.[92]

I emailed the ever-cooperative Julie Rivett, Hammett's granddaughter, to seek confirmation. She asked her mother and promptly replied: "She nodded. Yes, she saw his Party card. Not some other card I asked? For some other lefty group? No. Definitely his CP card."[93] And when would this have been? "She thinks she must have been at around 9 or 10 years old. She vaguely recalls her dad showing her the card and reading to her (or else she read) a quote on the card that, to the best of her recollection, implied fidelity to Lenin."[94]

That settles it. Jo Hammett would have been ten in 1936, but Hammett spent much of that year in New York, Tavern Island, Connecticut and Princeton, so it's more likely that Jo saw the card in 1937, after

Hammett returned Hollywood in March of that year, and where he would remain until May 1938.

In 1936, he had been researching the Pinkertons and had displayed a faulty knowledge of events in Germany and a tenuous grasp of CPUSA policy, referring to US communists in the third person.[95] By 1937 he would have made up his mind, possibly as a result of Soviet aid to Republican Spain; but it was also in that year when Hollywood was hit by a two-month strike by studio workers who, having received a ten-percent wage increase, now found that they were expected to work a double shift without overtime pay and enrich the corrupt leaders of the International Alliance of Theatrical Stage Employees with a two-percent levy on their wages; the strike was crushed by imported mobsters, and it is entirely possible this contributed to Hammett's decision.[96]

It's likely that he showed his card to Jo shortly after he joined, when it was as much a novelty to him as it would have been to her, so it turns out that all those people who, on the basis on no evidence at all, have claimed that Hammett joined the CPUSA in 1937 were probably right after all.

There remains, however, a question. If, as Mellen and Cline[97] assert, Hammett had been a "member at large," why did he have a card at all? This, as we have seen, was not the normal practice. We can only guess. Hammett, having searched so long for the belief that would give meaning to his life, gave himself wholly to this cause, to which he remained loyal for the rest of his life. To him, this was not just a political matter but also a deeply personal one, involving his own physical survival. So when they told him he need not carry a card, he probably demanded one.

≈

The political trajectory of Dashiell Hammett now seems clear. The boy who had been keen to understand how the world worked had by the late 1920s, having written story after story about the corrupt society in which he lived, arrived at the conclusion that life quite simply had no meaning.

While initially liberating, such a belief was ultimately dismal, for it brought with it a dark nihilism in which he could believe in nothing (it seems to us now, as possibly it did to him, that the "code" he had absorbed at the Pinkerton agency was perhaps a desperate attempt to believe in *something*, a poor substitute for a more noble form of commitment). When combined with sudden new wealth, his nihilism, doubtless conditioned by his tuberculosis, led to extremes of behavior and, in 1931, to the stated intention to commit suicide. Despite his continued search for meaning, and the "foggy glimpses" to which this led, there was still nothing. What was the point?

But the fog began to clear. He was living in a period when the Depression debilitated much of the world, demonstrating the correctness of Marx's theory regarding crises of overproduction. At the same time, a struggle was being waged for the future of mankind between socialism, which was under construction in a country covering one-sixth of the world's surface, untouched by the capitalist crisis, and fascism — capital's most reactionary response to the crisis.

There were encouraging developments in the USA, and Hammett began to identify with the organized working class, and in so doing to examine his own past. It was not the case, as Layman claims, that there "was little cause for optimism about workers' rights in the eighth and ninth years of the Great Depression, as long-term unemployment drained whatever sentiment people had for union organized work disturbances."[98]

In 1935 the Wagner Act had been passed, giving trade unions the legal right to recognition and the machinery by which it might be achieved; that same year saw the beginning of activity within the conservative American Federation of Labor which would lead to the formation of the more militant Congress of Industrial Organizations in 1938; it was in this very period that an effective new tactic was developed — the sit-down strike. In early 1937, this tactic won recognition for the United Auto Workers, formed as recently as 1935, at the mighty General Motors; by 1938, that union had grown in membership from 30,000 to 500,000. The sit-down tactic was widely emulated, the 48 such strikes in 1936 growing to 477 the following year.[99] There were ample grounds for labor optimism in the second half of the 1930s.

Then came Spain and the Civil War which, if won by the fascist forces, was sure to lead to another world war. At this point, Hammett committed himself as he had never done before. Dissuaded by the CPUSA from joining the Abraham Lincoln Battalion, the US contingent of the International Brigades which fought for the Spanish Republic, by arguing that he would be more useful at home,[100] Hammett became active in a host of anti-fascist and pro-Republic organizations.

Having moved beyond "foggy glimpses," he now found the world perfectly comprehensible. At last, life had meaning. His nihilism was in abeyance and he had found something in which to believe; he would cling to his new vision for the remainder of his life. True, his dissolute lifestyle would continue for some years, but the fact that he was on the wagon for the most of 1937 and part of 1938 was surely a sign that he was taking his political responsibilities seriously; and it is clear now that the worst of his excesses had occurred before this watershed.

It will be recalled that in *The Maltese Falcon*, Sam Spade says that Flitcraft, following his epiphany with the falling beam, "felt like somebody had taken the lid off life and let him look at the works." One wonders whether Hammett wished that he had saved that metaphor for the more powerful epiphany of 1937 when, having attended Marxist study classes in Hollywood, doubtless supplemented by his own reading, he must have felt, as did so many at the time, that he could actually *see* the forces of history at work. Suddenly, the anti-capitalist impulse which had led him to write the story "Nightmare Town" and the novel *Red Harvest* must have made more sense to him, and his new outlook transformed that mere impulse into real understanding. Possibly, he regretted that this understanding had not been present at the time he was writing, but one cannot imagine him spending much time in such pointless reflection.

And as he made the transition from writer to political activist, Hammett retained the hardboiled approach — something which, as we will now see, some admirers find so difficult to accept.

NOTES

1. William F. Nolan, *Dashiell Hammett: A Life at the Edge* (London: Arthur Barker, 1983), 136.
2. Hammett to Lillian Hellman, June 6, 1936, Dashiell Hammett; *Selected Letters of Dashiell Hammett, 1921-1960*, ed. Richard Layman with Julie M. Rivett (Washington D. C.: Counterpoint, 2001), 103.
3. Diane Johnson, *The Life of Dashiell Hammett* (US title *Dashiell Hammett: A Life*), (London: Picador, 1985), 135. Hearst had for many years shown progressive tendencies, adopting a pro-labor stance, defending the right to strike and crusading for regulation of the trusts. By the mid-1930s, however, he had turned sharply to the right, opposing Franklin Roosevelt in the 1936 election (partly because the New Deal legislation had encouraged his journalists to unionize) and accusing him of "communism." This backfired disastrously, and while Roosevelt was re-elected with the largest landslide in US history, Hearst's newspapers suffered serious declines in circulation. This would surely have ruled out any question of Hammett writing a screen story for Marion Davies, whose movie career was in decline. See David Nasaw, *The Chief: The Life of William Randolph Hearst* (Boston, New York: Mariner Books, 2001.)
4. Johnson, 106.
5. Ibid., 100.
6. Ibid., 103.
7. Joan Mellen, *Hellman and Hammett: The Legendary Passion of Lillian Hellman and Dashiell Hammett* (New York: Harper Collins, 1996), 75. Nolan (147), is mistaken when he says that Hammett rented the Harold Lloyd mansion. For one thing, Lloyd lived in it until his death in 1971. It was here that Hellman claimed to have smashed the basement soda fountain shortly after the opening of *The Children's Hour* when, having telephoned California, her call was answered by a woman claiming to be Hammett's secretary. But he never lived in the Lloyd mansion, the address of which is 1740, Greenacres Drive. However, he *did* live at 18904, Malibu Road, Pacific Palisades at this time, as he wrote to Hellman from this address on November 26, 1934 (*The Children's Hour* had opened six days earlier). See *Selected Letters*, 92-93.

8   Richard Layman, *Shadow Man: The Life of Dashiell Hammett* (New York and London: Harcourt Brace Jovanovich/Bruccoli Clark, 1981), 162.
9   Nolan, 161.
10 Johnson, 151.
11 Mellen, 130.
12 Nolan, 171.
13 Layman, *Shadow Man*, 164.
14 Mellen, 123. It was more than a mere question of rent arrears, for the three-floor, 17-room house contained expensive furnishings, some of them antique, and by the time Hammett left there were "cigarette burns in the hardwood floor and a large hole in the living room rug." See Carl Rollyson, *Lillian Hellman: Her Legend and her Legacy* (New York: St. Martin's Press, 1988), 95, 96.
15 Johnson, 107.
16 Mellen, 34.
17 Ibid., 90-91.
18 Johnson, 120.
19 Mellen, 193.
20 Joseph Freeman, *An American Testament: A Narrative of Rebels and Romantics* (London: Victor Gollancz, Left Book Club Edition, 1938), 438.
21 Ibid, 457-458.
22 See Robert P. Newman, *The Cold War Romance of Lillian Hellman and John Melby* (Chapel Hill: University of North Carolina Press, 1989).
23 Johnson, 121.
24 Layman, *Shadow Man*, 162.
25 Ibid., 129-130.
26 Gerald Horne, *The Final Victim of the Blacklist: John Howard Lawson, Dean of the Hollywood Ten* (Berkeley, Los Angeles and London: University of California Press, 2006), 274, n. 78. Howard Fast, having earlier stated that Fitzgerald was "willing to embrace" the party but that he did not know whether he did, a few years later declared that he had in fact joined. I am inclined to distrust this latter claim. See Howard Fast, *Being Red: A Memoir* (Boston: Houghton Mifflin, 1990), 79 and Natalie Robins, *Alien Ink: The FBI's War on Freedom of Expression* (New Brunswick: Rutgers University Press, 1993), 426. Both are cited by Horne, *The Last Victim of the Blacklist*, xx.

27 Mellen, 85.
28 Hellman, *An Unfinished Woman* in *Three*, (Boston: Little, Brown, 1979), 283-84.
29 Lillian Hellman, *Scoundrel Time* (London: Macmillan, 1976), 3. Overtures would surely have been made by John Howard Lawson also. Lawson, a Broadway playwright and the most influential communist screenwriter in Hollywood, considered Hellman to be "the most significant playwright of the later thirties." John Howard Lawson speech, 1961, Box 36, Folder 1, John Howard Lawson Papers, cited in Horne, *The Last Victim of the Blacklist*, 81.
30 Rollyson, 2, 319. According to Hellman's FBI file, she attended the CPUSA's national convention in 1938 (Rollyson, 146), but this may have been as a guest or visitor, as it is unlikely but not impossible that, having just joined the party in that year, she would have been elected as a delegate.
31 Draft, April 28, 1952, Library of Congress, Manuscript Division, Joseph Rauh Collection, quoted in Deborah Martinson, Lillian Hellman: A Life with Foxes and Scoundrels (Berkeley: Counterpoint, 2005), 138.
32 Mellen, 217.
33 Nolan, 14. On the same page, Nolan has Hammett reminisce: "I had no political conscience back in '17. I was just doing a job, and if our clients were rotten it didn't concern me. They hired us to break up a union strike, so we went out there to do that." But he gives no source for his quotation (it does not appear in Hellman's *Scoundrel Time*) which, if true, would have lent some credibility to the Frank Little story.
34 Dashiell Hammett, *The Dain Curse* in *Five Complete Novels* (New York: Avenel Books, 1980), 258.
35 Nolan, 98.
36 Richard Layman, commentary, Dashiell Hammett, *Selected Letters*, 59.
37 Layman, *Shadow Man*, 171, 135.
38 Mellen, 64, 113; Vince Emery, commentary, Dashiell Hammett, *Lost Stories*, ed. Vince Emery (San Francisco: Vince Emery Productions, 2005), 293.
39 Lillian Hellman, *An Unfinished Woman*, in *Three*, 204.
40 See Freeman, *An American Testament*, 336-337.

41 Alice Kessler-Harris, *A Difficult Woman: The Challenging Life and Times of Lillian Hellman* (New York: Bloomsbury Press, 2012), 77, 101.
42 Hellman, *An Unfinished Woman* in *Three*, 132. Hellman's former husband Arthur Kober would note in his diary that she seemed to have identified with progressive politics in 1935, as she had "just found the cause [and] speaks like expert & like all eloquent dogmatists will not allow anyone else to think or listen to what is being said." Quoted in Rollyson, 89.
43 Hellman, *Pentimento* in *Three* (Boston: Little, Brown, 1979), 422, 423.
44 Martinson, 130.
45 Mellen, 71, and endnote 477. Gallagher also argues that Hellman's schedule for 1934 simply does not permit the two months she claimed to have been in Europe. See Dorothy Gallagher, *Lillian Hellman: An Imperious Life* (New Haven and London: Yale University Press, 2014), 75.
46 Gallagher, 76.
47 Rollyson (106) tells us that she left for Europe the day after *Dead End*, for which she had written the screenplay, opened in New York, which is recorded as having been August 24. See http://www.imdb.com/title/tt0028773/releaseinfo?ref_=tt_ql_9, accessed May 22, 2015.
48 Hellman, *Pentimento* in *Three*, 403. Hellman had invited Hammett to accompany her to the Moscow theatre festival but, she says, he declined because he had "an amused contempt for Russian bureaucracy" — which Hammett cannot possibly have ever encountered. See also Nolan, 161.
49 Hellman, *Pentimento*, 443. Here, she says that the following year she telephoned Julia's grandmother and told her that she had seen Julia in October.
50 Hellman, *An Unfinished Woman* in *Three*, 91.
51 Ibid., 93.
52 Dashiell Hammett to Lillian Hellman, September 9, 1937; *Selected Letters*, 121.
53 "Theatre: Classic Festival," *Time*, September 27, 1937.
54 In 1980, Hellman would file a libel suit against Mary McCarthy after the latter, speaking on a television chat show, charged that every word that Hellman wrote was a lie. The case died with

Hellman.
55 Mellen, 114.
56 Gallagher, 45.
57 Hellman, *An Unfinished Woman* in *Three*, 133.
58 Rollyson, 274.
59 Rollyson, 550, says that they knew each other for 45 years; as Hellman died in 1984, this places their first meeting in 1939.
60 Mellen, 98.
61 Mellen, 100-101. The book by the "cowboy detective" was actually *Two Evil Isms, Pinkertonism and Anarchism*, by Charles A. Siringo. First published in 1915, this has been republished by Forgotten Books (London, 2013).
62 J. A. Zumoff, "Politics and the 1920s Writings of Dashiell Hammett," *American Studies Journal*, 52.1 (2012), 83.
63 Mellen, 109. The claim is curious, as a page earlier Mellen has informed us that Hellman did not join the CPUSA until 1938.
64 Patrick McGilligan and Ken Mate, "Allen Boretz," in Patrick McGilligan and Paul Buhle, eds., *Tender Comrades: A Backstory of the Hollywood Blacklist* (New York: St. Martin's Griffin, 1999), 97, cited by Kessler-Harris, 113.
65 Kessler-Harris, 123, 125, 258.
66 Rollyson, 314.
67 Kessler-Harris, 50.
68 Emery, commentary, in Dashiell Hammett, *Lost Stories*, 294, 295.
69 Ibid., 293-94.
70 Jonathan Miles, *The Nine Lives of Otto Katz* (London: Bantam Books, 2011), 62. On one occasion, Miles does refer to Katz as a "Comintern organizer." Ibid., 180.
71 Ibid., 65.
72 Ibid., 212.
73 Ibid., 227.
74 Ibid., 225.
75 Ibid., 345.
76 Gerald Horne, *Class Struggle in Hollywood, 1930-1950: Moguls, Mobsters, Stars, Reds and Trade Unionists* (Austin: University of Texas Press, 2001), 71.
77 Mellen, 107-108.
78 Howard Fast, *Being Red*, 86, 190.

79 Martin Gottfried, *Arthur Miller: His Life and Work* (Boston: Da Capo Press, 2003), 158.
80 Mellen, 123.
81 Layman, *Shadow Man*, 175; Layman, in Hammett, *Selected Letters*, 131, n. 3. This latter claim is repeated by Emery, commentary, in Hammett, *Lost Stories*, 296.
82 Johnson, 147.
83 Nolan., 178.
84 Mellen 113.
85 Kessler-Harris, 107.
86 Dashiell Hammett to Mary Hammett, February 21, 1936; *Selected Letters*, 99.
87 Dashiell Hammett to Mary Hammett, September 11, 1936; *Selected Letters*, 107-108, emphases added.
88 William Z. Foster, *History of the Communist Party of the United States* (New York: International Publishers, 1952); Chapter 23 available at williamzfoster.blogspot.com, accessed February 12, 2015.
89 Hammett, *Selected Letters*, 109-110.
90 Rollyson, 154.
91 Rollyson, 152.
92 Sally Cline, *Dashiell Hammett: Man of Mystery* (New York: Arcade Publishing, 2014), 145.
93 Julie M. Rivett to Ken Fuller, May 27, 2015.
94 Julie M. Rivett to Ken Fuller, May 29, 2015.
95 The following year, he would be referring to himself and his comrades as "we reds." See Dashiell Hammett to Mary Hammett, November 25, 1938; *Selected Letters*, 142. We catch a fascinating glimpse of Hammett in a reminiscence by John Howard Lawson concerning a picket line in support of striking publishing house office workers in New York. "One solitary figure was walking up and down — a tall, aristocratic individual wearing spats and twirling a cane in his gloved hands. His name was Dashiell Hammett. And I fell in behind him. The next day many writers answered the call." This was probably in 1936, when Hammett was on the East Coast, and it is obvious that the two men did not at first know each other, lending further weight to the possibility that it was in 1937 that Hammett joined the CPUSA — probably recruited by Lawson. See Horne, *The Final Victim of the Blacklist*, 106, citing

a speech by Lawson, November 12, 1955, Box 13, Folder 5, John Howard Lawson Papers, Southern Illinois University-Carbondale.
96 Horne, *Class Struggle in Hollywood*, 49.
97 Cline, 145.
98 Layman, commentary, Hammett, *Selected Letters*, 62.
99 Howard Zinn, *A People's History of the United States, 1492-Present*, revised and updated (New York: HarperPerennial, 1995), 391.
100 Layman, commentary, Dashiell Hammett, *Selected Letters*, 62.

Dashiell Hammett, 1939. At this time, he was engaged in a strenuous round of political activity that would continue until he rejoined the Army in 1942.

7 Hardboiled activist

Hammett's political beliefs have drawn fire from some of his (and Hellman's) biographers. Significantly, however, none of these writers even attempt to explain why Hammett (or Hellman) would have adopted these positions.

Why did he join the CPUSA during its "Popular Front" period? Why might he have considered the verdicts in the Moscow trials to have been correct? Why did he not take the George Orwell line on the Spanish Civil War? Why did he follow without protest the change in party line after the conclusion of the Soviet-German Non-Aggression Pact of 1939, apparently dropping his anti-fascism and raising his voice against the possibility of war?

We are left in the dark, for while these writers are all too anxious to display their own Cold War credentials (even if, in some cases, in a "left" guise) they succeed in telling us nothing about Hammett — unless it be that he was some sort of dupe, lured into "uncritical acceptance" of the Soviet line, who "lacked the energy and the will to discover the anti-Stalinist alternatives that did exist,"[1] or that he suffered "the intellectual blindness of the self-educated, the gaps in logic he had not been trained to avoid."[2] Thus, because these writers are apparently more interested in telling us about their own politics than those of their subject, we are presented with a distorted portrait of Hammett.

The real Hammett is further obscured by the fact that no attempt is made (perhaps the writers lack the "energy and the will" to do so) to place these admittedly controversial issues in any kind of historical context.

If we are to deepen our understanding of the man, therefore, we must revisit each of these issues, viewing them as they would have appeared to Hammett.

The Popular Front

Joan Mellen characterizes the CPUSA as "a crude transmission belt for Stalin's dictates, a carbon copy of his authoritarian rule." She says that by the time Hammett joined, "under orders from the Comintern" the CPUSA was "discarding its revolutionary ideology, abandoning the ideals of Communism and socialism and the class struggle, and instead proclaiming its Americanism, its patriotism, its New Dealism, and its antifascism." This, she says, was because the Comintern had "declared the Popular Front, which required every foreign Communist Party to subordinate itself to bourgeois parties."[3]

Richard Layman takes a similar line, describing the Popular Front period as one where "upon orders from the Comintern…national parties worked to promote social change within established political structures."[4] Furthermore, Mellen claims that Hammett, "a man of considerable intelligence, fell prey to uncritical acceptance of all this and more."[5]

Nowhere is there an appreciation of the need for, or the aims of, the Popular Front strategy.

Prior to 1935, the policy of the Comintern (the Communist International, formed in 1919, grouped together the communist parties of the world so that they might take a coordinated approach to the major questions of the day) was one of "class against class," allowing no compromise with the capitalist class, regardless of issue or circumstance. Social democratic parties were condemned as "social fascist," and communist trade unionists were expected to break with reformist organizations and establish "red alternatives." Such sectarianism proved disastrous in practice, usually resulting in the isolation of the communists, and thus in many countries the policy was allowed to quietly die.⁶ However, it was obvious to most parties that there was a pressing need not only for "class against class" to be formally discarded, but to be replaced with an alternative that took into account the rise of fascism.

The new policy was that of the united front, or Popular Front, and rather than being imposed on national parties by "orders" of the Comintern, it was arrived at by the delegates of those very parties when they met for the Seventh Congress of the Comintern in 1935. The inspiration came from France and Spain. In the latter, says an official history of the Comintern, "the Communist Party in the summer of 1935 succeeded in achieving real progress in the campaign for a popular front. The experience of the Spanish Communist Party's struggle played an important role in the framing of the decisions of the Seventh Congress of the Comintern."⁷ Here is Dolores Ibarruri ("La Pasionaria") on the same subject:

> The People's Front policy was not concocted in a Moscow laboratory, as claimed by the priests of anticommunism. It was a logical step, arising from the need to counteract the danger facing the working masses; and it was also the crystallization of the people's experience of various communist parties — in particular the Spanish and the French which, by different routes, had arrived at the same conclusions.⁸

The new orientation had, in fact, been adopted by the Spanish party's central committee as early as April 1933.⁹ Indeed, rather than being foisted on national parties by the Comintern, one prominent Comintern leader, whose pseudonym at the time was Chavaroche, took issue with the Spanish line, later admitting that he had been mistaken. "Since we knew the situation in Spain better than Chavaroche did," says Ibarrurri, "we continued to fight for an alliance of the workers and other democratic forces."¹⁰

Once adopted by the Comintern, the Popular Front policy had as its aim the building of a broad coalition of forces capable of checking the rise of fascism in each country, as to have persisted with the previous sectarian line would have left the way open for the advance of the extreme right.

The results were not long in coming, with communist parties throughout the world seeing increases in membership, and it was in this period that many intellectuals, anxious to combat fascism, adopted (albeit temporarily in some cases) a Marxist outlook. Hammett was one of those won to the cause. One might have expected this to pose a problem for Mellen, for while she is glad to label the CPUSA as a "a crude transmission belt for Stalin's dictates, a carbon copy of his authoritarian rule," she never poses the obvious question: how could such a dissolute and ill-disciplined character as Hammett have been accepted into such a straitlaced organization? One suspects that the question is not attempted because it implies that the CPUSA was not as she describes it.

The Moscow Trials

Gallagher considers with horror the fact that Hellman and Hammett signed a statement in April 1938 supporting the guilty verdicts in the Moscow trials. Hellman, she says, found during her visit to Moscow in 1937 that, when it came to the purges, diplomats and journalists, with the exception of Walter Duranty of the *New York Times*, talked "gobbledygook." But Duranty, Gallagher advises us, citing I. F. Stone, was known as the "unofficial spokesman for the Kremlin."[11] Mellen is equally horrified by the signing of the statement, charging: "No petition they signed was more virulent...than one which appeared at the end of April in support of the Moscow trials 'of the Trotskyite-Bukharnite [sic] traitors!'"[12]

It is commonly held that the trials of high-level dissidents held in Moscow between 1936 and 1938 constituted little more than Stalin's attempt to get rid of his opponents, and in particular those who followed Trotsky. The official Soviet version of events at the time, on the other hand, held that those found guilty had been involved in a conspiracy to aid a military attack on the Soviet Union by Germany and Japan, during which Stalin and Molotov would have been assassinated. The conspirators, it was alleged, were willing to settle for a smaller Soviet Union without Stalin for the price of ceding the Ukraine and the western part of Russia to Germany, while in the east the Pacific provinces would have gone to Japan.[13]

At the time, few communists, in the USA or elsewhere, accepted that the differences between the camps of Stalin and Trotsky (who had been first expelled from the Communist Party of the Soviet Union and then deported in 1929) were about a struggle for personal power. While Hammett left no written record of his views on Trotskyism, we can be assured that they did not differ from those of the CPUSA, as he signed the party's open letter opposing the American Committee for the Defense of Leon Trotsky.[14] Joseph Freeman, recalling his year in the Soviet Union (1926-27) but written a decade later, at the very time when Hammett joined the CPUSA, has this to say about the fierce debate raging within the Soviet party:

> The inner-Party crisis could have meaning only if you dissociated it from hysteria, ethical fainting spells, and invidious personal comparisons. Lenin said he who makes up his mind on political questions by hearsay, without reading the documents, was a fool. It was when you read the documents on both sides dealing with fundamental *economic* questions that the dispute assumed clarity.[15]

This view is shared by Alec Nove, a non-communist economic historian who, writing decades later, answers in the following manner the question of whether the debate was concerned wholly or mainly with political power:

> Such a conclusion would be totally misleading. The policy differences were deeply felt. It is true that Stalin later stole many of the clothes of the left opposition, but Bukharin's entire vision of Soviet development differed radically from that which came to be adopted by Stalin, despite the fact that they shared some common aims.[16]

As is well-known, the question around which the debate was centered was whether it was possible to build socialism in the USSR ("socialism in one country") while being virtually isolated from the West and without revolutionary allies. The Stalin camp took the view that it was indeed possible, while Trotsky and his adherents held that "permanent revolution" was required. (This might be the appropriate place to point out that Mellen's assertion that "Socialism in a single country meant socialism nowhere else"[17] is a crude distortion: it was not the case that socialism elsewhere was undesirable to Soviet leaders, but that it had proven impossible at that time; in practical terms, acceptance that socialism in one country was *not* feasible would have led to *no* socialism in the USSR.)

For communists in the USA and elsewhere at this time, the Soviet Union was a beacon — the land, covering one-sixth of the earth's surface, where socialism was being built against all the odds. Already ringed by hostile powers, by the mid-1930s there was, of course, an additional danger, as fascism had taken power in Italy and Germany and was growing elsewhere. In these circumstances, Trotskyism — posing as "left" but objectively aiding the right by its opposition to the Soviet Union — was viewed with little tolerance by communists.

Freeman views Trotskyists with amused contempt, recounting in his memoir that the very people on the editorial board of *New Masses* who had previously voted against publishing a political speech by Trotsky (not because it was by Trotsky — at this time his differences with Stalin were unknown or barely understood — but because it was considered too "communist" for the broad audience at which the magazine was then aimed), "were now Trotsky's verbal partisans. He had given them the excuse they needed to abandon and attack the movement. They could be 'communists' without being communists."[18]

And this is something that should be understood about Hammett: instead of choosing the opportunist option of being "a 'communist' without being a communist," he obviously felt that he had aligned himself with the genuine article — not because he "lacked the energy and the will to discover the anti-Stalinist alternatives that did exist," but because this was obviously more than a passing intellectual fad for him.

Yes, on a personal level the belief was a life-saver for him, but he surely would have understood that the very history of mankind was in the balance; indeed, the belief, the idea, *had* to be that big in order to *be* his life-saver.

While it is usually a mistake to identify an author too closely with his characters, in the case of Hammett the opposite is probably true. The man who wrote hardboiled prose about hardboiled characters had also worked for a strikebreaking agency, and so he knew better than most the lengths to which the ruling class would go to suppress the working-class movement.

Hammett would have recognized only too well that it would take a *very* hardboiled guy to stand up to Hitler and Mussolini. So was he ever likely to have spent time seeking "anti-Stalinist alternatives?" The very notion is laughable.

≈

The Moscow trials were sparked by the murder of Leningrad party secretary Sergei Kirov on December 1, 1934. This led first to the trial of Grigory Zinoviev, Lev Kamenev and 14 others in August 1936; revelations during this trial gave rise in January 1937 to the trial of Karl Radek and 16 others. In June, 1937 several Red Army generals were tried by court martial and sentenced to death, followed in March 1938 by the trial of Nikolai Bukharin and 20 others.

In order to understand Hammett's support of the trials, we need to set aside what we have been told in more recent decades: by Khrushchev in his "secret speech" at the 20th Congress of the CPSU in 1956, or by Gorbachev when his regime cleared the defendants in 1988 (although even more recently, with access to Soviet files in the post-1991 period, the veracity of Khrushchev's speech has come under question[19]). The important question is: how did these trials appear at the time? Were they condemned? Well, yes, much of the capitalist press condemned them, as one might expect. But did all credible observers believe them to have been unfair? No, they did not. Even Martinson notes that the verdicts were accepted by many outsiders.[20]

We are fortunate to have the record left by Joseph P. Davies, who was in Moscow in 1937 and 1938, and he describes the trials as fair. He attended each of the six days of the Radek trial in January 1937, and says that seats were actually reserved for foreign and local journalists and for members of the diplomatic corps.[21] At the conclusion of the trial, 13 of the defendants were sentenced to be shot, while Radek and three others, found to have been uninvolved in the direct commission of crimes, were sentenced to ten years' imprisonment. But surely the trial was stage-managed? Almost certainly not, says Davies, because to believe so "would be to presuppose the creative genius of a Shakespeare and the genius of a Belasco in stage production."[22]

Davies, who, significantly, had previously been a lawyer, arrived at the "reluctant conclusion that the state had established its case, at least to the extent of proving the existence of a widespread conspiracy and plot among the political leaders against the Soviet government, and which under their statutes established the crimes set forth in the indictment."[23] Moreover, "it would be difficult for me to conceive of any court, in any jurisdiction, doing other than adjudging the defendants guilty of violations of the law as set forth in the indictment and as defined by the statutes." But surely Davies must have been constituted a minority of one? No, because of the many members of the diplomatic corps to whom he spoke all, with a single possible exception, took the same view.[24] Furthermore, in March that year an unnamed diplomat remarked that although they both knew that the Radek trial was not a "façade," it was just as well that the outside world, relying on hostile press reports, thought otherwise.[25]

Come the trial of the generals which, as it was a court-martial, he could not attend, Davies noted that those diplomats who had been in Moscow the longest accepted that there had been a conspiracy in the Red Army,[26] thinking it

> scarcely credible that their [the defendants'] brother officers — Voroshilov, Egorov, Budenny, Blucher, and many other district military commanders — should have acquiesced in their execution unless they were convinced that these men had been guilty of some offence. It is generally accepted in the Diplomatic Corps that the accused must have been guilty of an offence which in the Soviet Union would merit the death penalty.[27]

In March 1938, Davies attended the Bukharin trial daily and reported that, "after daily observation of the witnesses, their manner of testifying, the unconscious corroborations which developed, and other facts in the course of the trial, together with others of which a judicial notice could be taken, it is my opinion so far as the political defendants are concerned sufficient crimes under Soviet law, among those charged in the indictment, were established by proof and beyond a reasonable doubt to justify the verdict of guilty of treason..." and that most diplomats thought it had been established that an "exceedingly serious plot" had existed.[28]

But who was this man Davies, who had access to the trials and to the diplomatic corps? He was the US Ambassador to Moscow, no less, whose views of the trials and much else were conveyed to the US Secretary of State in his diplomatic dispatches. These, along with entries to his diary and journal, were published in 1941 (the following year in the UK) as *Mission to Moscow*, a book which sold 700,000 copies. If the US Ambassador, a lawyer and an eyewitness to two of the trials, was convinced of the guilt of the defendants, it seems rather less surprising that Hammett, a member of the CPUSA, should have believed likewise.

Later, writing when she was seeking to distance herself from communism, Hellman would claim that when she "knew about the purges" (the trials were attended by Western journalists and she was in Moscow in 1937, so she would, in fact, have known about them at the time), she bought a history of the trials from which she and Hammett would read aloud, making sarcastic asides about the proceedings and Andrey Vyshinsky, the prosecutor.[29] Maybe she did, but it is unlikely that Hammett would have joined her, for as Rollyson says, when it came to support for the Soviet Union, "she could never feel as secure about it as Hammett evidently did."[30]

The Spanish Civil War

Support for the Spanish Republic was not as straightforward as might be supposed, for this involved the question of Soviet "interference." It is unlikely that the Hammett-Hellman biographers conducted serious research into the Spanish Civil War, and it is more likely that several of them were influenced, directly or indirectly, by the eyewitness accounts of George Orwell and Franz Borkenau, whose respective books *Homage to Catalonia* and *The Spanish Cockpit* made major contributions to mainstream anti-Soviet perceptions of the Spanish conflict and whose arguments prefigure those of the aforementioned biographers.

Significantly, following World War II Borkenau became a founder-member of the anti-communist (and CIA-funded) Congress for Cultural Freedom, the idea for which is said to have originated with Orwell[31]; the latter would gain posthumous notoriety for having handed a list of suspected communists to the Information Research Department, an anti-communist propaganda unit of the British Foreign Office, in 1949.[32]

Soviet aid to the Republic, says Kessler-Harris, led to "a disastrous and divisive Soviet effort to exert leadership over all Spanish Republican forces."[33] Julian Symons charges that "Stalin was interested in a Communist-controlled Spain, not in a Republican victory,[34] while Rollyson sees the communists as "sabotaging the Republic."[35] Gallagher also agrees with Orwell that the Soviet Union had its "own agenda" in Spain.[36]

Here is Mellen on the same subject:

> Conflict broke out in Spain. From July through October 1935, Stalin sent no help to the struggling Loyalists. He still hoped that England and France, with whom he had an alliance, would fight Hitler for him; a socialist revolution in Spain would jeopardize that goal and he set out to abort it even if it meant the victory of Franco.[37]

The biographers, then, take Hammett and Hellman to task not for supporting the Republic, but for sitting in the corner of the Spanish communists and Soviet assistance, as opposed to cheering for the anarchists and the Trotskyists.

By placing events in context (something which the biographers consistently fail to do) and presenting them as they would have been regarded by Hammett at the time, it can be seen that his position was perfectly logical and, from a left perspective, defensible.

In deploring the fact that the Soviet Union (or, as she has it, Stalin) sent no aid to republican Spain between July and October 1935, Mellen not only overlooks the fact that the Spanish Civil War did not commence until a year later (her error here, we may concede, is probably due to mere carelessness), but she grotesquely distorts the facts, possibly comfortable in the assumption that her readers will have little knowledge of the subject beyond that they may have gleaned by reading Orwell. For example, she omits to mention that the Soviet Union involved itself with the London-based Non-Intervention Committee in the hope that international pressure might be exerted on Germany and Italy, both of which sent Franco arms, troops and equipment at an early stage. When it saw that Ivan Maisky, its London ambassador and representative on the committee, was wasting his breath, and following a request from the legitimate Spanish government, the Soviet Union sent assistance immediately, while the Comintern called for volunteers from all countries to go to the aid of the Republic, leading to the formation of the International Brigades. That such assistance was effective is demonstrated by the fact that even the anti-Soviet Orwell concedes: "The Russian arms and the magnificent defence of Madrid by troops mainly under Communist control had made the Communists the heroes of Spain."[38]

The Popular Front government, which was elected in February 1936, only five months before Franco's military revolt, was fragile from the very start. The alliance between the Socialist Party, the republican parties and the Communist Party was a recent development (indeed, their unity pact had been signed as late as January 1936, just a few weeks before the elections[39]) and, it stands to reason, aside from a shared desire to strengthen the democratic republic, the approaches of the constituent parties, and their longer-term aims, differed from each other. Of particular concern to the communists was that the republican government, just like a previous republican-socialist government formed in 1931, dithered on the question of agrarian reform, "the very essence of the democratic revolution," which if carried through in determined fashion "would have resulted in winning millions of people for democracy and progress."[40]

General Francisco Franco, the leader of the military revolt against the Republic, was initially handicapped by the fact that he was based in the Canary Islands, with the result that when troops based on the mainland sought to join his revolt, in several parts of the country the people were able to rise up and overcome them. It was in these circumstances that, with the people under arms, the anarchists, who wielded considerable influence in some regions, but particularly in Catalonia, carried out sweeping confiscations.

When Franz Borkenau arrived in Barcelona in early August 1936, he found the extent of expropriation (hotels, large stores, factories) "almost incredible... All the churches had been burnt, with the exception of the cathedral..."[41] Orwell also notes that "churches were wrecked and the priests driven out or killed."[42] This, it must be emphasized, was the work of the anarchists, not the communists

Where they controlled villages, the anarchists attempted to abolish money, while the communists disliked "this playing at Utopia."[43] Where land was seized under anarchist leadership, it was collectivized, something that was rarely popular with the peasantry.

Entirely unacknowledged by Orwell and Borkenau, it was the communist minister Vicente Uribe who finally addressed the agrarian problem when, early in the government formed by the socialist Largo Caballero, he proposed a reform which, even after it had been diluted by the Cabinet, "gave the land of the large landowners involved in the fascist conspiracy to the peasants in permanent usufruct." President Manuel Azaña (a member of the Republican Left party) approved the measure without demur, thereby demonstrating, says Iburruri, "that even the ideas of men who are most strongly against radical reforms... can evolve and change when the masses' demands are sufficiently loud to be heard."[44]

After the upsurge of popular resistance to the military rebellion, in some areas local committees were formed to rule alongside, or in some cases instead of, the established authorities, and the anarchists saw these as soviets, intending that they should become the ruling power in the country.[45] Orwell describes the committees as "the rough beginnings of a workers' government," and then asserts: "The thing that had happened in Spain was, in fact, not merely a civil war, but the beginning of a revolution."[46]

It is in this context that we must consider claims by Orwell (who goes so far as to assert, with no supporting evidence whatsoever: "The thing for which the Communists were working was not to postpone the Spanish revolution till a more suitable time, but to make sure that it never happened."[47]) and Borkenau (echoed by the previously-cited biographers of Hammett and Hellman) that the communists played a right-wing, anti-revolutionary role in Spain.

The terms "right" and "left" are, of course, relative. It is perfectly correct that the Spanish communist party was to the right of the anarchists and the quasi-Trotskyist Partido Obrero de Unificacion Marxista (POUM, in whose militia Orwell served). But that could hardly be considered a sin, when the latter two organizations were advocating (and, at least in the case of the anarchists, attempting to wage) a social revolution at a time when the Spanish Republic was under attack by the Franco military rebellion, aided by Mussolini and Hitler, and when the greatest possible unity was required within the Republic against the military insurgents.

Critics of the communist role in Spain often claim that the Soviet Union exerted rightward pressure on the Republic, using its military aid as a lever, an argument that sometimes twists reality out of all recognition. For example, when Symons claims that Stalin was interested in a communist-controlled Spain rather than a republican victory, he does not attempt to explain how, even if this were true, the communists would achieve such a result without first defeating Franco!

In fact, as early as May 1936, i.e. before the outbreak of the Civil War, the leadership of the Spanish party and the Comintern secretariat "stated clearly that the chief aim of the Spanish working people was to fight for a democratic republic without at present setting itself the task of effecting a transition from the bourgeois-democratic revolution to a socialist revolution."[48] And, yes, the Spanish party continued to receive Comintern advice, but this can hardly be interpreted as pressure on the Republican government, in which the communists constituted a minority.[49] Sometimes, furthermore, this advice was such as to give the lie to the claim that, as Kessler-Harris would have it, the Soviets wished to exert leadership over all Republican forces. For example, although the Spanish party had proposed that it and the Socialist Party should work for organic unity as early as 1935,[50] the Comintern advice now was that there should be no attempt to "force amalgamation" as "the most important thing was unity of action by both parties within the government, in all government bodies, in the trade unions, in the army, in the leadership of industry, as well as in joint action at the parliamentary and municipal elections."[51]

Did the Soviets, after they extended diplomatic and military support, make policy suggestions to the Republican government? Yes, of course. Was such advice always accepted? No. In December 1936, Soviet leaders Stalin, Molotov and Voroshilov wrote to Spanish premier Largo Caballero, in part suggesting that peasants be drawn into the army or form guerrilla detachments behind enemy lines, a process which might be aided by pro-peasant decrees.[52] Such detachments were never formed, which Hobsbawm finds "a strange omission in the country which gave this form of irregular warfare its name."[53]

So how, precisely, did Spanish communists wish to influence the course of the Civil War?

Seeing real dangers in the unrealistic revolutionary romanticism of the anarchists and Trotskyists, they sought to halt the confiscations, summary executions and church-burnings, as these were unnecessarily driving people into the Franco camp; similarly, they sought to curtail the activities of the local committees, centralizing government — a surely sensible measure in a time of civil war. In order to prosecute that war more effectively, it was the communists' strong view that the militias (even Borkenau is forced to concede that the "military inadequacy" of the militias "is beyond doubt"[54]) should be dissolved and replaced by a national army, subject to normal military discipline. Undoubtedly, such practical measures were unlikely to have attracted the support of romantic revolutionaries, but the communists were more intent on winning the war than posturing. And it would be a mistake to assume that this approach did not command support: even Ernest Hemingway — an individualist if there ever was one — "accepted the Communist discipline in Spain because it was 'the soundest and sanest for the prosecution of the war.'"[55]

Those who are critical of Hammett's support of the international communist movement's position on the Spanish Civil War can only attribute this to shortcomings in his intellectual development, implying that he may have been misled. It is, apparently, inconceivable to them that he not only had a good understanding of this position, and of the objectively counter-revolutionary stance of the anarchists and the Trotskyists, but that he could have been in firm agreement with the measures urged by the Spanish communists, subordinating all to the task of winning the war on the grounds that unless this were achieved, all would be lost. Because they do not agree with this viewpoint, they deny the possibility that Hammett may have genuinely shared it. It therefore seems that they do not have much of an understanding of the real Hammett, the unsentimental man who in his writing on many occasions had his protagonists allow nothing to stand in the way of getting the job done. This was not a man whose lack of formal education caused him to stumble over "gaps in logic," but someone who in mid-life had finally found the means of identifying those gaps, allowing him to overcome the "intellectual blindness" of earlier years and adopt the *class position* which could have imparted much greater meaning to his work had he only achieved this level of understanding ten or 15 years earlier.

The Soviet-German Non-Aggression Pact

And then there is the Soviet-German Non-Aggression Pact of August 1939.

Rollyson makes no real attempt to explain the circumstances in which the agreement was signed.[56] Gallagher uses Muriel Gardiner, the real-life "Julia," to express her disapproval of the pact, claiming that the Soviet Union and Nazi Germany had "practically become one."[57] Kessler-Harris concedes: "Some argued that the Soviet Union signed the pact to buy time to build up its defenses," but then she quotes Hellman as saying that she "wholly disagreed with the position of the Communist Party in its glorification of Nazism" to which the pact gave rise.[58] Mellen says that after the signing of the pact Hammett and Hellman "became ardent pacifists, discarding their antifascism as warmongering and opposing the 'imperialist war' in Europe" as "opposition to fascism was no longer acceptable" after "Stalin decreed that antifascist activity should cease and Party faithful should work for peace."[59] Then, of course, having campaigned against war in Europe, the CPUSA, along with other communist parties, immediately switched to support for the war after Nazi troops invaded the Soviet Union in June 1941.

Mellen's above-quoted claim that Stalin "hoped that England and France, with whom he had an alliance, would fight Hitler for him" is shown, by a consideration of the circumstances in which the non-aggression pact of August 1939 was signed, to be little more than a threadbare falsehood. The reverse was the case.

It was Stalin's view, in fact, that Britain and France wished to create a situation in which the Soviet Union would be left to fight Nazi Germany alone. In a speech on March 10, 1939, he accused "certain American and European politicians and newsmen of inciting Germany to attack the USSR." The latter would support nations that, victims of aggression, were fighting for their independence, but its policy was "to be cautious and not allow our country to be drawn into conflicts by warmongers who are accustomed to have others pull the chestnuts out of the fire for them."[60]

Events were to demonstrate that this Soviet caution was fully justified. Joseph P. Davies wrote to his friend Sumner Welles on the day the Soviet-German pact was announced, reminding him that the

Soviet Union had been prepared to fight on behalf of Czechoslovakia (the Soviet Union had even cancelled its non-aggression treaty with Poland in anticipation of having to cross Polish territory in order to deliver on this promise[61]) but had been undermined by Chamberlain's agreement with Hitler at Munich in 1938, leading in March 1939 to the dismemberment of Czechoslovakia. Since Munich — "appeasement" — "there grew still greater distrust, so far as the Soviet Government was concerned, in either the capacity, the intention, or even the 'pledged word' of the Chamberlain government or the Daladier government...The suspicion continued to grow that Britain and France were playing a diplomatic game to place the Soviets in the position where Russia would have to fight Germany alone."[62]

On March 20, 1939, five days after the Nazi annexation of Bohemia and Moravia, the British press reported that the UK had asked the USSR to join a pact to resist further aggression. The text of this diplomatic note was not published at the time, but a Soviet communiqué issued the following day gave an indication of its content. The communiqué stated that neither Poland nor Rumania had sought Soviet assistance; neither did they advise the Soviet Union that they felt threatened. On March 18, the British government had asked the Soviet Union what its position would be in the event of an attack on Rumania. In response, the Soviets had proposed a conference of Great Britain, France, Poland, Rumania, Turkey and the Soviet Union, which could evaluate the dangers and make clear the position of the parties. Said the Soviet communiqué of March 21: "The British government, however, found this proposal premature."[63]

The British government now asked if the Soviet Union would, with Poland, France and Britain, issue a joint declaration denouncing aggression and consider an immediate meeting of all four after any further aggression. The Soviet Union found this too vague, but agreed to it, proposing that such a declaration should be signed not just by Foreign Ministers, but also the Prime Ministers. This went nowhere, as Poland refused to sign a declaration with the USSR. There was no further approach to the Soviet Union until April 15, but on March 31 British premier Neville Chamberlain announced that Britain and France would go to the aid of Poland if it was attacked.[64] To have taken such a step without Soviet participation was, according to the authors of *A History of Anglo-Soviet Relations*, "stark madness."[65]

On April 15, British Ambassador Sir William Seeds asked the Soviet Union to issue a unilateral declaration guaranteeing Poland and Rumania. Thus began talks which would last until August 26. On April 17, the Soviet Union presented an eight-point program calling for an alliance of Great Britain, France and the Soviet Union, a military convention and the "guaranteeing of all states between the Baltic and the Black Sea." Astonishingly, this went unanswered for three weeks.[66] In the meantime, Germany withdrew from the Anglo-German Naval Treaty and the German-Polish Non-Aggression Pact.

On May 9, Britain reiterated its request of April 15, modified to the extent that if the Soviet Union issued a unilateral declaration, Britain would decide where and when Soviet troops would be used. The Soviet proposal for a triple alliance was ignored. Five days later, the Soviet Union modified this proposal, stressing that it was essential to have a three-power pact, a military convention alongside the political agreement, and a joint guarantee as previously proposed. Even the conservative *Daily Telegraph* pointed out that if the British government wished to convince the Soviet Union that a Soviet declaration would result in British and French assistance, there could be no logical objection to a triple alliance.[67]

On May 27, the British Ambassador agreed to discuss a pact, but with the guarantees restricted to Poland and Romania. In a speech four days later, Soviet foreign minister Molotov pointed out that this was a virtual invitation for Hitler to leave these countries aside for now and attack other states bordering the Soviet Union — and he named Latvia, Estonia and Finland — "by the time-honoured Nazi methods of the instigation and financing of internal disturbances and revolts and then marching in on the 'invitation' of a puppet government."[68] It was at this juncture that the French Ambassador to Berlin advised his government that if the triple alliance negotiations were successful, Hitler would not attack. A few days later, Winston Churchill sounded a similar note, saying in a speech that "with a strong eastern front war may be averted altogether."[69]

In its reply to Britain, the Soviet Union repeated its request for the inclusion of the Baltic states, proposing that the pact should guarantee Latvia, Estonia, Finland, Rumania, Poland, Greece, Turkey and Belgium, and that the pact of mutual assistance and the military convention should come into force simultaneously.

Ostensibly, Britain now decided to speed up the negotiations, dispatching William Strang to Moscow on June 12. However, while Chamberlain had been only too willing to personally meet Hitler and Mussolini in 1938, Strang was "an unknown Foreign Office official."[70] In Britain, questions were asked by those opposed to appeasement of Hitler. Writing in the *Sunday Express* on July 23, former Prime Minister Lloyd George wanted to know why a mere Foreign Office bureaucrat had been sent to "represent us in an infinitely more powerful country which was offering to come to our aid?" He answered his own question thus: "There is only one answer. Mr. Neville Chamberlain, Lord Halifax [foreign secretary] and Sir John Simon [former foreign secretary and now Chancellor of the Exchequer] do not want any association with Russia."[71] Soviet Ambassador Ivan Maisky, obviously keen that the British should adopt a more serious approach to the negotiations, invited foreign secretary Lord Halifax to visit Moscow, but this was virtually ignored.

On June 16, the day after the negotiations commenced, Molotov suggested that if the Baltic states were not to be guaranteed there should be a defensive triple alliance pledging mutual assistance in the event of direct aggression. Britain and France ignored this and on June 21 put forward a formula regarding the Baltic states which the Soviet Union found unacceptable. Later in the month, Andrei Zhdanov, president of the Soviet Foreign Affairs Committee, wrote in *Pravda*: "It seems to me that the British and French governments are not out for a real agreement acceptable to the USSR, but only for talks about an agreement in order to demonstrate before the public of their own countries the alleged unyielding attitude of the USSR and thus facilitate the conclusion of an agreement with the aggressors."[72]

Britain and France finally put forward a proposal regarding the Baltic states on July 1 which the Soviet Union found acceptable, i.e. that their names appear not in the treaty but in an annex — but with the addition of Switzerland and Holland, which did not even recognize the Soviet Union. Even so, two days later the Soviet Union accepted this with the qualification that as this would mean additional obligations for itself, there should be further guarantees in the form of mutual assistance pacts with Turkey and Poland.

This was followed by two long meetings on July 8 in which Britain and France insisted on the inclusion of Switzerland and Holland, regardless of the provisions for Turkey and Poland. At these meetings, there was no meeting of the minds on what constituted "indirect aggression" and no agreement on when the military convention would come into play. On July 17, Britain and France dropped the proposal regarding Switzerland and Holland, but there was still no agreement on the other two questions.

On July 23, the Soviet Union insisted that the military convention come into force concurrently with the pact for the triple alliance. (The reason for such Soviet insistence was obvious: it wanted to avoid a situation in which its own troops would go to aid Poland immediately while France and Britain, on the other side of the continent, might drag their heels.) The Soviet side urged that talks along these lines commence immediately, in which case it was confident that a formula could be found regarding "indirect aggression." Two days later, Britain agreed to immediate "staff talks."

This latter formulation meant that the representatives at the negotiations would not have the power to agree, merely to talk. Further dismay was caused by the choice of leader for the military mission that Britain would dispatch to Moscow: Admiral the Hon. Sir Reginald Aylmer Ranfurly Plunkett Ernle-Erle-Drax, of whom few MPs had heard. Adding insult to injury, the British delegation was sent by sea, when it could have flown to Moscow in a day.

In recent years, declassified documents have revealed that the Soviet negotiators, War Minister Klementi Voroshilov and Red Army chief of staff Boris Shaposhnikov, offered 120 infantry divisions, 16 cavalry divisions, 5,000 pieces of heavy artillery, almost 10,000 tanks and around 5,500 bombers and fighter aircraft as its contribution to a determined bid by the proposed triple alliance to respond to further aggression by Hitler. The Soviet negotiators were nonplussed when Drax, asked what the British contribution would be, replied that only 16 divisions were currently combat-ready.[73]

But there would be no triple alliance, as it emerged that Poland stood in the way. When Britain and France asked the Soviets what they were prepared to do after an attack on Poland by Hitler, Voroshilov said that the Red Army was prepared to assist in Poland's defense, but that it would obviously need to cross Polish territory to do so. The Anglo-French team then consulted Poland, which said that as it had British and French support, it would not require assistance from the

Soviet Union, which should not enter Polish territory — although it would welcome Soviet supplies. The air of unreality prevailing in Polish government circles is perhaps best illustrated by the boast by an unnamed Polish minister, made a few months earlier to Davies, that Polish troops would be in Berlin three weeks after any German attack. "Poland did not need Russian aid; they could handle the Germans alone and easily."[74]

There was a break after August 17, and the talks resumed four days later, but no progress was made. That same day, it was announced that the Soviet Union had agreed a non-aggression pact with Germany, which would be signed on August 23. Nothing in this pact ruled out the Soviet Union signing a similar agreement with Britain and France, but the latter were not interested, and their delegations departed from Moscow on August 26.

Soviet distrust of Britain and France had been proved well-founded, as it was by now perfectly plain that the latter had no intention of entering an anti-Hitler political and military pact with Moscow, believing that they would be able to sit and watch as Hitler attacked not just Poland, but the Soviet Union as well. Had they been serious, they would surely have exerted the kind of pressure on Poland that they had brought to bear on Czechoslovakia in 1938, prevailing upon Warsaw to allow Soviet troops to cross its territory in order to stop Hitler.

≋

Having resisted German approaches for an agreement until it became obvious that a pact and military convention with France and Britain would not be possible, the Soviet Union now had little option, unless it was to find itself in the position into which the Anglo-French team had tried to maneuver it all along, but to deal with the Nazis.

Mellen records that Hellman explained the CPUSA position to Ring Lardner Jr. — "it was necessary for the Soviet Union to defend itself now that the British and French weren't coming through with their own alliance with Stalin." [75] Quite true, but this is neither explained nor placed in context, thus making it easier to misrepresent the pact which, it is sometimes claimed, meant that Germany and the Soviet Union were now "allies." Emery goes further than most when he refers to the "Hitler-Stalin team."[76] Both he and Mellen find some irony in the fact that Hammett and Hellman, nine days before the pact was signed, endorsed a statement condemning the "'fantastic falsehood that the USSR and the totalitarian states are basically alike.'"[77]

But, of course, the two countries were *not* basically alike, and the pact did nothing to change that. Neither did it mean that they were now "allies." Instead, the agreement was precisely what it claimed to be: a non-aggression pact in which both parties agreed "to desist from any act of violence, any aggressive action, and any attack on each other either individually or jointly with other powers" and from lending support to any third power which might attack the other party, or participating "in any grouping of powers whatsoever that is directly or indirectly aimed at the other party;" disputes or conflicts between the two parties would be settled by "friendly exchange of opinion" or arbitration. The pact would be valid for ten years and, unless either party gave notice of termination (the pact used the unusual formulation "denounce it"), extended for a further five years.[78]

There was, of course, a secret protocol in which it was agreed to divide Poland between the two powers, but even this becomes understandable when seen in the context of the failed negotiations for a triple alliance: had Poland agreed that Soviet troops, in coming to its defense, could cross its territory, how different things might have been! Hitler, with no triple alliance standing in his way, duly attacked Poland on September 1, whereupon Britain and France were compelled by their previous undertakings to declare war on Germany. World War II had commenced.

The line of the CPUSA, like that of communist parties elsewhere, now changed, shifting its emphasis from antifascism to opposition to the war. In a statement on September 19, the party characterized the latter as "the Second Imperialist War."

> The ruling capitalist and landlord classes of all the belligerent countries are equally guilty for this war. This war, therefore, cannot be supported by the workers. It is not a war against fascism, not a war to protect small nations from aggression…It is a war between rival imperialisms for world domination."

The statement proceeded to call for "maximum support to China and to all oppressed peoples in their struggle against fascism, for freedom and national independence." Nor did the Comintern suddenly become pro-Nazi, but in a manifesto issued on November 7 characterized the war as "an unjust, reactionary, imperialist war, which the ruling circles of Britain, France, and Germany are waging for world supremacy."[79] This, it can be seen, was practically identical to the left line on World War I.

Hammett, rather than becoming the "ardent pacifist" labeled thus by Mellen, supported the Soviet invasion of Finland,[80] by means of which the Soviet Union sought to secure the defense of Leningrad. (This effectively gave the lie to claims that the Soviet Union was now "allied" with Germany, for against whom, if not Hitler, was such a defense being prepared?) And Hellman's later claim regarding the CPUSA's "glorification" of Nazism after the signing of the pact was, of course, simply untrue. Mellen is right in one of her assertions, however, for Stalin did indeed call for a muting of antifascism. But was this because he had suddenly discovered the glories of Nazism? Of course not: it was due to the often over-cautious Stalin's fear that Hitler would use continued antifascist activity by Comintern affiliates as an excuse to void the pact and attack the Soviet Union.

That Hammett *actively* supported the new line, working on the League of American Writers' Keep America Out of the War Committee, suggests that this was not a man duped into blindly following every twist and turn of CPUSA or Soviet policy but someone who believed in — and understood — what he was doing. In a letter to his daughter Mary in October 1938, Hammett had explained that the most reactionary circles in Britain believed that:

> the next World War will be between the Fascist countries and Russia, and that Britain should do what it can to help the Fascists and to keep that war from spreading to Western Europe. It seems to them that the war will be a very long and fierce one that may result in the Fascists and Communists destroying one another, but will certainly result in considerable damage to both sides — leaving England sitting pretty, holding once more the balance of power.[81]

It is clear from this that Hammett would have fully understood what was at stake during the Soviet Union's negotiations with Britain and France in 1939. We can only regret that we do not have his reaction when it was announced that the Soviet Union had turned the tables on the latter two powers — a dramatic twist that might have been plucked from a Hammett novel!

NOTES

1. Joan Mellen, *Hellman and Hammett: The Legendary Passion of Lillian Hellman and Dashiell Hammett* (New York: Harper Collins, 1996), 111.
2. Ibid., 107.
3. Ibid., 102-103.
4. Richard Layman commentary, Dashiell Hammett, *Selected Letters of Dashiell Hammett, 1921-1960*, ed. Richard Layman, with Julie M. Rivett (Washington D,C,: Counterpoint, 2001), 59.
5. Mellen, 103.
6. See, for example, the case of the Communist Party of Great Britain in Ken Fuller, *Radical Aristocrats: London Busworkers from the 1880s to the 1980s*, (London: Lawrence and Wishart, 1985).
7. Institute of Marxism-Leninism, Central Committee of the CPSU, *Outline History of the Communist International* (Moscow: Progress Publishers, 1971), 363. Surprisingly, Hobsbawm falls into the same error as Mellen, et al, claiming that "the Spanish Left discovered the Comintern's Popular Front, which was being urged on it from neighbouring France." See Eric Hobsbawm, *The Age of Extremes: The Short Twentieth Century, 1914-1989* (London: Michael Joseph, 1994), 157.
8. Dolores Ibarruri, *They Shall Not Pass* (New York: International Publishers, 1976), 147.
9. Ibid., 155.
10. Ibid., 155-56.
11. Dorothy Gallagher, *Lillian Hellman: An Imperious Life* (New Haven and London: Yale University Press, 2014.), 59, 58. Joseph Davies takes a somewhat different view of Duranty, saying that he "told the truth as he saw it and has the eyes of genius." See Joseph E. Davies, *Mission to Moscow* (London: Victor Gollancz, 1942), 227.
12. Mellen, 129.
13. Davies, 181-182.
14. Mellen, 112, 167.
15. Joseph Freeman, *An American Testament: A Narrative of Rebels and Romantics* (London: Victor Gollancz, Left Book Club Edition, 1938), 495.
16. Alec Nove, *An Economic History of the USSR 1917-1991* (London:

Penguin Books, 1992), 126.
17 Mellen, 114.
18 Freeman, 547.
19 See, for example, Grover Furr, *Khrushchev Lied* (Kettering Ohio: Erythrós Press and Media, LLC, 2011). Roger Keeran's review of this book, "Khrushchev Lied but What Is the Truth?" on the *Marxism-Leninism Today* site provides valuable balance. See mltoday.com/article/1246-khrushchev-lied-but-what-is-the-truth/29. Also of interest is Furr's "Rejoinder to Roger Keeran" at mltoday.com/rejoinder-to-roger-keeran.
20 Martinson, 139.
21 Davies, 33, 34.
22 Ibid., 38-39.
23 Ibid., 38.
24 Ibid., 39.
25 Ibid., 83.
26 Ibid., 110.
27 Ibid., 136-37.
28 Ibid., 178-79.
29 Hellman, *An Unfinished Woman* in *Three*, (Boston: Little, Brown, 1979), 205.
30 Carl Rollyson, *Lillian Hellman: Her Legend and her Legacy* (New York: St. Martin's Press, 1988), 146.
31 See Cedric Belfrage, *The American Inquisition* (Indianapolis: Bobbs-Merrill Company, 1973), 138-39 and Giles Scott-Smith, "'A Radical Democratic Political Offensive': Melvin J. Lasky, *Der Monat*, and the Congress for Cultural Freedom," *Journal of Contemporary History*, Vol. 35 No. 2, April 2000.
32 See, for example, Timothy Garton Ash, "Orwell's List," *The New York Review of Books*, September 25, 2003.
33 Alice Kessler-Harris, *A Difficult Woman: The Challenging Life and Times of Lillian Hellman* (New York: Bloomsbury Press, 2012), 115.
34 Julian Symons, *Dashiell Hammett* (San Diego/New York/London: Harcourt Brace Jovanovich, 1985), 123.
35 Rollyson, 112.
36 Gallagher, 60-61.
37 Mellen, 114.
38 George Orwell, *Homage to Catalonia* (London: Folio Society,

1998), 202.
39 Ibarruri, 161.
40 Ibid., 89, 86.
41 Franz Borkenau, *The Spanish Cockpit: An Eyewitness Account of the Spanish Civil War* (London: Phoenix Press, 2000), 71. This was first published in 1937 by Faber and Faber.
42 Orwell, 187.
43 Borkenau, 60.
44 Ibarruri, 235, 236.
45 Borkenau, 27.
46 Orwell, 189.
47 Ibid., 207.
48 Institute of Marxism-Leninism, 415.
49 The Comintern assigned a small team of international leaders to assist the Spanish party, led by Italian communist leader Palmiro Togliatti. Hobsbawm says that Togliatti was among "the last to escape from the country in 1939." See Hobsbawm, 161.
50 Ibarruri, 160-161.
51 Ibid., 420.
52 Institute of Marxism-Leninism, 418.
53 Hobsbawn, 160.
54 Borkenau, 187.
55 Carlos Baker, *Ernest Hemingway: A Life Story* (London: The Literary Guild, 1969), 413. Baker gives the impression that these words were uttered by Hemingway, but in fact, although doubtless they reflected his own thinking, he put them in the mouth of his character Robert Jordan. See Ernest Hemingway, *For Whom the Bell Tolls* (New York: Collier Books, Macmillan, 1987), 163. The Spanish Civil War had a significant effect on Hemingway's maturity as a writer and on the belated dawning of his social consciousness. In this period, he cooperated — knowingly and without regret — with communists, as when on June 1937 he addressed the Writers' Congress, an event sponsored by the party-influenced League of American Writers, and at which party general secretary Earl Browder was a speaker. Baker, 376-377.
56 Rollyson, 151.
57 Gallagher, 78.
58 Kessler-Harris, 126, 127. This quote also appears in Deborah

Martinson, *Lillian Hellman: A Life with Foxes and Scoundrels* (Berkeley: Counterpoint, 2005), 140. Identification of its source, however, casts a different light on it, as it comes from Hellman's draft statement, which was never made, to the House Un-American Affairs Committee, and in which she was obviously trying to curry favor. See Rollyson, 320.
59 Mellen, 161, 162, 166.
60 W. P. and Zelda K. Coates, *A History of Anglo-Soviet Relations* (London: Lawrence & Wishart/The Pilot Press, 1943), 601.
61 Joseph P. Davies to Harry Hopkins, July 18, 1941; Davies, 316.
62 Joseph P. Davies to Sumner Welles, August 22, 1939; Davies, 290.
63 W. P. and Zelda K. Coates, 604.
64 Ibid., 605.
65 Ibid., 605-606.
66 Ibid., 606.
67 Ibid., 608, citing *Daily Telegraph*, May 18, 1939.
68 Ibid., 609.
69 Ibid., 610, citing *The Times*, June 5, 1939.
70 Ibid., 611.
71 Ibid., citing *Sunday Express*, July 23, 1939.
72 Ibid., 612.
73 Nick Holdsworth, "Stalin planned to send a million troops to stop Hitler if Britain and France agreed pact," *The Telegraph*, October 18, 2008.
74 Davies, 292.
75 Mellen, 166.
76 Vince Emery, commentary in Dashiell Hammett, *Lost Stories*, ed. Vince Emery (San Francisco: Vince Emery Productions, 2005), 301.
77 Ibid. and Mellen, 165-66.
78 The full text is widely available. See, for example, http://avalon.law.yale.edu/20th_century/nonagres.asp
79 These statements appeared in *The Communist*, October and December, 1939, and are quoted in William Z. Foster, *History of the Communist Party of the United States* (New York: International Publishers), 1952, Chapter 27, available at williamz.foster.blogspot.com.
80 Emery, 301. Emery chides Hammett for supporting the Soviet invasion of Finland in November 1939, as he was "normally a rooter for

the little guy." What Emery cannot see, because like other authors writing on Hammett's politics he makes no effort to understand his subject's viewpoint, is that Hammett *was* rooting for the little guy: the worker, in whose interest the Soviet Union was governed; that country was now, having postponed the threat of a Nazi invasion with its non-aggression pact, strengthening the defenses of the approach to Leningrad in preparation for the inevitable. (The Soviet Union attempted to achieve its aims by diplomatic means, but was rebuffed by the Finnish government. For a useful summary of the Finnish campaign, see the Coateses' *A History of Anglo-Soviet Relations*, 628-636.)

81   Hammett to Mary Hammett, October 13, 1938; *Selected Letters*, 138.

8 Hardboiled to the end

In November 1939, Hammett, concerned at the increasingly illiberal political climate in the USA, was active in seeking signatories to a public statement headed "In Defense of the Bill of Rights."[1]

He succeeded in getting 65 signatories, consisting mainly of scientists and academics, writers and artists who now publicly warned that the House Committee Investigating Un-American Activities, formed in 1938 under the chairmanship of Martin Dies Jr., and later to be popularly known as HUAC, was "talking openly of the suppression of dissident groups" and had won the support of several influential newspapers; that "open incitement to vigilante activity against labor, against minority groups, against national and religious groups is increasing in this country"; and that "various discriminatory and repressive measures against the foreign-born have been passed by the House of Representatives and have become law in many states."

In particular, the statement noted efforts to silence the CPUSA, and that its general secretary Earl Browder was being prosecuted on the basis of information that had been in the possession of the authorities for several years.

The Dies Committee and its aides had illegally raided CPUSA offices in several cities, and Detroit police had, by failing to provide adequate protection, allowed people attending a public meeting addressed by party chairman William Z. Foster to be attacked by organized thugs as they left the hall. The statement concluded by pointing to recent international experience:

> We have before us the example of many European countries where suppression of the Communist Party was but a beginning, followed by a campaign against trade unions, cultural groups, Jews, Catholics, Masons, and ending with the destruction of all freedom. It is in our own interest, therefore, and in the interest of those rights for which America has struggled these many years that we raise our voices in solemn warning against denying to the Communists, or to any other minority group, the full freedom guaranteed by the Bill of Rights.[2]

This statement, we must remember, was drafted by Hammett. And we see that, three months after the signing of the German-Soviet Non-Aggression Pact, there is no sign that he has suddenly become soft on fascism.

The threat posed by HUAC would recede after the USA entered World War II and found itself an ally of the Soviet Union, but even before that conflict was over the red-hunters would be back on the job, and Hammett would eventually be in their sights.

≈

By this time, Hammett had come to the attention of the FBI (although, of course, he had broken no laws); Layman says that his FBI file "documents his full schedule of active political interests from 1938 to 1942" and from 1945 to 1951.[3] J. Edgar Hoover's operatives must have had their hands full with Hammett, because his political duties were numerous, and there can be little doubt that they consumed considerable quantities of his time and energy.

Writing to his daughter Mary in December 1938, he said that he had just spoken at a meeting of 22,000 and that in the previous week he had spoken four times — at "the Commodore for Spain, at a dinner for the League for Peace and Democracy, at a Mecca Temple anti-Nazi mass meeting, and over the radio for Jewish refugees."[4]

He was president of the Professionals Conference Against Nazi

Persecution, protesting the treatments of Jews and Catholics in Germany, and chaired the Exiled Writers Committee.[5] He appears to have been a hardliner; when a dissenter argued at a meeting called by the Committee on Election Rights that the CPUSA sought to deny the election rights of Socialist Party members, Hammett used his position as chairman to silence him, saying that the man had violated the spirit of the meeting.[6]

Along with others, in May 1939 Hammett launched the monthly *Equality* magazine, followed by Equality Publishers in September. These ventures opposed racism and anti-Semitism, and we must assume that by now Hammett had come to understand the role of racism in the exploitation of working people. (One of Hellman's biographers notes that the FBI was suspicious of the magazine "for its intent to bring about racial harmony."[7])

Although the CPUSA did indeed scale down its anti-fascist activity somewhat, this did not necessarily lighten Hammett's load, for he then took a role on the Keep America Out of the War Committee, formed by the League of American Writers in January 1940. Also in 1940, he was involved in the launch of the afternoon newspaper *PM* published by Ralph Ingersoll, one of Hellman's lovers, but withdrew after Ingersoll invited government scrutiny of a list of staff, supposedly communist members or supporters, which had been circulated anonymously.[8] The following year, he became president of the League of American Writers.

Hammett still had his bad days. At a public meeting in February 1940, while sitting at the speakers' table pretending to take notes, he jotted down his immediate impressions in a letter to his daughter Mary:

> Some ass is talking about Finland as if he thought it was a breakfast food...Some old duffer is up on his tottering legs now mumbling so that there's no way in God's world of knowing what he is talking about, though I just heard him say "civil liberties." Some crackpot just passed me a note asking if I thought we ought to say something about F.D.R. and the Youth Congress. I'm going to suggest that we say something about Aztec pottery.

After the meeting Hammett intended to eat, then attend a meeting of German refugee writers. "At least I'll come as close to understanding them as I do these mugs."[9]

What was happening here? He may have been drunk, of course. We have no way of knowing whether the people he was satirizing were fellow-members of the CPUSA, or merely allies, but they were certainly not enemies. One is reminded of Hellman's recollection that Hammett "was often witty and bitingly sharp about the American Communist Party, but he was, in the end, loyal to them [sic]."[10] Maybe this is the sort of thing she meant. It is perhaps important to bear in mind that he was making fun of personalities, not policies. It is possible that Hammett, who seems to have committed himself to the international communist movement before he actually joined the CPUSA, sometimes felt that his US comrades (or some of them) were merely playing at being communists, particularly in their use of jargon, compared to those with experience of opposing fascism at close quarters or building socialism — hence his professed preference for the German refugee writers.

≈

Anti-communist (and particularly anti-Soviet) writers pour scorn on parties which, like the CPUSA, first adopted an anti-war position upon the conclusion of the Nazi-Soviet non-aggression treaty and then became pro-war once Nazi Germany attacked the Soviet Union in June 1941. Mellen and others picture Hammett as meekly following the party line, as if unable to think for himself. Once again, the picture we get of Hammett is grossly distorted; the real man is obscured from our view.

Hammett was guided by class politics. It was a long time since he had been a worker, and few if any of his acquaintances were workers, but the cause that he had embraced just a few years earlier placed him at the service of the working class. That seems too obvious to need stating, but the fact of the matter is that for many of his middle-class comrades it was not so clear; although believing themselves to be socialists, for many of them the vision of socialism was often based more on morality and their revulsion at the Depression and its effects than on the real desire to create a society in which the working class would wield power. That is one reason why many of them would acquire a new set of beliefs when the going got rough, whereas Hammett would weather the storm.

For those who believed that the working class *did* wield power in the Soviet Union, the adoption of an anti-war position upon the conclusion on the non-aggression pact and then the reversal of this when the Nazis invaded was not really that problematic. The Soviet Union was the only socialist country in the world, and for communists it was therefore important that nothing should jeopardize the first socialist state. War, obviously, was one such threat, and thus the 1939 anti-war policy which, mistaken though it may have been, viewed the conflict as merely another inter-imperialist squabble, had the virtue of being protective of the Soviet Union. And opposition to the war could not be described as being confined to an oddball minority.

Arthur Miller recalls that in 1940 he "saw the conflict between Germany and the Anglo-French as a new version of the old imperialist conflict of the previous world war, another last gasp of an expiring, self-destroying capitalist system."[11] Miller would later change his mind about both the anti-war policy and the Soviet Union (although unlike some other former communists in the postwar period, he staunchly opposed McCarthyism and refused to name names during his appearance before the HUAC), and it is easy to sympathize with him when he laments: "How could I possibly have tolerated the idea that a Nazi victory would be no worse than that of the British and French, corrupt and decadent as they were, and craven as they had been during the decade of knuckling under to Hitler's demands?"[12]

Come June 1941, the CPUSA immediately jettisoned its anti-war policy as, says Foster, it "realized that all possibility of limiting the war had vanished and that now there was a...full-fledged people's anti-fascist war."[13] Some will scoff at this formulation, but read in context it is reasonable enough, as Britain and France (the latter, of course, had been defeated in 1940) had, as Miller says, knuckled under to Hitler, and there were real fears that British ruling circles would come to a deal with Hitler; but with the Soviet Union now involved, there was no doubt that this would be an anti-fascist struggle.

Hammett, anyway, now had a war he could support, and one which, after the attack on Pearl Harbor in December 1941, the USA would join. Unlike at least one critic of his politics (Julian Symons, then a Trotskyist who unsuccessfully attempted to avoid the war by registering as a conscientious objector), Hammett, aged 48, overcame the Army's initial medical objections and re-enlisted.

≋

There were probably several reasons why Hammett rejoined the Army, some of which we will discuss briefly in the final chapter. However, it would be rash to discount the possibility that he was a patriot who wished to play a part in the defense of his country. Conservative opinion is all too ready to view communism and patriotism as polar opposites, but Hammett would not have seen it that way, as US progressives have always been anxious to assert that the USA and its history is not the sole property of reaction: it is *their* country as well.

However, it is also possible that Hammett felt that, in his initial rush of enthusiasm after 1937, he had over-committed himself — or, rather, his time — and that he was looking for some breathing space. He would not have been the first, or the last, political activist to have realized that he has volunteered so much of his time that he has little left for himself; sometimes, this realization is accompanied by the discovery that some of the tasks one has shouldered are not as exciting or vital as anticipated, and the letter to Mary in February 1940 quoted above may have arisen from just such a revelation. Enlisting in the Army would, Hammett might have estimated, more than compensate for the other pro-victory duties he was now unable to perform. But we should not exaggerate this factor; if it played a part in his decision, it may well have been a secondary one.

Once assigned to the remote Aleutian island of Adak, Hammett's duties were, in large part, those of the writer. Along with Robert Colodny, a veteran of the Abraham Lincoln Brigade which had fought in Spain, he was given the job of writing *The Battle for the Aleutians*, a 4,000-word pamphlet.

According to Layman, he sat back while Colodny wrote it and then, finding it too political, completely redrafted it himself;[14] Colodny is usually credited with providing the captions only. Hammett wrote Hellman that the "local army folk think it's hot stuff."[15] And when the question of a camp newspaper came up, there was obviously only one possible editor. Although the Army was still segregated, when

Hammett was allowed to select his own staff for the paper, he chose a mixture of blacks and whites. Apart from the readily-available news sources, Hammett was able to obtain *PM*, the left-wing New York newspaper he had helped launch, the CPUSA's *Daily Worker* and *New Masses*, and Claude Cockburn's irreverent *The Week*.[16]

When the camp chaplain complained that God's name was being taken in vain in the *Adakian*, Hammett told Hellman: "My feeling is that God's doing pretty well to be mentioned at all, space limitations being what they are, and He and His representative had better leave well enough alone."[17]

Hammett continued to read widely while on Adak. Towards the end of his military service, he told Hellman that he "happened to run across a copy of Lenin's *Theoretical Principles of Marxism* (Vol. XI in the *Selected Works*) and am looking forward to a very fine time indeed with it."[18] According to Johnson, Hammett also "reread Marx" (but how much of Marx would have been available on Adak?).[19]

Hammett did much to become "one of the boys," but there was also much which marked him as a privileged soldier. When, for example, he wrote to his daughter Mary on Christmas Day 1943 that beer was being issued, he noted, "In a box under my bed there are some cans of pate foi gras and caviar and lobster and smoked salmon in olive oil and one thing and another that ought to go pretty well with beer."[20] And when the opportunity offered itself, he would gamble. In July 1944, he asked Hellman to bet up to $2,500 for him on the outcome of that year's election. In September, he won "a couple of hundred dollars in a latrine crap game — the first time I've had dice in my hands in nearly a year." In November, the tables were turned when he lost almost $500 in a game in the non-com's club.[21]

≈

As the war wound down, forces were re-awakening which wasted no time in alerting Hammett to the kind of America which awaited him.

In March 1945, he and others were denounced by the *Chicago Tribune* for allegedly being communist propagandists in the Army. In July, shortly before Hammett received his honorable discharge, a congressional subcommittee was told that this editor of a camp newspaper was a communist. Hammett told Hellman that he wouldn't be surprised if the *Chicago Tribune* story "stirred up only the faintest of ripples," explaining to daughter Jo that the ludicrous implication was that he had been "scouting Alaska for the Soviet Union in case they wanted to take the Aleutians away from us..."[22]

Small wonder that for a while he even considered staying in Alaska after the war, buying a bar or club called the Carolina Moon in Anchorage. But he decided otherwise and, typically open-handed, gave the Carolina Moon to Corinne Benny, the black woman who ran it.[23] But he was still conflicted, and when he got home he on the one hand resumed his round of political activity, but on the other expressed the desire to purchase an island in Maine, if only he had the $160,000 required,[24] indicating a wish to resume something akin to the isolation he had just left behind him.

While Hammett had been in the Army, the CPUSA had suffered a major crisis.

At the January 1944 meeting of the party's national committee, general secretary Earl Browder put forward a thesis that the postwar period would see the continuation of the wartime cooperation between the USA, Britain and the Soviet Union, ushering in a time of peaceful coexistence internationally and of labor-capital harmony within the USA.

What need of a communist party in such circumstances? Browder proposed the dissolution of the CPUSA and its reorganization as a "political-educational association," and this was (due to the low ideological level prevailing in the party, according to William Z. Foster[25]) agreed by the districts and, in May, by the party's National Convention. Thus did the Communist Political Association come into existence.

As life demonstrated the incorrectness of each of Browder's propositions, however, opposition began to grow, and, aided by the publication of a fierce attack on Browderism by Jacques Duclos, a leader of the Communist Party of France, the national committee in June 1945 unanimously rejected the Browder line and removed the man himself from office; the following month, an emergency convention reconstituted the CPUSA and completely recast the policies of the organization. Browder was allowed to remain a member but, after he involved himself in factional activity, he was expelled in February 1946.

It is hardly surprising that these dramatic developments receive no mention in Hammett's published correspondence, as he was in the

Army at the time, but it is curious that the biographies are also silent, leaving us no clue as to his position. However, as he now resumed activity in party-led organizations, he is hardly likely to have supported Browder; such a possibility is also rendered doubtful by the fact that when discussing the rift between Yugoslavia and the Soviet Union with Yugoslav Deputy Foreign Minister Srdja Prica at Hardscrabble Farm in the late 1940s, Hammett sided with the Soviet Union.[26]

While the party had succeeded in fighting off Browderism, however, it would find the attacks by what became known as McCarthyism much more disabling.

≈

The House Un-American Activities Committee (HUAC) had been formed in 1938 and that year issued a report in which it was claimed that communism was widespread in Hollywood. The intellectual level of the committee may be gauged by a question put to a witness by committee member J. Parnell Thomas, who asked "which WPA [Works Progress Administration, in 1939 renamed Work Projects Administration] payroll is Christopher Marlowe on, New York or Chicago?" By 1947, Thomas would be chairing the committee; he was later convicted of accepting kick-backs from federal employees and sentenced to two years' imprisonment.[27]

The CPUSA was not illegal. However, in 1940 Congress passed the Alien Registration Act, or Smith Act, which apart from requiring all adult non-citizens resident in the USA to register with the authorities, provided criminal penalties for those advocating the violent overthrow of the US government. The Act was said to have arisen from concern regarding the presence of "fifth columnists" in countries overrun by the Nazis, but it was significant that its chief sponsor was Howard W. Smith, the Virginia Democrat who led an anti-labor grouping in Congress.

It should not be thought that the HUAC and the interests it represented were motivated solely by disapproval of a "foreign ideology," because in these early years their stance was largely based on opposition to Roosevelt's New Deal.[28] Equally, many Hollywood producers were only too glad to blacklist alleged communists as very often they were a thorn in their sides at the studios.

The entry of the USA into World War II at the end of 1941 called a halt to red-baiting, as the Soviet Union was a major ally — and, indeed, in this period some pro-Soviet films were made. That swiftly changed after the war, and as early as March 1946 Churchill, although out of office following electoral defeat, effectively launched the Cold War with his "iron curtain" speech in Fulton, Missouri. The following year saw the creation of the Central Intelligence Agency, US intervention in Greece, and the compilation of something called the Attorney General's List, a list of allegedly subversive organizations used to screen federal employees. The list of names was made public and this, says Garry Wills in his commentary on Lillian Hellman's memoir of her experiences during this "scoundrel time,"

> was a profound violation of civil rights in itself, and the basis for all kinds of later violations — by Congress, by individual employers, by entrepreneurial blacklisters. Without charging any illegal acts, without supplying the grounds for its proscription, without offering a machinery for individual reply, the government branded as putatively disloyal any citizen who belonged to one of a large number of organizations.[29]

Things would get worse. For example, the HUAC asked 70 US colleges and universities to furnish its investigators with a list of textbooks and supplementary reading, along with the names of the authors, used in a wide range of largely non-scientific subjects. Dalton Trumbo, himself a victim of the blacklist, had this to say of HUAC methods:

> As a matter of general policy it has flouted every principle of Constitutional immunity, denied due process and right of cross-examination, imposed illegal sanctions, accepted hearsay and perjury as evidence, served as a rostrum for American fascism, impeded the war effort, acted as an agent for employer groups against labor, set itself up as censor over science, education, and the cinema and as arbiter over political thought, and instituted a reign of terror over all who rely in any degree upon public favor for the full employment of their talents.[30]

In Hollywood, the anti-communist onslaught was not reserved for writers, directors and actors, for in 1946 the studios engineered a lockout of the militant (not communist-led, although that was the allegation hurled at it) Conference of Studio Unions (CSU), which the previous year had waged a bitter seven-month strike arising from a demarcation dispute involving the mob-influenced International Alliance of Theatrical Stage Employees. The lockout signaled the end of the CSU — and of militant trade unionism in Hollywood — and set the stage for the introduction of the blacklist, which, says screenwriter Abraham Polonsky, was aimed at the major unions and was wielded at them first.[31]

Similarly, when the turn of the writers came, it was as much for their trade union activity as for any attempt to convey "subversive" messages in their scripts — indeed, how would the latter have been possible, when they were "under the strict supervision of a top-heavy, usually conservative, studio hierarchy"[32] and subject to the Hays Code? Communist screenwriter John Howard Lawson was of the view that it was their Screen Writers' Guild activism that got progressive screenwriters blacklisted.[33]

In late October 1947 ten writers, producers and directors — the Hollywood Ten, one of whom was Trumbo — were indicted for contempt of Congress, having refused to divulge their political or trade union affiliations. They did this not merely for their own protection, because if, for example, they had answered the stock question "Are you now or have you ever been a member of the Communist Party?" they would have been obliged to answer subsequent questions regarding their friends, colleagues and acquaintances. The following month a conference of studio heads at New York's Waldorf-Astoria Hotel agreed that they would require their employees to give written assurances (suggested by the American Legion) that they were not communists, had no subversive acquaintances, and that that they regretted any past transgressions. All who refused would be placed on the blacklist and refused employment.

On the very day of the conference, Lillian Hellman was due to meet Roy Cohn at the Waldorf-Astoria to sign a very generous contract. He came up from the conference and handed her the contract, to which was now attached the "loyalty oath" formulation which she was expected to rewrite in her own hand. She argued about it with Cohn, refused to sign and walked out.[34] Although later, as lives were often irreparably damaged, Hellman would adopt a more cautious approach, she was quite courageous at this early stage, asking in *Screenwriter*, "Has it anything to do with Communism? Of course not. There has never been a single line or word of Communism in any American picture at any time. There has never or seldom been ideas of any kind." At this stage even Sam Goldwyn was bold enough to issue a statement in which he said, "The most un-American activity which I have observed in connection with the hearings has been the activity of the Committee itself."[35]

In its 1949 decision denying the appeals of the Hollywood Ten, the Court of Appeals talked of films being a "potent medium of propaganda dissemination which may influence the minds of millions of Americans," leading Trumbo to retort: "Freedom of speech is thereby reserved only for unimportant speech, ineffectively communicated. Since the instruction of youth is a vital matter and the profession of teaching an effective means of communication, the schools and universities of the country — by order of the court — must yield up not only their textbooks, but their instructors as well."[36] Arthur Miller recalls that in the early 1950s he was casually advised by the orientation professor at his alma mater that "the FBI was actually enlisting students to report any radical remarks by their professors and at the same time asking professors to inform on students who expressed dangerous thoughts."[37]

The Hollywood Ten were sentenced to the maximum of one year in prison and fined $1,000 dollars each. Worse than this was the fact that their careers were ruined, at least for a lengthy period. It would be 1960 before Trumbo's name appeared in the credits of a Hollywood film — significantly, *Spartacus*, based on the novel by Howard Fast, a communist (he would break with the CPUSA later in the 1950s) who began planning the novel in prison, having in 1950 been sentenced to three months for refusing to name names before HUAC.

Others would follow, but the effects of the witch-hunt would reach beyond those on the blacklist to what Trumbo called the "gray list," consisting of "scores of men and women whose ideas and politics might possibly give offense to the committee. And beyond the gray list lies a wide and spreading area of general fear in which unconventional ideas or unpopular thoughts are carefully concealed by self-censorship."[38]

And, Trumbo pointed out, the very quality of liberal thought had become degraded as a result, with the "non-communist left" becoming in practice the "non-anti-fascist left," its dogma consisting of "nine parts anti-Communism to one part anti-Toryism, or anti-reaction..."[39] Thus, by way of example, these "New Liberals," fearing that to call for the elimination of slums on simple humanitarian grounds would brand them as communists, argued that slums should be eliminated because they bred communism! Writing a quarter of a century after her own brush with HUAC, Hellman also laments the failure of liberals to speak out against the committee. "*Partisan Review*," she wrote, "although through the years it has published many pieces protesting the punishment of dissidents in Eastern Europe, made no protest when people in this country were jailed or ruined."[40]

Hellman should not have been surprised by the supine stance of *Partisan Review*, as it received funds from the CIA, as did a number of cultural magazines throughout the world. Indeed, the "non-communist left" was itself something of a CIA project.[41]

In 1949, the Smith Act was used to sentence eleven CPUSA leaders to five years' imprisonment; scores of other party members were prosecuted in subsequent years until, in 1957, the Supreme Court ruled that some convictions were unconstitutional, whereupon prosecutions ceased. Although the CPUSA was formally outlawed by the Communist Control Act of 1954, in 1961 the Supreme Court ruled that the party was not barred from New York's unemployment insurance system, following which the Act was no longer enforced. The HUAC was not abolished until 1975.

As a result of the 1949 convictions, Hammett would himself spend some time in prison.

≈

After a three-week binge following his discharge,[42] Hammett returned to Hardscrabble Farm and shortly thereafter once again became openly involved with left-wing causes, seemingly unworried about being linked to the CPUSA. Layman says that Hammett's postwar political role was played with "less fervor," a claim that appears to be contradicted five pages later when he notes that in December 1949 the *New York Journal-American* reported that Hammett was involved in 35 groups "named as Communist fronts by Congressional or State Committees."[43] Even allowing for some exaggeration, that would seem to be quite a lot of fervor — or if not fervor, certainly commitment. Layman cites a twenty-page report by a New York FBI agent which, submitted to Washington in January 1950, detailed Hammett's observed political activity between February 1946 and December 1949.[44] Not totally reliant on direct observation, the report also cited newspaper and magazine reports, sometimes referring to pre-war activity. The organizations and publications which Hammett currently supported or was involved in were claimed to be:

- American Youth for Democracy
- Jefferson School of Social Science
- Civil Rights Congress-New York
- Oust Bilbo Campaign
- American Labor Party
- Veterans of the Abraham Lincoln Brigade
- Friends of Italian Democracy
- Voice of Freedom
- Contemporary Writers
- *Soviet Russia Today*
- Joint Anti-Fascist Refugee Committee
- Action Conference on Indonesia
- *Daily Worker*
- Film Audiences for Democracy
- National Conference on American Policy in Greece
- Council for the Advancement of the Americas
- American Committee for the Protection of the Foreign Born
- National Council of the Arts, Science and Professions
- American Continental Congress for Peace
- Cultural and Scientific Conference for World Peace
- Communist Party of the USA
- West Side Citizens Committee to End Discrimination on the City-Owned Docks

According to Joan Mellen, although he signed up for a number of causes, "it was clear that he was capable of no more than offering his name," and even his role in the Civil Rights Congress (CRC) was a "titular" one.[45] Based on the evidence, once must conclude that such claims are incorrect.

It's true, of course, that some of his commitments involved little more than turning up, as when, in October 1946, he attended the launch of the new quarterly magazine *Mainstream* (in 1948 this would merge with *New Masses* to become *Masses and Mainstream*).[46] And, yes, some of the activity, like signing petitions, took little effort: there was the October 28, 1947 public letter on behalf of the CRC announcing that over 300 labor groups and "organizations of the people" had attended its conference two weeks earlier demanding the abolition of HUAC[47]; a March 1948 appeal to President Truman seeking clemency for one of HUAC's contempt victims[48]; the March 1, 1949 public letter, again from the CRC, in support of six innocent black men sentenced to death for murder; a call to the mayor of New York to halt police brutality against blacks[49]; and later, after he had served his prison term, a petition to save the Rosenbergs from the electric chair.[50]

Sometimes, it was as Mellen says: he offered his name — not because that was all he was capable of, but because that was all that was asked of him — and several of the organizations listed above received his support as sponsor. He gave money: according to an FBI informant, $1,000 went to the campaign to oust the thoroughly racist Senator Theodore Bilbo of Mississippi, and, on the word of an FBI informant of "unknown reliability," the same amount went to the CPUSA each month.[51] Then there were speaking engagements — to the Veterans of the Abraham Lincoln Brigade, the 1946 New York state convention of American Youth for Democracy, a "Town Meeting for Freedom"[52] and others. Now and again, he had an off-day, as when, according to the aforementioned FBI report, he was "allegedly reported to the Communist Party Headquarters for his inability as a speaker and inability to be persuasive" after appearing as the main speaker at an American Youth for Democracy meeting at Buffalo University.[53] But this was 1947. Maybe he was drunk. (Or maybe the informant was wrong: speaking of the same meeting, Hammett told his daughter Mary that it had gone very well, with six new members joining.[54])

In 1946, Hammett was registered as a member of the largely New York state-based American Labor Party (ALP) which, founded ten years earlier, tended to endorse those candidates of either major party who adopted a pro-labor stance. One of the ALP's most notable achievements was the election, six times in a row, of Vito Marcantonio, a former Republican, to the US House of Representatives between 1936 and 1948. Both Hammett and Hellman also joined the Progressive Citizens of America (later known as simply the Progressive Party), but Hammett dropped out rather than, despite it being CPUSA policy, support Henry Wallace, of whom he had a poor political opinion, as the Progressive presidential candidate in the 1948 election. There was considerable activity by CPUSA members in both the ALP and the Progressive Party.

There were two commitments to which Hammett gave considerable time and energy. One of these was the Jefferson School of Social Science, established by the CPUSA in 1944, where he taught mystery writing once a week. This was a political as well as a literary task, as one aim was to get students to consider the genre as a vehicle for progressive ideas (which is ironic, as Hammett had rarely if ever used his own writing to convey political ideas). One student, Samm Sinclair Baker, had a low opinion of Hammett's teaching methods after Baker read one of his stories in class, a satire on advertising, only to have Hammett make a single, vapid comment; Frederick Dannay, co-author of the Ellery Queen stories, whom Hammett had invited to the class, gave practical advice, as a result of which Baker got the story published.[55] Given the fact that Hammett continued to teach at the Jefferson School for many years (the school was forced to close in 1956 after significant and prolonged pressure from the government's Subversive Activities Control Board), it is evident that most students did not share Baker's reservations.

Hammett's other major commitment was to the Civil Rights Congress (CRC), formed in April 1946 by the merger of International Labor Defense, the National Negro Congress and the National Federation for Constitutional Liberties,[56] all CP-inspired organizations; Hammett was elected president of the CRC-New York and, says Layman, built "the most successful American communist organization of its time, with a bail fund that had some $760,000 in cash by 1951."[57]

Hammett was hardly the enfeebled "titular" leader. He writes to tell Mary that he went into the city (from Hardscrabble Farm) on September 23, 1946 to attend a national board meeting of the Independent Citizens' Committee of the Arts, Sciences and Professions, and the next day he would be at a CRC-NY executive board meeting. At the end of the week he would be travelling to Chicago for a conference of labor groups and "various progressive political organizations" with the aim of formulating a "unified political program" for the forthcoming elections.[58] Having reported the result of the Chicago conference to Mary, he tells her that the city has him "trapped" this week: a board meeting on Tuesday, the launch of *Mainstream* magazine on Wednesday, and a further board meeting on Thursday; on October 17th, he would be speaking at a dinner held by the campaign to oust the racist Senator Bilbo (another CRC cause).[59] Even before he gave up drinking, then, Hammett often had a heavy schedule. And with regard to the CRC's bail fund, Layman points out that documents subpoenaed by the court in the 1951 case demonstrated that he had "a major role in formulating the policy of the bail fund committee."[60]

As we saw above, in 1949 11 CPUSA leaders were tried under the Smith Act. Hammett seemed totally unconcerned by the rising tide of repression, and viewed the fainthearted with amused contempt, writing his daughter Jo: "Red-baiting's kind of rife these days in these parts and it keeps the space between floors and beds fairly well filled with otherwise intrepid characters."[61] He wrote a forward to George Marion's *The Communist Trial: An American Crossroad*, in which he charged: "From the indictment of the Communist leaders on July 20, 1948 — just as the presidential election campaigns were getting well under way — until the verdict of Guilty on October 14, 1949, politics was the whole show. The indictment was political, the verdict was political. Only the defense was not allowed to be political."[62]

The CRC bail fund, which hitherto had most often been used to free arrested strikers, had provided $260,000 in bail for the eleven leaders, but when their appeals were exhausted in July 1951, four of them — Gus Hall (a future general secretary), Henry Winston (a future chairman), Robert G. Thompson and Gilbert Green — absconded. A week later Hammett, as chairman of the bail fund committee, was in court.[63] He proceeded to refuse to answer most questions put to him by the prosecution or the judge: whether he was a bail fund trustee, recognized the bail fund's minute book or his own initials or handwriting therein; whether he had assisted the four absentees in failing to appear in court, or knew any of them, had seen any of them in the last few days or knew of their present whereabouts. When asked when he was last in New York City, after consulting his counsel Hammett did supply an answer, but when the questioning returned to the bail fund he once more pled the Fifth Amendment. When asked whether he was willing to produce bail fund records with details of deposits and the sources of those deposits, he replied that, without conceding that he had the ability to produce them, he would not do so. At the conclusion of this somewhat tedious process, the judge found Hammett in contempt of court, placing him in custody until 7.30pm that evening, at which time he would be returned to court for sentencing. At that second session, when asked by the judge whether he had anything to say as to why judgment should not be pronounced, Hammett replied, "Not a thing."[64] He was sentenced to six months' imprisonment, which would commence immediately.

Years later, the myth-making Hellman sought to weave her own version of events surrounding the trial. One of Hammett's lawyers, she claimed, passed her a note containing a message from Hammett which read: "Do not come into this courtroom. If you do, I will say I do not know you. Get out of 82nd Street and Pleasantville. Take one of the trips to Europe that you love so much. You do not have to prove to me that you love me at this late date." His lawyers, however, had no recollection of this note. Hellman, says Jo Hammett, "fabricated" it.[65] Hellman claims to have dashed around New York and Martha's Vineyard, mortgaging property and pawning jewelry in an attempt to raise $100,000 bail money,[66] whereas in fact bail, pending appeal, had been set at a tenth of that figure. Johnson, the Hammett biographer authorized by Hellman, later said that the latter's bail-raising attempts had been inserted into her manuscript at Hellman's insistence.[67] Hellman did, however, book a trip to Europe. It was Hammett's secretary, Muriel Alexander, who went to court with the $10,000 bail money, but the judge refused to accept it because she refused to divulge its provenance, as it had come from a wealthy comrade insisting on anonymity.[68] Later, upon the instigation of the federal prosecutor, bail was refused regardless of its origin.

Julian Symons, one of Hammett's "left" critics, strikes a surprising pose regarding Hammett's behavior in court:

> It is difficult to see what the judge could have done but sentence him for contempt when confronted by this total intransigence, adhered to in spite of frequent instructions

by the court to answer. High-flown language about "what democracy is" seems wholly inappropriate.⁶⁹

As Symons himself concedes, the "high-flown language" came via Hellman, as in her first memoir she has Hammett tell her on the night before the trial, "I better tell you that if it were more than jail, if it were my life, I would give it for what I think democracy is, and I don't let cops or judges tell me what I think democracy is."⁷⁰ This, says Symons, sounds like a speech from a Hellman play, and so it does. But many a speech in a Hellman play had been written by Hammett, and it would surely be difficult to argue that the content of this one diverged much from Hammett's own thinking.

Hammett's view was that the identities of the bail-fund donors was no business of the court, and in this he was at one with those who, like Dalton Trumbo, had argued that the witch-hunters of HUAC had no constitutional right to demand that witnesses reveal who among their friends and colleagues had been CPUSA members in the 1930s. If Symons thought otherwise, it was surely his view that was "wholly inappropriate." Nor should we overlook the fact that on this occasion Hammett's political views coincided with the professional code he had assigned to Sam Spade all those years ago. Just as a private detective would be short of business if it was known that he had allowed the killer of his partner to go free, so few people would be persuaded to donate time and money to a progressive organization if confronted with the spectacle of its president divulging the identities of previous donors and activists to a court of law.

Hellman tells of an occasion when she and Hammett bumped into Howard Fast on the street, and Fast talked about his own impending jail term. Hammett told him, "It will be easier for you, Howard, if you first take off the crown of thorns."⁷¹ While Hellman conveys the impression that this advice was proffered on the basis of experience, the fact of the matter was that Fast had already served his three-month' sentence in 1950; nevertheless, the anecdote does give an indication of Hammett's approach to the prospect of prison. His sentence surely confirmed his world-view: this was class justice. It was to be expected in capitalist society and there was simply no point in taking it personally. Hence his reply (accompanied, maybe, by a shrug) to the judge when asked if he had anything to say before sentencing: "Not a thing."

What would have been the point?

Within days of the trial, the sensationalist "free" press was at work, one rag dubbing Hammett "one of the red masterminds of the nation, with main headquarters in Hollywood and a sub-office in New York."[72] Just as off-target was the New York *Herald Tribune* column which predicted the following year that Hammett "will renounce his Red companions by issuing a torrid denunciation of communism." In response to this, Hammett assured his daughter Jo, "You can't believe everything you read in the newspapers."[73]

≋

Hammett served his time, less two weeks for good behavior, but came out of prison to changed circumstances. There was little indication that his tastes were more proletarian as a result of his incarceration, as Hellman greeted him with a supper of quail and oysters, the latter apparently at his request, although he was not well enough to eat it.[74] His health was one of the things that had changed, and he would be frail for the remaining decade of his life; another was that the Internal Revenue Service had filed a case against him for $100,629.03 in unpaid taxes for the years 1942-45.[75] This was compounded by a demand for back property taxes levied on Hellman, resulting in her sale of Hardscrabble Farm. He therefore lived most of the time in the small house in Katonah provided by friend Samuel Rosen for a peppercorn rent. After all the years of excess, poverty had returned.

Officialdom was still not finished with Hammett, but if it expected to find him chastened, it was in for a disappointment. In March 1953, Joseph McCarthy's Senate subcommittee called him to a hearing regarding books by actual or suspected communists being stocked by overseas libraries under the auspices of the US Information Service. Hammett took it in his stride, and where he did not plead the Fifth Amendment (on questions relating to his membership or financial support of the CPUSA), he answered honestly. When, for example, asked whether he had ever engaged in espionage or sabotage, he gave a forthright "No." Asked whether he knew the whereabouts of the four communist leaders who had jumped bail in 1951, he cooperated fully, advising McCarthy's counsel Roy Cohn of the whereabouts of Gus Hall: prison. Did he know the whereabouts of the other three?

No, he did not. When McCarthy asked questions calling for a political judgment, Hammett appeared to be having a little fun with him, answering honestly, but in so doing demonstrating that, as many may have long suspected, Joseph McCarthy was not a particularly bright man.

Did Hammett believe that "communism as practiced in Russia" was superior to the US form of government? Well, it wasn't as straightforward as that, as "one is better for one country, and one is better for the other." Had McCarthy used the term "socialism" (the system in place in the Soviet Union, and regarded by Marxism as the stage prior to full communism), he might have received an answer closer to the one he was looking for. Instead, he continued to employ the term "communism" and to press Hammett on the matter, allowing him to confess some bafflement. "Theoretical communism is *no* form of government. You know, there *is* no government." McCarthy obviously *did not* know, and so asked whether Hammett favored the adoption of communism in the USA. Very cleverly, Hammett responded, "You mean now?" and, when McCarthy replied in the affirmative, said no, he did not, because it would be impractical, as most people didn't want it — a perfectly sensible and honest answer for a communist to have given in the USA of 1953. But it left McCarthy with nowhere to go, and so this line of questioning was abandoned. McCarthy handed over the questioning to Senator John McClellan (D, Arkansas),[76] who asked Hammett whether he felt that his refusal to answer certain questions was a "voluntary act of self-incrimination before the bar of public opinion." Hammett replied that "the bar of public opinion did not send me to jail for six months."

Minutes later, McCarthy made the mistake of feeding Hammett his most witheringly effective line yet, and one that would signal the close of the hearing. If Hammett were in charge of the campaign to fight communism, McCarthy asked, would he "purchase the works of some 75 Communist authors and distribute their works throughout the world, placing our official stamp of approval upon those works?" Hammett told him that if he were fighting communism he would not give people any books at all.[77]

In early 1955, he testified again. This time, the New York Joint Legislative Committee wanted to know whether there were communists in the Civil Rights Congress. "Communism to me," he told the committee, "is not a dirty word. When you are working for the advance of mankind it never occurs to you whether a guy is a communist."[78]

Politically, he was as active as his health allowed. Asked to chair the Committee to Defend V. J. Jerome, who faced a prison sentence for an article he had written in *Political Affairs*, the party's theoretical journal, he agreed, organizing a cultural protest event in March 1952 and a statement of protest the following month.[79] He joined the campaign to end the Korean War, but Johnson advises us that at this stage he rarely attended meetings and rallies, a notable exception being the rally to protest the death sentence meted out to Ethel and Julius Rosenberg.[80] While Johnson is undoubtedly correct when she says that Hammett "believed a man should stick to his views," it is difficult to see how, in view of these demonstrations of continued belief, she can claim that "he didn't believe in anything too much" (unless, of course, Hellman was hovering at her shoulder). Hammett insisted on continuing to teach at the Jefferson School, and when in 1953 Hellman tried to persuade him to forsake it because of the risks involved, he told her (according to her recollection) that if he had become a burden to her she should leave; alternatively, if she wanted their friendship to continue she must never raise the matter again.[81]

But the Jefferson School would fold in three years' time, and by that stage there was little scope for activity by a prematurely elderly man in declining health in a party that was struggling for survival in the face of state repression which, had it occurred elsewhere, would have been condemned by Washington. The CPUSA was a shadow of its former self, with a membership which had shrunk from around 80,000 in 1944[82] to 5,000 in the mid-1950s, at which time almost a third of those members consisted of FBI informers.[83] Just as well, then, as Johnson tells us, that Hammett took the long view of politics, a subject that, according to his friends the Rosens, "formed the topic of many discussions with Hammett as late as 1957."[84]

For Hammett himself, of course, anything beyond the next few years would have constituted "the long view," for he must have known that there was not much time left to him; indeed, he may well have been surprised that he had lived as long as he had. It would almost certainly be a mistake to think that his wish to be buried at Arlington National Cemetery constituted a last-minute relapse into sentimental patriotism, because just as progressives had long argued that the USA was not solely the property of the reactionaries who ran it most of the time but *their* country as well, so Hammett would have taken the view that Arlington, rather than being the preserve of those who had fought in imperialist wars, should be the appropriate burial place for anti-fascists. He wanted to be buried there for much the same reason that J. Edgar Hoover wanted him excluded from it: it was one more piece of the USA to be fought over, and this time Hammett, hardboiled to the end, won.[85]

NOTES

1. Hammett's letter of November 13, 1939 in which he sought the support of Theodore Dreiser can be found in Dashiell Hammett, *Selected Letters of Dashiell Hammett, 1921- 1960*, ed. Richard Layman with Julie M. Rivett (Washington D. C.: Counterpoint, 2001), 155.
2. The full text of the statement, and the list of signatories, can be found at *Selected Letters*, 157-159. Interestingly, the signatories profess: "We are not Communists, and we are not concerned at this moment with the merits or demerits of the doctrines advocated by the Communists." That was doubtless true of most of the signatories, and even of a borderline case like playwright Clifford Odets, who had been in the CPUSA between 1934 and 1935, but it was not true of Hammett and Hellman.
3. Richard Layman, *Shadow Man: The Life of Dashiell Hammett* (New York and London: Harcourt Brace Jovanovich/Bruccoli Clark, 1981), 181.
4. Dashiell Hammett to Mary Hammett, December 19, 1938; *Selected Letters*, 144.
5. Diane Johnson, *The Life of Dashiell Hammett* (US title *Dashiell Hammett: A Life*), (London: Picador, 1985), 163.
6. Ibid., 162.
7. Deborah Martinson, *Lillian Hellman: A Life with Foxes and Scoundrels* (Berkeley: Counterpoint, 2005), 249.
8. Ibid., 163.
9. Dashiell Hammett to Mary Hammett, February 15, 1940; *Selected Letters*, 160.
10. Lillian Hellman, "Introduction," Dashiell Hammett, *The Big Knockover: Selected Stories and Short Novels*, ed. Lillian Hellman (New York: Vintage Books, 1989), xii.
11. Arthur Miller, *Timebends: A Life* (London: Methuen, 2005), 81.
12. Ibid., 84.
13. William Z. Foster, *History of the Communist Party of the United States* (New York: International Publishers, 1952), Chapter Twenty-Nine; available at williamzfoster.blogspot.com, accessed February 2, 2015.
14. Layman, *Shadow Man*, 193.

15 Dashiell Hammett to Lillian Hellman, November 25, 1943; *Selected Letters*, 254.
16 Layman, commentary, in Dashiell Hammett, *Selected Letters*, 182.
17 Dashiell Hammett to Lillian Hellman, July 16, 1944; *Selected Letters*, 345.
18 Dashiell Hammett to Lillian Hellman, March 18, 1945; *Selected Letters*, 419.
19 Johnson, 189. Mellen, 206, says that an army colleague told Layman that Hammett read Marx's *Capital* for the third time while on Adak. One assumes this is a reference to the first volume.
20 Hammett to Mary Hammett, December 25, 1943; *Selected Letters*, 257.
21 Hammett to Lillian Hellman, July 27, 1944, Hammett to Mary Hammett, September 3, 1944, Hammett to Prudence Whitfield, November 3, 1944; *Selected Letters*, 351, 368, 385.
22 Dashiell Hammett to Lillian Hellman, March 15, 1945; Dashiell Hammett to Jo Hammett, March 22, 1945; *Selected Letters*, 417, 422.
23 Jo Hammett, *Dashiell Hammett: A Daughter Remembers*, ed. Richard Layman with Julie M. Rivett (New York: Carroll & Graf Publishers, 2001), 122. Although elsewhere it is described as a bar, Jo Hammett says that the Carolina Moon was a night club.
24 Johnson, 211.
25 William Z. Foster, *History of the Communist Party of the United States*, Chapter Thirty, available at http://williamzfoster.blogspot.com, accessed February 12, 2015.
26 Joan Mellen, *Hellman and Hammett: The Legendary Passion of Lillian Hellman and Dashiell Hammett* (New York: Harper Collins, 1996), 262. Julie Rivett, Hammett's granddaughter, disagrees with my conclusion, saying, "Browder's ousting may well have been the beginning of his [Hammett's] disillusionment with the CPUSA. I suspect he'd have generally favored Browder's Communist Political Association and his more moderate, pragmatic version of communism, though Party allegiance would certainly have complicated his response…Like Browder, DH was an advocate for education and informed choice. That must have left him in a tough spot when Stalin and his faithfuls turned on Browder." Julie M. Rivett to Ken Fuller, April 21, 2015.
27 Dalton Trumbo, *The Time of the Toad: A Study of Inquisition in*

America (London: Journeyman Press, 1982), 10.
28 James Cameron, "Introduction," Lillian Hellman, *Scoundrel Time* (London: Macmillan, 1976), 16. Hellman makes the same point herself at ibid., 26.
29 Garry Wills, "Commentary," in Hellman, *Scoundrel Time*, 149.
30 Trumbo, 6.
31 Gerald Horne, *Class Struggle in Hollywood, 1930-1950: Moguls, Mobsters, Stars, Reds and Trade Unionists* (Austin: University of Texas Press, 2001), 5.
32 Clayton R. Koppes and Gregory D. Black, *Hollywood Goes to War: How Politics, Profits and Propaganda Shaped World War II Movies* (New York: Free Press, 1987), 70, cited by Gerald Horne, *The Final Victim of the Blacklist: John Howard Lawson, Dean of the Hollywood Ten* (Berkeley, Los Angeles and London: University of California Press, 2006), xix. And the role of the banks should not be overlooked: producer Walter Wanger's plan to follow 1938's *Blockade* with an indictment of Nazi Germany (written, like *Blockade*, by John Howard Lawson) was blown out of the water two days before filming was due to start when the bank "informed him that he would never receive another loan if he proceeded." See ibid., 111. The banks, particularly the California-based Bank of America, held major interests in the studios and, Horne says, "reportedly initiated the blacklist." See Horne, *Class Struggle in Hollywood*, 7-8.
33 Horne, *The Final Victim of the Blacklist*, 140.
34 Hellman makes two points about the studio heads who enforced the blacklist: that the possibility of losing the often fabulous wealth they had acquired in Hollywood made them willing dupes for the red-baiters and, rather more perceptively, that many of them had simply never been a part of the Anglo-American culture in which individuals insisted on their rights. "I don't think," she writes, "the heads of the movie companies, and the men they appointed to run the studios, had ever before thought of themselves as American citizens with inherited rights and obligations. Many of them had been born in foreign lands and inherited foreign fears." See *Scoundrel Time*, 56.
35 Lillian Hellman, "Judas Goats," *Screenwriter*, December 3, 1947; Martinson, 218.
36 Trumbo, 32.

37 Miller, 227.
38 Trumbo, 48.
39 Ibid., 36-37.
40 Hellman, *Scoundrel Time*, 74.
41 See James Petras, "The CIA and the Cultural Cold War Revisited," *Monthly Review*, November 1999. Petras is here reviewing Frances Stonor Saunders' *Who Paid the Piper: The CIA and the Cultural Cold War* (London: Granta Books, 1999).
42 Dashiell Hammett to Jose Dolan Hammett, October 25, 1945; *Selected Letters*, 453.
43 Layman, *Shadow Man*, 206, 211.
44 See Layman, *Shadow Man*, 206-212. As an example of the FBI's often careless investigations, Layman points out that although considerable space was taken to support the allegation that *Soviet Russia Today* was a communist publication, and a confidential source had reported that Hammett was on its advisory board, the report completely overlooked the fact that on the magazine's masthead Hammett was quite openly identified as an editorial board member. Ibid., 208. One is reminded of Hammett's tale of the description of a suspect he was once given that, while meticulously detailed in every other regard, failed to mention that the man had only one arm.
45 Mellen, 249, 281.
46 Dashiell Hammett to Mary Hammett, October 6, 1946; *Selected Letters*, 483.
47 *Selected Letters*, 494-495.
48 Layman, *Shadow Man*, 209.
49 Ibid., 207.
50 Johnson, 258.
51 Layman, *Shadow Man*, 207, 210.
52 Ibid., 207, 209 American Youth for Democracy was the new name given to the Young Communist League during the Communist Political Association period; this was superseded by the Labor Youth League in 1949. See http://www.yclusa.org/about-the-yclusa/history-of-the-young-communist-league-usa/.
53 Ibid., 208.
54 Dashiell Hammett to Mary Hammett, April 30, 1947; *Selected Letters*, 487.

55 Layman, *Shadow Man*, 212. Baker published several detective stories and novels before embarking on a decades-long career as the author of self-help books. He came to national attention in 1968, however, with the publication of his *The Permissible Lie*, an expose of the advertising industry, in which Baker had been employed for many years.
56 Dashiell Hammett, *Selected Letters*, 470, n.1.
57 Ibid., 450.
58 Dashiell Hammett to Mary Hammett, September 24, 1946; *Selected Letters*, 479.
59 Dashiell Hammett to Mary Hammett, October 6, 1946; *Selected Letters*, 482-483.
60 Layman, *Shadow Man*, 220.
61 Dashiell Hammett to Josephine Hammett Marshall, April 18, 1949; *Selected Letters*, 512.
62 Johnson, 239. Johnson says Hammett wrote the forward in 1950, although the book appears to have been published in 1949.
63 Arthur Miller says that a few years later, in Reno to secure his divorce from his first wife, his lawyer advised him that an investigator from HUAC was in town to serve him with a subpoena. Coincidentally, in the law office at the same time was a Texas rancher who voiced his opposition to HUAC and told Miller that he had served in the Aleutians with Hammett, who taught him everything he knew. He had hidden Hammett on his ranch when "they were after him, but then he got foolish and left, and that's when they got him." He now made the same offer to Miller who, although tempted, declined. See Arthur Miller, *Timebends*, 390-392. Given the fact that there was just a week between the four men jumping bail and Hammett's appearance in court, the rancher's story strains credulity.
64 A complete transcript of Hammett's testimony can be found in Layman, *Shadow Man*, 248- 262. It will be seen here that claims that Hammett refused to give his name (Layman, commentary, Dashiell Hammett, *Selected Letters*, 452, for example) are mistaken.
65 Dorothy Gallagher, *Lillian Hellman: An Imperious Life* (New Haven and London: Yale University Press, 2014.), 96; Jo Hammett, 151.
66 See Johnson, 245-47.
67 Gallagher, 97; Diane Johnson, "Obsessed," *Vanity Fair*, May 1985.

68 Mellen, 287.
69 Julian Symons, *Dashiell Hammett* (San Diego/New York/London: Harcourt Brace Jovanovich, 1985), 146.
70 Lillian Hellman, *An Unfinished Woman* in *Three*, (Boston: Little, Brown, 1979), 282.
71 Hellman, "Introduction," Dashiell Hammett, *The Big Knockover*, xi.
72 *Hollywood Life*, July 13, 1951, quoted in Johnson, 249-250.
73 This was Hy Gardner's column, New York *Herald Tribune*, October 20, 1952. See Johnson, 332.
74 Johnson, 254; Mellen, 293.
75 Johnson, 248.
76 McClellan, then a new member of the subcommittee, would later break with McCarthy over the latter's outrageous methods.
77 The transcript of Hammett's testimony before McCarthy appears in Johnson, 265-272. It is clear from this that Cline's claim that he refused to give his name to McCarthy is mistaken. See Sally Cline, *Dashiell Hammett: Man of Mystery* (New York: Arcade Publishing, 2014), x.
78 Johnson, 278-279.
79 See Hammett, *Selected Letters*, 580, 581.
80 Johnson, 258-259.
81 Hellman, *An Unfinished Woman* in *Three*, 134.
82 Anthony Summers, *Official and Confidential: The Secret Life of J. Edgar Hoover* (New York: G. P. Putnam, 1993), 191.
83 Kurt Gentry, *J. Edgar Hoover: The Man and the Secrets* (New York: W. W. Norton and Company, 1991), 442.
84 Johnson, 319, n. 14.
85 In her will, Lillian Hellman provided for the establishment of a fund named after Dashiell Hammett, stipulating that the revenue be distributed "in accordance with 'the political, social and economic beliefs, which of course were radical, of the late Dashiell Hammett who was a believer in the doctrines of Karl Marx." See Alice Kessler-Harris, *A Difficult Woman: The Challenging Life and Times of Lillian Hellman* (New York: Bloomsbury Press, 2012), 350. However, in 1989 the trustees named by Hellman "asked Human Rights Watch to devise a program to help writers who were targeted for expressing views that their governments oppose, for

criticizing government officials or actions, or for writing about subjects that their governments did not want reported." See http://www.hrw.org/hhgrants/nominations. From this, laudable though such aims may be, it is far from clear that Hellman's original intention for the fund is currently being fulfilled.

9 Dry

There remains one major question before us: why did Dashiell Hammett never write another novel or story after the mid-1930s? There is, of course, not one single answer. Writers who have spent time laboring in the Hammett-Hellman industry have advanced their theories, several of which have been part-right, but most of them overlook the more mundane explanations, and few if any relate the question to his political development or the nature of his political commitment.

≈

Between September 1936 and July 1953, just over 50 of Hammett's published letters, most of them to his daughters, his wife and Hellman, feature a claim that he is writing or intends to do so. It would seem that his daughter Mary (a troubled young woman who, he possibly thought, needed to believe that her father was industrious[1]), was the only person he genuinely tried to convince that he was still writing, although in the beginning he also attempted this with his wife Jose. With his daughter Jo, with Hellman and less close acquaintances, on the other hand, he was far more truthful, often referring to his writing plans and activity in a self-deprecating manner, as if knowing that he would be unable to fool them.

There were occasions, it is true, when he seemed to be attempting to fool himself, although Layman concedes that he may have come close to completing one novel, "though no evidence survives except for the mention of it in his letters."[2]

There are 11 letters between September 1936 and Hammett's re-induction into the Army in which he claims to be still writing, and seven of these are addressed to his daughter Mary.

- September 1936: Hammett tells wife Jose that he's "hard at work on the book;" three days later he tells daughter Mary that he'll find somewhere in New York to finish the book which, although not a detective story, may be called *Death is for Suckers*.[3]
- June, 1938: He tells Mary that he hopes to have his book finished by the end of November; five days later, he tells Hollywood agent Nat Deverich that he's "dug out the partly finished book, *My Brother Felix*, and hope to get it done here [Tavern Island, Conn.] this summer."[4]
- August, 1938: Mary now hears that a book, provisionally entitled *Toward Z*, is "coming along not too badly."[5]
- After a spell in hospital, in early 1939 Hammett remains in New York and tries to work on a novel, leading Random House, to which he has turned after leaving an exasperated Knopf, to believe that it is on the way.[6]
- March 1939: He tells Mary that he hasn't worked on "the book... for days," and is unable to think of a title, although ten days later he assures her that he's been "up in the country banging away on the book..."[7]
- November, 1940: Mary is told that he has just spent "a couple of weeks up in the country working on the book..."[8]
- February 1941: He assures Mary that he is still "plugging away at the book," and hopes to finish it the following month.[9]
- April 1941: "The book — thank Christ — will soon be finished," Mary hears, "apart from some changes I want to make."[10]
- January, 1942: Hammett tells his wife, "I've put the book aside for a while. Tonight I have to make up my mind whether to do the movie adaptation of *Watch on the Rhine* or a play that I have been talking over with [director Herman] Shumlin."[11]

- May 1942: After the screenplay of *Watch*, he tells Jose, he has to decide whether to do another movie or, maybe, some short stories.[12]

The above chronology is chillingly evocative. Seen solely in this context (a mistake, I think), Hammett becomes a sad, tragic figure. Writers, many of whom now and again make excuses not to cover a blank page with words, will find it frightening, and when one reads the sequence of falsehoods and excuses Hammett wrote to his daughter Mary one is reminded of that scene (surely the most frightening in the movie; it did not appear in Stephen King's novel) in *The Shining* where Jack Torrance, who has apparently beavered away day after day on his writing project, is discovered to have merely typed over and over again the line "All work and no play makes Jack a dull boy."[13]

It was not all falsehoods and excuses, however, for there exist two fragments of *My Brother Felix*.[14] The first of these, entitled "Time to Die," appears to be a first attempt at a story about a man who has returned from Latin America, where he has acquired a suntan and facial scars.

Felix sits in the lounge of a New York hotel. At midnight, he rises to greet Michael and Julie who, attired in evening clothes, enter from the street. Michael wonders why Felix has not replied to his letter, which the latter now denies having received. Neither has he seen Tomas, the bearer of the letter. It seems that Michael did not receive Felix's letter either. Felix, saying that he does not believe the couple, takes out a knife and holds it against Michael's chest as he demands "Cornejo's letter."

Eventually, Michael concedes that he has the letter, whereupon Felix pockets the knife and slaps his face. Michael, although the larger man, pleads for an opportunity to explain and Felix agrees, telling Michael that he has never liked him. When Julie tells Felix that the big man has a pistol in his pocket, Michael says that he can hardly shoot his own brother. Here the fragment ends, and it is possible that Hammett was dissatisfied with his work, finding it too reminiscent of the tough-guy stuff of his previous stories and novels. Deciding on a different approach, he started anew.

In late 1936, Hammett told the *Daily Princetonian* that he was working on a novel concerning a family of 12 children on an island and that he hoped this would see him leaving the detective novel behind.[15]

Hammett's first biographer was under the impression that nothing survived of this attempt,[16] and many of his readers (including this one) would have assumed that Hammett had casually fobbed off the student publication with an off-the-cuff invention. We were mistaken, for that project is recognizably the second version of "My Brother Felix," the surviving fragment of which is headed "September 20, 1938."

This time, Hammett employs the first person, using Felix's brother Morgan as narrator. Morgan watches Felix arrive on their island home (modeled, says Julie M. Rivett, on Tavern Island, where Hammett spent the summers of 1936 and 1938) after five years away. As in his previous incarnation, Felix is scarred and sun-browned. Besides Morgan, Felix's siblings (and half-siblings) are Viv, Jim (the eldest, and six-feet-seven), Wally, Sue, Alice, Ellen, Bob (absent, having departed home for city life), Ted, Olive and Humboldt; in addition, the crowded cast of characters includes his father and his 31-year-old step-mother Christina; there is also mention of Inés, who has been sick and, we gather, is married to Jim, but she never appears.

The newspapers Felix has brought with him bear headlines concerning the agreement by Britain and France — appeasement — by means of which Czechoslovakia will be handed to Hitler. This news mocks the statue in the room assigned to Felix, showing St. George slaying a "small inoffensive-looking dragon."[17] The gathering war-clouds are reflected symbolically as three of Felix's siblings speculate on which path will be taken by the hurricane which Christina has been reading about in one of Felix's newspapers.

Morgan doesn't know whether to be a painter or a farmer, or both, given the unstable international situation. Felix lets him nibble at the edges of a conversation concerning such weighty matters, but then postpones it.

When Jim asks Felix how things are down south, the latter tells him that his (Jim's) friends von Marees and Ibañez are in jail, thus virtually accusing Jim of supporting fascism in Chile,[18] and here we can see that Hammett intends that Jim should perform the role assigned to Michael in "Time to Die." Jim describes Felix as "hard to get along with as ever," as a result of which Christina, their step-mother, indicates to Morgan that she has a poor view of Jim.

Julie M. Rivett speculates that Hammett's plot may have been thwarted by the election to the Chilean presidency of the Popular

Front's Pedro Aguirre Cerda in October 1938,[19] but we have no way of knowing. Whatever the reason, it is to be regretted that Hammett abandoned the project, because the surviving fragment of "September 20, 1938" certainly demonstrates that he had indeed left the detective genre behind and was engaged on what promised to be his most mature work, setting the dynamics of a large family against a background of international politics at a specific time and place.

However, if we consider this work in the context of the letters cited above, questions abound. Was the first version of *Felix*, "Time to Die," the book he was working on in September 1936? It seems probable, as just two months later he was to outline what was obviously the second version to the *Daily Princetonian*. He was obviously discussing *Felix* in his June 1938 correspondence, but one wonders how much of the "partly finished" book then existed, as the political events discussed in it would not occur until September. And even before that, he claimed to be working on something called *Toward Z*. Possibly he had considered renaming *Felix*, but it is equally possible that he was not being entirely truthful with Mary.

In March 1945, Hammett would explain to Mary (quite possibly in response to a direct inquiry from her) that *Felix* had become *There Was a Young Man*, which was half-finished.[20] Julie M. Rivett suspects that this was an exaggeration, speculating that "Time to Die" and "September 20, 1938" might have been all there was to it.[21]

≋

In the next two years, Hammett's published letters make no mention of his own writing. It could be argued that, certainly since he rejoined the Army, writing had not been a realistic option, but this is not so. Not only was writing his job on Adak, but there seemed to be ample time for private correspondence. The obvious question arises: why did he re-enlist?

Hellman told Hammett's authorized biographer that although he claimed that when he was accepted it was the happiest day of his life, she thought that it was "a silly stunt to escape real-life problems."[22] While here mystified as to why a free spirit like Hammett should find Army life so congenial, in her first volume of memoirs she takes a slightly different line:

Maybe a life ruled over by other people solved some of the problems, allowed a place for a man who by himself could not seek out people, maybe gave him a sense of pride that a man of forty-eight could stand up with those half his age; maybe all that, and maybe simply that he liked his country and felt that this was a just war and had to be fought.[23]

According to an Army comrade, "The reason he joined up had to do with his personal campaign to fight Fascism, a fight he'd been engaged in since 1937, and to which he'd devoted most of his time and money."[24]

Quite possibly, all of this was correct. But is difficult to avoid the impression that Hammett was hiding in the Army — from publishers, from the false people who populated Hollywood and the literary circuit in New York, from personal difficulties. While Hellman may have been right in thinking that he was escaping "real-life problems," it is equally likely that he found Army life, and the people populating it, more real than the one he had been living. And the sense of belonging he would mention to Hellman in 1944 (see Chapter 1) should not be underestimated, for maybe this was a feeling he'd never experienced before. By serving in the military he was also acquitting himself of his political responsibilities, chief of which was to combat fascism (never really a "personal" campaign, as his comrade called it). It is perhaps surprising that the CPUSA had never (as far as we are aware) censured Hammett for his often outrageous behavior; now, his excesses were, at least until his final months in Alaska, held in check, and his life had a clear purpose — and this, for a very long time, was what he had craved.

For present purposes, however, it must surely have been the case that, aside from its other attractions, military service provided a perfect alibi for not writing. Suddenly, the pressure was relieved, and he was no longer required to meet other people's expectations. This, and the fact that he had found a meaningful role for himself, doubtless explains why he saw no reason to mention his writing until May 1944. At this point, he seemed to realize that the several excellent reasons for not writing would not be available for much longer, and so the subject reappeared in his correspondence; the fact that it features in twelve letters over thirteen months is perhaps an indication of some anxiety about what his civilian role would be. It was to Mary that he first broached the possibility of a return to writing. His remarks on this matter to Prudence Whitfield in July 1944 and February 1945 were rather more honest, as was his first letter to Hellman in March, although by the end of that month he seemed to be fooling himself again. In April, the serious note was maintained in the letter to Mary, slipped when he mentioned the novel to Prudence Whitfield, and descended into an excuse in his next two letters to Hellman. After his return to civilian life, this would continue to be the pattern.

- May 1944: "Every once in a while," he writes Mary from the Aleutians, "I bring out the notion of writing some fiction while I'm here, but so far all that's come of it is that I've dusted off the notion and put it back where it came from. Maybe someday..."[25]
- July 1944: He tells Prudence Whitfield that he'd like to turn a letter he's received from a former Army comrade into a short story — but probably only because the circumstances rule against this. "I haven't willingly done a short story in God knows how many years and must conclude therefore that this desire now is just perverse."[26]
- February 1945: If he remains in the Aleutians, he writes Prudence Whitfield, "I'll get around in a little while, out of a sort of boredom, to at least starting to write a book. That would be a shock to me. I haven't written a book since 1933."[27] Here, he is virtually confessing that his correspondence to others has, since 1936, been less than honest.
- March 1945: He tells Hellman that he has a number of things to think about. "I'm even thinking about maybe perhaps it might be possibly writing a novel, for which I've got a kind of feel if not exactly any very clear idea." Later that month, he says: "I'm still fumbling around with rosy nebulae, most of which I hope will presently merge to form a novel, and it's a lot of fun." If his transfer to Fort Richardson doesn't materialize, he says at the end of the month, he will "settle cozily down to do a novel, probably about a middle-aged painter in the Army. I've got a couple of other notions, but at the moment like that one best."[28]
- April 1945: Hammett tells Mary, "I'll fuss around with the novel I'm going to do — if I stay on the island this summer — about an artist in Alaska. It's at that nice stage now when I've got nothing to

do but fool around with notions and feelings and don't yet have to commit myself to anything by putting it down on paper." Similarly, he writes Prudence Whitfield: "After loafing on the job for a few days, pretending there was no use trying to do anything on the book till I know definitely whether I was going to stay here and finish it, I'm now back in harness, though still not ready to pin it down on paper." A few days later, however, he tells Whitfield that he's engaged on Army work and "it doesn't look as if I'm going to have any time to work on the novel, but I don't mind that so much: I more or less thought of the novel as something to keep me busy down on the island, where I didn't have a great deal to do…" He gives Hellman a similar line, telling her that his transfer and the consequent workload mean that "there'll be no time to work on the new novel in the immediate future."[29]

- May 1945: He probably won't, he repeats to Hellman, have time to work on the novel "in the immediate future. I'm not too disappointed, since I had from the beginning thought of it in terms of *if* I stayed on the island." The very next day, however, he tells her that if, rather than doing his current job the way he thinks it should be done, he sulks in his tent, he may turn to the novel again.[30]

≈

The period between Hammett's return to civilian life in the fall of 1945 until he gave up drinking in late 1948 was the darkest since the early 1930s.

Over an evening drink, presumably after the Jefferson class, he told his student Samm Sinclair Baker: "Most days, I see no point in getting up in the morning."[31] Lillian Hellman would later write that the years 1945 to 1948 "were not good years; the drinking grew wilder and there was a lost, thoughtless quality I had never seen before."[32] When a woman he had known in Alaska visited him in New York, he took her to club after club, abusing waiters. When she, having suffered enough of this, was about to get into a cab, Hammett pleaded, "Please don't leave me alone."[33] That woman's husband, E. E. Spitzer, an *Adakian* colleague, said that in postwar New York: "It seemed to me as if he felt a lack of interest in his life."[34] From this it would seem that the nihilism of earlier years was threatening to return, and that his victory of the late 1930s was not necessarily permanent. This can only be understood by considering his situation at the time.

Despite not having worked on a film for almost five years or published a book in over a decade, he still had a comfortable income — continuing royalties from the books and revenue from the radio shows based on characters he had created. Quite apart from the inclination, then, he had no *need* to get up in the morning. This would not necessarily have been viewed by Hammett in a positive light. He was living on the proceeds of work completed at a vastly different time in his life, such that it might have been written by another person. What sort of life was that? All of his published work had been completed before he became a Marxist. After Marxism had shown him that the world was not, after all, meaningless, he must have looked back at that work with a very critical eye, possibly amused that some people placed a Marxist interpretation upon portions of it, but knowing that most of it was, in fact, politically irrelevant. And it was on the proceeds of this work and its offshoots that he now lived.

Depressing as that realization may have been, the external situation was hardly cheerier. For the left in the USA, this was a time of retreat as, the monster of Nazism slain, the representatives of big capital turned to demonizing the one country that had done more than any other to secure the victory against Hitler, fomenting a phobia against domestic communism, and behind this smokescreen recouping as much as they could of the concessions granted to labor under Roosevelt's New Deal. Unlike the second half of the 1930s, when Hammett had joined the party, this was not a time of optimism. And on top of this, he was not writing — or at least not writing anything that he had a hope of completing. True, with his continuing income he didn't really *need* to write, but this must have imparted a sense of unreality, or lack of authenticity, to his life.

"Pessimism," he had written Hellman in 1944, when she was expressing doubts regarding her play *The Searching Wind*, "is the opium of the middle-class intellectual and you are to stop it."[35] Maybe it was this which now gnawed at Hammett himself, threatening the return of the bleak nihilism of old. And it *was* a middle-class ailment: had he been a worker, compelled, say, to stand at a lathe five or six days a week in order to keep the wolf from the door, and yet deriving satisfaction from creating new value with his skills, he probably would have seen such pessimism for what it was, just as he had viewed it in 1944 — an unaffordable luxury. He must have scolded himself just as he had scolded Hellman, because he seems to have fought the return of nihilism. Although he may initially have seen alcohol as one avenue of escape, it worsened his condition, and in 1948 that prop would be kicked away when he was told to either stop drinking or die in a matter of months.

The choice he made — to live — can only mean that he had won the battle against renewed nihilism, banishing all thought of suicide. And this victory was achieved by employing the same weapons he had used in the 1930s: political belief and activism, the details of which we discussed in the previous chapter. It was not the case, therefore, that he was distracted from writing by his political activity, but that his failure to write made the political activity all the more necessary, for this was his life-saver.[36]

In this period, there are 16 letters in which Hammett mentions his attempts to write — an average just short of one every two months, half the previous average but high enough to justify the suspicion that his block, if block it was, played a part in pushing him into extremes of behavior last seen in the 1930s. The letters progressed from apparent sincerity to self-deception, and finally to disarming honesty.

In October 1945, all was seriousness after his discharge-happy binge as he wrote to wife Jose and daughters Mary and Jo. By December, however, he was admitting to Jose that he hadn't written much of his novel, while he told Mary that he was taking a break to write a short story, but in January predicted that he would be finished in a few months — only to admit, the following month, that he hadn't even finished the short story. There was then a five-month lull before he assured his daughter that he was working on the novel again. The truth came out in September when he wrote more distant acquaintances.

In March 1947, it was no longer "the novel;" but "the play," a pretense he kept up with Mary in April, while being more honest with Jo, his younger daughter — a pattern repeated in July.

By 1948, there was no more play, but an idea for yet another novel — although he now joked to Jo about his lack of productivity. Almost a year later, he was still trying to get a book started. Was it the same one? We don't know.

- October 1945: He confesses to his wife Jose that he went on a binge for three weeks after his discharge from the Army before going to Hardscrabble Farm, where he has "decided to go on the wagon until I've finished a novel that I hope to start putting on paper either this week or the beginning of next." Six days later, he writes Mary that he's working on a book which "won't be a mystery. It's about a middle-aged painter who comes home from the wars and I'm not too sure what all's going to happen to him, though it isn't going to be one of those hard luck stories about how the returning soldier does or doesn't adjust himself to civilian life again. I haven't found a title yet. I'd use The Changed Lock if it weren't so hard and ugly to pronounce. The meaning fits, but that D-L sound is pretty bad."[37]
- December 1945: He's found a small apartment in New York, he tells Jose, where he thinks he will be able to finish his book. "I'm speaking kind of boldly about 'finishing' the new book, when the truth is I'm not a hell of a long way into it. The temptation to stay outdoors in the country has kept me away from the typewriter most of the time. But anyhow I've got a title now, or at least one I'm pretty sure I'll use. It's from a poem by Peacock and is, or will be, *The Valley Sheep Are Fatter.*" Six days later, however, he tells daughter Mary that he's leaving off work on the novel to do a short story for *Salute*, a news magazine to be launched by "some of the *Yank* lads in February." Towards the end of the month, he predicts to Jo that in January he should be in his New York apartment "until the book's finished, which I hope won't be too many months away. I've a couple of more in my head and may actually do at least one of them the same year. All right, all right, I know that sounds alcoholic, but I haven't had a drink since October 1..."

"...When folks ask me what a book or story is about I usually tell them the first thing that pops into my head... The book *is* about a man who has just come out of the Army, but his family — such as he has — doesn't play a very large part in it...though I'm not exactly sure what does. All I know about him so far is he's an artist named Helm and has been on a drunk since his discharge and has just been locked out of his hotel and he's got a son who's a Captain in the Eighth Air Force. I'm just finishing a short story about a couple of men just discharged from the Eighth Air Force,

one of whom wants the other to marry his sister so they can hang around on the farm together and shoot ducks and stuff..."[38]
- January 1946: *"The Valley Sheep Are Fatter,"* he writes Mary, "goes along smoothly but without any great speed, probably because I've been putting in a good deal of my time on other things." After a long weekend at Pleasantville "I hope to settle down to a more or less day after day attack on the book till it's done ... which I think will be before the winter ends."[39]
- February 1946: "Tomorrow," he tells Mary, "I hope to get that god-damned short story out of the mothballs and into the mail. It should have been done weeks ago. It'll only take a couple of hours to finish it. That's what the trouble's been: I always hate like hell to work on things when I know ahead of time what I'm going to say and have no little problems to worry my old white noggin. But this time I'm going to do it so I'll have nothing to keep me from getting back to *The Valley Sheep Are Fatter.*" He concludes the letter by announcing that he will now do a little reading of Shapley's *Galaxies* — "I'm doing some astronomical research for my next-after-this novel before I hit the sack."[40]
- July, 1946: After a five-month lull, he writes Mary that he is working again on "the novel," telling her once again, perhaps forgetting that he has imparted the information twice already, that it is "tentatively entitled *The Valley Sheep...*"[41]
- September 1946: Hammett is rather more honest with Nancy Bragdon, confessing, "I still murmur insincerely that I'm going to get back to work on TVSAF (*The Valley Sheep Are Fatter*)." He is similarly open with Marjorie May: "Once in a while, but not often enough to spoil the novelty, I add a line or two to *The Valley Sheep Are Fatter*, which by no means approaches *Men of Good Will* [Jules Romains' 27-volume novel cycle published between 1932 and 1946] in bulk."[42]
- March 1947: He's been in the country, he tells Mary, "trying to get in some honest licks on the play. I'd hoped to have it finished long before this, but I kept putting it aside for too many other things, but I'm going to get it finished this spring or else. I still think it's going to be pretty good ... maybe."[43]
- April 1947: Hammett tells Mary that he may write her sister Jo "to keep from having to work on my play," and, sure enough, in a

letter of the same date he tells Jo that he's been thinking of a short story — "anything, it seems, to keep from working on the play I've promised Kermit Bloomgarden..."[44]

- July 1947: He's just returned from Chicago and tells Mary that he hopes to stay in Pleasantville "till I get the play finished." Later in the month he tells Jo that "I've just finished what I call a hard day's work on the play — which means I fooled around for a while this evening after I got through listening to baseball games on the radio..."[45]
- February 1948: To his sister Reba, he writes: "Poverty and debts having descended on me in equal proportions, I now have to settle down to doing some short stories or something, not a nice prospect after all these years of evading that kind of stuff...It's nearly one in the morning, so maybe I'd better stop this and pretend I'm going to think about the short stories or something I've got to manufacture."[46]
- August 1948: By this stage Hammett is a little more honest with daughter Jo, telling her jokingly: "I thought up a plot for a novel, which I hope one day to get around to doing. Meanwhile it's swell having a new novel not to do. I was getting pretty bored just working on that half a dozen or so old ones..."[47]

≈

Between his achievement of permanent sobriety and his court appearance and prison term there were just four letters — three of them to daughter Jo — in which Hammett talked of his attempts to write. After the self-deprecatingly humorous tone of the previous letter, he seemed more serious now, although perhaps he gave the game away when, 15 months after telling his daughter that he had started another book (and this ten months after he had told her that he had conceived of a plot!), he confessed that he had yet to complete the first chapter.

- June 1949: Jo hears that Hammett is "trying to get a book — tentatively entitled *Man and Boy* — started and am fumbling around with a couple of television shows for the fall, so I guess I can call myself fairly busy."[48]

- January 1950: Now back in Hollywood to try to work on adapting *Detective Story* for the screen, he tells Jean Potter Chelbov, "I let myself be talked into putting aside my book — now entitled 'December First'..."[49]
- September 1950: He confesses to Jo that he hasn't finished the first chapter of his new book, although "in my torpid way, I'm kind of high on the book: it's a monstrously good conception, if only I don't bitch it up more than eighty per cent." Later that month he tells her that work on the novel is slow but he's fairly satisfied; "it's not at all like anything I've done before."[50]

If Hammett had persevered with the screenplay for *Detective Story*, it is quite possible that he would have encountered problems, as the main focus of the play (and of the eventual screenplay by Philip Yordan and Robert Wyler) is the psychological crisis of Detective Jim McLeod. McLeod is a driven man, haunted by the memory of his father who, with his "criminal mind," drove his mother into a mental asylum.[51] This has dictated McLeod's unwavering, hardline approach to police work, but his world collapses when, as he pursues the prosecution of an abortionist (transformed by Hollywood into a baby farmer), he learns that his wife Mary had made use of his services before he met her. As McLeod turns his puritanical ire on Mary, it becomes clear that he has much in common with his father. The depiction of such a crisis called for precisely the kind of introspection and psychological insight that Hammett had avoided in his writing. And perhaps this would have been a little too close to home in any case for Hammett who, although he had vowed not to follow his father in his drinking and the way he had treated his wife, Hammett's mother, had ended up doing precisely that.

It was not until October 1952 that Hammett again mentioned the book to Jo, but now it was only less than half-finished, although he hoped to have it done by Christmas. Here, for really the first time, he tried to fool Jo the way he used to attempt to fool Mary. At least we know that this would be the last attempt, for this was "Tulip," which by mid-1953 was "untouched for a long time," even though it only needed two months' work. But now he used his tax problems as an excuse.

- August 1952: The book, he tells Hellman, "might turn to be very worth while having done, though I'd be the first to admit that my optimism may be based more on what I intend and hope to inject into it than what I've managed to get into it this far..." Two days later, though, he writes: "It's not too late to still do some of that work I'm bragging about not having done, but the chances are I'll find some more or less Proustian reason for not doing it." He jokes that his watch has stopped and upset him. "Do you think I can do my best work when I'm upset? (Do you think I can ever do my best work?)"[52]
- October 1952: He had expected to have the book finished by now, he tells Jo, but it's less than half-completed; eleven days later he has hopes of getting back to it the following day, with the aim of being "out of the trenches" by Christmas, although to have a first draft by then will satisfy him. It's called "Tulip."[53]
- June 1953: The Christmas deadline has long passed, and Hammett tells Jo that "Tulip" has been "untouched for a long time now," although it only needs a couple of months' work. He feels there's not much point publishing anything until the tax problems are resolved, although "I could finish the book without publishing it. And I really ought to because I've got another book in my mind that I should get at..."[54]
- July 1953: He has taken out the "Tulip" manuscript "after a long holiday" and intends to work on it tonight — "but there will be the Yankee-Washington ballgame on TV and some boxing — from Los Angeles this time — and...well, we'll see how things work out. There is — fortunately — always tomorrow!" A week later, he claims to Jo that he's been "working a little — I never seem to work very hard, and do you want to make something of that? — on the book." Come the end of the month, however, he says that he had better finish "Tulip" so that he can work on another novel.[55]

But that was the end of the line. "Tulip" would never be finished and he would never attempt another novel. Hammett not only ceased writing, but he also abandoned the pretense that he was doing so.

Layman points out that the fragment of "Tulip" which survives ends with: "If you are tired you ought to rest, I think, and not try to fool yourself and your customers with colored bubbles." "By all the evidence," Layman concludes, "with that thought Hammett ended his writing career in the summer of 1953."[56]

When Hammett had written Jo in October 1952 that it was "less than half-completed," this was true enough, but this gave the impression that, say, at least a third of it was on paper. Similarly, when in July 1953 he claimed that it only required two months' further work, he was not being particularly truthful. The surviving fragment occupies just forty-seven pages of *The Big Knockover*, the collection edited by Hellman.

The story is obviously autobiographical. "Pop" (Hammett's nickname in the Army) is a former two-time soldier, tuberculosis survivor, writer and reformed drunkard. He's just out of jail and his radio shows have been cancelled. He is now having trouble writing and is arguing the point with Tulip, a friend of 20 years and his colonel in the Aleutians.

> "And where in the name of God do you get the notion that writers go around hunting for things to write about? Organizing material is the problem, not getting it. Most of the writers I know have far too many things on tap; they're snowed under with stuff they'll never get around to."
>
> "Words," he said. "If you've got so much stuff to write about, how come you haven't done any writing for so long?"
>
> "How do you know how much writing I've done?"
>
> "It can't be much. Magazines used to be lousy with you. All I ever see now is reprints of your early stuff, and less and less of that."[57]

Some of this material had been in Hammett's head for a while. It will be recalled that in July 1944 he had told Prudence Whitfield that he was thinking of turning a letter he had received from an Army comrade into a story; then we saw that in December 1945 he wrote

Mary that he was writing just such a story, "about a couple of men just discharged from the Eighth Air Force, one of whom wants the other to marry his sister so they can hang around on the farm together and shoot ducks and stuff..." And now that material turns up in "Tulip," as the title character tells Pop a story about visiting an Army buddy in the country; the buddy has a sister, the widow of a war hero. At one point she asks whether her brother is trying to buy him with her; she thinks he did the same with her husband. But Tulip tells Pop: "I never did any wondering about that. Look, Pop, whatever homo there is in Lee I don't think he ever knew about. He's not a bad kid."[58]

Much of the fragment concerns writing, as in this exchange:

> Tulip said, "I don't always know what you're talking about, Pop. But couldn't you just write things down the way they happen and let your reader get what he wants out of 'em?"
>
> "Sure, that's one way of writing, and if you're careful enough in not committing yourself you can persuade different readers to see all sorts of different meanings in what you've written, since in the end almost anything can be symbolic of anything else, and I've read a lot of stuff of that sort and liked it, but it's not my way of writing and there's no use pretending it is."[59]

At the end of the fragment, Pop says that he had a "wary feeling" that Tulip might come to represent a side of him.

> His being a side of me was all right, of course, since everybody is in some degree an aspect of everybody else or how would anybody ever hope to understand anything about anybody else? But representations seemed to me — at least they seem now, and I suppose I must have had some inkling of the same opinion then, devices of the old and tired, or older and more tired — to ease up, like conscious symbolism, or graven images. If you are tired you ought to rest, I think, and not try to fool yourself and your customers with colored bubbles.[60]

And that's where he stopped. When she included this fragment in *The Big Knockover*, Hellman added a few paragraphs which, she said, Hammett had intended to be the last page. Here, Pop visits Tulip in hospital and gives him the story (which we have just read). Tulip says he thinks it misses the point, but he'll give it a careful rereading. Cline, however, rather convincingly argues that this "last page" is something of a concoction, one paragraph of which Hellman may have written herself.[61]

≈

The major question is still unanswered: why was Hammett unable or disinclined to write, or at least to finish what he had begun?

Prosaic explanations are usually overlooked or discounted, but they probably played their part. Hammett was, as he would sometimes acknowledge, a lazy man. Why write when you can fish or hunt at Hardscrabble Farm? Why beat your brains out at a typewriter when you might be spending your time reading or listening to the radio? But you had to at least *pretend* to write because that's what people expected of you, so for appearances' sake you might knock out a page or two now and then and claim in the occasional letter that you were grappling with a novel in progress. Those who visualize Hammett as a tormented soul, wrestling with his writer's block, make the unspoken assumption that writing for him was some kind of missionary work. There being absolutely no evidence that this was the case, it is easy to dispense with the notion, at which point it becomes much easier to accept more mundane, but now plausible, explanations for his lack of productivity. But if writing was not missionary work, if he was not trying to win his readership to a particular view of the world, why had he written in the past?

According to his friend, the Hollywood writer and producer Nunnally Johnson, the only thing that interested Hammett in writing was the money, and Hammett told him that he stopped because he had all the money he would ever need. "He had none of the usual incentives that keep writers at their typewriters for as long as they have the strength to hit the keys. He had no impulse to tell any more stories, no ambition to accomplish more as a writer..." And once he had made his pile, that was all there was to it. Out went the typewriter and he never wrote another book or story. If there is a precedent for a decision like this in a writer I have never heard of it, and as a writer myself, with all the urges and secret vanities of a writer, it took me a long time to be convinced of the truth of it. But time provided the proof. And I can tell you how awed I was and always have been by such astonishing resolution.

However, says Johnson, Hammett's decision was based on a miscalculation, i.e. that he would not live "much beyond next Thursday."

I suppose that by the time he came to realize that he would in all likelihood be here not only next Thursday but for many Thursdays to come it was too late to sit down at the typewriter again with much confidence. When the end approached, it was thirty years later than he expected it, and Death owed him a genuine apology when eventually it made its tardy appearance.[62]

Given the fact that in his correspondence Hammett began to talk of writing again as early as 1936, it is more than possible that he had been less than honest when, just a few years earlier, he had told Johnson of his "decision." But there also must have been more than a grain of truth in it, for it had been many years since he had harbored lofty literary aspirations, submitting material to *The Smart Set*, and if nowadays he was neither aiming for "art" nor seeking to convey a "message," that left the financial motive.

Hammett himself gave a further explanation for his situation. A few years before his death, he claimed that he stopped writing because he had ruined himself by working a 30-hour stretch on the last third of *The Glass Key*. Ever since, he told James Cooper of the London *Daily Express*, "I've told myself I could do it again if I had to. And, of course … I couldn't."[63] But why would he have to? His claim leaves out of account the fact that after *The Glass Key* came *The Thin Man*, a number of screen stories and, when he was short of money, a few short stories. So, for a few years, was still writing.

Hammett's (and some of Hellman's) biographers and critics have a stab at explaining why he went dry.

Layman dismisses the 30-hour claim, saying that what ruined Hammett was "liquor, the women, the money, and the celebrity."[64] These undoubtedly played a part, but for the last dozen or so years of his life Hammett hardly drank at all, women were not an option and, thanks to the cloud of anti-communism that had descended on American life, there was neither money nor celebrity.

Mellen takes the view that Hammett was unable to go beyond the detective genre because of his "aversion to introspection" and, having "set too severe a limit on the degree of intimacy he was willing to allow his reader to share with him," this "finished him as a writer."[65] "Dreading the self-analysis that would have led him to new fiction," she later comments, "he stopped writing."[66] Given her own political inclinations, Mellen cannot help claiming that Hammett "stopped writing virtually in tandem with his confounding of Stalinism with a socialist ideal of justice,"[67] as if these two things were connected (they were, but not in the way that Mellen assumes). The same author claims that, "out of respect for the craft," Hammett chose to write little else because the "despair that suffused Hammett's own life had invaded his work..."[68]

This thesis is hardly convincing. It would appear to be true enough that Hammett's vision, in both his work and his life, had for some time been one of despair, but as argued previously his turn to politics was both an acknowledgement that individual solutions to the problems of the society in which he lived were simply not possible (either for the detective protagonist or himself), and an attempt to overcome this despair. Salvation lay in the collective solution of society's problems. Hammett's "aversion to introspection" — or, at least, to making its results public — doubtless prevented him from writing a particular kind of fiction, but there were other possibilities.

Nolan posits two reasons for Hammett's failure to produce:

> Hammett's problems were twofold. Having abandoned detective fiction, he had nothing to put in its place. Even more crippling, he had shut himself down emotionally, erecting an inner wall between himself and his public. He had lost the ability to communicate, to share his emotions.

As the years slipped past him, he drank, gambled, womanized, and buried himself in Marxist doctrines. His only creative outlet was his work on Hellman's plays.[69]

There are a number of problems with this explanation. Yes, Hammett had nothing with which to replace detective fiction, but as we shall see this really need not have been the case. The inability to "share his emotions" was not an insuperable bar to *all* the forms of writing of which Hammett would have been capable, and while the drinking, gambling and womanizing were undoubtedly diversions while he had the ability to pursue them, this was not really the case with his immersion in Marxism because, as argued earlier, this was the lifeline which allowed him to pull himself out of despair, and one which he grasped all the more determinedly *because* of his failure to write.

George Thompson says that in *Red Harvest* and *The Dain Curse*, Hammett had been asking whether "a moral man... in a corrupt world" can act "without himself becoming infected" and that the answer had been supplied in *The Maltese Falcon*: "yes, although the price — skepticism and alienation — is high."[70] He detects "a growing pessimism in Hammett's view of modern society, and a clear-eyed view of the dilemmas of a man of integrity in an immoral universe" in *The Glass Key*, which renders more concretely than any of Hammett's other novels "the attempt of the hero to get outside of himself by acting on what is best within himself for someone else, only to find, painfully, that the attempt merely proves the impossibility of such behavior."[71] And finally there is *The Thin Man* in which, despite its lightness of tone, all are corrupt, all is dark. Thus, concludes Thompson, Hammett never wrote another novel because "he had no more to say. He had worked out as far as he could the possibilities of the questions he had raised concerning individual man and society."[72]

Thompson is undoubtedly right, and he identifies the central problem: the novels all center on the *individual* in a corrupt society and his dilemma of how to survive *within* that society, rather than transform or transcend it. Hammett came to a dead end with such material because, like Raymond Chandler and his white knight Philip Marlowe, he realized that a single private eye could only treat symptoms, and that some force far greater was needed to tackle the basic condition. But the novels were written before Hammett became a Marxist, and so it would be a mistake to suppose that he would have identified that force already.

But what of post-1937? An entirely different kind of novel would be required now, but it seems that Hammett was not equal to the task, leading Thompson to assert that his "inability to change direction or to revivify his perceptions mark him as a minor writer."[73]

Rollyson remarks accurately enough that by the early 1930s Hammett had "exhausted the material over which he could be an undisputed authority."[74] By this he means the detective genre, of course. Diane Johnson says that in 1939 he was unable to write, "it seemed to him, because he had nothing to write about. His life, in some sense, had ended when he left San Francisco and obscurity..."[75]

But why, after he adopted a Marxist outlook, did he still fail to write? (It is not strictly true that he did not write at all, of course, because he wrote in the Army, as this was his job; it was fiction that was beyond him.)

≈

Let us now assume, with these other commentators, that Hammett, rather than being *merely* lazy or interested *only* in money, genuinely wanted to write and suffered from the inability to do so. Why did he not switch genres? The memoir and historical fiction spring to mind as distinct possibilities. (In addition to these, Hammett might have considered writing popularizations of the major issues of the day, using his simple, direct prose to render them more comprehensible to working-class readers. But perhaps he thought that his friend Leo Huberman was already doing a fine enough job in that market.)

As pointed out in Chapter 2, the unpublished "Seven Pages," written in 1926, held out the possibility that he would have been capable of writing an impressionistic set of memoirs. But he never again wrote anything that directly autobiographical, although "Tulip" comes close. It is perhaps significant that "Seven Pages" covers events well before his heyday, while "Tulip" is set in his twilight years, whereas the more interesting material was to be found in the two or three decades in between. But would a memoir have been possible without the self-examination to which he seemed to be so averse? If impressionistic, giving glimpses of the author amid the events that shaped him, then yes. Maybe he thought that a memoir covering those years would have been impossible without "naming names" (including his own). Or he possibly thought that his own life was of little interest.

At one point in "Tulip," Pop says that he's always avoided writing about his own life. "I've never written a word about any of these things."[76] Well, he had now! Or, at least, he had tried, because the problem with "Tulip" is that, by pulling its punches, it *does*, as the title character charges, miss the point. Hammett's failure to write had little to do with his "way of writing" and more to do with the fact that he either could not discover the cause of his disability or avoided the self-examination that might have led him to that discovery. It was surely a mistake to have embarked upon "Tulip." For a blocked writer who had shied away from self-examination throughout his writing career to set about writing a novel about a man who is unable to write was highly unlikely to set the creative juices flowing!

"Tulip" is the equivalent of Raymond Chandler's "A Couple of Writers," a short story, unpublished at the time, in which failing writer Hank Bruton reflects on his own plight. This contains a passage which, as Bruton realizes that his hopes as a writer will never be fulfilled, bears a remarkable resemblance to the General Griggs speech which Hammett refined for Hellman's *The Autumn Garden*. Even more remarkably, that play appeared in 1951, the same year that Chandler wrote his story.[77] There is, however, one major difference: Chandler, beset by self-doubt though he may have been, then rolled up his sleeves and wrote *The Long Goodbye*, his best book. He was able to do so because that novel was, as I will try to show in a forthcoming study, a veritable exercise in self-examination. Thereafter, he was to produce just one more work before his death — the potboiler *Playback*, an adaptation of a discarded screenplay.

Nolan says that by the time Hammett was 34, "Cynicism had been replaced by bitterness; troubling visions of a meaningless universe possessed him — and his method of dealing with such visions was to write about them."[78] Having written about *them*, what was he to write now that the universe was no longer so meaningless to him? It is probably a mistake, however, to assume that his search for meaning had triumphed completely. It is far more likely that his life from the mid-1930s onward consisted of periods during which the new sense of purpose was clear (as when his enthusiasm for political activity was uncompromised by either doubt or the apparent artificiality of some who campaigned alongside him, or when he served in the Army, and even when he went to prison), and those when the black tide of doubt and nihilism once more threatened to engulf him. The latter periods were most likely those in which he was tormented by the meaninglessness not of existence itself but of his own lifestyle, when alcohol (until 1948) both provided solace and acted as the source of further nihilistic behavior. Yes, he could in theory have used that internal struggle as the basis for a novel, but Hammett was hardly one to expose his own weaknesses to public view.

But there were also periods, when alcohol and philandering were no longer possibilities, during which he might have written. He did, it is true, begin "Tulip," but this merely states the problems; to complete the novel, he would have had to write about their causes and the possible solutions.

Perhaps Hammett was aware of the root of his dysfunction, and it filled him with shame. Writers who allied themselves to the working class in the 1930s and 1940s used their work to provide their readers with another way of looking at social conditions in their country, and sometimes to attempt to illustrate the transformation in consciousness that they had themselves experienced — what Julia Dietrich has called "conversion narratives."[79] But that also requires self-examination. Could Hammett have used his own experience to write such a novel, tracing the path of his own political development to illustrate the awakening of his central character? Probably not. It would have been possible in theory, but this would have meant that Hammett would have had to come to terms with what he had once been. And he had once been, or so he claimed, a strikebreaker. Not simply a misguided worker who thought that his interests and those of his employer coincided, but a *professional* strikebreaker, employed by an organization reviled by the US labor movement, knowingly paid by the employers to break strikes — and skulls. Hammett, once keen to invoke the Pinkerton agency as his badge of authenticity, would now have wanted to bury that part of his past.

And, if Nunnally Johnson's recollection is accurate, maybe Hammett would have been put off by the likelihood that such novels would pay little. (It is worth bearing in mind that even after joining the CPUSA, he had still written for money, as evidenced by the 1938 screen story *Another Thin Man*.)

The experience of John Steinbeck demonstrated, however, that such was not always the case. Although Steinbeck was never committed to a left-wing organization, he knew how to sound a radical note, as when he wrote in 1938: "I am treasonable enough not to believe in the liberty of a man or a group to exploit, torment, or slaughter other men or groups. I believe in the despotism of human life and happiness against the liberty of money and possessions."[80] His novel *In Dubious Battle* (1936) dealt with the organization of fruit-pickers, with a communist as a leading character. The 1939 novel *The Grapes of Wrath* won the National Book Award and a Pulitzer Prize, and by February 1940 434,000 copies had been printed.

There was another genre that Hammett could have considered if he was serious about continuing his writing career: the progressive historical novel.

While in the Aleutians, Hammett read Howard Fast's *Freedom Road*, which he thought "on the right side, but over-simplified to death." Even so, he found that "that sort of stuff does have a place, though: I know at least a couple of readers whose, you might say, eyes were opened by the book and who at least think they'd like to know more about what actually went on down there in the Old South, suh."[81]

Fast's novel is set on the fictitious former plantation of Carwell during the Reconstruction era. The indebted plantation, its owner having departed during the Civil War, has passed into the hands of the government. A loan having been obtained from a Boston abolitionist, freed slaves and poor whites ("white trash" or "scalawags") purchase 3,000 acres when the land is auctioned, living side by side and educating their children together. This bold experiment comes to an end when the Ku Klux Klan is given its head as a result of the "Compromise of 1877." (Democrat Samuel Tilden needed 185 electoral college votes to take the presidency, but 20 electoral votes in four states were disputed; a deal was done whereby the Republican Rutherford B. Hayes, who had 164 electoral votes, was handed the presidency on condition that he withdraw federal troops from the South, thereby ending Reconstruction.)

The central figure in the novel is Gideon Jackson, who graduates from illiterate freed slave to first delegate to the South Carolina constitutional convention, then to state assemblyman, and finally to congressman — the kind of dialectical development which Hammett appeared to be incapable of, or averse to, rendering in his own novels.

In an afterword, Fast poses and answers two questions. First, is there any truth in his tale?

> There was not one Carwell in the south at that period, but a thousand, both larger and smaller. All that I have told about as being done at Carwell was duplicated in many other places. White men and black men lived together, worked together, and built together, much as I have described here. In many, many places, they died together, in defence of what they had built.[82]

Second, why has the story not been told before?

> When the eight-year period of Negro and white freedom and co-operation in the south was destroyed, it was destroyed completely. Not only were material things wiped out and people slain, but the very memory was expunged.[83]

What Fast does in this novel, then, as in several others, is to lay before the reader a description of progressive historical developments which have been either buried or distorted by mainstream historiography, allowing US readers to discover their country's past in a completely new way. His novels were often the fictional equivalents of Leo Huberman's justly celebrated *Man's Worldly Goods*, which a few years earlier had presented Marxist political economy in a straightforward and entertaining fashion.[84]

Fast was enormously popular in the USA, in addition to which his novels were reprinted in huge editions in the Soviet Union. In the 1950s he was a victim of the blacklist, which he survived by publishing his own work. In his autobiography, he recalls that, years after leaving the CPUSA, he remarked to his Zen teacher that his party membership had thrown him "into literary obscurity and made me the hate target of the literary elite," whereupon the teacher "looked at me with contempt and said, 'You dare to complain of something that saved your own soul!'"[85]

Hammett's embrace of progressive political causes and a Marxist outlook had also saved *his* soul, overcoming the bleak, nihilist outlook with which he was cursed while writing his stories, novels and screen treatments. Then why, rather than sneering condescendingly at Fast's work, did he not tackle that genre himself? As he himself said, "eyes were opened" by Fast's *Freedom Road*. Isn't that what most progressive novelists would hope to achieve, leading their readers to a new way of looking at the world? Why was Hammett unable or unwilling to do this?

The answer to this might lie in the nature of Hammett's commitment, which was probably quite selfish. Yes, he would be generous with his time and, when it was available, his money, but the progressive cause had been a *personal* lifesaver for Hammett. He was not, it seems, particularly interested in proselytizing, which is what the writing of Fast-like novels would have amounted to. His daughter Jo says that Hammett "perfected a façade of utter confidence that was uncrackable and could be very intimidating. Part of it was that he really seemed indifferent to what other people thought, just shrugged off any arguments and never tried to convert anyone to his side."[86] Such an air of all-knowing superiority is certainly not unknown among those who, having adopted a Marxist outlook, are like Hammett immediately assigned leading positions in mass organizations but play no part in the day-to-day struggle in the lower echelons of the movement.

Also, Hammett was, now that he understood how the world worked, often content to sit back and watch it. Yes, he may have thought, it might just be worthwhile hanging around to see how this works itself out. And this offers a further explanation of his remark to Samm Sinclair Baker: if you are more interested in observing the world work than writing about it, there is little urgency about getting out of bed in the morning.

NOTES

1. Like Hammett, Mary developed behavioral problems associated with drink — something to which he seems to have contributed when she stayed with him in New York, for they sometimes got drunk together, and Hammett beat her. As we have seen, there are claims that Mary was not Hammett's biological daughter, and Mellen goes so far as to say (citing Hellman but without providing a reference) that while in New York together they developed "an almost incestuous love," and on one occasion indulged in "sexual fondling." See Joan Mellen, *Hellman and Hammett: The Legendary Passion of Lillian Hellman and Dashiell Hammett* (New York: Harper Collins, 1996), 256. It is surely significant that after Mary's New York visit in 1947 Hammett never again tried to persuade her that he was making a serious attempt to write. Instead, he turned his attention to Jo, although in the 1950s, as he worked sporadically on "Tulip," it is possible that he was actually serious.
2. Richard Layman, commentary, Dashiell Hammett, *Selected Letters of Dashiell Hammett, 1921-1960*, ed. Richard Layman with Julie M. Rivett (Washington D,C,: Counterpoint, 2001), 450.
3. Hammett to Josephine Dolan Hammett, September 14, 1936; *Selected Letters*, 110; Hammett to Mary Hammett, September 17, 1936; *Selected Letters*, 111.
4. Hammett to Mary Hammett, June 20, 1938; *Selected Letters*, 132; Hammett to Nat Deverich, June 25, 1938; *Selected Letters*, 135-136.
5. Hammett to Mary Hammett, August 26, 1938; *Selected Letters*, 136.
6. Diane Johnson, *The Life of Dashiell Hammett* (US title *Dashiell Hammett: A Life*), (London: Picador, 1985), 115.
7. Hammett to Mary Hammett, March 19, 1939 and March 29, 1939; *Selected Letters*, 150, 162.
8. Hammett to Mary Hammett, November 26, 1940; *Selected Letters*, 164.
9. Hammett to Mary Hammett, February 12, 1941; *Selected Letters*, 168.
10. Hammett to Mary Hammett, April 24, 1941; *Selected Letters*, 169.
11. Hammett to Josephine Dolan Hammett, January 16, 1942; *Selected Letters*, 174-175.

12 Hammett to Josephine Dolan Hammett, May 11, 1942; *Selected Letters*, 177.
13 Perhaps appropriately, director Stanley Kubrick co-wrote the screenplay for *The Shining* with Diane Johnson, who a few years later would publish her biography of Hammett.
14 Both fragments appear as bonus material in the e-book edition of Dashiell Hammett, *The Hunter and Other Stories*, ed. Richard Layman and Julie M. Rivett, (New York: The Mysterious Press, 2013).
15 William F. Nolan, *Dashiell Hammett: A Life at the Edge* (London: Arthur Barker, 1983), 157.
16 Ibid., 158.
17 *The Hunter and Other Stories*, location 5568.
18 Julie M. Rivett explains:

> "Carlos Ibañez del Campo headed a military dictatorship in Chile between 1927 and 1931. Jorge Gonzalez von Marées, called "El Jefe," was leader of *Movimiento Nacional de Chile*, a fascist group that staged a failed comeback coup attempt on Ibañez's behalf on September 5, 1938, in which most of the insurgent fighters were brutally slain by police. Radical Pedro Aguirre Cerda was at that time Chile's Popular Front candidate for president. He narrowly defeated Ibañez [in fact, the imprisoned Ibañez received only 0.03 percent of the vote; Aguirre's main opponent was the conservative Gustavo Ross] in the October 1938 election and held office until his death in 1941." Ibid., location 4956.)

19 Ibid., location 4972.
20 Hammett to Mary Hammett, March 15, 1945; *Selected Letters*, 418. In fact, Hammett had proposed this title to Bennett Cerf at Random House as early as 1938. See Nolan, 164. Cerf advanced him $5,000, which Hammett, explaining that he feared the book would never be written, returned two years later. See Julian Symons, *Dashiell Hammett* (San Diego/New York/London: Harcourt Brace Jovanovich, 1985), 122. Symons, following Nolan (168, footnote), almost certainly errs in saying that in August 1938 Hammett had claimed in a letter that he had completed 160 pages of the book. This is probably a misreading of his letter to agent Nat Deverich in which he says: "I'm in first rate physical shape again — got

myself up to the 160 pound mark — and the book seems to be going along nicely..." See Hammett to Nat Deverich, August 26, 1938; *Selected Letters*, 135-36.
21 *The Hunter and Other Stories*, Location 4972.
22 Diane Johnson, 171.
23 Lillian Hellman, *An Unfinished Woman*, in *Three*, ((Boston: Little, Brown, 1979), 294.
24 Nolan, 184.
25 Hammett to Mary Hammett, May 13, 1944; *Selected Letters*, 310.
26 Hammett to Prudence Whitfield, July 30, 1944; *Selected Letters*, 352-353.
27 Hammett to Prudence Whitfield, February 27, 1945; *Selected Letters*, 412.
28 Hammett to Lillian Hellman, March 4, 1945, March 20, 1945, March 29, 1945; *Selected Letters*, 414, 421, 423.
29 Hammett to Mary Hammett, April 4, 1945; Hammett to Prudence Whitfield, April 9, 1945 and April 13, 1945; Hammett to Lillian Hellman, April 23, 1945; *Selected Letters*, 425, 428- 429, 429-430, 430-431.
30 Hammett to Lillian Hellman, May 3, 1945 and May 4, 1945; *Selected Letters*, 435, 436.
31 Mellen, 249. Mellen mistakenly calls Baker "Samm Baker Sinclair."
32 Hellman, *An Unfinished Woman*, in *Three*, 296.
33 Richard Layman, *Shadow Man: The Life of Dashiell Hammett* (New York and London: Harcourt Brace Jovanovich/Bruccoli Clark, 1981), 204.
34 Nolan, 200.
35 Hammett to Lillian Hellman, July 27, 1944; *Selected Letters*, 351.
36 In 1948, when asked by his brother Richard whether he was a communist, Hammett replied, "I am a Marxist." Layman, *Shadow Man*, 203. In her account of this conversation, Mellen expands Hammett's reply into: "I'm not a Communist. I'm a Marxist." Mellen, 264. Had this been the case, it would have indicated that Hammett, while retaining his beliefs, was at this stage no longer a member of the CPUSA, and that this may have been a further symptom of the threatened return of his nihilism. It seems, however, that Mellen is mistaken, for whereas she cites

a Layman interview with Bill Glackin, one of Hammett's *Adakian* comrades, as her source, Layman says, "Joan has it wrong: my quote came not from Glackin, but from Richard Hammett's wife" and he insists, "I stick with my version." Richard Layman to Ken Fuller, June 11, 2015.

37 Hammett to Josephine Dolan Hammett, October 25, 1945; Hammett to Mary Hammett, October 31, 1945; *Selected Letters*; 453, 454.
38 Hammett to Josephine Dolan Hammett, December 5, 1945; Hammett to Mary Hammett, December 11, 1945; Hammett to Josephine Hammett, December 27, 1945; *Selected Letters*, 455, 456, 458.
39 Hammett to Mary Hammett, January 26, 1946; *Selected Letters*, 459-460.
40 Hammett to Mary Hammett, February 3, 1946; *Selected Letters*, 461, 462.
41 Hammett to Mary Hammett, July 4, 1946; *Selected Letters*, 467.
42 Hammett to Nancy Bragdon, September 4, 1946; Hammett to Marjorie May, September 10, 1946; *Selected Letters*, 474, 476.
43 Hammett to Mary Hammett, March 26, 1947; *Selected Letters*, 484-485.
44 Hammett to Mary Hammett, April 30, 1947; Hammett to Josephine Hammett, April 30, 1947; *Selected Letters*, 487, 490. Hammett was a script consultant for Bloomgarden, but did not write a play.
45 Hammett to Mary Hammett, July 10, 1947; Hammett to Josephine Hammett, July 29, 1947; *Selected Letters*, 491, 492.
46 Hammett to Reba Hammett, February 1, 1948; *Selected Letters*, 496.
47 Hammett to Josephine Hammett Marshall, August 29, 1948; *Selected Letters*, 498.
48 Hammett to Josephine Hammett Marshall, June 30, 1949; *Selected Letters*, 516.
49 Hammett to Jean Potter Chelbov, January 23, 1950; *Selected Letters*, 532.
50 Hammett to Josephine Hammett Marshall, September 9, 1950, September 28, 1950; *Selected Letters*, 543-544, 544.
51 Sidney Kingsley, *Detective Story* (New York: Dramatists Play Service, Inc.)
52 Hammett to Lillian Hellman, August 18, 1952 and August 20, 1952; *Selected Letters*, 585.

53 Hammett to Josephine Hammett Marshall, October 9, 1952 and October 20, 1952; *Selected Letters*, 588-589, 591.
54 Hammett to Josephine Hammett Marshall, June 14, 1953; *Selected Letters*, 592.
55 Hammett to Josephine Hammett Marshall, July 11, 1953, July 18, 1953 and July 30, 1953; *Selected Letters*, 595-596, 597, 597-598.
56 Richard Layman, commentary, Hammett, *Selected Letters*, 598.
57 Dashiell Hammett, "Tulip," in Dashiell Hammett, *The Big Knockover: Selected Stories and Short Novels*, ed. Lillian Hellman (New York: Vintage Books, 1989), 304.
58 Ibid., 313.
59 Ibid., 340.
60 Ibid., 347.
61 See Sally Cline, *Dashiell Hammett: Man of Mystery* (New York: Arcade Publishing, 2014), 197-98 Cline also insists that Hammett continued to work on "Tulip," which may or may not have been the case.
62 Nunnally Johnson, *The Letters of Nunnally Johnson*, ed. Doris Johnson and Ellen Leventhal (NY: Knopf, 1981), 187-188. This letter, which was addressed to Julian Symons, appears in Diane Johnson, 315, n. 14. According to his daughter Jo, Hammett *did* wish to "accomplish more as a writer." She says that "what Gershwin had accomplished in his field — bridging the gap from Tin Pan Alley to the concert hall — was precisely parallel to what Papa wanted to do in his own." See Jo Hammett, *Dashiell Hammett: A Daughter Remembers*, ed. Richard Layman with Julie M. Rivett (New York: Carroll & Graf Publishers, 2001), 92.
63 Nolan, 233.
64 Layman, *Shadow Man*, 115.
65 Mellen, 63, 65.
66 Ibid., 306.
67 Ibid., 111.
68 Ibid., 63.
69 William F. Nolan, "Introduction." Dashiell Hammett, *Nightmare Town*, eds. Kirby McCauley, Martin H. Greenberg, Ed Gorman (New York: Vintage Crime/Black Lizard, 1999), xi.
70 George J. "Rhino" Thompson, *Hammett's Moral Vision* (San Francisco: Vince Emery Productions, 2007), 131.

71 Ibid., 136, 138.
72 Ibid., 201.
73 Ibid., 202.
74 Carl Rollyson, *Lillian Hellman: Her Legend and her Legacy* (New York: St. Martin's Press, 1988), 43.
75 Diane Johnson, 155. Johnson writes that her "speculation about the underlying causes of Hammett's failure to write after 1934 is based on Hammett's discussions with a psychiatrist, who prefers not to be mentioned by name, who treated Mary Hammett, and whom Hammett also consulted for his own benefit." Johnson, 318, n.3. Rollyson also claims that Hammett would "seek out a psychiatrist." Rollyson, 158. According to Mellen, however, Hammett at first consulted Gregory Zilboorg, the psychiatrist treating Hellman, on Mary's behalf, but she was eventually treated by Edward Teicher in Los Angeles. Mellen, 256-257. It is unlikely, though, that Hammett, being averse to self-analysis, consulted an analyst on his own behalf; he was probably enough of a Marxist to look askance on this new "science." Nolan is quite clear that Hammett refused to submit to analysis. Nolan, 198. The furthest Hellman goes in this regard is to say that she discussed her own analysis with Hammett — "not very much but a little bit. Hammett used to say he learned more about himself through my analysis than I learned about myself." Christine Doudna, "A Still Unfinished Woman: A Conversation with Lillian Hellman," *Rolling Stone*, February 24, 1977; Jackson R. Bryer, ed., *Conversations with Lillian Hellman* (Jackson and London: University Press of Mississippi, 1986), 201.
76 Hammett, "Tulip," *The Big Knockover* 331.
77 See Raymond Chandler, "Á Couple of Writers," in Dorothy Gardiner and Kathrine Sorley Walker, eds., *Raymond Chandler Speaking* (Berkeley, Los Angeles and London: University of California Press, 1997), 99-112.
78 Nolan, 87.
79 Julia Dietrich, *The Old Left in History and Literature* (New York: Twayne Publishers, 1996), 70.
80 John Steinbeck to Elizabeth Otis, May 1938, quoted in John Steinbeck, *Working Days: The Journals of* The Grapes of Wrath, ed. Robert DeMott (New York: Viking, 1989), liv, note 12.

81 Hammett to Lillian Hellman, March 1, 1945; *Selected Letters*, 413.
82 Howard Fast, *Freedom Road* (London: John Lane The Bodley Head, 1946), 255.
83 Ibid., 255-256.
84 Leo Huberman, *Man's Worldly Goods* (London: Victor Gollancz, Left Book Club edition, 1937).
85 Howard Fast, *Being Red* (Boston: Houghton Mifflin Company, 1990), 74.
86 Rollyson, 144-145.

Bibliography

Ash, Timothy Garton. "Orwell's List." *The New York Review of Books*, September 25, 2003.

Baker, Carlos. *Ernest Hemingway: A Life Story*. London: The Literary Guild, 1969.

Bazelon, David T. "Dashiell Hammett's Private Eye." *The Scene before You: A New Approach to American Culture*. Edited by Chandler Brossard. New York: Rinehart, 1955.

Belfrage, Cedric. *The American Inquisition*. Indianapolis: Bobbs-Merrill Company, 1973.

Borkenau, Franz. *The Spanish Cockpit: An Eyewitness Account of the Spanish Civil War*. London: Phoenix Press, 2000.

Carr, E. H. "The Russian Revolution and the West." *New Left Review*, 1/111/September- October, 1978.

Chandler, Raymond. *The Big Sleep/Farewell My Lovely/The High Window/The Lady in the Lake/The Long Goodbye/Playback*. London: Wm. Heinemann/Chatto & Windus/Octopus Books, 1977.

— "Á Couple of Writers." *Raymond Chandler Speaking*. Edited by Dorothy Gardiner and Kathrine Sorley Walker. Berkeley, Los Angeles and London: University of California Press, 1997.

— *The Little Sister*. New York: Vintage Crime/Black Lizard, 1988.

— *Selected Letters of Raymond Chandler*. Edited by Frank McShane. New York: Columbia University Press, 1981.

Cline, Sally. *Dashiell Hammett: Man of Mystery*. New York: Arcade Publishing, 2014.
Coates, W. P. and Zelda K. *A History of Anglo-Soviet Relations*. London: Lawrence & Wishart/The Pilot Press, 1943.
Cooper, James. "Lean Years for the Thin Man." *Washington Daily News*, March 11, 1957.
Davies, Joseph E. *Mission to Moscow*. London: Victor Gollancz, 1942.
Dietrich, Julia. *The Old Left in History and Literature*. New York: Twayne Publishers, 1996.
Everett, George. "The Seeds of *Red Harvest*: Dashiell Hammett's Poinsonville," *Only in Butte*, http://butteamerica.com/hist.htm. Accessed May 2, 2015.
Fast, Howard. *Being Red*. Boston: Houghton Mifflin Company, 1990.
— *Freedom Road*. London: John Lane The Bodley Head, 1946.
Foner, Philip S. "Jack London: American Rebel," *Jack London/American Rebel*. Edited by Philip S. Foner. New York: Citadel Press, 1964.
Foster, William Z. *History of the Communist Party of the United States*. New York: International Publishers, 1952.
Freeman, Joseph. *An American Testament: A Narrative of Rebels and Romantics*. London: Victor Gollancz, Left Book Club Edition, 1938.
Fuller, Ken. *Radical Aristocrats: London Busworkers from the 1880s to the 1980s*. London: Lawrence and Wishart, 1985.
Furr, Grover. *Khrushchev Lied*. Kettering Ohio: Erythrós Press and Media, LLC, 2011.
— "Rejoinder to Roger Keeran," *Marxism-Leninism Today*, December 7, 2011. www.mltoday.com/rejoinder-to-roger-keeran.
Gale, Robert L. *A Dashiell Hammett Companion*. Westport: Greenwood Press, 2000.
Gallagher, Dorothy. *Lillian Hellman: An Imperious Life*. New Haven and London: Yale University Press, 2014.
Gentry, Kurt. *J. Edgar Hoover: The Man and the Secrets*. New York: W. W. Norton and Company, 1991.
Gibbons, Fiachra. "Blacklisted writer says illness clouded Orwell's judgment." *Guardian*, June 24, 2003.
Gottfried, Martin. *Arthur Miller: His Life and Work*. Boston: Da Capo Press, 2003.
Halper, Albert. *The Foundry*. New York: Viking, 1934.
— *Good-bye, Union Square: A Writer's Memoir of the Thirties*. Chicago:

Quadrangle Books, 1970.

Hammett, Dashiell. "The Advertisement is Literature." *Western Advertising*, October 1926.

— *The Big Knockover: Selected Stories and Short Novels*. Edited by Lillian Hellman. New York, Vintage Books, 1989.

— *Crime Stories and other Writings*. New York: The Library of America, 2001.

— *The Dashiell Hammett Megapack*. Wildside Press LLC, 2013.

— *Five Complete Novels*. New York: Avenel Books, 1980.

— *The Hunter and Other Stories*. Edited by Richard Layman and Julie M. Rivett. New York: The Mysterious Press, 2013.

— *Lost Stories*. Edited by Vince Emery. San Francisco: Vince Emery Productions, 2005.

— *Nightmare Town* Edited by Kirby McCauley, Martin H. Greenberg and Ed Gorman. Introduction by William F. Nolan. New York: Vintage Crime/Black Lizard, 1999.

— *The Return of the Thin Man*. Edited by Richard Layman and Julie M. Rivett. London: Mysterious Press for Head of Zeus, 2012.

— *Selected Letters of Dashiell Hammett, 1921-1960*. Edited by Richard Layman with Julie M. Rivett. Washington D.C.: Counterpoint, 2001.

Hammett, Jo. *Dashiell Hammett: A Daughter Remembers*. Edited by Richard Layman with Julie M. Rivett. New York: Carroll & Graf Publishers, 2001.

Hellman, Lillian. *The Collected Plays*. Boston, Toronto: Little, Brown and Company, 1972.

— *Conversations with Lillian Hellman*. Edited by Jackson R. Bryer. Jackson and London: University Press of Mississippi, 1986.

— *Scoundrel Time*. London: Macmillan, 1976.

— *Three*. Boston: Little, Brown, 1979.

Hemingway, Ernest. *For Whom the Bell Tolls*. New York: Collier Books, Macmillan, 1987.

Hobsbawm, Eric. *The Age of Extremes: The Short Twentieth Century, 1914-1989*. London: Michael Joseph, 1994.

Holdsworth, Nick. "Stalin 'planned to send a million troops to stop Hitler if Britain and France agreed pact'," *The Telegraph*, October 18, 2008.

Horne, Gerald. *Class Struggle in Hollywood, 1930-1950: Moguls, Mobsters,*

Stars, Reds and Trade Unionists. Austin: University of Texas Press, 2001.

— *The Final Victim of the Blacklist: John Howard Lawson, Dean of the Hollywood Ten.* Berkeley, Los Angeles and London: University of California Press, 2006.

Huberman, Leo. *Man's Worldly Goods.* London: Victor Gollancz, Left Book Club edition, 1937.

Ibarruri, Dolores. *They Shall Not Pass.* New York: International Publishers, 1976.

Institute of Marxism-Leninism, Central Committee of the CPSU. *Outline History of the Communist International.* Moscow: Progress Publishers, 1971.

Johnson, Diane. *The Life of Dashiell Hammett* (US title *Dashiell Hammett: A Life*). London: Picador, 1985.

Johnson, Nunnally. *The Letters of Nunnally Johnson.* Edited Doris Johnson and Ellen Leventhall. New York: Knopf, 1981.

Keeran, Roger. "Khrushchev Lied But What Is The Truth?" *Marxism-Leninism Today,* November 23, 2011, mltoday.com/article/1246-khrushchev-lied-but-what-is-the-truth/29.

Kenney, William Patrick. "The Dashiell Hammett Tradition and the Modern Detective Novel." Diss., University of Michigan, 1964.

Kessler-Harris, Alice. *A Difficult Woman: The Challenging Life and Times of Lillian Hellman.* New York: Bloomsbury Press, 2012.

Kingsley, Sidney. *Detective Story.* New York: Dramatists Play Service, Inc.

Larrabee, Eric. *Commander In Chief: Franklin Delano Roosevelt, His Lieutenants and Their War.* London: Andre Deutsch, 1987.

Layman, Richard. *Shadow Man: The Life of Dashiell Hammett.* New York and London: Harcourt Brace Jovanovich/Bruccoli Clark, 1981.

McCoy, Horace: *They Shoot Horses, Don't They?/Kiss Tomorrow Goodbye/No Pockets in a Shroud/I Should Have Stayed Home.* London: Zomba Books, 1983.

McGilligan, Patrick and Ken Mate. "Allen Boretz." *Tender Comrades: A Backstory of the Hollywood Blacklist.* Edited by Patrick McGilligan and Paul Buhle. New York: St. Martin's Griffin, 1999.

McKenna, Thomas M. *Muslim Rulers and Rebels.* Manila: Anvil Publishers, 2000.

Manchester, William. *Goodbye Darkness: A Memoir of the Pacific War.*

New York: Dell Publishing Co., 1982.

Marion, George. *The Communist Trial: An American Crossroads*. New York: Fairplay Publishers, 1949.

Martinson, Deborah. *Lillian Hellman: A Life with Foxes and Scoundrels*. Berkeley: Counterpoint, 2005.

Mellen, Joan. *Hellman and Hammett: The Legendary Passion of Lillian Hellman and Dashiell Hammett*. New York: Harper Collins, 1996.

Miles, Jonathan. *The Nine Lives of Otto Katz*. London: Bantam Books, 2011.

Miller, Arthur. *Timebends: A Life*. London: Methuen, 2005.

Nasaw, David. *The Chief: The Life of William Randolph Hearst*. Boston, New York: Mariner Books, 2001.

Newman, Robert P. *The Cold War Romance of Lillian Hellman and John Melby*. Chapel Hill: University of North Carolina Press, 1989.

Nolan, William F. *Dashiell Hammett: A Casebook*. Santa Barbara: McNally & Loftin, 1969.

— *Dashiell Hammett: A Life at the Edge*. London: Arthur Barker, 1983.

North, Joseph. "Still on the Fence." *New Masses*, September 25, 1934.

Nove, Alec. *An Economic History of the USSR 1917-1991*. London: Penguin Books, 1992.

Orwell, George. *Homage to Catalonia*. London: Folio Society, 1998.

Petras, James. "The CIA and the Cultural Cold War Revisited." *Monthly Review*, November 1999.

Rollyson, Carl. *Lillian Hellman: Her Legend and her Legacy*. New York: St. Martin's Press, 1988.

Siringo, Charles A. *Two Evil Isms, Pinkertonism and Anarchism*. London: Forgotten Books, 2013.

Summers, Anthony. *Official and Confidential: The Secret Life of J. Edgar Hoover*. New York: G. P. Putnam, 1993.

Symons, Julian. *Dashiell Hammett*. San Diego/New York/London: Harcourt Brace Jovanovich, 1985.

"Theatre: Classic Festival." *Time*, September 27, 1937.

Thompson, George J. *Hammett's Moral Vision*. San Francisco: Vince Emery Productions, 2007.

— "The Problem of Moral Vision in Dashiell Hammett's Detective Novels." Diss., University of Connecticut, 1971.

Trumbo, Dalton. *The Time of the Toad: A Study of Inquisition in America*. London: Journeyman Press, 1982.

Ward, Nathan. *The Lost Detective: Becoming Dashiell Hammett*. New York: Bloomsbury, 2015.
Wolfe, Peter. *Beams Falling: The Art of Dashiell Hammett*. Bowling Green: Bowling Green University Popular Press, 1980.
Zinn, Howard. *A People's History of the United States, 1492-Present*, revised and updated. New York: HarperPerennial, 1995.
Zumoff, J. A. "Politics and the 1920s Writings of Dashiell Hammett," *American Studies Journal*, 52.1 (2012).
— "The Politics of Dashiell Hammett's *Red Harvest*," *Mosaic*, 40.4 (2007).

Index

Adakian, The, 14, 258, 290
After the Thin Man (screen story), 124, 133-140, 151, 194
Alexander, Muriel, 270
Allentown, Pennsylvania, 113, 200
American Federation of Labor, 215
American Labor Party, 266, 267-68
American Magazine, The, 50
American Testament, An (Freeman), 195
Anaconda, 5, 69, 70, 71, 115n25, 198
Another Part of the Forest (Hellman play), 175-78, 189n52
Another Thin Man (screen story), 21n41, 144-50, 154n40, 163, 306
Anouil, Jean, 184
Arbuckle, Fatty, 5, 19n16
Argosy All-Star Weekly, 28, 72
Autumn Garden, The (Hellman play), 179-83, 305
Azaña, Manuel, 236

Baker, Samm Sinclair, 268, 280n55, 290, 309, 312n31
Bay, Howard, 204
Benny, Corinne, 260
Berkeley, Martin, 206
Bernal, J. D., 203

Bernstein, Leonard, 184
Big Knockover, The (collection), 179, 298, 299
Big Sleep, The (Chandler), 67
Bilbo, Theodore, 266, 267, 269
Black Mask, 3, 6, 7, 8, 9, 10, 20n22, 23, 24, 25, 26, 27, 28, 29, 34, 36, 39, 43, 44, 45, 46, 47, 48, 49, 55, 56, 57, 63, 66, 79, 89, 97, 103, 116n32, 128, 143
Blechman, Burt, 186
Block, Harry, 50, 79, 85
Blomberg, Werner von, 210
Blond Venus (film), 123
Bloomgarden, Kermit, 15, 16, 295, 313n44
Blucher, Vasily Konstantinovich, 232
Blue Book, 44, 48
Bolivar, Simón, 178
Boretz, Allen, 205
Borkenau, Franz, 233, 235, 236, 238
Bragdon, Nancy, 294
Brief Stories, 6, 24, 25, 55
Browder, Earl, 198, 211, 212, 250n55, 253, 260, 261, 277n26
Budenny, Semyon, 232
Budenz, Louis, 206
Bukharin, Nikolai, 231, 232

Caballero, Largo, 236, 237
Candide (Hellman play), 184
Carr, E. H., ix
Cawelti, John, 26,
Central Intelligence Agency (CIA), 262, 265
Cerda, Pedro Aguirre, 286, 311n18
Chamberlain, Neville, 240, 242
Chandler, Raymond, 10, 26, 28, 31, 55, 60n53, 65, 67, 74, 79, 87, 88, 98, 100, 101, 103, 125, 131, 143, 150, 190n67, 303, 305
Chavaroche, 227
Children's Hour, The (Hellman play), 155, 156, 157-59, 161, 183, 185, 217n7
Christie, Agatha, 26
Churchill, Winston, 241, 262
City Streets (film), 123
Civil Rights Congress, 16, 265, 266, 267, 268, 269, 274

Cline, Sally, 19n16, 19n20, 20n22, 117n70, 118n89, 213, 214, 281n77, 300, 314n61
Cockburn, Claude, 259
Cody, Phil, 17, 23, 24, 28, 29, 30, 36, 39, 40, 43, 55, 56
Cohn, Roy, 263-64, 273
Collected Plays, The (Hellman), 164
Collier's, 50, 51, 53
Colodny, Robert, 258
Comintern (Communist International), 203, 207, 208, 226, 227, 235, 237, 246, 248n7, 250n49
Communist Party of Spain, 227, 237, 250n49
Communist Party of the USA (CPUSA), ix, 15, 142, 143, 150, 170, 193, 194, 197, 198, 201, 205, 206, 208, 209, 210, 211, 212, 213, 214, 215, 219n30, 221n63, 222n95, 229, 233, 253, 255, 256, 257, 259, 264, 265, 267, 268, 271, 272, 274, 276n2, 288, 306, 308, 312n36; and Communist Political Association, 260-61, 277n26; and Non-Aggression Pact, 239, 244-46; and Popular Front, 226, 228; legal status of, 261, 265, 269
Communist Trial: An American Crossroad, The (Marion), 269
Conference of Studio Unions, 263
Congress for Cultural Freedom, 233, 249n31,
Congress of Industrial Organizations (CIO), 215
Cooper, Gary, 123
Cooper, James, 301
Cosmopolitan, 9-10

Daily Worker, 170, 259, 266
Dain Curse, The, 7, 8, 20n36, 31, 44, 47, 48, 49, 50, 59, 63, 72-82, 97, 163, 199, 303
Daly, Carroll John, 6
Dannay, Frederick, 268
Davies, Joseph P., 231-33, 239, 244, 248n11
Davies, Marion, 20, 193, 217n3
Days to Come (Hellman play), 143, 159-65, 205
Death is for Suckers (abandoned novel), 284
Detective Fiction, 44, 49
Detective Story (film), 16, 124, 125, 296
Devil's Playground (screen story), 124, 132-33
Dies, Martin Jr., 253

Dietrich, Julia, 306
Dietrich, Marlene, 123, 208
Dimitrov, Georgi, 208
Double Indemnity (film), 131
Doyle, Arthur Conan, 26
Drax, Reginald Aylmer Ranfurly Plunkett Ernle-Erle, 243
Duclos, Jacques, 260
Duranty, Walter, 228, 246n11

Egorov, Alexander, 232
Emery, Vince, 5, 6, 26, 27, 99, 158, 166, 201, 206, 208, 244, 251-52n80
Engels, Friedrich, 201, 202, 204
Equality, 255
Esquire, 51
Everett, George, 70
Experience, 29, 32

Fast, Howard, 15, 218n26, 264, 271, 307-09
Federal Bureau of Investigation (FBI), 9, 12, 13, 129, 206, 219n30, 254, 255, 264, 266, 267, 275, 279n44
Fitzgerald, F. Scott, 24, 197, 218n26
Ford, James W., 212
Foster, William Z., 211-12, 253, 257, 260
Foundry, The (Halper), 124, 125, 140-44
France, Anatole, 41
Franco, Francisco, 205, 234, 235, 236, 237, 238
Freedom Road (Fast), 307-08, 309
Freeman, Joseph, 142, 195-96, 229, 230
Freeman, Judith, ix

Gale, Robert L., 123, 152n4
Gallagher, Dorothy, 12, 155, 161, 189n52, 204, 220n45, 228, 239
Gardiner, Muriel, 202-03, 239
Gardner, Erle Stanley, 39, 102
Garrett, Oliver H. P., 123
Giroux, Richard, 185
Glackin, Bill, 312-13n36
Glass Key, The, 7, 8, 45, 47, 49, 63, 79, 88, 90, 91, 93-101, 163, 200, 301

Goebbels, Joseph, 210
Goering, Hermann, 210
Goldwyn, Samuel, 159, 264
Good Meal, The (abandoned play), 15
Goodrich, Frances, 138
Gordon, Ruth, 186
Gottfried, Martin, 209
Grapes of Wrath, The (Steinbeck), 307
Green, Gilbert "Gil," 269

Hackett, Albert, 138, 139, 144, 150, 151, 194
Haldane, J. B. S., 203
Halifax, Lord (Edward Wood), 242
Hall, Gus, 269, 273
Halper, Albert, 124, 140, 141, 142, 143
Hammett, Annie, 3
Hammett, Dashiell, and advertising, 5-6, 7, 41-42, 57, 81; and *Black Mask*, 6-7, 9, 24-49 (first stories, 24-28; in Phil Cody period, 28-40; under Joseph Shaw's editorship, 43-49); contributions to Lillian Hellman's plays, 154-183; dry period of, 283-309; early life of, 2-5; earliest stories of, 6, 23; extravagant lifestyle of, vii, 2, 4, 9, 10, 15, 194-95, 290, 292, 301; final years and death, 16-17, 272-275; and Frank Little, 69-71, 115n23, 198, 205; health of, 4, 5, 7, 10, 17, 194-95; in Hollywood, 8, 10, 16, 51, 113, 123-51, 171-72, 194-95, 200, 205-06, 209, 213-14, 216, 272, 295-96; influence of Hellman on his politics, 200-04; and Jefferson School of Social Science, 15, 266, 268, 274, 290; and Moscow Trials, 225, 228-33; nihilism of, vii, 56, 72, 127, 131, 150, 172, 199, 214, 215, 216, 291, 292, 306, 312n36; novels of, 7-9, 63-113; as a Pinkerton, 4, 5, 19n16, 19n18, 26, 33, 69, 70-71, 115n24, 162, 193, 205, 214-15, 306; political beliefs and activity of, 12, 197-200, 225-247, 253-258; postwar political activity of, 16, 204-216, 265-72, 274; and Soviet-German Non-Aggression Pact, 225, 239-47, 252, 254, 256-57; and Spanish Civil War, 205, 225, 233-38; stories after *Black Mask*, 50-54; and suicide, vii, 10, 194, 215, 292; testimony before Joseph McCarthy, 272-74, 281n77; trial and prison sentence of, 16, 269-72; and unpaid income tax, 272, 296-97; in U. S. Army, 12-15, 258-61, 272, 287-90;
Hammett, Josephine "Jo," ix, 7, 8, 11, 12, 15, 17, 18-19n13, 82, 92, 144, 157,

166, 189, 197, 213, 214, 260, 269, 270, 272, 292, 293, 294, 295, 296, 297, 298, 309, 310n1, 314n62
Hammett, Josephine Annis Dolan, 4-5, 7, 8, 70, 87, 194, 283, 284, 292, 293
Hammett, Richard, 3, 18n4
Harper's Bazaar, 50, 51
Haultain, Phil, 4
Hayes, Rutherford B., 307
Hearst, William Randolph, 9, 20n36, 20n38, 162, 193, 211, 212, 217n3
Hellman, Lillian, on Hammett's contributions to her plays, 156, 158, 161, 166-67, 179-80; and "Julia," 202-03; plays of, 155-186; political development of, 200-04
Hemingway, Ernest, 238, 250n55
Hill, Joe, 1
History of Anglo-Soviet Relations, A (W. P. and Zelda K. Coates), 240, 252n80
Hitchcock, Alfred, 125
Hitler, Adolf, 175, 210, 231, 234, 236, 239, 240, 241, 242, 243, 244, 245, 248, 257, 286, 291
Hobsbawm, Eric, 237, 248n7, 250n49
Hollywood Ten, 197, 264
Homage to Catalonia (Orwell), 233
Hoover, Herbert, 110
Hoover, J. Edgar, 9, 13, 17, 254, 275
House Un-American Activities Committee (HUAC), 12, 198, 251n58, 253, 254, 257, 261, 262, 264-65, 267, 271, 280n63
Huberman, Leo, 304, 308
Hughes, Howard, 123
Hunter and Other Stories, The (collection), 31, 40, 41, 48, 125, 131
Huxley, Aldous, 24

Ibarurri, Dolores, 201, 227
In Dubious Battle (Steinbeck), 307
Industrial Workers of the World (IWW), 1, 5, 29, 41, 64, 67, 69, 70
Ingersoll, Ralph, 158, 161, 255
International Alliance of Theatrical Stage Employees, 214
International Brigades, 215, 235

Jerome, V. J., 198, 205, 274

John Reed Club, 201
Johnson, Diane, 11, 13, 17, 41, 90, 91, 170, 209, 259, 270, 274, 275, 280n62, 304, 311n13, 315n75
Johnson, Nunnally, 92, 195, 300-01, 306
Judge, 44, 46

Kamenev, Lev, 231
Katz, Otto (aka Otto Simon, Rudolph Breda), 203, 206-09
Kazan, Elia, 209
Kessler-Harris, Alice, 210, 211, 234, 237, 239
Khrushchev, Nikita, 231
Kirov, Sergei, 230
"Kiss-Off, The" (screen story), 123, 125-27
Knight, Jack, 4
Knopf (publishers), 9, 47, 50, 53, 79, 85, 109, 284
Knopf, Alfred, 8, 158, 194
Knopf, Blanche, 28, 49, 63, 66
Kober, Arthur, 10, 161, 213, 220n42

Ladies' Man (film), 123
Landon, Alfred, 211, 212
Lang, Fritz, 208
Langley, Noel, 143
Lardner, Ring Jr., 197, 206, 244
Lark, The (Hellman play), 183-84
Larrabee, Eric, 111
Lawson, John Howard, 209, 219n29, 222-223n95, 263
Layman, Richard, x, 5, 7, 8, 9, 13, 15, 19n18, 20-21n41, 21n53, 28, 29, 31, 39, 40, 43-44, 52, 54, 55, 58n2, 60n51, 61n76, 68-69, 70, 72, 79, 91, 99, 115n23, 120n140, 123, 125, 141, 144, 158, 180, 194, 195, 200, 209, 215, 226, 254, 258, 265, 268, 269, 279n44, 284, 298, 302, 312-313n36.
League of American Writers, 13, 170, 246, 255
Lenin, V. I., 201, 202, 213, 229, 259
Lewis, Mildred, 195,
Lewis, Sinclair, 24
Liberty, 51
Little Foxes, The (Hellman play), 165-169, 170, 175, 177, 178, 189n52
Lloyd, Harold, 217n7

Lloyd George, David, 242
London, Jack, 3, 26
Long Goodbye, The (Chandler), 100, 305
Lorre, Peter, 208
Loy, Myrna, 124, 151

MacArthur, Douglas, 110-11
McCarthy, Joseph, 184, 196, 206, 257, 261, 272-74, 281n76
McCoy, Horace, 99, 127
McClellan, John, 273, 281n76
Maisky, Ivan, 234, 242
Maltese Falcon, The, 4, 7, 8, 34, 35, 43, 44-45, 47, 50, 63, 79, 82-93, 101, 110, 113, 114n10, 121n155, 159, 163, 164, 199, 216, 303
Mamoulian, Rouben, 123
Man and Boy (abandoned novel), 295
Man's Worldly Goods (Huberman), 308
Marcantonio, Vito, 268
Marion, George, 269
Martin, Nell, 7, 8
Martin, Max, 123
Martinson, Deborah, 19n13, 155, 161, 165, 170, 171, 180, 192n122, 203, 231
Marx, Karl, 69, 201, 202, 215, 259, 277n19, 281n85
Masses and Mainstream, 267
Matthau, Walter, 186
Maugham, Somerset, 24
May, Marjorie, 294
Mayakovsky, Vladimir, 201
Melby, John, 196
Mellen, Joan, 19n13, 61n72, 123, 153n40, 156, 1558, 161, 163, 167, 170, 171-72, 174, 175, 180, 185, 195, 197, 201, 202, 204, 205, 209, 210, 214, 221n63, 226, 228, 230, 234, 239, 244, 256, 266, 267, 277n19, 302, 310n1, 312n31, 312n36, 315n75
Mencken, H. L., 6, 20n22, 24
Men of Goodwill (Romain), 294
Miles, Jonathan, 207, 208, 221n70
Miller, Arthur, 209, 257, 264, 280n63
Mission to Moscow (Davies), 233
Mister Dynamite (film), 124, 152n4

Molotov, Vyacheslav, 237, 241, 242
Montserrat (Hellman play), 178-79
Moyers, Bill, 156
Mussolini, Benito, 172-73, 175, 231, 236, 242
My Brother Felix (aka *There was a Young Man*; abandoned novel), 166, 285-287
My Mother, My Father and Me (Hellman play), 186
Mystery League Magazine, 51
Mystery Stories, 44, 47

Nathan, George Jean, 6, 20n22, 24
New Masses, 142, 230, 267
New Yorker, 44
Nightmare Town (collection), 155
Nolan, William F., 5, 13, 17, 18n4, 20n21, 26, 60n53, 68, 71, 87, 97, 103, 152n1, 154n42, 155, 158, 166, 194, 198, 199, 210, 217n7, 219n33, 302, 305, 311n20, 315n75
North, Joseph, 142, 143
Nove, Alec, 229

On the Make (screen story), 123, 127-32, 162, 163, 165
Orwell, George, 225, 233, 234, 235, 236
O'Toole, Peggy, 87

Packer, Alfred G., 112
Partido Obrero de Unificacion Marxista (POUM), 236
Partisan Review, 265
Pentimento (Hellman), 202, 220n49
Perelman, S. J., 109
Pinkerton's National Detective Agency, 1, 2, 4, 5, 18n11, 19n16, 19n18, 26, 29, 33, 41, 69, 70, 71, 115n24, 115n26, 162, 193, 204, 205, 214, 215
PM, 255, 259
Political Affairs, 274
Polonsky, Abraham, 263
Powell, William, 123, 124, 151
Prica, Srdja, 261
Progressive Party, 268

Radek, Karl, 231
Random House, 284
Redbook, 9, 51, 53
Red Harvest, vii, 7, 8, 44, 49, 50, 58n2, 63, 64-72, 79, 85, 89, 90, 91, 93, 96, 115n25, 115n29, 139, 163, 199, 200, 216, 303
Return of the Thin Man, The (collection), 139, 149, 150
Rivett, Julie M., ix, ix-x, 125, 138, 150, 155, 213, 277n26, 286, 287, 311n18
Robeson, Paul, 198
Robles, Emmanuel, 178
Rollyson, Carl, 19n13, 20n25, 51, 162, 172, 180, 204, 213, 219n30, 220n47, 221n59, 233, 234, 239, 304, 315n75
Roosevelt, Eleanor, 13
Roosevelt, Franklin Delano, 210, 211, 212, 217n3, 261, 291
Rosen, Samuel, 17, 171, 275
Rosenberg, Ethel and Julius, 267, 274

Salute, 293
Saturday Evening Post, 32
Saturday Review of Literature, 44
Samuels, Albert, 7, 50, 57, 72, 87, 95, 197
Schwabacher, Wolf, 203
Scoundrel Time (Hellman), 69, 198
Screenwriter, 264
Screen Writers' Guild, 162, 209, 263
Searching Wind, The (Hellman), 155, 172-75, 177
Secret Agent X-9, 9, 193
Secret Emperor, The (abandoned novel), 42, 43
Seeds, William, 241
Sequel to the Thin Man (screen story), 150-51
Shaposhnikov, Boris, 243
Shaw, Joseph T., 7, 23, 29, 43, 47, 57, 60n51, 79
Shining, The (film), 285
Shumlin, Herman, 171, 202, 284
Sidney, Sylvia, 123
Simon, John, 242
Smart Set, The, 6, 24, 25, 27, 55, 60n52, 301
Smith, Howard W., 261
Socialist Party (US), 1, 255

Spanish Civil War, 187n1, 205, 208, 215, 225, 233-38, 250n55
Spanish Cockpit, The (Borkenau), 233
Spartacus (Fast/Trumbo), 264
Spitzer, E. E., 290
"Stalinism," viii, ix, 225, 231, 302
Stalin, Joseph, 2, 187n1, 226, 228, 229, 230, 234, 237, 239, 244, 246, 277n26
Steinbeck, John, 206
Stone, I. F., 228
Strand Magazine, The, 50, 53
Strang, William, 242
Strangers on a Train (film), 125
Stromberg, Hunt, 124, 138, 139
Sunset Magazine, 29, 32, 35
Symons, Julian, 4, 5, 57, 60n52, 64, 79, 88, 91, 92, 103, 120n141, 234, 237, 257-58, 270-71, 311n20

Teicher, Edward, 315n75
Thaelmann, Ernst, 211
These Three (film), 159
Thin Man, The (film), 124
Thin Man, The (novel), 7, 9, 10, 51, 101-13, 120n141, 139, 147, 150, 151, 200, 301, 303
Thomas, J. Parnell, 261
Thompson, George J. "Rhino," 68, 69, 111, 112, 116n50, 303, 304
Thompson, Robert G., 269
Tilden, Samuel, 307
Tolstoi, Leo, 174
Toward Z (abandoned novel), 284, 287
Toys in the Attic (Hellman play), 185-86
Trotsky, Leon, 228, 229, 230, 234, 236, 238, 258
True Detective Stories, 28, 39
Truman, Harry, 267
Trumbo, Dalton, 262, 263-65, 271
Tulip (abandoned novel), 296, 297, 298-300, 304, 305, 306, 309n1, 314n61

Unfinished Woman, An (Hellman), 197, 201
Uribe, Vicente, 236

Valley Sheep are Fatter, The (abandoned novel), 293, 294
Van Dyke, W. S., 138
Viane, Elise de, 195
Voltaire (François-Marie Arouet), 184
Voroshilov, Kliment, 232

Waite, Arthur Edward, 31, 58-59n14
Wallace, Henry, 210, 213, 268
Wallis, Hal, 171
Warner, Eltinge, 39
Watch on the Rhine (Hellman play), 169-71, 175, 208, 210
Watch on the Rhine (screenplay), 124, 125, 171-72, 284
Week, The, 259
Welles, Sumner, 239
West, Nathaniel, 197
Western Advertising, 41-42, 81
Whitfield, Prudence, 289, 290, 298
Wilder, Billy, 131, 208
Wills, Garry, 262
Winston, Henry, 269
Wister, Owen, 26
Wizard of Oz, The (film), 143
Wolfe, Peter, 11, 54-55, 68, 81, 88, 90, 91, 92, 99, 100, 119n130
Wolff, Eleanor, 204
Wright, James, 4, 18n11
Wyler, William, 16, 124, 125

Yank, 293

Zhdanov, Andrei, 242
Zilboorg, Gregory, 315n75
Zinoviev, Gregory, 231
Zumoff, Jacob A., x, 62n83, 70, 71, 90, 114n19, 115-16n32, 205

About the author

Ken Fuller is the author of *Radical Aristocrats: London Busworkers from the 1880s to the 1980s* (London: Lawrence and Wishart, 1985). His three-volume history of the Philippine Left is published by University of the Philippines Press: *Forcing the Pace: The Partido Komunista ng Pilipinas, from Formation to Armed Struggle* (2007); *A Movement Divided: Philippine Communism, 1957-1986* (2011); and *The Lost Vision: The Philippine Left, 1986-2010* (2015). In 2013, his e-book *The Long Crisis: Gloria Macapagal Arroyo and Philippine Underdevelopment* was published by Flipside (Quezon City).

A former trade union official from London, Ken Fuller has lived in the Philippines since 2003.

www.ingramcontent.com/pod-product-compliance
Lightning Source LLC
Chambersburg PA
CBHW050333230426
43663CB00010B/1842